Uncollecting Cheever

Uncollecting Cheever

The Family of John Cheever vs. Academy Chicago Publishers

ANITA MILLER

ROWMAN & LITTLEFIELD PUBLISHERS, INC.
Lanham • Boulder • New York • Oxford

ROWMAN & LITTLEFIELD PUBLISHERS, INC.

Published in the United States of America
by Rowman & Littlefield Publishers, Inc.
4720 Boston Way, Lanham, Maryland 20706

12 Hid's Copse Road
Cumnor Hill, Oxford OX2 9JJ, England

British Library Cataloguing in Publication Information Available

Library of Congress Cataloging-in-Publication Data

Miller, Anita, 1926–
        Uncollecting Cheever : the family of John Cheever vs. Academy
Chicago Publishers / Anita Miller.
                p.   cm.
        ISBN 0-8476-9076-8 (alk. paper)
        1. Cheever, John—Publishers.   2. Publishers and publishing—Law
and legislation—United States.   3. Authors and publishers—United States
—History—20th century.   4. Literature publishing—United States—History
—20th century.   5. Small presses—Illinois—Chicago—History.   6. Academy
Chicago Publishers.   7. Cheever, John—Family.
I. Title
PS3505.H6428Z78   1998
813'.52—dc21   98-7425
                                                                    CIP

Printed in the United States of America

⊗ ™ The paper used in this publication meets the minimum requirements of American National
Standard for Information Sciences—Permanence of Paper for Printed Library Materials, ANSI Z39.48-
1984.

For Jordan
and
Mark, Bruce, and Eric

Contents

Preface

There are ten different ways to intimidate a small press . . . . They can't afford a substantial insurance policy and they probably can't afford the quality of lawyer that the [larger] publishers have. As the major publishing companies, for economic reasons, start to publish fewer books and fewer controversial books, the smaller presses have to pick up that load. If the smaller presses are facing these kinds of pressures, you're going to have a whole range of books that cannot find a publisher.

Martin Garbus
The Village Voice
January 13, 1998

On its most basic level, this is the story of a lawsuit described by David Streitfeld in the *Washington Post* as "the most expensive, protracted and vicious court battle to take place in recent years over a book." The story is, I believe, dramatic, with twists and turns of plot and unusual characters who reveal themselves through their words as well as their actions. Everyone likes a good story: "We are all like Scheherezade's husband," said E. M. Forster, "in that we all want to know what happens next."

But the story of this lawsuit involves more than the story itself, fascinating as the press found it to be. This was a legal battle that generated four judicial judgments, all of which invaded the traditional relationship between publisher and author. One, from the Chicago Chancery Court, actually prescribed the contents of a projected book. Even more far-reaching was the last of these judgments: a state supreme court decision that, if it were to be implemented literally, would substantially alter the way business is traditionally done between book publisher and author. It would nullify hundreds, if not thousands, of book contracts and prevent many publishing agreements from being entered into in the future because its specificity requirements would disrupt the unique logic of these contracts. This Illinois Supreme Court decision sparked an immediate protest from the Association of American Publishers and the Association of American

University Presses; both protests provoked a counterargument from the Authors Guild. The decision stands.

But this is not simply the story of two parties fighting over a book: one must bear in mind that John Cheever is considered one of the major American writers of the century, the recipient of every important literary award, including the Pulitzer Prize and the National Book Award.

The Cheevers argued in federal court that publication of the projected book of short stories would hurt John Cheever's reputation because these stories were poor. This argument, a key element in the federal suit, would seem to call upon the court to render an aesthetic judgment, setting a questionable precedent. The Illinois Supreme Court also ventured into aesthetic territory with its rejection of the standard acceptability clause in the publishing agreement: the clause, the court held, "did not define criteria which would render the work satisfactory to the publisher in form and content." The prospect of judicial judgments of editorial criteria is not a happy one.

I think it is important that the background to these judicial findings be detailed because they are findings that affect an industry crucial to the functioning of our democracy and because one cannot learn too much about legal processes and about the actions of lawyers and judges in an open society.

Another issue that came to the fore in the discussion of this case is the role of the small press and the university press in the publishing community. In this connection, a disturbing theme emerged in the course of litigation. This was the at times explicit inference that small presses are inefficient, inept, and even dishonest. Cheever lawyers argued the "total" incapability of our small press to perform contractual obligations already entered into, implied strongly that "a small university related press" could not be expected to publish a book of any significance, and stated that there is no difference between a small independent press and an antiquarian bookseller that produces a few hundred signed, numbered collectors' editions in fine bindings of a previously published story.

After litigation ended, Cheever lawyers defended their arguments by pointing out that Academy Chicago referred to itself "in its own trial exhibits as 'a small publishing house,' 'a little house' and 'a small press.'" In the Winter 1992 Authors Guild Bulletin, Martin Garbus, who represented the Cheevers in this case, warned writers to beware of small publishers: they might not have much money, and even if they are solvent, he said, there have been "troubling cases" in which they did not "follow standard industry practice in editing, publishing or marketing the book." In the Spring 1993 Authors Guild Bulletin, authors are warned again against small presses: some of these publishers are "well-intentioned but have terrible cash flow problems—and others are just plain deadbeats."

This denigration of small presses extended during this litigation and even after it, to the work of authors published by small presses. Mrs. Cheever argued that books produced by Academy Chicago and other clients of our publicist Franklin Dennis were "small, obscure" works and that small presses paid "small advances for small books for small audiences." The federal judge rendered an opinion in which he called Academy Chicago "a small press . . . specializing in literary works of limited popular appeal." And John Updike referred to the "obscure Academy Chicago Publishers," a "mom-and-pop operation."

I have included as an epigram to this introduction Martin Garbus's recent words on this very subject. "A whole range of books," he says, will not find publishers if small presses are pressured by "ten different" kinds of intimidation. He is quoted here in an article about Grove Press, which published books that challenged censorship laws. But he speaks of "a whole range of books," and he is correct. As well as controversial books, small publishers publish works that have been rejected or put out of print by what the Cheever lawyers called "major houses with larger advances and wider audiences." Mr. Updike himself bought from us our edition of Sylvia Townsend Warner's *Lolly Willowes.* His subsequent essay on Sylvia Townsend Warner was reprinted in his book *Hugging the Shore,* with a footnote crediting my introduction to *Lolly Willowes.*

It should be noted that this Academy/Cheever litigation began in the 1980s, a time often referred to as "an age of greed"—as though the end of that decade signaled a substantial change in the general economic climate. Certainly the 1980s saw a strong increase in the influence of large, powerful companies on book publishing, as well as on bookselling. The conglomerates that absorbed publishing houses brought many resources into the field, not the least of which was financial. The legal struggle detailed in this book reflects the high expectation of monetary rewards by agents and writers because of conglomerate wealth.

But the evident need of "major houses" to pay large advances and seek wider audiences has caused some concern among book buyers and many booksellers, who fear that those books that will not generate "mass" sales will not be published or, if they are published, will not be kept in print for long. This concern has surely increased the value to society of the small or independent publishing house. As I have said, much insightful nonfiction and many first novels as well as out-of-print works (many of them used in the classroom) have been made available by independent and university presses. The concept of the book "superstore" originated in the perceived need of the public for bookstores that can provide a whole range of books apart from the mass appeal volumes that were the mainstay of the mall chain bookstores. The recent rise of Internet bookselling underscores that perceived need. Publishers' catalogs are placed before book buyers, who can choose whatever they like.

In any case, it seems to me that the denigration of small and university presses that surfaced in this lawsuit reflects a disturbing mind-set that values bigness and power over enduring quality.

It should be noted, too, that many of the issues raised in this case have implications that go beyond book publishing: these are issues that can affect any small business attempting to coexist with massive competitive entities. Any small business can be "intimidated" by a lawsuit.

This is a cautionary tale as well as an issue-oriented one. Anyone considering litigation should not move ahead without deep consideration of the possible consequences. As most lawyers are aware, almost anything can happen in a lawsuit. I think this case illustrates that, and it points also to the role specialization can play in law: as a rule a lawyer should be a specialist in the particular area of litigation, no matter how sophisticated he or she might be in general. But the reader will find areas in this case where even the specialists demonstrated some lacunae in their own grasp of their specialty.

Finally, this is a personal tale. It happened to my husband and me and by extension to our sons. I have to state strongly that at no point have I injected any fictional elements into it. I had a true tale to tell, and I have told it.

Anita Miller
Chicago, Illinois

1

Prelude: "This Is Really Easy"

In 1976, my husband Jordan and I set out to build an old-fashioned publishing house. We wanted to bring back worthwhile out-of-print books and to introduce new books by writers who had been rejected by the big presses. We intended to edit and design the books ourselves, store and pack them on our premises, invoice them and deliver them to bookstores.

Wasn't that what Leonard and Virginia Woolf had done?

Well, yes. Of course, they had done it in London, a literary center filled with independent bookshops, and they had done it in the 1920s, when life was certainly simpler. We knew that. But we still thought a good book could make its own way.

And our first book *did* make its own way. It was *A Guide to Non-Sexist Children's Books*, with an introduction by the actor Alan Alda, then still starring in the popular television series *M*A*S*H*. There was no guide like it available in 1976; it received a good deal of publicity because some newspapermen thought it was a ludicrous project and wrote articles disparaging it. Inevitably these articles—coupled, of course, with excellent reviews—helped to sell the book. We sold out our initial five thousand paperback copies in a few months, mostly by mail order, and printed five thousand more.

"This is really easy," we said to each other.

Like many of the things we say to each other, this was wrong.

We were misled because we were selling a reference work that many people wanted; it became apparent later that this was a very different thing from selling the quality reprints and new fiction that we envisioned as the core of our press. Neither of us had a background in trade publishing. I was an academic; Jordan had founded the Poetry Seminar and the poetry magazine *Choice*. For years he had been publishing an annual directory of Illinois media in connection with the press clipping bureau he had founded in 1956. We did not at first grasp the magnitude of the task we had set for ourselves. We began to discover how difficult it is for a new publisher to get books into bookstores and even into libraries. Librarians must depend on reviews, and reviews are not easy for novice publishers to get. Booksellers rely on publishers' representatives: salespeople in various regions of the country who act as liaisons between publisher and bookseller by sitting down with buyers each season, by appointment, and going through publishers' catalogs with them. Most big publishers have their own salaried salespeople; medium-sized and small publishers use salespeople who work on commission and represent many publishers. In 1976, when we began, these salespeople were in great demand; it took us two years of hard work to get our first sales rep.

Before that, we took our books around to local booksellers ourselves. But we quickly learned that it was definitely déclassé for publishers to go around showing their own books.

"Very nice, dear," one veteran bookseller said to me. "But you gotta get a rep."

But most salesmen—there were few women in the field then—seemed to be looking for presses with big backlists (books from previous seasons that went on selling indefinitely) or presses oriented toward the potential Big Book. We approached them with humility: reps on both coasts, in the Midwest, in New England, in the South. Some refused us politely; others did not bother to reply. The few who actually took us on never sent us any orders. There was, for instance, the respected Old Hand who covered only New York City. Every six weeks or so Jordan would call him and plaintively ask why we never got orders from any New York booksellers. "They're watching you," the Old Hand said kindly. "Don't worry. They're watching you."

If we had known about this salesman situation, we might have hesitated to become trade publishers. And we would certainly have hesitated if we had known—as we discovered to our sorrow—that many booksellers habitually paid new small presses last and that some booksellers did not pay new small publishers at all, especially when there was no publishers' representative to urge payment. One bookseller in Ohio bubbled with mirth when I called to ask for our $18. "I have to pay Random House," she said jovially. "You go on the back burner."

We discovered, too, that in the late 1970s, the term "small press" carried a sort of stigma. New publishing houses had sprung up across the country in the midst of the social turmoil resulting from the Vietnam War. Many of these publishers had small budgets and big axes to grind. Some cultivated an appearance of eccentricity and gave their presses odd names. I remember in particular Down There Press and Shameless Hussy. At our first American Library national convention—I believe it was in Detroit in 1976 or 1977—the owner of Shameless Hussy put a large, handprinted sign on her table that read "NO MORE TURKEYS." She sat after the first day with her back to the aisle and refused to talk to librarians. That sort of thing caused many booksellers and salesmen to look askance at new small presses.

But we persevered. Under an imprint called Cassandra Editions, we issued neglected classics by women and brought out so many previously unavailable books by George Sand that the few people who noticed us said that we were a house built on Sand. For a few years, we were the American distributors for Virago, a new feminist press in England whose books dovetailed nicely with our Cassandra Editions. In the fall of 1979, we made a distribution arrangement with Granada Paperbacks, a large English publisher. Granada's rich, varied list enabled us to add important history titles to our own growing backlist.

We published the only children's book by Sen. Eugene McCarthy, *Mr. Raccoon and His Friends.* When we learned that many titles by Robert Graves were out of print, we contacted his agents and bought world rights to four of his books for advances (against royalties, of course) of about $250 apiece. Graves was still alive at the time and signed the contracts. Many of our writers, like Graves, were on the brink of death when we contacted them. Sylvia Townsend Warner, for one, promised us an introduction to our edition of *Lolly Willowes,* but unfortunately died before she could write it. Another septuagenarian who passed on shortly after we approached him was Rupert Croft-Cooke, who wrote mysteries under the pen name Leo Bruce. It occurred to us that our letters of inquiry might be considered a sort of death warrant.

But we signed living authors as well. Our list eventually included Fay Weldon, Malcolm Bradbury, Alix Kates Shulman, Francis Steegmuller, and H.R.F. Keating, among many others. Our first original mystery, *Murder at the Red October* by Anthony Olcott, was well received; paperback rights to it were sold to Bantam by our New York agent. In the fall of 1981, we brought out *The Fair Women,* a heavily illustrated history of the Woman's Building at the Chicago World's Columbian Exposition of 1893. It received major review attention, all positive.

Gradually, we gathered a national commissioned sales force—our two younger sons Bruce and Eric represented us in the Midwest—along with a Canadian one and developed a good relationship with booksellers and distributors. We passed a kind of milestone when our existence was recognized by Ray Walters, who wrote the "Paperback Talk" column for the *New York Times Book Review*. Jordan had sent him our catalogs, along with cheery notes, and phoned him from time to time. I thought this was pushy. But during the fourth or fifth call, Mr. Walters said he had decided it was time he wrote something about us. And he did. We felt that with this column we had somehow arrived.

By the mid-1980s, we had a staff of ten, a backlist of over two hundred titles, and had sold about $100,000 worth of subsidiary rights. Despite various ups and downs, we thought we must be doing something right.

2

"A Splendid Idea"

It was in 1986, at the American Booksellers Association (ABA) annual convention, that Franklin Dennis first broached the subject of Cheever stories to Jordan. Franklin said that many stories had appeared in magazines over the years which had never been collected in any Cheever volume—not even in the omnibus volume of Cheever stories published by Knopf in 1978. Franklin had been collecting Cheever material for years: proofs and galleys and a few limited editions of single stories. He still lived in Montrose in Westchester County in the house where he had grown up; he knew people who had known John Cheever, and he had met Cheever himself. The Cheevers lived in Ossining, not far from Montrose. Franklin had read many of the uncollected stories and thought they were excellent.

I had begun to read Cheever's stories in the *New Yorker* when I was in high school. I had given copies of the 1978 collection to our sons Bruce and Eric as gifts; Bruce, especially, admired Cheever's work. But in 1986, Jordan and I were distracted by other projects, and we thought the Cheever suggestion was probably an unrealistic one.

We had first met Franklin in 1980 at a Modern Language Association convention in New York. At that time he was a publicist for Continuum Publishers, whose booth was across the aisle from ours. They were promoting the work of Elias Canetti, who had recently surprised them by winning a Nobel Prize. The decisions of the Nobel Committee have led to many stories about wild-eyed publishers leaping out the door to stop trucks about to drive off, laden with the works of obscure European writers, to the pulping mills.

"Get your Elias Canetti books here," Franklin said to passing academics. He was in his early thirties—a slight person with a mop of unruly black hair and a wry sense of humor. I liked him at once and spent a lot of time talking shop with him in the Continuum booth.

A couple of years later, when he left Continuum to set up his own publicity firm, Franklin called us and came out to Chicago to discuss representing us in New York. I remember that on that initial visit, when we picked him up at his hotel, he mentioned Cheever's death and remarked sadly that Cheever was a great American writer.

Franklin seemed to be an ideal publicist because he did not seem at all like a publicist. He represented several independent publishers and one university press in a soft-spoken manner that inspired confidence. He actually read the books he was presenting, and since most of his publishers turned out quality books, media people trusted Franklin's word. We arranged that, in return for a monthly stipend and expenses, he would present our lists to book review editors in New York, D.C., Boston, Philadelphia, Los Angeles, and San Francisco. He also visited Chicago, where we did our own publicity.

In 1987 at ABA, Franklin brought up the subject of the Cheever stories once again. He said that a friend of his, Tom Glazer, knew Ben Cheever, the middle son, and could arrange a meeting between Ben and Franklin to discuss the project. This gave the idea some solidity, and when we got home from ABA, Jordan remarked that Franklin had great faith in these uncollected stories. I said I knew that Franklin was a devoted Cheeverite but if these stories were really any good, someone else would have collected them by this time. And besides, the Cheevers would probably want a lot of money up front.

"Well, maybe," Jordan said. "But it certainly wouldn't hurt to try, would it?"

These were the fateful words that had gotten us into publishing in the first place. And once more there were no rumbles of thunder, no dead birds falling through the roof, no spectral figure detaching itself from the shadows to warn us off. So I responded the way I always responded to Jordan's ideas.

"That's true," I said. "It can't hurt to try."

Accordingly, on June 15 Franklin wrote the following letter to Ben Cheever:

> Dear Mr. Cheever:
> I work for Academy Chicago Publishers, a literary publisher of quality now in its eleventh year. A catalog is enclosed.
> I much admire your father's short stories. One of my most valued possessions is a set of galleys and a first edition of the 1978 omnibus. Back then I was living over Sally Swope's garage, and Mr. Cheever very kindly inscribed them. To complete

the local connection, I add that my tennis pal Tom Glazer passed on your address.

Tom thought that you would be helpful advising Academy Chicago on how to proceed with a volume of stories not in the 1978 edition. That edition includes "stories [that] date from my Honorable Discharge from the Army after World War II," to cite the delightful preface.

I know from interviews that your father noted the existence of some two hundred stories written after "Expelled." Surely there must be excellent ones among these; in fact, I found "The National Pastime" in a short story anthology and it was a wonder. I also have two limited editions: "Homage to Shakespeare" and "The Leaves, the Lion Fish and the Bear."

Would you advise us on, or maybe even be the editor of, these "uncollected" stories? Perhaps you could focus on the project after finishing the book of letters Tom tells me you are working on.

You may be concerned about the effect of publication on your father's literary reputation. It seems to me that at the very least readers will come to appreciate the astounding evolution of his talent. More likely, there are neglected gems. After all, the author has already picked his favorites and so let the critics know his choices for posterity.

I thank you in advance for any help on the enterprize [*sic*]: how to proceed with permissions and copywrite [*sic*]; the appropriate people to contact; perhaps even the stories to feature.

Sincerely,
Franklin Dennis
for Academy Chicago

Both Sally Swope and the "tennis pal" Tom Glazer, a noted folksinger, were longtime residents of Westchester County. Mary Cheever was later to refer to Mrs. Swope, in a deposition, as "a woman of wealth and importance." Franklin evidently hit all the right notes in this letter because Ben telephoned him on July 2. He said he thought the idea of the uncollected stories was a good one, although he himself was too busy to edit them as Franklin had suggested he do; he was taking a "sabbatical" from his job as an editor at *Reader's Digest* to edit the collection of his father's letters that Tom Glazer had mentioned to Franklin. But he had no objection to Franklin's editing the stories, and he told Franklin to write to Mrs. Cheever and to Maggie Curran at International Creative Management (ICM), his mother's agents, and to send copies of the letters to him. (Ben was under the mistaken impression that ICM "controlled" some Cheever material.) He also suggested that Franklin write to Joy Weiner at the *New Yorker,* which held publishing rights to the bulk of John Cheever's stories. The two men arranged to meet for lunch toward the end of July.

Franklin dutifully wrote to Mary Cheever on July 10:

> Dear Mrs. Cheever:
> I was delighted to hear from your son Ben that the idea of publishing "uncollected" John Cheever stories is feasible.
> Certainly, there are many, many stories to choose from and I feel certain that a number are excellent. At the very least, a new volume will allow readers to appreciate the remarkable evolution of Mr. Cheever's talent.
> Academy Chicago Publishers reiterates its interest in publishing previously uncollected stories; that is, short stories Mr. Cheever did not select for the 1978 omnibus.
> Academy Chicago looks forward to discussing with you and other family members such questions as locating the stories, deciding on those appropriate for publication, resolving copyright questions, the introduction and the foreword.
> The publishers underscore their concern with producing a volume—or even volumes—which meet your collective approval. I mean, in particular, matters of format and design. Academy Chicago, of course, will take on all editorial, copyright and production work.
> Although Academy Chicago, a high quality literary publisher, cannot afford a large advance, they will pay full royalties on all stories in the volume(s) irrespective of their copyright status.
> At lunch next week, Ben and I will explore this exciting project more fully. I trust you will pass on to him any questions or concerns you may have.
>
> Sincerely,
> Franklin Dennis

Franklin copied this letter to Ben and followed it on July 14 with one to Maggie Curran, as Ben had told him to do. Maggie was assistant to Lynn Nesbit, who had been at ICM for twenty-three years and was a vice president of that large and prestigious literary agency. Mary Cheever was Lynn Nesbit's client, but it was Maggie who usually dealt with her.

> Dear Ms. Curran:
> Ben Cheever, the son of the late John Cheever, suggested that

I write you to request information about the writer's short stories. International Creative Management controls copyright for many of these.

To debrief you a bit, I have enclosed a recent letter to Mary Cheever. This letter spells out the interest Academy Chicago Publishers has in doing volume(s) of "uncollected" John Cheever stories.

Ben Cheever had asked me to write a formal letter of intention to Mary Cheever after I had previously contacted Ben and told him about the book idea of "uncollected" stories. Both Ben and Mary Cheever had given Academy Chicago a positive response.

Because John Cheever was so prolific, there are many stories to review for possible inclusion in the "uncollected" volume. It was Ben Cheever's idea that I start the inventory of the short stories by asking exactly what works International Creative Management controls; I mean which stories International Creative Management holds the copyright for.

In the near future, Ben Cheever and I are going to meet to review this project. I hope that you can conveniently provide copyright information about his father's short stories.

In closing, I want to pass on greetings from Jordan Miller of Academy Chicago. Your paths have crossed agreeably and he wanted to be remembered to you.

Sincerely,
Franklin Dennis
for Academy Chicago

Ben had given Franklin to understand that ICM controlled some copyrights: it would have been unusual for an agent to do this, especially in this case because ICM had not represented John Cheever when he was alive.

Mary Cheever did not reply to Franklin's letter, but on July 24, Maggie Curran wrote to him.

Dear Franklin Dennis:

I think the idea of a collection of John Cheever's short stories not previously published in volume form is a splendid idea. However, ICM is at a slight disadvantage in this area as we never represented any of the published collections including the recent Knopf THE STORIES OF JOHN CHEEVER. We have some records, including the result of a Copyright search done by John's attorney that goes back to 1951, a record of two early collections, SOME PEOPLE PLACES AND THINGS THAT WILL NOT APPEAR IN MY NEXT NOVEL and THE WAY SOME PEOPLE LIVE and the listing of stories in the Knopf THE STORIES OF JOHN CHEEVER.

What we do not have is the names and publishers of the various collections other than those (and our listing for SOME PEOPLE . . . and THE WAY SOME PEOPLE LIVE does not include the names of the stories collected therein.)

I've just discovered a copy of THE WORLD OF APPLES on my shelf and include a Xerox of the table of contents.

To the best of my knowledge we never sold a single story of John Cheever. I think that you and Ben are going to have to do a search of the collections in John's library, compare the table of contents especially with the Knopf volume and after eliminating the stories collected, see what is left.

If there is any way that I can be of help to you, please let me know.

Best wishes,
Maggie Curran

Enclosures. P.S. Please return greetings to Jordan Miller.

She enclosed the contents pages of some Cheever short story collections.

To my surprise, things seemed to be moving along smoothly. On July 28, Franklin, Ben, and their mutual friend Tom Glazer met for lunch at Chez Vong, a Chinese restaurant on East 46th Street. The meeting was cordial. Ben said that his mother liked the idea of the book, and so did he. Tom Glazer liked it, too, but he wondered, since Franklin represented Princeton University Press, why Franklin didn't want to give the book to Princeton.

Franklin responded that he was representing Academy Chicago in this and that in any case the book was too commercial for a university press. He said that he had heard that the 1978 Knopf collection of Cheever stories had sold about 125,000 copies.

Ben said it was closer to 118,000.

"If we could sell half that number," Franklin said, "I would be pleased." Ben said a quarter of that number would be fine.

The question of an introduction came up. The writer most often thought of in connection with Cheever was John Updike. Franklin said that he deeply admired Updike's work, but he did not think Updike would be a good choice to write an introduction because he had already written so much about Cheever. Ben agreed with Franklin, who went on to say that he thought either John le Carré or Raymond Carver might be a good choice. Franklin had once sent Le Carré a galley of Father George Hunt's critical study of Cheever's work; Le Carré had responded that the Hunt book was "hard work" and "a bit forbidding" but that he was willing to put his name to anything that might secure Cheever a wider readership: "for example a reissue of Cheever's work." Ben said he thought Le Carré might be a good bet.

Raymond Carver, Franklin said, had written a story called "The Train" that he had dedicated to Cheever because its protagonist was taken from Cheever's story "The 5:48." Carver thus obviously admired Cheever's work, and an introduction by him might, Franklin thought, bring younger readers to Cheever. Ben said that was a good idea.

Franklin asked Ben whether he thought the *Letters* and the short story collection should appear in the same season. Ben said he didn't know. He thought the *Letters* would be published in late fall 1988 or early spring 1989, but he said he would have to ask Allen Peacock, his editor at Simon & Schuster, whether it mattered if both books came out in the same season. Franklin reminded Ben that Scott Donaldson's biography of Cheever was scheduled for 1988; its publication had been delayed by the Cheevers' objections to it. Ben said the Donaldson book wasn't worth consideration.

The conversation ranged over books of military history, in which Franklin and Ben shared an interest, and Ben's new house in Pocantico Hills, where Franklin's aunt had lived on Ben's block. Franklin gave Ben a current Academy Chicago catalog and copies of feature stories about Academy from the *Washington Post* and the *Christian Science Monitor* so that Ben would know what kind of books Academy published. The *Monitor* article put emphasis on our mysteries. Ben told Franklin to have Academy send his mother a contract or "an option letter."

Franklin picked up the tab for lunch. He told Ben it was the least Academy could do.

3

"I Suppose You Could Say They Haven't Been Delivered"

After the lunch, things moved rapidly. Following Ben's suggestion, Jordan drew up an option letter for Mrs. Cheever. But after some thought, neither he nor Franklin could see any point in sending it. It was obviously simpler just to send her a contract.

It did not occur to any of us to talk to a lawyer about the contract. We had our standard contract form that we always tinkered with to fit the individual case, crossing out this clause and that word, adding things in the margins. At least until the advent of desktop publishing, this was the common practice in publishing houses.

Jordan tinkered with the contract in the office we shared. He filled in the title: "The Uncollected Stories of John Cheever." Then he came to the line, "The Author will deliver a manuscript . . . " When we had a manuscript in hand at the time the contract was being drawn up, we often crossed out "will deliver" and wrote "has delivered" above it. Now Jordan asked me whether we should cross out "will deliver" on this contract, since Mrs. Cheever, in addition to not being the Author, was clearly not going to deliver anything except the right to publish this book. It was understood that *we* were going to find all the stories. What Mrs. Cheever was delivering was the right to publish them.

I was editing a book called *The Trial of Levi Weeks*. I looked up and applied my accursed literal mind to Jordan's question. "Well," I said, "we don't have all the stories yet. So I suppose you could say they haven't been delivered."

Jordan accepted this idiotic reply and did not cross out "'will deliver." He crossed out "Author" and wrote in "The Estate of John Cheever." Then he asked me what I thought we should offer for an advance. I was still not convinced that this contract was going to be signed. I suggested our usual $1,000 advance. This was, after all, reprinted material—all of it had been published before—and Franklin had explained in his first letter to Ben that we could not afford a large advance.

Jordan hesitated. He said this was a special book; they might think $1,000 wasn't enough. He thought we should offer $1,500, half on signing the contract and half on publication of the book. I agreed. Then he said he thought we should give up something in the contract. I said I thought the agent would take everything away anyway—all subsidiary rights. But Jordan said we should make a gesture and cross something out. Maybe film rights.

So he crossed out film rights. And he crossed out the clause that allowed us to turn down the book if we didn't like it when it was submitted—after all, we were the ones who were going to compile it.

Then there was the question of Franklin's compensation. He was designated as Editor in the contract. In the past, editors who had compiled short story collections for us had received royalty payments and split them with the authors. So we thought the contract should give Franklin part of the royalty. But which part? Half? That seemed like a lot, but Jordan pointed out that this project was Franklin's idea; he had gotten it together. If Maggie Curran at ICM didn't want him to have half, she could change the percentage. It was all open to negotiation: the contract was subject to whatever changes Mrs. Cheever's agents wanted.

That seemed sensible to me. "Maggie must know what's customary," I said.

So Jordan split the royalty between the Estate of John Cheever and Franklin Dennis. The royalty rate was standard: 10 percent of the cover price of the book on the first five thousand copies, escalating to 12.5 percent on sales from five to ten thousand copies and 15 percent on sales over ten thousand. Since the cover price of the book was going to be in the $25 range, royalties would represent a lot of money.

Franklin was going to send the contract to Mrs. Cheever, so Jordan sent a packet of copies of the contract to him, along with a letter to Mrs. Cheever, the first Jordan had written her, dated August 14.

> Dear Mary Cheever:
> I'm delighted to send you the attached agreements for our projected volume, THE UNCOLLECTED STORIES OF JOHN CHEEVER. It's a project which we find very exciting and worthwhile.
> There are several copies attached, since you may want to distribute them to others. I'll be glad to discuss any of its terms

with you or with whomever you designate.

As you will see, we have divided royalty payments evenly between the Estate and Franklin Dennis who is acting both as packager and editor.

I have already mentioned to Franklin that we stand ready to help in finding some of the stories which may have appeared in now-hard-to-find publications. The Chicago Public Library used to have an excellent collection of 20th century magazines but I don't know what condition they're in at the moment since the CPL plans to move in the next year or two. In any event, we'll do everything we can to pitch in on research.

I'm sure someone has already thought of this, but will someone be checking Mr. Cheever's letters for references to stories and where they were to appear or had appeared? I know that when my wife did her massive bibliography of Arnold Bennett's journalism, she found AB's letters tremendously helpful in turning up the material. In any event, we're very excited about all this, as I said, and I look forward to hearing from you and/or one of your representatives.

Best wishes.

On August 20, Franklin added a letter of his own to Jordan's packet before sending it on to Mrs. Cheever in Ossining. Franklin's letter was to be quoted by Cheever counsel in innumerable briefs and affidavits because of the statement that terms would be discussed in detail and because of Franklin's offer of cooperation.

Dear Mrs. Cheever:

I am sending along a contract from Academy Chicago Publishers for THE UNCOLLECTED STORIES OF JOHN CHEEVER for your consideration.

The packet also contains a letter to you from Jordan Miller, co-director of Academy. Your son Ben, advised that I forward all this to you directly.

Academy Chicago obviously views the particulars of the contract as appropriate. But you should understand that the document is intended primarily to get things underway, and that Academy Chicago expects to discuss the terms in detail.

As I underscored during my lunch with Ben, the publisher and I as editor will cooperate with the Cheever family on all matters of publication.

For instance, I direct your attention to the fifth (#5) particular of the contract. Academy Chicago is aware that Ben is editing a volume of Mr. Cheever's letters and that he does not want the short stories to appear at the same time. Of course I will consult with you (the Cheever family collectively) on the final selection of stories for publication.

If you wish to speak with me, my Montrose telephone number is 739-1735 and the New York office is (212) 684-1608. I will be out of town, however, until Friday, August 28. Naturally, Jordan Miller expects to discuss the details of the contract with you or your representative in the near future.

You will be interested to learn that I am in the process of writing John le Carré to see if he would contribute an introduction to the volume. I have previous correspondence from Le Carré which makes evident his admiration for Mr. Cheever's talent. On the other hand, do let me know if other candidates occur to you.

Sincerely,
Franklin Dennis

Mrs. Cheever did not respond to either of these letters.

Jordan had sent her several copies of the contract because Ben had given Franklin the impression that the Cheever children would want to read it and discuss it with their mother and with each other. But Mrs. Cheever— who was later to testify that she relied solely on her agent in these matters—simply sent the contract on to Maggie Curran, who checked it and phoned Jordan requesting some minor changes. "Estate of John Cheever" was changed to "Author"—those kinds of changes. Maggie did not question Academy's control of foreign rights or the royalty split between Mrs. Cheever and Franklin. Jordan readily agreed to these changes, telling Maggie to make them on the contract; she did not need to send him a memo.

He hung up feeling very pleased, especially since Maggie had told him how much she respected Academy Chicago. We had published some ICM authors in the past.

"Those Cheevers must be wonderful people," I said, surprised that there were only minor changes. "They obviously don't care about money. All they want is to have these stories brought out by a reputable, conscientious house."

Jordan said the Cheevers probably didn't need money, and anyway we had offered to do all the work, and they would certainly make money on the book. After all, the small advance was just against royalties, which would probably be impressive.

I agreed that the Cheevers probably considered it found money, since the stories had just been lying there.

"Franklin said there might be two hundred stories," Jordan said dreamily. "Do you think we should do two volumes?"

I said I didn't know. "How many stories are in the Knopf collection?"

So we went on, talking to each other.

Jordan had offered to "pitch in" on the research, but the lack of response from Ossining made it obvious that if any research was going to be done, we would have to do it. Ben Cheever made no attempt to pitch in himself by going through the Cheever library, as Maggie Curran had suggested he do, and he seemed to have no opinion about any of the questions Franklin put to him: should there be one volume or two? How should the stories be arranged? We thought chronological order might be best—what did he think? Everything Franklin suggested seemed to sound good to Ben: a big volume would be good, but two smaller volumes might be good, too. Chronological order sounded good.

We started doing research before Maggie returned the signed contracts. More than half the stories, it seemed, had been published in the *New Yorker*. Many had appeared in mainstream magazines like the *Atlantic Monthly, Harper's, Esquire, Good Housekeeping, Collier's,* and *Mademoiselle*. Some had been published in small, obscure journals in the 1930s. The magazines held the publishing rights—and in some cases the copyrights—to the stories, and we contacted them for permission to reprint.

Franklin contacted the *New Yorker* and received a letter, dated September 21, 1987, from Joy Weiner of their editorial department, saying that she understood that Academy Chicago Publishers wanted "to publish all the John Cheever stories that have yet to appear in book collections." She enclosed copies of ten cards listing all the Cheever stories that had originally appeared in the *New Yorker* and offered to provide copies of stories Franklin selected, depending on "work involved and the photocopying costs."

As Joy Weiner's letter indicated, we believed that we had contracted for the right to publish all the uncollected stories we could find. We thought that the title in the contract of our projected book—"The Uncollected Stories of John Cheever"—made clear that intention. We could not call the book "The Complete Uncollected Stories of John Cheever" because we could never be sure that we could locate, or even identify, all the stories. In addition, there was nothing in the contract that suggested there would be any selection process by anyone—this despite the fact that we were not sure we would want to exercise the right to publish all the uncollected stories we could find. We assumed—mistakenly, as it turned out—that Cheever himself had deliberately excluded stories from his collected editions, and particularly from the 1978 collection. So we thought that some of these stories might not be worthy of inclusion in our book. We were to learn later that Cheever had not made value judgments on the stories in the 1978 collection, and it is apparent to us now that it would have been inexcusable, from a scholarly point of view, for us to exclude early published stories. As it evolved, we were to find no reason to eliminate any stories from our collection except those that had later been incorporated as chapters in Cheever's novels.

We had left the publication date open in the contract because we did not know how long our research would take. We hoped to publish in the fall of 1988, but we did not know how difficult it would be to compile an accurate list of the uncollected stories and then to locate the stories—and, of course, we assumed there would be a process of evaluation, possibly involving the Cheevers. We began the research by checking the tables of contents of the seven Cheever collections against Franklin's bibliographies, none of which was definitive. On weekends we went to our local library to xerox, from old magazines, those stories that we knew for sure had never been collected.

As I have said, we began work before we received signed contracts: these arrived, signed by Mary Cheever and Franklin, on September 24, 1987. Jordan signed them and returned them to Maggie Curran with a note:

> Dear Maggie:
> We're delighted to attached [*sic*] two copies of a fully executed agreement for THE UNCOLLECTED STORIES OF JOHN CHEEVER, along with our check for the first half advance.
> There are a couple of questions you might be able to answer.
> (1) We're tentatively planning to publish in the fall of 1988. Does this conflict with any other publication plans for the Cheever oeuvre?
> (2) Do you have a list—or know where I might get one—of foreign houses which have published Cheever's work? We're primarily interested in the stories collection [*sic*] of course, but any information would be useful.
> Thanks again for your reply to these.

Once again, let me say how pleased we are to be participating
in what we consider to be a major literary event. Best wishes.

By October 1, we had culled titles of fifty-seven stories that had apparently never been collected in a Cheever volume. We had read some of these
and were particularly struck by the quality of the early stories that had not
been published in the *New Yorker.* They had an interesting flavor that reminded me a little of Dreiser; Sarah Leslie of our office said it reminded
her of Edward Hopper. These stories reflected a political consciousness not
usually associated with Cheever's work. By the end of the first week of
October, we were convinced that all the stories were interesting and should
be republished. I had reservations about three stories that had appeared in
Collier's magazine in the late 1930s—the so-called racetrack stories:
"Saratoga," "The Man She Loved," and "His Young Wife." I thought these
were so commercial that they should perhaps be isolated from the others in
an appendix.* Franklin liked them; Jordan thought they should remain in
the chronological arrangement because they illustrated a point in Cheever's
development. Ben had no opinion.

I think that my attitude toward these three stories was influenced by
Collier's slick illustrations and, again, by my belief that Cheever had deliberately excluded them from his other collections. But as time went by and
stories flowed in steadily, the idea of an appendix withered away, so to
speak. I realized that the cumulative impression of Cheever's work would
not be weakened by a few contrived stories: we had a book that would be
indispensable to any consideration of Cheever's accomplishment as a writer.
We began to wonder why these stories had not been republished before and
why no stories published before 1947 had been included in the Knopf
omnibus.

We were now convinced that we had a really impressive book. Jordan
was so filled with enthusiasm that he fired off a letter to Bill Haas, who
handled foreign rights for us at the Scott Meredith Literary Agency. Jordan
had a friendly relationship with Bill, and he probably told Bill more than
he wanted to hear about what we were doing: that so far we had found
fifty-seven uncollected stories, that we were checking various bibliographies and reference works "in addition to having the cooperation of the

---

*Ironically, these three stories were later singled out by reviewers for special praise.

Cheever family," and that we had found two stories in the *New Yorker* that contained significant "textual variants" from the *Wapshot Chronicle* chapters they later became.

Jordan expected Bill to sell foreign rights for the collection, since the contract gave us those rights. At the outset, Franklin had told Ben that the Scott Meredith Agency sold foreign rights for us, since Franklin wanted Ben to know that these rights were in experienced hands. Ben had said that was good.

On October 6, Jordan, still bemused by textual variants, wrote to Joy Weiner at the *New Yorker:*

> Dear Ms Weiner:
>
> Thanks very much for your quick response to my inquiry about permission to reprint the Cheever stories. Thanks, too, for making it as easy as possible for us to acquire them.
>
> I've attached a copy of our publishing agreement with Mary Cheever and Franklin Dennis, a list of stories we plan to use and a copy of *Publishers Weekly* for August 28th. I thought you might like to know a little more about us and the *PW* piece is quite thorough.
>
> A word about the stories. There are 37 we expect to include in our collection plus 2 possibles: CLEAR HAVEN and THE JOURNAL OF AN OLD GENT are both excerpts from THE WAPSHOT CHRONICLE. But the interesting thing about them is that their text in the magazine is in several ways markedly different from that of the novel. We'll have to examine them a little more carefully, but we just might publish these two pieces in an Appendix. So if you can include these two as well I'd appreciate it.
>
> As I mentioned on the phone, we're collecting these stories now and already have copies of several. It shouldn't take more than another week to find and photocopy the others.
>
> Again, many thanks for your cooperation.
>
> Best wishes.

On that same day, Jordan also wrote to Mary Cheever. He lived in hope that she was going to answer him some day.

> Dear Mary Cheever:
>
> I wanted first of all to tell you how delighted we are to be publishing the uncollected stories. Apparently there are more than 60 of them and we're looking for others that may not be

listed in any of the sketchy bibliographies that are now available. It's a very exciting and challenging project.

We're planning to publish next fall and I wondered if I could trouble you for some information. Is it possible for us to look at the journals and any collections of letters which may be available? Our only interest is to find clues about story publication and we thought the journals, letters to and from friends and agents could be invaluable. The [Malcolm] Cowley letters are at the Newberry, as you know, and that should help, but whatever other collections there are and to which we can have access would help as well.

In any event, Franklin Dennis will also be in touch with you in due course; we're dividing up the research chores and want to do as complete a job as possible. We're very excited about this book and would be grateful for whatever guidance you may be able to offer.

You probably don't read *Publishers Weekly*, so I've attached a copy of the August 28th issue which has a story about our house which I thought might interest you. I've also enclosed our complete backlist catalogue. I'd be pleased to send you reading copies of whatever books you'd like.

Best wishes.

This letter did provoke a response, although apparently not from Mary Cheever. It was returned to Jordan by Maggie Curran on October 9, with a note scrawled across the top in green ink:

> Dear Jordan—I don't care what Mary says, this is an absolute NO, NO, I've left a message for her—. Both the letters and the Journals are being worked on by Ben Cheever* and are under contract for publication. As you say, there is information in libraries, but what you're asking for is under wraps until publication. Best, Maggie.

Horrified at his inadvertent transgression, Jordan rushed to the phone to apologize to Maggie. As always, she was friendly; she said that of course he couldn't have known that the material was classified. To make him feel better, she read him the list of eight foreign houses that had bought rights to Cheever works. We were glad that no one was angry with us, but we found the tone of her note unsettling. The opening phrase—"I don't care what Mary says"—puzzled us.

---

*Robert Gottlieb edited the journals.

Meanwhile, we were busily reading Cheever stories. The pressure on us had lifted considerably when a librarian in our suburban library noticed Jordan lugging large, bound volumes of magazines to the copy machine. She suggested we give her a list of the stories we needed and the magazines that had published them; she would then order copies of the stories from Inter-Library Loan. Since at that moment we were sitting on tiny chairs in the Children's Room—the Reference Room was overcrowded—sharing a low, round table with a set of building blocks, we gratefully made out lists of story titles, magazine dates, and page numbers and left them on her desk. All treks to libraries could now cease.

At the end of October, we were to have a stroke of good fortune when Franklin, browsing in a San Francisco bookshop, discovered that Dennis Coates had compiled a reliable Cheever bibliography that had been published in the *Bulletin of Bibliography* for 1979. This was not an easy periodical to find. Eventually, Sarah Leslie of our office located it in the library at Northwestern University, where she was taking graduate courses in English. When we were finally able to check the Coates bibliography, we noted that we had already painstakingly found most of the information ourselves—although not all of it.

Jordan had written Mary Cheever on October 6 that we thought there were sixty stories available to us. On October 13, Franklin, as he had told the Cheevers he would, wrote to John le Carré about the proposed volume, which "would gather all the works not previously published in the omnibus volume of 1978 . . . . We estimate conservatively that our research will yield some sixty stories. We will arrange them chronologically; John Cheever's fifty-year career reflects a remarkable evolution." Now, after consulting Coates, we raised the number of available stories from sixty to sixty-eight.

On October 19, 1987, Joy Weiner of the *New Yorker* sent Jordan copies of a document called "Confirmation of Copyright" for the thirty-eight stories he had told her would be included in our book. She enclosed a copy of a letter she had sent to Mary Cheever, telling her that she was enclosing confirmation of copyright for thirty-eight stories by John Cheever originally published in the *New Yorker.* "As per your agreement with Jordan Miller, publisher of Academy Chicago Publishers," Ms. Weiner wrote, "the thirty-eight *New Yorker* stories will appear in a forthcoming book collection."

Along with this letter, Ms. Weiner sent Mrs. Cheever a list of the thirty-eight stories that would appear in the book.

On November 3, Jordan wrote to Joy Weiner again, asking for permission to reprint four stories listed by Dennis Coates: "The Habit" (which would later turn out to have been included in the 1978 omnibus under another title), "Keep the Ball Rolling," "The People You Meet," and the sixth story in the "Town House" series. On November 6, Ms. Weiner sent Confirmation of Copyright for these four stories, asked for the scheduled date of publication for *The Uncollected Stories,* and requested a review copy. On November 19, Jordan wrote thanking her for the permissions and telling her *The Uncollected Stories* was scheduled for fall of 1988.

Thus, by the end of the first week of November 1987, Mary Cheever had been given the titles of forty-two stories that would be included in our collection.

4

"A Perfect Agent for the Eighties"

Franklin kept in close touch with Ben, asking him his opinion on everything we were doing and giving him glowing reports on our progress. Ben said he thought everything we were doing was fine; he was eager to read the stories—especially the "Town House" series of six, which had run in the *New Yorker* in the mid-1940s. These were based on the Cheevers' experiences sharing a Manhattan townhouse with three other couples during the war years. Ben said he remembered hearing his parents talk about the house. But he told Franklin he did not want to read those stories yet; he wanted to wait until we had gotten the whole collection together and read all the stories in sequence.

On November 3, Franklin went up to see Ben in his office at *Reader's Digest* and told him that we had definitely decided to include all the stories and that we had, in fact, expanded the title: the book was to be called *The Uncollected Stories of John Cheever, 1930–1981*. It would be irresponsible from a scholarly viewpoint, Franklin explained, to exclude stories; in addition, if the collection was inclusive, critics would not single out stories they considered weak and complain about their inclusion. And he reminded Ben that a chronological, inclusive collection would demonstrate the "evolution of John Cheever's talent." Franklin always took great pains to make everything clear to Ben, whom he regarded as the representative of the Cheever family. But he did not really need to do a selling job: Ben readily agreed. Including all the stories was fine with him. And he told Franklin that Allen Peacock, his editor at Simon & Schuster, saw no conflict in the *Letters* and *Stories* coming out in the same season. So it was all right to plan publication for the fall of 1988.

Franklin brought gifts for Ben: some books from publishers he represented (one was our collection of lawyer stories, called *The Judge's Chambers*) along with a photocopy of the early Cheever story "Bock Beer and Bermuda Onions" (*Hound and Horn*, Spring 1932), which Ben said he had long wanted to read. Ben asked Franklin for a favor: he had written Yevgeny

Yevtushenko that he wanted to include the poet's correspondence with John Cheever in his book of letters but had received no answer. Since Yevtushenko was published in England by Franklin's friend and client Marion Boyars, would Franklin mind asking Mrs. Boyars's help in this matter? Needless to say, Franklin was delighted to help. As a return favor, Franklin asked Ben to keep an eye out, as he edited the letters, for mention of any stories we might have missed. Ben agreed to do this, and to make it easier for him, Franklin offered to provide an alphabetical list of the stories we had found so that Ben could quickly check the titles against stories mentioned in the letters.

The upshot of the Yevtushenko business was that Yevtushenko told Marion Boyars he had no letters from Cheever; he thought he must have thrown them away. Franklin duly reported this to Ben, who was later to use this incident as an example of Franklin's ineptitude. The upshot of the alphabetical list business was that Jordan provided Franklin with a hand-written list of the stories; Franklin had to leave for San Francisco, so he gave the list to his wife, Mary, to type. Not surprisingly, Mary had trouble reading Jordan's handwriting, but she guessed at what it said, assuming that even if she got the titles wrong, they would still be recognizable enough for Ben's purposes. And they were: for "Autobiography of a Drummer," Jordan had hurriedly written "Auto of a Drummer," which Mary read as "Arts of a Drummer"; "Bock Beer and Bermuda Onions" was typed as "Birch Beer and Bermuda Onions." It was one of those things no one gives a thought to at the time.

Thus in November 1987—before Ben saw the manuscript of the collected stories—all was happiness and goodwill. Everything was going so well, in fact, that we should probably have guessed that the Furies were tuning up offstage; for purposes of dramatic unity, some pity and fear had to be injected into this tale. But we went blithely on, feeling perhaps the way Oedipus felt when he first met Jocasta; sounding like Lady Macbeth's mother telling her friends about this terrific thane who wanted to marry her daughter. Franklin especially tempted Fate: in order to reassure Ben— who really had not questioned it—that his father's work was going to be well served, Franklin kept telling him about the financial rewards that would probably accrue from this book, thanks to our efforts and those of the Scott Meredith Agency: sales of paperback reprint rights and foreign rights, to say nothing of bookstore sales.

Ben told Franklin he was really eager to read the whole collection. Franklin suggested, since Jordan and I had to be in New York for sales conferences in early December, that we bring along a couple of copies of the manuscript so that Ben could read it over the Christmas holidays. Jordan thought that was a good idea. He decided to xerox three copies of all the stories we had to date—one copy for Ben, one for Franklin, and one for the people at Scott Meredith. We now had a list of sixty-eight stories, but Inter-Library Loan had so far provided only sixty of them. Jordan and Franklin decided to list the titles of the missing stories in the table of contents, enclosed in parentheses to differentiate them from the stories included in the manuscript.

Our semiannual sales conference in New York was scheduled for December 8. The purpose was to show our twenty-two commission salespeople the spring catalog and explain our spring list, which they would start to sell in January. We intended to mention the Cheever book to the reps, but there was no reason to discuss it in any detail until our next sales conference in May, when we would describe our fall 1988 list. Since Ben was going to visit his mother in Ossining during the December 12 weekend, he asked Franklin to drop the manuscript off at her house—Ossining was a relatively short drive from Franklin's home in Montrose—on that Saturday, so that Ben could pick it up from her. He told Franklin to phone his mother in advance any time except between 1:00 and 2:30 in the afternoon, when she took what she apparently referred to as her "writer's nap."

We were leaving for New York on Tuesday morning, December 8. At 5:00 on Monday afternoon, Jordan and our publicist, Mary Jo Reilly, were still sorting papers at the copy machine. They sorted and copied until 9:00 that night, when they bound the finished manuscript into three two-volume sets: our spiral bindings were not wide enough to hold all sixty stories in one volume. I was annoyed at this rushed work and even more annoyed at not being able to eat dinner until 10 P.M. I said I couldn't see the point of our knocking ourselves out to provide Ben with stories, many of which, with some effort, he could have gotten for himself years before. Jordan, unlike me, was happy to accommodate Ben. I did not see why we could not have mailed the manuscripts to Franklin a few days after we got back from New York—preparing them at our relative leisure.

I was still irritable the next morning when we clambered aboard the plane, encumbered by six volumes of Cheever stories. After we had settled into our seats, I sought to distract myself with a copy of *Vanity Fair* magazine, which I had bought in the airport over Jordan's mild objection; he considered it a frivolous publication. I soon became engrossed in an article about a literary agent named Andrew Wylie, of whom I had never heard, who was sending "shock waves through the publishing world by demanding outrageous sums of money for his clients—and often getting what he wants."[1]

The article, written by Michael Schnayerson, began with an anecdote about Wylie spitting on a copy of a new Saul Bellow novel, calling it "utter drivel," and extinguishing a cigarette on it. "Is the rising literary agent just obnoxious?" Schnayerson asked. "Or is he changing the rules of the game?" Schnayerson's conclusion seemed to be that Wylie was not just obnoxious, he was also changing the rules of the game by raiding other agents' lists, ignoring option clauses, misleading publishers about exclusive arrangements, and—most important—demanding outrageously high advances for his clients, who were "literary" writers whose work did not, as a rule, earn back that kind of money. Both Jason Epstein of Random House and Sonny Mehta of Knopf, a division of Random House (the owner of which also owns *Vanity Fair*), had good things to say about Wylie. Other editors called him confrontational and paranoid. One said, "He's a horrible person—if he's a person at all," and wondered aloud why he had not been run out of town. Another said Wylie was "utterly without principles. I suppose in that respect he's a perfect agent for the eighties."

The article, warts and all, was not entirely negative. Wylie "flashed" a schoolboy's "mischievous smile"; in his low-pitched voice, he spoke in the "clipped, concise tones of an arrogant Oxford don"; and he came of "Yankee blueblood" stock. Indeed, a former Harvard classmate said he was "terribly well-born," and Adam Saroyan called him "a young Shelley . . . very sweet-natured and loving . . . the tall, silent type."

Not only was Wylie tall, charming, and blue-blooded, he appeared to be terrifyingly erudite as well. Schnayerson reported that upon graduating from Harvard, Wylie won the Boylston Elocution and Rhetoric Prize, "a Latin-translation prize—*and* a Woodrow Wilson Fellowship." In the early 1970s, he was driving a cab in New York, apparently unsuccessfully because he was forced to live on "family money—not a lot." He turned his storefront living quarters into a bookstore, stocked, unfortunately, with his "library from Cambridge"—editions, for example, of Heraclitus in German, French, and Italian—for which, as he put it with self-deprecating charm, "there was, let us say, a noncompetitive market." And no one, he said, would hire him as an editor because he had to admit that the last author he had read was Tacitus!

Turning to a career as an agent, he was able to capture I. F. Stone as a client by singing Homer to him over the telephone.

Wylie capped these interesting revelations by saying that he was not motivated by money; if he were, he could have taken over his uncle's bank and, he said, made more money in one year than he could in ten years as an agent. What he really wanted, he said, was to learn, and to that end he pursued only the writers he admired and the subjects that intrigued him.

Gary Glickman, a Knopf author, joined Sonny Mehta and Jason Epstein in praise of Wylie, whose financial demands Glickman found justifiable: "Editors represent huge corporations and huge corporations have lots of money to spend." The advances Wylie demanded, Glickman said, would not break "some little editor's back. The real little person is the writer working in his little house."

The last sentence, or bottom line, of the article was: "For better or for worse, Andrew Wylie is here to make that writer's little house a bigger one."

On the first page of this piece was a photograph of an unsmiling person with an elongated head, staring fixedly through oversized, black-rimmed spectacles. What hair he had was slicked tightly back. He wore dark trouser and a sort of black polo shirt, and he was holding a cigarette. The photograph certainly seemed to support the comment of one editor, who said with a shudder, "He looks . . . . evil," and of another, who remarked, "I sense a violence in him—those watery, pale-blue eyes." The caption read, "I don't break the law. And I don't tell lies."

I found this article fascinating and passed it on to Jordan to read while I turned to the Cheever manuscript. Jordan and Franklin had read all the stories, but I had not. Some of the xeroxed pages were crooked and dark—the result of working under pressure—but they were certainly readable, and I thought the collection was gratifyingly impressive.

Jordan's reaction to the *Vanity Fair* story was the same as mine. He thought Wylie sounded awful.

"Well," I said, "anyway, we'll never hear from *him*. He's just after big bucks."

We both laughed heartily.

5

"John's Poor Little Stories"

On Saturday afternoon, December 12, 1987, Franklin drove to Ossining to bring Mary Cheever the two-volume set of xeroxed stories, which we had bound in dark-blue covers. He had phoned her twice that day, once in the morning to check on her schedule and again at noon to make sure that 2:00 was still a good time for him to arrive.

Mrs. Cheever, accompanied by her Labrador retriever, greeted Franklin at the door of "Afterwhiles," the Cheever house. Franklin had brought her some books he thought would hold a special interest for her. Two of them had been published by Academy Chicago. One was *Ramage in South Italy*, a classic travel book that Franklin had chosen because the Cheevers had lived for a while in Italy; in fact, their younger son had been named Federico in memory of that sojourn. The other Academy book was the first volume of the *Lyttelton/Hart-Davis Letters*: Franklin had chosen it because he thought Mrs. Cheever might be interested in lively book talk. The other books were volumes of poetry from some of his other publishers; he thought that since she was a poet, Mary Cheever might like to read some poetry.

They sat down at the dining room table, which was near the front door, and Franklin went over the front matter of the manuscript with her. He pointed out the addition to the title: "1931–1981." She nodded. Inside the front cover of the manuscript, Franklin had placed a copy of a letter to the Scott Meredith Agency; he explained that that agency sold subsidiary rights for us. She nodded. He went over the table of contents, explaining that the last eight titles in that list were enclosed in parentheses because we had not yet been able to locate the stories. One of these, "Bayonne," had appeared in the spring of 1936 in an obscure magazine, now defunct, called *Parade*. "Oh," Mrs. Cheever said nostalgically, "I remember 'Bayonne.'" A novella called "Behold a Cloud in the West" had been included as the only Cheever work in a collection of stories called *New Letters in America*, published by Norton in the late 1930s. We had ordered this relatively rare volume from Inter-Library Loan, but we had not yet received it.

Mrs. Cheever said she thought she had a copy of *New Letters* upstairs. Franklin accompanied her up to the library, where a portrait of the young John Cheever hung over the fireplace. She found the book quickly and gave it to Franklin; she said she was very pleased to have found it because John had given away a lot of books to friends and admirers. She was afraid he might have given that one away, too.

They went downstairs and resumed their seats at the table. Mrs. Cheever commented that it was so nice that "John's poor little stories" were going to be published. For scholars. Franklin, taken aback, said that they were not poor little stories; some of them were "wonderful," and not only scholars would want to read them: John Cheever had thousands of devoted readers outside the academy. Mrs. Cheever, apparently unconvinced, nodded and smiled at Franklin.

He broached the subject of the introduction to the book, about which he had already written her. Mrs. Cheever said she thought that John Updike was the best person to write the introduction. Franklin said that both he and Ben believed that Updike would be more helpful as a reviewer of the book for the *New Yorker* and that Raymond Carver would attract a new generation of readers to Cheever. Mrs. Cheever said she did not know anything about Carver's work. Franklin told her that he would like to use, as a foreword, the piece called "Why I Write Short Stories," which Cheever had written for *Newsweek* in 1978. Mrs. Cheever said she thought that was a good idea.

The conversation touched on Scott Donaldson's biography of Cheever. Mary Cheever said she thought Scott Donaldson was a perfectly pleasant man and "harmless." Her children, she said, thought otherwise.

Franklin told her that we were going to include in the book all the uncollected stories we had found. He repeated the reasons he had given Ben: for the sake of scholarship and completeness and to head off any reviewers who might carp about the inclusion of some of the weaker stories. Mary Cheever accepted that without discussion. She said she would pass the stories on to Ben; she knew he wanted to read them, especially the "Town House" series, because he had heard a lot about his parents having lived in a town house in New York with other couples during World War II. She made it clear that she had no intention of reading the stories herself.

Franklin reassured her, as he had Ben—although neither of them had asked about it—that Academy Chicago had an excellent sales force: he mentioned specifically the legendary southern rep George Scheer, who had been profiled in the *New Yorker*. And the Scott Meredith Agency would, he said, do a good job selling book club and other subsidiary rights.

After Franklin had been there for about forty-five minutes, two of the three Cheever children—Susan, the eldest, and Federico, the youngest—arrived with the journalist Warren Hinckle, who was to become Susan's third husband. Franklin and Susan had met when Susan worked at *Newsweek*. "Oh, Franklin," she said. She seemed surprised to see him there. Franklin introduced himself to Warren Hinckle and to Federico. Then, since he did not want to intrude further on a family gathering, he said his good-byes and departed.

He called us that evening and reported that he had had a good meeting with Mrs. Cheever; she was rather "ethereal," he said, as befitted a poet. At that time she represented the Cheever mystique for Franklin; he was all too willing to overlook any little lapse on her part. It was only months later, when the iron had entered into his soul, that he mentioned that she had not offered him even a cup of coffee during his visit.

Several times before Christmas, Franklin spoke to Ben, who had retrieved the manuscript from his mother and was reading it; he was especially fascinated by "Autobiography of a Drummer," a 1935 *New Republic* story that we had found extremely poignant. Ben said that John Cheever had always told his children that their grandfather had owned a shoe factory, but now, after reading this story, Ben thought that his grandfather might really have been a shoe salesman. Ben's only criticism of the manuscript was that the photocopies were not very good. Franklin reassured him that these were copies of copies, made only for Ben and for Scott Meredith. No one else would see them. And Ben mentioned to Franklin that he was reading the contract.

"Ben says he's reading the contract," Franklin told us cheerfully, "and he told me he thought I was going to do well financially out of this. I told him that yes, I really think this book is going to be a success. I told him about the paperback auction and the foreign rights and everything. He's really pleased." Ted Chichak at the Scott Meredith Agency had told us when we were in New York that we should hold an auction for the paperback reprint rights to the book, soon after the American Booksellers Association convention in late May. "I told him what Ted Chichak said about the auction and all that, and he told me—" Franklin chuckled, "—he told me that he mentioned this book to Allen Peacock at Simon & Schuster and Allen said, 'Why didn't you bring this book to us?'"

"Did he really?" we said. "No kidding! Isn't that great!"

We told everyone what Allen Peacock had said; it highlighted our great perspicacity and business acumen. We were behaving like a couple of first-century real estate agents selling lots in Pompeii and pointing out the wonderful view of Mount Vesuvius.

John le Carré had not responded to Franklin's two letters; we assumed that he must have changed his mind about joining a Cheever project. So, after checking with Ben, Franklin wrote to Raymond Carver about writing an introduction, and Carver responded, expressing interest. Franklin asked Jordan to send Carver the manuscript, which Jordan did, just before Christmas: the two volumes now contained photocopies of sixty-five stories, in addition to Mary Cheever's copy of "Behold a Cloud in the West."

We went off to the academic conventions we always attended between Christmas and the New Year—the Modern Language Association and the American Historical Association—with, we thought, everything in place. We had copies of almost all the stories and were delighted, by and large, with their quality; we had plans for promotion—we planned to give bound "samplers" containing two or three stories to booksellers at the ABA convention in May—and now we seemed to have solved the problem of the introduction. Both our eldest son Mark and our middle son Bruce agreed with Franklin that Raymond Carver's name on the book would attract younger readers to John Cheever's work. Ted Chichak of Scott Meredith, whom we thought must certainly be knowledgeable, was pleased with the book, and everyone who heard about it responded enthusiastically. We had planned a print run of seven thousand copies; now we wondered whether we might not be able to sell ten thousand.

It looked as though 1988 was going to be a great year.

6

"Serious Inequities in the Contract"

On a Monday morning in the middle of January 1988, Jordan woke me with a bulletin. "Franklin just called," he said. "He says something very disquieting has happened. Ben wants to break the contract. And Andrew Wylie is going to call us."

I was half asleep. "Who's Andrew Wylie?" I said.

Franklin had gotten off the phone without giving Jordan any details. On our drive downtown, we suggested to each other that, on the one hand, Franklin might be blowing the thing out of proportion, but, on the other hand, maybe it hadn't been such a hot idea to tell Ben all that great stuff about paperback auctions and big money. It was certainly understandable that Franklin would want the Cheevers to know that we were going to do a good job for them. But now Ben had been reading the stories—and the contract—and suddenly Andrew Wylie had appeared on the scene. Very odd.

We arrived at the office to find that Andrew Wylie had phoned twice. He had asked for me. I was, of course, president of the company, but Jordan had handled all the arrangements and signed the contract. I had only witnessed his signature.

Jordan called ICM to find that Maggie Curran was no longer there. She had retired. Since Maggie had been assistant to Lynn Nesbit, one of New York's more high-powered agents and a vice president of ICM, Jordan asked for Lynn Nesbit. She wasn't available, but her assistant, Lew Grimes, said that he didn't know anything about this development and suggested that we ask Wylie to write us a letter.

A few minutes later, Wylie called again and asked for me.

"My name is Andrew Wylie," he said. "I'm a literary agent. I have been retained by the Cheevers to terminate their contract with you."

"Write me a letter," I said. There was a pause, and I added, "But I'm not going to terminate."

"You aren't?" he said. He sounded surprised.

"No, I'm not. Why would I want to do that?"

"There are serious inequities in the contract," he said. "Surely you must be aware of that."

I said I wasn't at all aware of that, and I asked him what he meant.

For one thing, he said, "Franklin Dennis misrepresented himself to the Cheevers. When he approached them, he did not tell them he worked for you."

I said I couldn't believe that; I was sure it was not true.

"The Cheevers are very unhappy," Wylie said.

I asked him whether he had spoken to Mrs. Cheever.

"Yes," he said. "I have."*

"And is she unhappy?"

"Yes, she is. Very unhappy."

"Well," I said, "write me a letter."

"All right," he said. "You will hear either from me or from my lawyer, *Martin Garbus.*"

The name sounded vaguely familiar to me. Wylie's emphasis told me he considered it to be intimidating.

After I hung up, I looked at a copy of Franklin's first letter to Ben, dated June 15, 1987. The first sentence read, "I work for Academy Chicago Publishers." And the letter was signed, "Franklin Dennis for Academy Chicago Publishers." So Franklin had clearly not "misrepresented" himself. It seemed obvious to us that Wylie was looking for a way to take this book from us and from ICM and renegotiate a new contract with a big publisher for a big advance, of which he would get 10 percent or more.

Efforts to reach Franklin were fruitless that day. Jordan did reach Lynn Nesbit, who said she knew nothing about any of this. Jordan asked her if the name *Martin Garbus* rang a bell. "Oh yes," she said, "I know Marty Garbus." She said she would call Susan Cheever, who was out of town, and try to find out what was going on. It did not occur to us to wonder why she did not call Mary Cheever, her client.

We could not figure out what might have happened to trigger this. About

---

*Mrs. Cheever was later to testify that she had not spoken to Wylie.

ten days earlier, an article by John Blades had appeared in the *Chicago Tribune,* discussing the forthcoming *Letters* and the Scott Donaldson biography of Cheever and including a brief interview with Franklin about the *Uncollected Stories.* Was it possible, we wondered, that Wylie had somehow seen the Blades piece, which was the first public announcement of our book, and had gotten in touch with Ben . . . . ? And why would Mrs. Cheever suddenly become unhappy? She had been perfectly cooperative when Franklin had seen her a month before. And if she was unhappy, why hadn't she told her own agent, Lynn Nesbit?

On Tuesday, Franklin still did not answer his phone. Jordan reached Lynn Nesbit again, and this time she sounded annoyed. She said she had talked to Susan Cheever, who told her she didn't know anything about all of this but that Wylie was an old friend of Ben's. "That's a ridiculous advance," Ms. Nesbit said to Jordan. "Fifteen hundred dollars."

Jordan replied that we had paid what we could afford. She repeated that it was ridiculous. The Cheevers, she said, had received "many hundreds of thousands of dollars" for the journals. She said she had called Maggie Curran and asked her why she had allowed Mrs. Cheever to sign that contract; Maggie had said that Mrs. Cheever wanted to do it. "I'm not going to get embroiled in a mess," Lynn Nesbit said. "I'll just drop this contract."

About 5:00 that Tuesday afternoon, Franklin resurfaced, to our great relief. He explained that on Monday morning, he had decided to hire a lawyer and had gotten a name from Eric Rohman at the Princeton University Press. The lawyer, Bob Stein of Pryor, Cashman, Sherman & Flynn, had told Franklin not to talk to anyone, including us, until he, Stein, had had a chance to read the contract. Now Stein had read it and had told Franklin he could contact us. The most important thing Stein had done, Franklin said, was to call Wylie and tell him to stop phoning Franklin. That had been a great relief.

"Has Wylie been phoning you?" Jordan asked. "What for?"

Franklin said that on the previous Friday afternoon, Ben Cheever had phoned him at his office and invited him to go out for a drink; he said he wanted to introduce him to an agent he knew. Since Ben had told Franklin several times that everyone thought Franklin was a genius for coming up with the Cheever story project, Franklin assumed that Ben was going to introduce him to an agent who might want to work with him on future projects.

So Ben collected him, and they went into the bar at the Algonquin Hotel, where Andrew Wylie was waiting for them. Franklin had never heard of Wylie, but it didn't take him long to decide that he didn't like him. Ben had brought along the two-volume manuscript in blue bindings. Wylie picked the volumes up, hefted them with a grunt of approval, and said that he could take this book to any publisher in New York and get $100,000 immediately. He added with pride that none of his authors ever earned back their advances. He said he knew how to get a lot of money.

While Ben sat silent, Wylie went on to say that Academy Chicago was the wrong publisher for this book. He was flying to London in a few days to see Sonny Mehta—the head of Knopf, a division of Random House—and on his way back he would stop off in Chicago and speak to the people at Academy. When he explained to them that they weren't wanted, they would surely back off. Now in the meantime Franklin had to go to Wylie's office first thing Monday morning and sign a contract with the Cheevers for this book, and they would give him 25 percent of their royalties.

Franklin, desperately confused by Ben's silence, said that Academy Chicago had twenty-two salesmen across the country; the publisher could do an excellent job, they were eager to do it, and he didn't think they would be willing to bow out.

Ben spoke up at this point. He said that his mother agreed with him that the contract should be canceled and a more appropriate publisher should be found. He said that when they started, he had no idea that this was going to be such a big project. No matter how many salesmen Academy had, Knopf or Random House could certainly sell more copies than they could; so, Ben said, even though the Cheevers were proposing to give Franklin 25 percent instead of the present 50 percent, he—Franklin—would come out the same financially. And, Ben said, Andrew here will be able to get an appropriate advance of at least a hundred thousand, so you'll get money up front. He added earnestly that Franklin deserved this because he had had such a clever idea.

Wylie said that Academy was just "hopeless" and Scott Meredith was only an "order taker." And neither Raymond Carver nor John le Carré was the right person to write the introduction. Saul Bellow was the man to do it.

Franklin, as can be imagined, was extremely upset. He did not know how to deal with this situation. Wylie was insistent: Franklin must go to his office on Monday morning and sign an agreement. Finally, to get out of there, Franklin said he would do that. He went home, too distraught and confused to call us. On Monday morning, Wylie called him and demanded a copy of the contract and reminded him that he expected him at his office shortly. Franklin said he would not go until the afternoon, but he did messenger a copy of the contract to Wylie, who, incidentally, had no right to ask for it. Later in the morning Wylie called Franklin again and, sounding somewhat less peremptory, told him that the Cheevers "wanted to do right" by him. It was at this point that Franklin decided to consult a lawyer.

Bob Stein told him not to go to Wylie's office. He said he would call Wylie and tell him to stop phoning Franklin. After he had looked at the contract, Stein said that it was good and enforceable.

Jordan and I decided that we had better get in touch with our own lawyer, Paul Freehling. Paul was not an intellectual properties lawyer, but he had handled some bizarre problems for us with aplomb. We sent him the contract, all correspondence, and a written summary of events. We also phoned Ted Chichak at the Scott Meredith Agency. He was soothing. He said we had an airtight contract—we had given him a copy in December—and we shouldn't worry: "This sort of thing goes on in New York all the time."

On Thursday afternoon Franklin called to say that he wanted to phone Ben and offer to give up 25 percent of his royalty share to the Cheevers. "I look upon the Cheevers as an extension of John Cheever," Franklin said. "I respect them enormously. I hate the idea that they're not happy with me." Bob Stein, Franklin's lawyer, had suggested that Franklin offer the 25 percent in return for a legal document promising that the Cheevers would not sue us. Stein suggested that we might make other relatively small concessions, on foreign rights and so on. It was nitpicking, he said, but these points might help.

We ourselves were distinctly annoyed with the Cheevers because of the conversation in the Algonquin bar; we thought making concessions at this stage might only encourage Ben and Wylie. Franklin said he would not do anything until we had discussed it with Paul Freehling, but he would like to talk to Ben while Wylie was away in London. When we asked him about it, Paul said that he thought it would be a mistake for Franklin to approach Ben or to ask him for an undertaking that he would not sue us. The contract looked okay to him, assuming that Mary Cheever had the proper authority to sign it and that she was compos mentis. Neither Ben nor Andrew Wylie could sue us without being sued in turn for interfering with a contract, he said, and even if Franklin signed a contract with them, he could not abrogate our contract with Mary Cheever. Paul told us to behave normally and not do anything "out of the routine" with this book. And if Wylie or Ben phoned, we should refuse to speak to him.

We felt somewhat reassured, although the admonition to "behave normally" called up memories of the instructions Kim Philby got from the Russians just before they sent a ship for him.

We reached Franklin with some difficulty—radio celebrity Sally Jessy Raphael lived across the street from him, and broadcasts from her house had tied up his phone lines. He and Bob Stein, Franklin said, were alone in thinking he should get in touch with Ben. Franklin's wife Mary and everyone else he knew were dead set against it. But he wanted to think it over.

We got back to the many things that needed our attention. For one thing, the old piano warehouse on the Chicago River that housed our offices and books was going to be torn down. We had to find new quarters before September. Then there were necessary repairs to our house. One of them was a new electronic garage door that responded to a portable gizmo: one day it responded a little too enthusiastically and destroyed the rear window of our hatchback. So on a bright Wednesday morning, January 27, we went to a suburban auto parts garage, where Jordan phoned the office to find out if anything was new. Something was. Martin Garbus had called me.

It had been ten days since I had heard from Andrew Wylie. We had relaxed.

When we got to the office, I called Paul Freehling. He said he would answer Garbus's call. I said I thought they were trying to intimidate us. Could they legally keep calling and bothering us?

Not indefinitely, Paul said: there was a thing called "laches" that could protect us. If they kept threatening and delayed filing beyond a reasonable time, their plea for an injunction would be disallowed. (It was a relief to hear that, although that was the only relief laches afforded us. When I brought the principle up later, in a time of need, Paul said laches was inappropriate in that instance.)

The next morning Paul called us at home to report on his conversation with Garbus. Paul had started that conversation in a friendly way—telling Garbus how much he enjoyed reading his column in the *New York Law Journal*. Then Garbus told Paul that he represented Ben Cheever and Andrew Wylie and his clients felt that Academy Chicago was not the right publisher for the collection under discussion because Academy Chicago had no experience with mass publishing. The Cheevers needed a publisher with mass experience who had published Cheever before and who had a relationship with the Cheever family. Maybe the publisher should be Knopf, Garbus said, maybe it shouldn't be Knopf . . . .

While Paul made notes, Garbus went on: the stories were uneven; some were very bad. John Cheever had not wanted these stories published, and certainly the man's wishes should be respected. An experienced, sophisticated editor was needed to fix these stories up, to improve them. Maggie Curran at ICM had thought this was going to be a "scholarly" book, and certainly no publisher in the country was better suited to do a scholarly book than Academy Chicago. In fact, Garbus said, the contract was perfectly proper, and Academy had behaved properly. The Cheevers had no quarrel with Academy. But Academy should now back out, and they would be compensated for out-of-pocket expenses. ICM's Lynn Nesbit was going to drop this book. And by the way, he had seen the Xeroxes in the blue binders, and they were very bad, very sloppy work. Finally, there was the weighty question of whether Mary Cheever had the authority to sign this contract, and there was the question of her competency. Maybe she's competent, Garbus said, maybe she's not competent . . . .

The suggestion that Mary Cheever did not have the authority to sign the contract was the only thing Garbus said that Paul thought had any relevance. We assured him that Mary Cheever was John Cheever's legal heir. We had no proof, but we had to believe she was the heir. We told Paul that she had to be the heir because, for one thing, ICM had allowed her to sign the contract. In that case, Paul said, he believed that they were going to hold a competency hearing for Mrs. Cheever. We told him we considered that unthinkable. But he repeated Garbus's words: "Maybe she's competent, maybe she's not competent . . . . " "I believe," Paul said, "that what he's telling us is that they are going to have a competency hearing and they expect her to be found incompetent."

He had to get back to Garbus, Paul said, on whether we were going to give up the contract. We said that we found Garbus's demand outrageous and without foundation. I was particularly insulted by the comments about the Cheevers needing an "experienced and sophisticated editor" and by the suggestion that someone should tinker with these stories to "improve" them. Paul told us not to decide without giving the matter careful thought. He had the impression from Garbus, he said, that we had "stumbled" on "a diamond in the rough"—he was referring to the stories—but we had to be aware that this could be a very ugly situation; everything we had ever done would be laid out for everyone to see. As an example, he mentioned a famous case involving Occidental Petroleum and Mead Paper, the upshot of which was that Mead Paper had linked Occidental Petroleum to the Love Canal pollution scandal and things looked so bad for them that Occidental backed off.

In the end, Paul said, he thought we would prevail; the whole thing would probably be over by May. If Mary Cheever really was the heir and if she proved competent, we would probably win. But we would have to travel a long, rocky, ugly road. We should be sure that we wanted to do it. He was a litigator, he said; he loved a fight. He prowled alleys looking for a chin to punch. But he wanted us to know what we were getting into.

We told him we saw no reason to back off. We had no scandal in our background; we did have a contract signed in good faith by someone who we were convinced had the right to sign it. It had been vetted by one of the most prominent literary agencies in the world. We knew the book was good, and we thought it was shocking that Garbus would suggest that these stories could be "edited" to make them better. And the talk about Knopf was silly; apart from anything else, Knopf was not a "mass" publisher. We told Paul to tell Garbus that we were not going to bow out.

When Franklin heard about Paul's conversation with Garbus, he told us that he had a copy of John Cheever's will, which he had obtained at his lawyer Bob Stein's suggestion, and that Mary Cheever was unquestionably the sole heir. He could not imagine that anyone would question her competency. "She drives a car," he said. "She lives alone. She writes poetry. She recognized the title of 'Behold a Cloud in the West' and went right upstairs and got it for me. She's sort of ethereal, but she's certainly competent."

Paul was surprised but pleased to hear about the will. He said he thought "the Mary Cheever issue" was all Ben and Wylie had, and he still believed that Garbus intended to pursue the question of her competency. He had called Garbus and informed him that his clients were excited about the book and were going to go ahead with it. Garbus had replied, slowly and ominously, "I'm sorry to hear that. I'm *really* sorry to hear that."

"We're going to hear from them in about ten days, I think," Paul said briskly. "We're going to be in court."

7

"They're My Only Children"

It was on Friday, January 29, that Paul told Garbus we intended to go ahead with the book. We expected to hear from the Cheevers again the following week because a pattern of weekly communication seemed to have been established. Sure enough, the next Friday, February 5, Ben called me. I forgot that Paul had told me not to speak to any of them and accepted the call. I was careful to make notes. My response was terse, and Ben became angry immediately. If I was not going to be pleasant, he said, he would hang up on me.

"All right," I said pleasantly. "Go ahead."

He said that his lawyer had assured him that he would win this case, but he believed that people communicating directly could do better than lawyers, who cost a lot of money and frequently made things worse. So he and his sister wanted to come to Chicago and meet with us, and maybe we could work things out.

"What do you mean?" I said. "Terminate the contract?"

"Well," he said, "yes." But we could talk about that. So I agreed to meet on the following Tuesday. "Just you and your sister," I said.

"Yes, and I might bring Mr. Wylie."

"Oh no," I said. "I won't meet with Mr. Wylie."

He said all right, he wouldn't bring Mr. Wylie. He gave me two phone numbers where he could be reached if anything came up before Tuesday. I wrote them in my diary on the date of the meeting. We chatted a bit about Chicago; he said he had not been there since he was a small child. Then he remarked, "You know, Franklin never told me when we talked that he worked for Academy Chicago. He gave me the impression that he was going to take this book to various publishers and see what kind of deal he could get."

"I don't think that's possible," I said. "I have a copy of his first letter to you, and the first sentence says, 'I work for Academy Chicago.'"

"I really would like to know what Franklin has done here," Ben said. "I'd like to know why he is part of this."

I said the book was Franklin's idea—

Ben cut me off with a scornful laugh. "Oh," he said, "I suppose if I decide I'm going to design a Ford car, I should get all the money Ford gets?"

"Franklin knows all about John Cheever," I said.

"Franklin doesn't know anything about John Cheever," Ben said. "He may have picked up a few things about John Cheever from me. Franklin has not handled this thing right at all; he's not a straightforward person. He's not reputable. And he has no connections. First he talked about getting John le Carré to do an introduction, and I guess that fell through. Now he's talking about Ray Carver, and I'm not convinced that Ray Carver is the right one for this. I just don't like the way this thing is being handled. Those were terrible-looking Xeroxes."

I agreed that the Xeroxes could have been better. But I said that he should understand that we had made them from other Xeroxes in a hurry because we were rushing to New York for a sales conference.

"Oh, but you don't go around *showing* something like that," Ben said.

I told him we hadn't shown it; it was too early to show anything to the salespeople. We had made the Xeroxes only for him and the people at the Scott Meredith Agency.

"I just don't like the way that this is being handled," Ben said. "And you don't have all the stories anyway."

"We don't?" I asked. I was surprised to hear that.

"No, you don't."

"But didn't you tell Franklin that you would look out for other stories when you were reading the letters and tell him if you found anything?"

"Who's editing this book?" Ben said. "Franklin or me?"

I could see that this conversation wasn't going anywhere.

"He even went to see my *mother*," Ben said. "He doesn't know what he's doing. He doesn't know the stories."

"Did *you* know the stories?" I asked.

"Of course I did. I knew them all," Ben said. "I wasn't paying any attention. I thought this was going to be a nice little book . . . . "

"Well, if you knew the stories, you must have known that this could not be a little book," I said. "There are too many of them for a little book."

"I don't mean physically," he said, "I mean about a ten-thousand run."

"That's what we plan," I said. "A run of about ten thousand."

"And then I start to hear about paperback auctions," Ben said. "I hear about foreign rights sales."

"Are we talking about money now?" I asked.

"No, but now I hear about all these things. And I wasn't paying any attention. And—well, you got away with something."

"I resent very much being told that I got away with something, Mr. Cheever," I said. "If you're going to talk to me like that, I think it would be better if we didn't meet."

"Maybe we shouldn't meet," he said in a disheartened tone, and we both hung up.

During this conversation, Jordan phoned Paul Freehling. "She's talking to Ben Cheever now," he said in a low voice, like a sports announcer reporting on a golf game in progress. After I hung up, I told Paul what Ben had said. We all agreed that it was odd that we had received nothing in writing.

About two weeks later, Franklin had lunch with Bill Goldstein, then trade news editor for *Publishers Weekly (PW)*. Goldstein told Franklin that he was going to write a story about our Cheever book, and he had called Ben Cheever at Simon & Schuster because he wanted to include information about the *Letters*. Allen Peacock, Ben's editor, took the call; he was delighted to hear from Bill Goldstein and went off to hunt up Ben. But Allen returned to the phone to tell Goldstein that Ben had a message for him: he refused to speak to *PW*, and he was going to sue Academy Chicago. Goldstein asked Franklin what was going on.

Franklin told Goldstein that all he could say at the moment was that Andrew Wylie had come on the scene, and as a result there was some tension. Bill said he thought he got the message.

On February 20, a Saturday, we were in the office as usual, coping with the mail, when Paul Freehling called. He had been away and had just come into his office to find a message from Garbus saying that he had written us "a contentious letter."

"Every week there's something," I said. "This is a war of nerves."

The contentious letter arrived, by registered mail, on Monday. It was dated February 17 and addressed to Jordan. I no longer seemed to be the focus of attention.

> Dear Mr. Miller:
> We are attorneys for the Estate of John Cheever (the "es-

tate"). Our clients inform us that Academy Chicago Publishers ("Academy") intends to publish the "uncollected" stories of John Cheever pursuant to an agreement purportedly reached between Academy and Mary Cheever, executor of the Estate. Benjamin Cheever also made efforts to meet with you to discuss the proposed publication. We were told that you declined to meet with him.

Our client informs us that the agreement was obtained through fraudulent representation by Franklin Dennis and the Academy [*sic*] and, thus, is void. Moreover, according to our client, Mr. Dennis and Academy are *totally* incapable of performing and, indeed, have not performed their obligations pursuant to any such agreement.

Thus, the Estate demands that Academy confirm to us that it has no intention to publish any of the works of John Cheever. If we do not receive such confirmation within five days of your receipt of this letter, we will have no alternative but to bring an action against you for a judgment declaring the agreement void and seeking appropriate damages.

Nothing contained in this letter should be construed as a waiver of any of our client's legal or equitable rights in this or any other matter.

Very truly yours,
Martin Garbus

cc: Mary Cheever

Since we were unused to receiving threatening missives from lawyers, we took this letter at face value. We considered it an ultimatum and told Paul we thought we should act immediately to forestall being sued in New York; we expected that a suit would be filed against us there by the following Monday. Paul said that we should not go off half-cocked. He was not at all sure that the letter meant what it said.

He was surprised to see that Garbus, having told him he represented Ben Cheever and Andrew Wylie, was now claiming to represent the "Estate of John Cheever." By the way, Paul asked, when did Cheever die? He registered amazement when we told him that Cheever had died in 1982.

"Nineteen eighty-two!" he said. "Then the estate has to be closed. How can Garbus represent the estate?" He noted that Garbus's letter was copied to Mary Cheever. "I wonder if she really got a copy," he said.

Since, as I have mentioned, Paul was not an intellectual properties lawyer, he asked our permission to consult with a Chicago firm that specializes in copyright and related matters. Consequently, he spent a morning in the offices of Pattishall, McAuliffe & Hofstedder, where he was assured that he had the matter in hand; there were, as he put it, "no hidden shoals." They did want to bring up one point: the question of the children's rights. The Pattishall people explained that after an author's death, any of his or her work that comes up for copyright renewal becomes, when it is renewed, the property of his or her children as well as of the spouse, regardless of what the will says. Any of the children, as well as the spouse, can assign rights in these renewed works without officially notifying the other heirs, but compensation must be shared among them.

There were three stories in our collection that had come up for renewal after 1982, the year of Cheever's death: "The True Confessions of Henry Pell" (*Harper's Magazine*, June 1954); "The Journal of a Writer with a Hole in One Sock" (*The Reporter*, December 29, 1955); and "How Dr. Wareham Kept His Servants"(*The Reporter*, April 5, 1956). There was no problem for us here because Mary Cheever had the legal right to assign these stories to us. But Pattishall felt Paul should be aware of this situation.

There was no reason, Pattishall said, why we could not file for a declaratory judgment that our contract was valid. We had been presented with a written ultimatum, they said, and we ought to protect ourselves against being sued in New York. They had one other suggestion: someone should call Mary Cheever and confirm that she had in fact hired Garbus, because we had only his word for that. Since he had mentioned representing the estate and also Ben and Wylie, they were not clear about whom he actually represented.

Jordan said he would call Mrs. Cheever. Everyone in the office, including me, thought he was very brave. And when she answered the phone, Mary Cheever was most pleasant. Martin Garbus did, indeed, represent the estate, she said, but "only on this one matter." Jordan asked her whether she had received a copy of Garbus's letter to us; as Paul had suspected, she had not, and she knew nothing about it.

Jordan asked her if she was unhappy with us. "Yes," she said promptly, "we're unhappy." She said she shouldn't have signed the contract without looking into it more carefully. "What are you going to do?" she asked.

"We're going to publish the book," Jordan said. "We've already put a lot of work into it—"

"Oh come *on!*" she said. "It wasn't even properly xeroxed."

Jordan explained, as I had tried to do with Ben, that the manuscript consisted of copies of copies, that only three sets were made and they were not for general distribution.

Mrs. Cheever commented in her thin, reedy voice that "What's-His-Name"—Franklin—had come to see her, and she had given him a book with a story in it. She added morosely that she would probably never see the book again.

Jordan, taken aback, said that Franklin would certainly return the book. "Why didn't he find it *himself*?" she asked, with some vigor.

Jordan explained carefully that we were in the process of finding all the stories. It was a months-long process, the stories were in various places, and that particular story had not yet been sent to us by Inter-Library Loan.

"I signed the contract in November, didn't I?" she asked.

No, Jordan told her, she signed it in August.

"Oh," she said. "August?" Then she said that they were afraid "the book wouldn't be properly promoted and—made . . . . "

Jordan responded with an impassioned description of the good things we had done and our excellent reputation.

She agreed that Maggie Curran had told her we were highly regarded. "That's why I signed the contract," she said. She laughed rather sadly. That was her only excuse for the children, she said; she told them what Maggie had said.

Jordan acknowledged that one had one's feelings for one's children.

"They're my only children," Mrs. Cheever said.

Jordan said he had children of his own and he understood.

She seemed disturbed about the letter Garbus had sent us. "I'm kind of dumb about lawyers and things like that," she said. Had Martin Garbus sent us a summons?

"No," Jordan said. "A letter accusing us of fraud and misrepresentation."

She said they had more or less decided that "Martin Garbus is a very expensive, high-powered New York lawyer. We haven't gotten together yet, but I think we're going to tell him to stop pretty soon."

"You're going to tell him to stop?" Jordan asked. The entire staff was standing around his desk, listening to his end of the conversation. His words elicited sighs of relief.

"Maybe," Mrs. Cheever said. She laughed. "I probably shouldn't be telling you this," she said. She went on to say that she was "kind of dumb about contracts. What clause was it that caused so much trouble?" She added, "You have to admit that the advance is minute."

Jordan had nearly forgotten that his purpose in calling her had been only to find out whether she had actually hired Martin Garbus. Now he felt rather awkward; he did not want to take advantage of what appeared to be her confiding nature by talking about the contract with her. It did not seem right. So he talked instead about his feelings toward her, which at the moment were genuinely warm. "We have no animus against you," he said. "No matter what happens. Please believe that."

"I don't want to be unfriendly either," she said.

Jordan hung up and looked at all of us. "She's such a nice woman," he said.

8

"Cheever Clout"

Paul began to work on our complaint,* the first pleading of our case, with some reluctance. He was not sure that a lawsuit was the way to go; he did not want to destroy any possibility of an amicable agreement with Mary Cheever.

But after Jordan's conversation with Mrs. Cheever, it seemed clear to us that her opinion carried little, if any, weight. She had not been sent a copy of the ultimatum and had not been told about it. She did not even seem to know what the dispute was all about: she had asked what "clause" in the contract was responsible for "so much trouble." We remembered also Maggie Curran's note saying, "I don't care what Mary says," and the fact that Lynn Nesbit had not called Mary to ask what was going on. Jordan and I felt sure that Mrs. Cheever would never have initiated this hassle; she had seemed genuinely pleased that her husband's "poor little stories" were going to be published.

Bob Stein, Franklin's lawyer, called Paul to say that he thought Garbus should be approached with Franklin's offer to give the Cheevers 25 percent of his share of the royalties. Mary Cheever would then get 75 percent, and Franklin would be left with the 25 percent that Ben and Wylie had offered him in the Algonquin bar. Stein said he knew Garbus; Stein had opposed him on a case and believed that Garbus saw himself as a businessman; he loved to negotiate, and he was almost always successful. "He wins all his cases," Stein said. He offered to negotiate with Garbus for us.

Both Jordan and I thought that any approach to the Cheevers would be perceived by them as a sign of weakness. I was sure, after my conversation with Ben, that they would not accept Franklin's offer. For one thing, there was Andrew Wylie's presence in this affair. Wylie could not profit in any way as long as ICM held the contract. He could profit only if he agented a new contract for Mary Cheever with another publisher—"maybe it would

---

*The complaint in a civil suit is the plaintiff's first statement in legal terms of the facts on which the plaintiff's case is based.

be Knopf; maybe it wouldn't be Knopf . . . . "—and he had told me that Martin Garbus was his lawyer. Garbus had told Paul that he represented both Ben *and* Wylie. Ergo, we did not think that Wylie would advise Ben to take an additional 25 percent and let the ICM contract stand.

Apart from that, we thought that Martin Garbus saw himself as more a crusader than a businessman. He wished to be seen as a staunch defender of civil rights. He had defended Lenny Bruce and Timothy Leary in court, as well as various black, Native American, and Hispanic victims of society. He points out in his autobiography that he has "spent time" with Cesar Chavez, for instance, and that he is particularly outraged by the presence in the courtroom of "the structure of power and privilege" or by the suggestion that anyone would sacrifice "moral principle for self-interest."[1] Garbus was impelled to take up the practice of law, he says, because of "the promise of change through the judicial process." Both *Publishers Weekly* and Studs Terkel had compared him to Clarence Darrow. We thought that a posture as the defender of the rights of the hapless widow of a great American writer might be attractive to him.

Paul agreed with us that any concession could encourage the opposition, but he did not feel he could interfere between Franklin and his lawyer. So he told Bob Stein to go ahead and make the offer if he thought it was best to do it. Stein acted accordingly and reported to Paul that Garbus had said he would take the offer to the Cheevers but—surprise!—he could not hold out any hope that they would accept it. Stein replied to Garbus that Academy was adamant, but a look at Garbus's case might shake them loose: he asked Garbus what his aces were. Garbus responded that without the "Cheever clout," Academy would never get anyone to write an introduction for the book and would never get permissions from the magazines to reprint the stories. And, he added, no matter what happened, Ben would never allow us to publish more than two or three stories.

As "aces," these left something to be desired. We had had the necessary permissions for months. And Raymond Carver had agreed to write the introduction. He told us he was ill, but he would be happy to provide a relatively brief appreciation for the book.

On Friday, February 26, Paul filed the complaint in chancery court in Chicago. He could have filed in federal court, but he told us he chose chancery because he knew the judges there better. This was, to put it mildly, the wrong decision. The complaint said, among other things:

In about January, 1988 various persons contacted representatives of Academy, stated the Contract was null and void, and threatened to institute legal action against Academy. . . . Unless this Court declares that the Contract is valid and enforceable, Academy will be required to take enormous risks in publishing the Work in the face of the threats made purportedly on Mrs. Cheever's behalf or, otherwise, to abandon the project.

Academy has no adequate remedy at law.

Paul delayed the service of this complaint on Mrs. Cheever. He was hoping that he would not have to do it.

On Wednesday, March 2, we received our weekly shove from the Cheevers in the form of a strange letter from Martin Garbus. It had not been sent by registered mail, and it was addressed only to Academy Chicago Publishers. The salutation was "Gentlemen." Both Jordan and I seemed to have faded out of the picture.

Garbus wrote that he had recently spoken to "Mr. Wise, the attorney for Mr. Dennis" and had told him what he had already told Academy's attorney, which was that even if Academy were "to prevail on the question of the validity of the contract that the course of conduct since the contract was entered into makes it difficult for me to believe that Academy can publish a book of the kind it wants." He listed "several disagreements": what should be included in the collection; whether "all the copyrights" could be "obtained"; how the book should be edited; how the introduction "should relate to the book"; "how and by whom the introduction should be written"; and "how the book should be presented." He wrote further that he had told "Mr. Wise . . . that given what I had understood what had happened, I saw no possibility of the Cheevers and Academy cooperating in publishing a book that will satisfy both of them."

We found this letter puzzling. There had never been any "disagreements" about anything: we had never been able to drag any opinions out of either Ben or Mrs. Cheever. We had to assume that "Mr. Wise" was Bob Stein; someone made the facetious suggestion that Garbus might have been thinking of a lawyer named Wisenstein. The phrase "given what I had understood what happened" caused endless amusement.

Paul said the whole case was beginning to remind him of P. D.Q. Bach: a series of announcements of a nonevent.

9

"Franklin Thinks Maybe the Cheevers Won't Like It"

Early in January, before the fateful meeting at the Algonquin Hotel, Jordan had written to Scott Donaldson, Cheever's biographer, to ask him whether he knew of any uncollected stories we might have missed or that Dennis Coates, the bibliographer, might have missed. Jordan enclosed copies of the table of contents of our book and of Franklin's editor's note. Professor Donaldson wrote back that he thought Coates, who was extremely thorough, had probably "caught all the stories." He added that he himself had read them all and he thought Franklin's note did not make all the necessary "connections" between the stories. Jordan had mentioned that we were having trouble locating the early story "Bayonne," and Donaldson very kindly enclosed a copy of it with his reply; he said he knew it was the story most difficult to locate.

Franklin had, of course, no intention of making literary judgments in his note; he expected to leave those to the writer of the introduction. The tone of Donaldson's letter gave us the impression that he would be interested in writing the introduction, for which we now had an agreement with Raymond Carver. But in late February, we received an unsettling letter from Mr. Carver: his lung cancer was "acting up a bit again now," and he was going to have to spend some time in the hospital. He said he could not concentrate even on his own work, and so he was afraid we could not count on him for anything. We were extremely touched that he had troubled to write this apologetic letter; of course, it saddened us immensely. And he had even taken the time to suggest the name of another writer who might write the introduction for us.

It was now March. Our fall advertisements and other announcements had to be prepared weeks in advance; we had to have catalogs ready for the American Booksellers Association Convention in Anaheim at the end of May, and all this literature should include the name of the person writing the introduction. Following Paul's advice to proceed routinely, we had sent the manuscript out to be typeset so that we could give bound galleys to reviewers and booksellers at the convention.

Mrs. Cheever had received notice of our suit on March 9. Some time after that, Garbus told Paul Freehling that the Cheevers wanted to settle this suit, to put an end to it. He said he was busy with other matters, so he was turning this case over to Maura Wogan of his office. On March 28, Maura Wogan called Paul, who was out of town; she told Dana Deane, a lawyer in Paul's office, that the Cheevers were going to go along with our contract, but she needed six weeks to pull everything together. The next day, Dana Deane sent her a confirmation of the phone conversation:

> Dear Ms. Wogan:
> On March 28, 1988, you contacted me by telephone stating that your client was willing to commit to settlement of the above-captioned matter which included her acknowledgment of the validity of the August 15, 1987 contract between our clients. You also indicated that Mr. Ben Cheever was willing to "sign off" on any settlement to which our clients agreed. Pursuant to your representations, Academy Chicago has agreed to your request for expansion of time to file Defendant's Answer in the above-captioned matter until May 6, 1988.
> Mr. Freehling will be in the office again next week and he will contact you at that time in order to make arrangements for settlement of this matter.
>
> Very truly yours,
> Dana S. Deane

Of course, we were relieved to hear that this thing was going to be settled. But we wondered why these people needed six weeks. We asked Paul whether it was a good idea to grant them an extension until May. Paul said it was; the judge would undoubtedly insist that we grant it, so we might as well do it. And by the way, we had been assigned to a terrific judge: his name was Roger Kiley, Paul said, and he was just about the best on the bench. Paul explained that the Cheevers needed an extension because they had added Chicago counsel to their team—one M. Leslie Kite, a lawyer who apparently specialized in pension work, and M. Leslie Kite needed time to familiarize himself with the case. Kite had confirmed to Paul that the Cheevers were going to settle.

We wondered why the Cheevers would add a Chicago lawyer to their team and pay him to familiarize himself with the case if the case was not going forward. And we wondered why nobody had brought up settlement terms. But we didn't want to bother Paul with dumb questions, and anyway, we had a lot of things on our minds. Our new offices were on the second floor of a renovated loft building, once the Schwinn bicycle factory, in the River North area of Chicago. The space was completely open and had to be built out, so we were busy with plans and contractors.

Then there was the question of the introduction. I decided that the simplest, easiest thing to do was to ask Scott Donaldson to write it. He obviously wanted to do it; he probably already knew most of the stories, so there would not be a long delay while he went through the manuscript; and an introduction by a knowledgeable academic would surely shed more light on the stories than a laudatory piece by a novelist. In addition, Donaldson's biography of Cheever was coming out in a few months, and everything would fit together nicely.

Jordan thought my arguments were convincing, but Franklin did not agree. He said he had heard that there were bad feelings between the Cheevers and Scott Donaldson; he did not know exactly what had happened, but he did know that the Cheevers had caused the biography to be postponed and that Donaldson had been forced to rewrite some of it. He thought it might have been a J. D. Salinger kind of threat, with the Cheevers refusing to allow Donaldson to quote from unpublished letters and journal entries. I said that things must have been worked out because Random House was about to publish the biography. I had a bee in my bonnet, as they say, about Scott Donaldson.

Jordan was uncertain. "Franklin thinks maybe the Cheevers won't like it," he said.

I pointed out that the Cheevers had given us no direction in the matter of the introduction—or anything else. They had never voiced an opinion, except that Ben had agreed with Franklin that John Updike should not write it and that Mrs. Cheever had said she thought Updike should write it.

Jordan called Donaldson and asked him directly whether there were bad feelings between him and the Cheevers and whether they would be angry if he wrote the introduction. Jordan explained to him that we were already having trouble with the Cheevers. No, Donaldson said, there were no bad feelings. He considered that he had a good relationship with the Cheevers;

in fact, that relationship was important to him because his book was coming out in the fall. He was not upset about our difficulties with the Cheevers. Mary Cheever, he said, was a little volatile, and these things happened. He wasn't surprised to hear that the affair was about to be settled. He would be happy to write the introduction, and he didn't need a copy of the manuscript because he had already read all the stories listed in the table of contents that we had sent him.

This was a relief to me. But Franklin was still not happy about it. In mid-March, he and his wife Mary arrived in Chicago to help edit and proofread the galleys, which were coming in batches from the typesetter (this was before we adopted the practice of desktop publishing). We had to make decisions about regularized spelling, since the journals in which these stories had ap-peared had their own house styles, and spellings varied from story to story. We had to decide, for instance, whether it should be "whisky" or "whiskey" and whether "into" should be two words or one—things like that. And we suspected that some strange sentences might be typesetting errors at the magazines; we had no manuscripts to check against. Franklin and Mary proofread copies of galleys in their hotel room, and then we all gathered at a conference table in our offices to coordinate our efforts and make final decisions. Garbus was later to refer to this process as a gathering of "the editorial council," with the strong implication that we were a kind of cabal.

At about this time, our Cheever imbroglio became public knowledge, much to Paul's dismay. He had urged us from the beginning to avoid the press at all costs: "You can never tell what they're going to say about you. They can take all kinds of different tacks." But when the boyfriend of one of our staff members leaked the story to "INC," a *Chicago Tribune* gossip column, we answered the columnist's questions when she called because we thought it was better to get our viewpoint to the press than to leave the field to the other side by refusing to comment. Jordan has a considerable talent for public relations, as befits the founder of a press clipping agency, but publicity of any kind was anathema to Paul. He took no comfort from the fact that the "INC" item, when it ran, was completely sympathetic to us: "Publishing types, evidently annoyed that they didn't think of the collection idea first, are bending Mrs. Cheever's ear and encouraging her to go for Bigger Bucks . . . . "[1]

It was Ben, however, who was responsible for the news appearing in New York. He must have realized that would happen when he told Bill

Goldstein that he was going to sue Academy Chicago. Bill left *PW* soon after that to write a column called "Inside Books" for a new (and now unhappily defunct) magazine called *7 Days,* and at the end of March, Bill's story appeared under the heading "Cheever Feud." The Big Bucks theme was mentioned here, too. Mary Cheever, Bill wrote, had been "game" when Franklin approached her in June and had even given him "her personal copy of a rare Cheever story." Everything seemed set by September when Mary, represented by ICM, had signed a contract:

> Enter Ben Cheever—represented by bad boy agent Andrew Wylie and lawyer Martin Garbus . . . . It evidently dawned on Ben that more money would be poured into the Cheever coffers if a larger publisher handled the uncollected stories—with himself, perhaps as editor . . . . Ben began rumbling about a lawsuit.
>
> Suddenly, though, Ben's not the only one threatening legal action. In response to "harassing phone calls" from Ben and Wylie, as well as two threatening letters from Garbus, Academy Chicago has itself filed for declaratory judgment . . . [2]

The story quoted Jordan saying, "We want the courts to declare our contract valid. This is a means of basically getting someone off your back," and calling Mary Cheever "the innocent victim." There was no mention of a settlement, so we were surprised a few days after this story ran, to receive a note from Maggie Curran thanking and congratulating us for "the speed with which you sent them scuttling." She said she had heard that it was going to be "a splendid book." The "whole ghastly lawsuit" had upset her terribly, she said. Now it was a great load off her mind, and she wished us the best of everything.

10

"The Cheevers' Concern about Premature Publicity"

Scott Donaldson's introduction arrived on the last day of March, two weeks before his deadline. He began by pointing out that these stories had originally been seen into print by John Cheever and were not "discarded dross tricked out as . . . legitimate work as had been the case with some of Ernest Hemingway's 'leftover stories.'" We were pleased with this statement because we wondered whether some critics might think—as we ourselves had done at first—that these stories had remained uncollected because they were not good. Some of them, Donaldson said, were short sketches, some were written to a predictable pattern, but "even the slightest radiate an occasional glow . . . that marks them as uniquely Cheever's." He went on to say that, apart from this, the stories "throw considerable light on Cheever's art and life." After touching lightly on Cheever's "apprenticeship and formative years"—which he believed the writer had "repudiated"—Donaldson launched into a biographical, rather than an analytical, discussion of the stories.

We would have preferred an analytical approach, but we were glad to have the introduction because we wanted to include part of it, along with three stories, in the sampler we were preparing for the booksellers convention. We were extremely busy, producing promotional material, proofreading Cheever galleys, and getting ready to move to our new offices.

Franklin, too, was busy that April. He had sent the book clubs what he called "interim galleys"—copies of the uncorrected galleys spiral-bound in our offices. The "final galleys" or "prepublication galleys" would be bound into a paperback by a printer; these would be ready later in the summer and would be given to reviewers and subsidiary rights people. The Book-of-the-Month Club was enthusiastic about the project; the Literary Guild was not interested.

Franklin sent the interim galleys to the *New York Review of Books* and the

Washington Post, where David Streitfeld, who writes the "Book Report" column, was planning a big story on all the Cheever books scheduled to come out that fall: Donaldson's biography, the *Letters,* and the *Stories.* Franklin wrote, too, to Herbert Mitgang, who reviewed books and reported cultural news for the daily *New York Times,* telling him that he would soon receive a copy of the interim galleys for review.

Toward the end of April, one week before the continuance was due to run out, Paul got a call from Maura Wogan of Garbus's office, requesting complete information about the book. Her tone, Paul said, was not friendly. He sent her a packet that included copies of the table of contents, Donaldson's introduction, Franklin's editor's note, and a forthcoming *Publishers Weekly* ad that featured a picture of the planned cover of the book. These documents, he wrote her, "are not being sent to you for your approval or disapproval. You asked that they be forwarded and we agreed to do so."

Two days after he mailed this packet, Paul received a letter from Martin Garbus. Garbus said that he had been "advised" that Paul had told reporters that the "dispute" was settled and that Mrs. Cheever had withdrawn her objections to the "proposed publications." This, Garbus said, was wrong: there was no final settlement, and further, Maura Wogan had "clearly communicated the Cheevers' concern about premature publicity" on this matter, which could "only complicate" efforts to resolve it. In addition, it had been noted that in Paul's material, Franklin was referred to as editor. Garbus asked that he be informed "immediately of the nature and extent of such editorial work." And he wanted a prompt reply—apparently as well as an immediate one. This missive was copied to "Benjamin Hale Cheever," Andrew Wylie, and Maura Wogan.

We had not seen any publicity saying that matters were settled, and certainly none of us had told the press that, since we knew there had been no settlement—and no discussion of one. It had, of course, been Ben who had announced the "dispute" to the *Publishers Weekly* reporter Bill Goldstein in New York. Paul, who never spoke to the press if he could help it, was naturally annoyed by this letter; he was forced to reply defensively that he had "no recollection of talking to reporters about resolution of the case" and further, he made it "a practice not to discuss pending litigation with the media." He had already told Maura, and was now repeating, that Franklin's "editing" consisted of "helping to locate stories, proofreading galleys and preparing an editor's note. The only changes made in the text of Mr.

Cheever's stories were to regularize the spelling of certain words."

While we were sorting our six-year accumulation of books and papers, Jordan got a phone call from the *New York Times* cultural reporter Herbert Mitgang. We had met him once a few years earlier at a booksellers convention, and he had been sympathetic to the plight of small presses. Jordan had told him how a kind word from the *New York Times* had launched our Leo Bruce mysteries. He had shaken his head and murmured that the power of the *Times* was too great.

But he did not sound sympathetic now. He said that Ben Cheever had called him and raised some questions in his mind about our dealings with the Cheevers. Jordan, taken aback by his tone, asked what these questions were and said he would be glad to answer them. Mitgang repeated the accusation that both Ben and Wylie had made to me: that when Franklin approached Ben, he had not told him that he represented Academy Chicago. This accusation was, of course, disproved by one look at the first sentence of the letter Franklin had written Ben on June 15, 1987: "I work for Academy Chicago." Jordan told Mitgang that. Mitgang answered by quoting Ben: Ben said we had gone off on our own, and he did not know what we were doing.

Jordan said that wasn't true either. We had copies of letters from Franklin and Jordan to Ben, Mary Cheever, and Maggie Curran, and Franklin had been in constant touch with Ben. Did Mr. Mitgang want to see copies of those letters?

Mitgang said he wanted to see them.

Jordan hung up and said he thought he should fax copies of all the letters to Mitgang. "Then," he said, "he'll see that I've told him the truth." I agreed that he should send the letters, but I said it sounded to me as though Mitgang had made up his mind. "When people of that sex and that generation take that attitude," I said, generalizing unfairly, "you can usually forget it."

We had just bought our first fax machine, and we were all overwhelmed by its capabilities. Jordan spent part of the afternoon faxing twelve pages of copies of letters to Mitgang at the *Times*. In his innocence, now lost forever, Jordan thought that as a newspaperman Mitgang was genuinely seeking clarification. So he felt relieved when all the material was faxed. We returned to our sorting and packing, having ignored Paul's admonition to have nothing to do with the press.

11

"It's a Matter of Honor"

Bright and early on Monday morning, May 8, 1988, we arrived at our shiny new offices to find that we had no telephone service. A couple of picketers turned up outside the building every three weeks or so to protest something to do with the elevators; the man from the phone company had seen them that morning and had left, refusing to cross a picket line.

But the mail was delivered. In it was a copy of David Streitfeld's column that had run in the *Washington Post* the day before. Streitfeld had altered his focus from the three books that would have made this a "Cheever year" to a discussion of the controversy revealed by Bill Goldstein in *7 Days*. Streitfeld put some emphasis on the role of Andrew Wylie, who, he said, was known in publishing circles as "The Jackal" and who had refused comment on the Cheever matter. Franklin and Scott Donaldson did comment. Franklin said, "It was as if these people in New York thought this was just a small Midwestern publisher that would be intimidated by big New York agents and big New York lawyers." Donaldson said half a dozen of these disputed stories ranked with Cheever's best work and that was "enough to justify the work right there. Maybe another fifteen or twenty are canonical Cheever." A number of the stories, he said, were only "sketches," but they were still interesting.

Streitfeld commented that "these sixty-eight stories will have the salutary effect of demythologizing Cheever as the quintessential *New Yorker* writer." Both the *Letters* and the *Journals*, he said, were going to offer juicy disclosures about Cheever's private life. Ben was quoted as saying that in editing the letters, he was being unflinching in his determination to look at "the whole man" and that the *Journals* were going to contain "intimate details of Cheever's alcoholism, phobias, parents and marriage."[1]

The next morning—while we still had no phone—the Mitgang article about the affair appeared in the *New York Times*. We had been braced for open hostility from Mitgang, but we found something more subtle, along with a surprise: Mrs. Cheever was going to sue us! Apparently they had not really intended to settle—they had only wanted time to prepare a case! The story's headline was "Cheever's Widow Suing to Stop Publication of Story Collection: The author's wife rejects interpreting the fiction as personal history."

Mrs. Cheever, Mitgang announced, was going to sue that week in "both Federal District Court and State Supreme Court in Manhattan" to stop "a small Chicago publishing house" from bringing out what he called "The Uncollected Short Stories of John Cheever." Martin Garbus was identified as the lawyer leading "a Cheever family effort to declare the contract invalid on the ground of false representation—including lack of promised consultation and control over the book's contents"; he was quoted as observing that the advance came to less than "$10 a story" and that after ICM's commission was deducted, Mrs. Cheever "received half the advance or $337.50."

The only quote from Franklin, who was identified as "a New York–based press agent," was that "one book club is interested in acquiring the book for what could be a six-figure sum," a remark that Franklin had not made to Herbert Mitgang, who had briefly interviewed him on the phone. Franklin had said that there was "strong interest" from a book club. Jordan's only contribution to Mitgang's piece was that he intended "to go ahead and publish" in order "to give people a new view of Cheever as an involved author in various causes." Academy Chicago, Mitgang noted, was "best known as an importer of British mysteries."

Mrs. Cheever was quoted copiously. "Bringing the case out into the open," she said, "is a matter of honor. Either we take action to stop it or we'll have to live with this book." She said she objected particularly to Franklin's editor's note and to Scott Donaldson's introduction. Mitgang quoted from a May 3 letter she had apparently written to Donaldson, in which she laid out the themes that were to be played again and again in the ensuing months—and years. "Academy Chicago," she announced, "wants no information or comment of any kind from the Cheever family." The stories in the 1978 omnibus edition had been selected by Robert Gottlieb and "approved" by John Cheever; the early stories had been dropped from that book because they were "embarrassingly immature"; Cheever and Gottlieb had "agreed on that" in 1978 because "unlike Academy Chicago," Gottlieb "valued the views and tastes of the copyright holder." Further, she objected to Donaldson's interpreting what Mitgang called "the fictional stories" as "personal history." This was unacceptable: "John fought against that kind of reading all his life . . . . 'Fiction is not crypto-autobiography,' he repeated again and again. It is the merit of a work of fiction, not its genesis."

The article ended with a comment from Scott Donaldson, who sounded considerably less enthusiastic about the uncollected stories than he had sounded when he talked to David Streitfeld. He hastened to make clear that he had "nothing to do with the quarrel over the book's publication" and had no wish to become involved in it. He agreed with "Mary" that "the merit of a work" was all-important. He was "pleased to have her comment" and found it "well taken." He "did want to point out that the stories shed some light on Cheever" and were "useful to have published."[2]

After this, Professor Donaldson was to embark on a series of emendations to his introduction, which he sent us in a futile attempt to palliate Mrs. Cheever.

From this article we learned many things for the first time. One was that Mrs. Cheever did not like the introduction or the editor's note. Certainly we would have dropped them if she had told us this before, although it was not clear to us what she found objectionable in Franklin's note. We were also surprised to learn that she considered the stories "embarrassingly bad," since five months earlier, she had told Franklin that she was glad "John's poor little stories" were going to be published. And she had, of course, signed the contract for their publication. Further, we could not see how we could be accused of ignoring her "views and tastes" when she had never expressed them to us, although she had been pelted by letters from Jordan and Franklin requesting guidance. She had said nothing to Jordan about the book's content during their phone conversation in February.

Ben had never told Franklin that he thought these stories should not be published; certainly he had said nothing to me about it on the phone. Wylie hadn't said anything about that either. What Ben had said was that he had started to hear about paperback auctions and foreign rights sales and that he had not been paying attention. To Franklin's questions about whether the "racetrack" stories should be eliminated or put in an appendix, Ben had responded that Franklin should do whatever he thought best. The implications in Mitgang's article disturbed all of us—especially since we knew that reporters would be trying to call us and we had no phone. But Franklin was particularly upset. He valued his good relationship with the book publishing community—indeed, his livelihood depended upon it— and he did not know what effect this sort of publicity would have on that relationship. He had been called a "press agent," which raised the image of a fast talker in a 1930s movie, wearing a loud sports jacket and chomping on a cigar. It would have been completely out of character for Franklin to have told Mitgang that a book club might buy the book for "what could be a six-figure sum"; in his well-meant attempt to assure the Cheevers that we could do a good job for them, Franklin had told Ben that he was "hopeful" that the Book-of-the-Month Club would take the book for a "respectable" sum, although he had no idea how much, because he had no experience in that area. Franklin worried, too, about the effect of this article on his neighbors in Westchester County; he himself had always had a deep respect for the Cheever family, and he believed that respect was universal. His world was tottering.

The mail that day brought a copy of Mrs. Cheever's letter to Scott Donaldson, with no cover letter to us. Her prose was heavily flavored with quaint sarcasm: Academy's lawyers had "deigned" to send her the introduction; Paul had "sweetly" told her he did not want her approval or disapproval, and so on. Referring to the 1978 Knopf collection (which she mistakenly called "the Collected Stories"), she said flatly that her husband had not been consulted about its contents. Beyond giving "a rather grudging permission" to Gottlieb to publish it, Cheever had done nothing but write a preface: "The selection of the stories was Gottlieb's alone. Ask Gottlieb!" Then she immediately contradicted that statement by repeating her statement to Mitgang that "Cheever and Gottlieb" had agreed to drop the early stories from that collection because they were "embarrassingly bad."

She asked Donaldson whether he thought his "preface" would cause a "rush to buy the book the way shoppers buy tabloids at supermarket checkouts, as if John was like a movie queen or a rock star?" We remembered these words five months later when we saw a banner on the cover of *Esquire* magazine: "The Intimate Letters of John Cheever," and when we read interviews in *People* in which Mrs. Cheever said that John had tried to rape one of her students and Ben said he often wondered whether his father lusted for him.[3] Farther in the future, of course, were the depressing selections from the *Journals* featured in the *New Yorker;* the publication of the *Journals* themselves, accompanied by interviews with the Cheevers; and Susan's new "revelations" about her parents in her own book, *Treetops.*

The next day, to our intense relief, the elusive worker turned up with a colleague and connected our telephones. But some damage had been done. The Associated Press, unable to reach us, had sent out a story embroidering on Mitgang's theme. In that morning's *Chicago Sun-Times* we read that we were known primarily "for importing British mystery novels" and that Martin Garbus had said, "Mrs. Cheever objects to the very cavalier treatment she has been given by this publishing company and the cavalier treatment to Mr. Cheever's work." He said he was seeking to have the contract declared invalid because "the publisher had failed to consult Mrs. Cheever about the book's contents as promised." The suit, he went on, would be filed "by week's end in either Federal or state court in Manhattan."[4]

My brother read this item and was impressed by the reference to "cavalier treatment." He phoned to tell me that we had brought this calamity upon ourselves by being arrogant toward the Cheevers. If he had been in our position, he said, he would have been "humble. Very, very humble."

A few reporters called us that Wednesday. One was from the Westchester County Gannett newspaper, Mrs. Cheever's local paper. It was Franklin's local paper, too, but he was never contacted by any of its reporters, then or later. Jordan, still naive, talked to the Gannett person with friendly animation, as was his wont. He explained that nobody realized how valuable the stories were when we first signed the contract, although we knew that there were many good stories that had never been collected. But, Jordan said to the pleasant interviewer, when the Cheevers saw that these stories were "a virtual treasure trove, a literary gold mine," they had second thoughts about the contract.

At the end of the week, the Westchester paper carried a story adorned with a picture of Mary Cheever wearing a floppy hat and sneakers, sitting on a sort of patio with a large dog identified as "her Labrador Cocoa." She was quoted as saying that she was only trying to respect her late husband's wishes and money was not an issue. Jordan was quoted as saying, "Frankly, I think what they realized is that they didn't know such a treasure trove of stories was out there and that what we were getting our hands on may turn out to be a gold mine."[5]

The phrase "what we were getting our hands on" was the reporter's embellishment; Jordan had not used it. The reporter also deleted the word "literary" before "gold mine." This seems rather petty, but Garbus accused Jordan over and over again, in court and in briefs, of considering the stories to be a "treasure trove" and a "gold mine," and two judges would later quote these words in their legal opinions. Paul was to point out, in mild and mournful reproof, that he had warned us not to babble to the press.

But at the moment of this interview, Jordan believed, as he had when he spoke to Herbert Mitgang, that any sensible person who heard the whole story would realize that the Cheevers had no case. "They have no case," we kept saying to each other. "They simply have no case."

12

"The Work Is of Grossly Substandard Quality"

In the third week of May, Garbus sent Paul a check for $375 in an attempt to rescind the contract by returning Mrs. Cheever's half of the advance. Paul returned the check with a brief note rejecting what he called Mrs. Cheever's "offer." That same week, Mary, Susan, Benjamin Hale, and Federico Cheever filed suit in the U.S. District Court for the Southern District of New York against Academy Chicago Publishers, Franklin Dennis, and Franklin's company, Book Promotions, charging violations of the Copyright Act of 1976 and the Lanham Federal Trade Act.

The copyright violation claim held that Mrs. Cheever did not deliver a manuscript and did not deliver any stories; Academy and "Dennis" had acted "without her knowledge and consent" to prepare a manuscript that contained "an unauthorized and unlawful misappropriation of the Cheever Stories."

The Lanham Act claim involved unfair competition and trademark violation. This claim would have been appropriate if, for instance, we had invented a soft drink, called it Boca Cola, and packaged it in a familiar red can with familiar type. Or if we had bought the rights to a TV program and edited it so that its intent was distorted, as had happened when an American television company had purchased and edited some Monty Python programs. Monty Python had sued the TV company under the Lanham Act and won. The contract was rescinded. Now the Cheevers, attempting to use this act, asked for "redress" for "the use, in commerce, of false designations or origin, false descriptions and false representations": Academy and "Dennis" were causing "goods, namely the Work, to enter into interstate commerce, falsely using the Cheever name and association . . . to deceive persons in the publishing industry and among the general public into believing that the Work was authorized, sponsored and/or approved by the Cheevers when, in fact, it was not." Further, "the Work is of grossly substandard quality and contains false and misleading interpretations of the Cheever stories, as well as disparaging comments with reference to John

Cheever. . . . " Its effect would be "the loss and impairment of plaintiffs' good will and reputation."

Mrs. Cheever claimed, too, that Franklin and Academy had intended to "defraud and deceive her" by causing her to believe that the contract "pertained" only to "a small edition of a scholarly venture aimed at identifying and rescuing a few obscure stories which would otherwise have fallen into the public domain,* when in truth the defendants were scheming to acquire cheaply and exploit the entire body of John Cheever's uncollected stories, numbering in excess of sixty-eight." And Franklin and Academy "had no intention of consulting with her or her family or involving the Cheevers in any way in publication of the Work."

In connection with the children's copyright interest, which had been explained to Paul by the Pattishall people, Susan signed a complaint saying that the Cheevers had joint interest in two stories: "The Temptations of Emma Boynton" and "The People You Meet." This was wrong. As noted earlier, the Cheevers had joint interest in *three* stories, not two, and the three were "The Journal of a Writer with a Hole in One Sock," "The True Confessions of Henry Pell," and "How Dr. Wareham Kept His Servants"— because these three stories had come up for copyright renewal after John Cheever's death.

There were other errors in the Cheever papers. Maura Wogan of Garbus's office filed a motion for a preliminary injunction enjoining Academy from infringing the Cheever copyrights "in and to the following short stories . . ." There followed a list of five stories. In addition to "The Temptations of Emma Boynton" and "The People You Meet," already mistakenly claimed by the children, Wogan listed "The Habit," "The Leaves, the Lion-Fish and the Bear," and "The Folding Chair Set." Why these five were the only ones listed was a mystery to all of us, since Mrs. Cheever owned copyrights to many more than five stories.

In a memorandum filed May 16, the same day as the complaint, Garbus wrote: "defendants are, in essence, stealing the work of John Cheever in a crude effort to reap a financial windfall and put themselves 'on the map' in the literary world at the expense of the Cheever family and the memory of John Cheever." Academy's "substandard production of the Work, their

---

*Apart from anything else, stories about to fall into the public domain cannot be rescued by being included in a book. If copyrights are not properly renewed, work will fall into the public domain whether reprinted or not.

unauthorized editing," and the inclusion of "disparaging comments" about John Cheever constituted, he said, "a mutilation" of the stories "actionable under the Lanham Act." In yet another motion, Maura Wogan asked the court to waive the usual thirty-day waiting period that follows the filing of a complaint "because of the imminent danger of continuing copyright infringement and violation of the Lanham Act." Gerard Goettel, the federal judge in White Plains, New York, responded the next day by calling a hearing for May 20 and issuing an order for expedited discovery of documents from Franklin and Academy and for expedited depositions of Franklin and Jordan.

Paul had gone to Harvard with a partner in Kronish, Lieb, Weiner & Hellman, a New York firm specializing, we later learned, in real estate law. Paul hired them to represent us in New York. He also asked a New York lawyer about Judge Goettel. The response was that the judge was "not exactly a rocket scientist" but he had a good reputation. He had also a strong interest in publishing. He had once formatted one of his decisions into a little book, with a dedication and tiny chapters.

"My God," I said. "He'll never dismiss this case."

Paul said that Judge Goettel was well respected and Judge Kiley, who was assigned to our case in Chicago, was one of the best judges in the chancery division. Paul knew that for a fact; he had been before him countless times.

"What a relief," Jordan said. "What a relief to know that we have two sensible judges."

We gathered papers for discovery: all documents connected in any way at all with the Cheever case. Paul warned us that it would be illegal to hold anything back. There was no need for this warning; since we knew we were innocent of any wrongdoing, we did not even look at the papers as we collected them. We just lifted them from the files—all letters to Franklin, for instance, whether they were about the Cheever book or not—bundled them together, and sent them by messenger to Paul, who sent them on to Garbus. We were distracted because we were busy working on our fall catalog, which announced the Cheever book and about twenty others.

On the cover of the catalog was a rather depressing black-and-white photograph of John Cheever, purchased by us from Sylvester & Orphanos, a California antiquarian bookseller that, while Cheever was still alive, had produced two expensive, signed limited editions of single Cheever stories, for bibliophiles and Cheever enthusiasts. There had been no contract with Cheever for these editions; just letters of agreement. Now Sylvester & Orphanos was going to bring out a limited edition of Cheever's first story, "Expelled." There was certainly a contract for this edition; it had been vetted by ICM, and Maggie Curran had told us that it was a severely limited contract, completely different from our standard commercial publishing agreement with Mary Cheever.

Adam Walinsky, our Kronish, Lieb lawyer, filed a long memorandum in White Plains, arguing that there is a sharp distinction between a contract suit and a suit for copyright infringement: the contract question had to be settled before there could be a question of copyright infringement. He attacked the Lanham Act claim on the ground that the contract had specifically allowed the use of the Cheever name in connection with the book— and that would be true even if the Cheever name were a trademark, which it is not. The Cheevers, Walinsky pointed out, were not trying to sell a competing product, so the book could not hurt the sales of other Cheever story collections "or in any material way damage the Plaintiffs."

Walinsky claimed, too, that Garbus had erred by including Franklin and Book Promotions in the suit, because federal law has jurisdiction when every defendant is a citizen of a different state from the plaintiff. Franklin and the Cheevers (except for Federico, who lived in Colorado) were all citizens of New York State, and Book Promotions was a New York business.* In addition, Walinsky argued that the Cheever suit should be dismissed because a suit on contract was pending in Chicago and our contract stipulated that any suits arising from the agreement must be filed only in Chicago—the so-called forum selection clause.

Franklin's lawyer, Tom Ferber, the litigator for Bob Stein's firm Pryor, Cashman, Sherman & Flynn—which specialized in intellectual property law—stated that expedited discovery should, by precedent, be granted only in "the exceptional case." Since the book was not scheduled to be published for four months, there was no necessity for expedited discovery. The proposed work was, Ferber said, "precisely what it purports to be—a collection of the genuine works of John Cheever," so there could be no Lanham Act claim. Finally, he expressed what we thought was the heart of the case:

---

*We were later told that federal courts do not require diversity in cases concerning copyright, trademark, patent, and other matters of federal jurisdiction.

"Long after the contract was entered into, plaintiffs became dissatisfied with its monetary provisions, even though a skilled agent had represented them in its negotiation. This action represents nothing more than a contractual dispute, by means of which plaintiffs hope to force an increase in their share of the proceeds from the proposed book."

A hearing before Judge Kiley in Chicago was set for June 3 on Mrs. Cheever's motion for dismissal of our suit against her. Paul said that he wanted an agreement from Garbus that the Cheevers would do nothing "disruptive" before that hearing. Without an agreement, Paul said, an attempt might be made to prevent us from going to the convention in Anaheim at the end of May and promoting the Cheever book there. He said it was better to try and work things out ahead of time than to charge forward and get involved in senseless arguments.

Jordan and I thought the whole Cheever case was senseless, but we told Paul he could go ahead and negotiate an agreement with them. We were looking forward to Anaheim: the response to the Cheever book had been so encouraging that we had raised our announced print run from ten thousand to fifty thousand. So Maura Wogan wrote an agreement that Cynthia Johnson, Paul's assistant, said was acceptable: it stipulated that the Cheevers' motion for a preliminary injunction against the book would not be set for hearing until after June 3, 1988. In return Academy agreed not to distribute any Cheever stories prior to June 3, including but not limited to reviewers' copies. The Cheever sampler was an exception: it could be distributed, but it could contain only three stories. This was not a hardship for us because we had planned from the beginning that the sampler would contain three stories: "Bayonne," which was in the public domain, and "The Habit" and one "Town House" story, for both of which we had reprint permission from the *New Yorker*.

There was the further stipulation that Academy "may distribute no more than 2000 [samplers] (as opposed to the 50,000 originally planned)." We had never planned to print fifty thousand samplers: it would have been crazy to print fifty thousand copies of anything for distribution at the ABA convention, where the total attendance ran to about fifteen thousand, of which generally no more than six thousand were booksellers. We had, as I have said, announced a print run for the actual *book* of fifty thousand. We told Cynthia to delete this stipulation. But on several occasions in the future, Garbus was to announce triumphantly that he had forced us to reduce our fifty thousand samplers to a measly two thousand—which was the amount we had planned in the first place.

The Cheevers stipulated further that "each such sampler include a disclaimer that 'THIS SAMPLER IS NOT AUTHORIZED BY THE FAMILY OF JOHN CHEEVER.' Such disclaimer shall be placed in a conspicuous location on the front cover of the sampler and will be at least 1½ by ¾ inches in size and red in color."

A second exception in the agreement allowed Academy to "distribute free and on a 'confidential and not for distribution basis' copies of The Uncollected Stories of John Cheever to persons with whom they are negotiating to sell subsidiary rights to the work." Maura added the caveat that, despite the agreement, the Cheevers "were not acquiescing in and object strenuously to the distribution of the sampler and copies of the work to persons for purposes of negotiating subsidiary rights, as they consider such distribution to be a violation of any copyrights which they may have."

I found it baffling that the Cheevers would agree to allow the distribution of material that they claimed violated their copyright—especially since they had asked for expedited legal action because of the "imminent danger of continuing copyright infringement and violation of the Lanham Act."

In any case, we ordered the mandated stickers with "THIS SAMPLER IS NOT AUTHORIZED BY THE FAMILY OF JOHN CHEEVER" printed in large, red type on a white background. They cost $85.

13

Hearing in White Plains: "They Are Not the Stories of John Cheever"

On May 20, Judge Goettel held his hearing into Mrs. Cheever's complaint. Adam Walinsky represented us; Paul did not attend. Tom Ferber of Bob Stein's firm represented Franklin, who wasn't there, and neither were we.

The hearing began with Garbus attempting to explain the case to the judge, who eventually said, "Let's stop right there and get our facts pinned down a little better. John Cheever was an author. He is dead."

"Yes," Garbus said.

"He wrote novels and short stories," the judge said.

"Yes," Garbus said.

"I gather from the papers," the judge went on, "that a number of the short stories were never published in book form, and there is almost some suggestion that they were never published in a magazine or otherwise. Is that correct?"

"Most of that is correct," Garbus said tactfully. "They were all published elsewhere and the copyrights then—They were all published elsewhere, in response to your question."

"And there are about fifty of them?"

Garbus said there were "roughly" sixty-eight.

"All right," Judge Goettel said. "And I understand that the copyrights to virtually all of these is owned by persons other than the plaintiffs and that the plaintiffs only own copyrights in a handful." The judge was basing this question on the misstatement in Garbus's own brief: Maura Wogan had said that Mrs. Cheever owned only five stories. Despite this, Garbus went on to say, "That's a deliberate misstatement in their brief. That is totally wrong. She holds forty-five roughly, out of the sixty-eight, she and the children. So that's the beginning of the kind of stuff they're telling the Chicago court."

The judge, still trying to pin down the facts, said that at some point "somebody" decided to collect these "previously unpublished-in-book-form works." He said he gathered that the defendants collectively were responsible for that task and that there was a signed contract to accomplish it. But, he said, it wasn't clear to him whether all the plaintiffs were co-owners of copyrights or what the situation was there.

"I will clarify that," Garbus said, with what proved to be unjustifiable optimism. "I think I'll also clarify how you've described what the contract is because there are letters that deal with this issue and I think the contract is something different. That is the interpretation they put on it."

Continuing his clarification, Garbus said, "The reason that the complaint indicated four, five copyright stories is because we learned roughly on April twenty-seventh that, in fact, they were distributing to book reviewers and other people copies of these stories, although they had no permission of any kind, no copyright assignments from either Susan Cheever, Benjamin Cheever or Fred Cheever. In fact the document, the publishing agreement, is not a document that assigns a copyright."* Then Garbus began to talk about the mutual agreement to suspend most legal action until after the June 3 hearing before Judge Kiley. "They agreed," he said, "not to publish the book, distribute the book until June third. Their understanding is, we are going to make a record here to ask the Court to extend that injunction.† They have agreed not to send around any further copies of the book to any book reviewers. They had intended, at the American Book Association Fair [*sic*] which is coming up in two weeks now, to distribute fifty thousand copies of something called 'A Cheever Sampler,' which we have to stop. They have agreed to cut that down to two thousand . . . . In other words, I think there is a recognition here that the copyright claims, the Lanham Act claims, are serious and substantial."

The judge did not seem to share that recognition. "What specifically," he asked, "is the Lanham Act claim?"

"There is a book out now called *The Stories of John Cheever*," Garbus replied. "This is a book published by Knopf. As you will find when we get into this case that John Cheever and his editors made a decision back then

---

*As a rule, publishing agreements do not assign copyrights to the publisher. The copyright stays with the copyright holder. Publishing agreements normally assign *publishing rights*.

†This was not an injunction but an agreement freely entered into by both sides.

not to have certain of these stories published. They made a decision these stories were available. This is not a book suppression case. This is not stopping the publication of anything. These stories are available to anyone who wants to see them. They're in the *New Yorker*, in *Mademoiselle*, in other places."

The judge asked how many stories were in *The Stories of John Cheever*. "Oh, I don't know. Sixty or seventy."

"How many of them overlap, are involved in this?"

"None," Garbus said.

"They are all different?"

"They are all different. And what happened was, *The Stories of John Cheever* then, or the stories that Mr. Cheever selects as the stories that he wants to see go out as any author does and any author decides what he wants to be remembered by and what he decides his collection shall be, and he says— and you're getting to the Lanham Act claim. These are not all stories. These are stories that Mr. Cheever and Mrs. Cheever never wanted to see published, and these are stories that Mrs. Cheever doesn't have the right to allow somebody to publish."

"She doesn't own the copyright?"

"She does not have the exclusive right to many of these stories,"* Garbus said. "And we'll get into that."

"Who does?"

"Susan Cheever, Benjamin Cheever and Fred Cheever are the children," Garbus said.

"The plaintiffs collectively own some of the copyrights?" the judge asked, and upon receiving an affirmative reply, inquired again, "What is the Lanham Act claim?"

"The Lanham Act claim," Garbus said, "and I would have to—we would go to the advertising for the book here. The advertising for the book passes this book off—and I'll go straight to the language—as first of all, the uncollected stories of John Cheever. They are not all stories. There are sketches. There are other things that are not stories at all. Secondly, they pass that off as a collection by Mr. Cheever. In the copyright page, for example, of this book they're now handing out, called *The Uncollected Stories of John Cheever*,

---

*She had exclusive rights to all but three of them at that time, and she does have the right to license any of them for publication.

has on the copyright page, as does the Knopf book, that these copyrights all come from Mrs. Cheever. And anyone would think that this then is the authorized version or version put out by Mrs. Cheever, the copyright holder. That's not true. They also say—"

"You're losing me completely," the court said. "If somebody owns a copyright, they either assign it for publication or they don't. And they don't have a copyright claim. And if they do, there's no Lanham Act claim."

"No," Garbus said. "If you pass off—I think it's a two-step thing. First of all there's no assignment of copyright with respect—"

"You don't have to assign the copyright," Judge Goettel said. "All you have to do is authorize the publication by the copyright owner."*

"There's no such authorization here," Garbus said. "And if I can go through the documents, I would like if I could to go into it somewhat chronologically, because I think it's a history that relates to all of these things."

"I'm still trying to find out what the Lanham Act claim is," said Judge Goettel.

"The Lanham Act claim," Garbus said, "is that their book is being advertised as the stories of John Cheever. They are not the stories of John Cheever."

"Who wrote them?" the judge asked.

"They are not the stories of John Cheever," Garbus repeated. "What they are, are some descriptive passages. And this book is being described as some of the best stories of John Cheever, some of the best-kept secrets of John Cheever. John Cheever, like any author who has a right to protect his reputation, specifically decided that these stories would not be printed in another volume. And he made that decision, first of all, by not including it [*sic*] here." He held up the Knopf collection.

"Let me stop you right there," the judge said. "John Cheever is dead. He has no rights personally that he can enforce."

"The rights are Mrs. Cheever's," Garbus said, "and Mrs. Cheever reserved to herself the right to define which stories should ultimately be published. And you can see both—"

"That's a contract claim," the judge said.

---

*See p. 88 for Judge Goettel's reference to "assignment of copyright" in his opinion accepting the case.

"No, it's not a contract claim. In other words, the question here is, does the copyrighted material, does the stuff that is being published, go beyond the particular contract, that is a copyright claim. And the law is very clear, and I can quote Professor Nimmer, and I can also refer to the very cases that they [*sic*] cited. Professor Nimmer says, 'Notwithstanding the existence—' and this is an Eastern District case which is later cited by the Ninth Circuit and is the law of this jurisdiction, and we can show you the case they rely on, the Berger case."

"I've had a few cases in this area before," the judge responded, "including the Ann-Margret case. I'm familiar with the law."

Garbus shot back with a case of his own involving celebrities. "And I tried the Isley Brothers case," he said, "and we went through the stuff or related stuff at great length. You have third-party infringers, which I think we'll get—"

"You had an issue of when a composition was created," Judge Goettel said. "I recently mistakenly referred to them as the Everly Brothers, much to Mick Jagger's dismay," he added, dropping a few more names.

"I saw that," Garbus said, "and I was upset. I thought the difference was clear."

"It came back to me after ten seconds," the Court said.

"I was going to call you, but I decided not to," Garbus responded.

After this pleasant interlude, he returned to Professor Nimmer, whom he quoted as saying, "Notwithstanding the existence of a contractual relationship between the parties, if a defendant's conduct is alleged to be without authority under such contract and to further constitute an act of copyright infringement, then Federal jurisdiction will be invoked." That, Garbus said, was precisely this case.

"I thought we were talking about the Lanham Act claim," the judge said. "I'm still looking to understand what the Lanham Act claim is."

"That deals," Garbus said, "with the attempt to pass this book off as a book of the collected stories of John Cheever. It is not. It is an attempt to pass this book off as the best stories of John Cheever. It is not. I'm now referring to the advertising and promotional material for this book. It is an attempt to pass off the book as one which is authorized by Mary Cheever. And that's what the book says."

"How does it say it's authorized?" the judge asked. "Read me the words about 'authorized by Mary Cheever.'"

"What it says is—and this is no different than *The Stories of John Cheever*," Garbus said. "It doesn't say 'authorized by John Cheever.' The copyright owner is the person who is authorizing it. They are claiming—"

"I suggest to you," the judge said, "that a reader of the book wouldn't care who owned the copyrights or whether Cheever had authorized the stories. He would be interested, in fact, only in the fact that Cheever wrote the stories."

"I suggest to you something different," Garbus said. "For example, last week in the *Times*, they had an article on the collected stories of Raymond Carver. And the understanding is, if a person who owns the copyrights puts them in a book, then that person is saying that these stories are stories—that these stories stand for something. It's the copyright owner who is holding forth these particular stories. In other words, it's known in the publishing world that if stories come out where the preface is written, let's say by John Cheever, that he is holding these things out to be his stories and he is saying something about it—"

"I thought we agreed that John Cheever is dead," the court said, "and has no rights."

"Here it is Mary Cheever who is the copyright owner. And their claim is that—and if you pick up this book then—it's Mary Cheever, the copyright owner, it is the uncollected stories of John Cheever. She is not holding out that these are either the stories of John Cheever, nor is she holding out the material—and I think we have to get into this. There is a preface to this book, there is some editing notes. Nor is she holding out that these things are in any way accurate. In other words, what happened is—"

"Let me stop you for a second," the judge said. "Can a publisher, who has rights to publish and doesn't own the copyright, publish without acknowledging the copyright at the front of the volume? Are the copyright indications required as a matter of law?"

"I believe they are," Garbus said. "And that was part of the deal. The deal here was—"

"I think they are," the judge said.

"Yes," Garbus said.

"So," the judge went on, "any time anybody publishes something, he has to acknowledge who owns the copyright. And to assume that the mentioning of the copyright carries with it some implicit endorsement of some sort by the copyright owner, I find that to be rather baffling. For example, you've told me that some twenty or so of these stories, the copyrights are not owned by the Cheevers. I don't know who does own them. I don't think it's particularly pertinent. But I don't think anyone would assume from the fact that the owner of these copyrights is mentioned as the copyright owner in the front of the book in any way connotes any approval of the project other than from a copyright standpoint by the copyright owner."

"I must say I disagree with you," Garbus said. "And let me tell you why. In a publishing agreement—and I'll just get to the agreement now—for evidence of something, when an author owns a copyright—if I write a book and I deliver it to you to publish, and I have the copyright on it, then anything in the book is mine. I take responsibility for it. If the book is written by John Cheever, Martin Garbus, Judge Goettel, it's your book."

The judge said that now Garbus was getting into something different. "Anybody who claims to own a copyright, in effect says, 'This is an original work. I wrote it. I have the rights.' There are other representations implicit by a copyright owner. But that's not what we're talking about here."

"I think you're going over two different things, if I can," Garbus said. "You have a publishing contract here. What Mrs. Cheever agreed to do— and you don't yet have, and let me give you—the letters, if I can, the documents. Because what I'm saying is consistent with the history of what went on in this case. Mrs. Cheever knew, and she bargained, and she negotiated and she discussed that 'You are not publishing what are the uncollected stories.' She doesn't own all the uncollected stories. What she is going to do is pick and choose which of the uncollected stories are then going to be published. So this is what she negotiated . . . 'I feel that a certain number are excellent and that's true. If you wanted to publish one or two or three of the stories, that's one thing. If you want to publish sixty-eight, that's different.'"

Garbus went on to produce a scenario of what "Academy" was supposed to do. "They were supposed to say, 'There are some sixty or seventy stories. Now let us sit down, Mrs. Cheever, and decide which you will give us the copyrights to, where we can get other copyrights, whether your children will permit these.'" In addition to violating this scenario, Garbus went on to say, Franklin had written an introduction "which talks about these stories as being or exhibiting the best-kept secrets of John Cheever. In other words, that these stories are hot stuff, stuff that he somehow tried to repress.* Now, an author has the right—and this is a Lanham Act claim." It was outrageous, he said, for Academy to think it could just come on April 27 and say, "'Here is the book. It is coming out. You have no control over time. You have no control over the introduction. You have no control over which stories are in there.' This is a copyright claim, this is a Lanham Act claim—"

"This sounds to me very much like a contract dispute," the judge said.

"Absolutely not. And if you look at the cases they cite . . . and I've read you Nimmer and I can give you cases endlessly—"

The judge cut him off. "Move to some other point in your argument," he said.

Garbus then delivered a lengthy disquisition, studded with quotes from Franklin's letters and Mrs. Cheever's letter to Scott Donaldson. "No one can stop Academy from publishing what is in the public domain," he said. "They have an absolute right to do that."

"You say five or ten?" the judge asked, referring to the public domain stories.

"I think it's about ten or twelve," Garbus said.

"They are not going to put out a book with ten or twelve stories," Judge Goettel said.

Garbus said that no one could stop Academy from publishing stories that "other people" held copyrights for—*Mademoiselle, The New Republic, Harper's Bazaar, Esquire, Good Housekeeping*: "That's another ten stories. No one is saying that they cannot publish those twenty stories.† What they are saying is that they cannot publish stories of people from which they have not gotten copyright, the Cheever children. And they cannot publish the stories, any stories, that they claim to come by virtue of this particular agreement."

---

*The "hot stuff" Garbus talked about was Franklin's comment in his editor's note: "Nowhere in the *Newsweek* piece ["Why I Write Short Stories"] did Cheever mention the Depression era, strike-busting, foreclosed mortgages, barracks life, apartment shortages or bleak boarding houses. But, in one of American literature's best-kept secrets, John Cheever had made such subjects his concern, and written about them extensively for many years . . . many of the stories now published together for the first time prove once again that Cheever's imagination embraced an even wider segment of our 'intense and episodic' experience than we had thought."

†In September, Garbus was to write to these magazines, demanding that they withdraw permission from Academy to publish these stories on the ground that that permission had been fraudulently obtained.

Eventually, the judge became restless. "You're getting much too detailed," he said. "And you're arguing a summary judgment motion. Can you come down to a conclusion with this?"

Garbus said that the conclusion was that "they have agreed to hold back the publication of the book." He complained about the Chicago litigation: it was "inappropriate" because "Mrs. Cheever was never in her life in Chicago," and furthermore, the children did not "submit themselves to the jurisdiction in Chicago" because they did not sign the contract.

"And do the children own completely any of the copyrights?"

"No. As I understand it, they are joint copyright holders with Mrs. Cheever. I'm trying—"

"Were those assignments made by the author's death or were they part of the estate?"

"There were no assignments," Garbus said. "Which assignments? The renewals?"

"No. The copyright ownerships could have been conveyed to the heirs by the author before his death, or they could have been conveyed by will, or they could be part of his estate. Which are they?"

"By will," Garbus said.

"By will," the judge said. "And the widow has at least part of every copyright that the children have an interest in . . . . And there are some that she exclusively has?"

"Yes," Garbus said. "But she doesn't have the right to give the exclusive right to any copyright that the children share in, and she understood that."*

"I don't see how she could," the judge said, mulling it over, "unless . . . . "

"That's what they're claiming," Garbus said. "They're claiming that— and that's what these stories are [*sic*]. They're claiming that she gave them the right, and that's what the contract deals with. The contract talks about the exclusive right that she gave. She never did. She couldn't."

"All right," the judge said. "Let me hear from your adversary."

Adam Walinsky, who had been silent to this point, began by saying that Mrs. Cheever had freely signed the contract through International Creative Management, "one of the major literary representational agencies," and the

---

*Mrs. Cheever had inherited the right to give the exclusive publishing rights for all those stories in the original copyright period. She can give rights for all renewal periods of her ¼ share, which would pragmatically block another transfer.

contract provided that Academy Chicago would "publish the uncollected stories of John Cheever." That meant generally, he said, all of the uncollected stories, not some of them. And Mrs. Cheever had represented, in paragraph twelve, that she had full power to enter into the agreement "and that all rights conveyed were free of encumbrances of any kind. And, in fact, we know from Mr. Garbus this morning that indeed she does have at least a share of all of these."

The judge pointed out that she didn't have a share of twenty of them, which were in the public domain or owned by other publishers.

Walinsky agreed that the judge was "absolutely correct." He went on to complain that Garbus had accused him of saying that Mrs. Cheever owned copyrights to only five of the stories when, in fact, it was Garbus's own complaint that alleged that she owned only five. He quoted from the *Berger* case as a precedent: in that case the judge had ruled that "once a decision is made on the contract, there is nothing to decide on infringement." Unquestionably, Walinsky said, this was a contract, not a copyright, case.

The judge did not accept this. The children, he said, owned copyright to some of the stories, and they did not sign the publishing agreement. So the dispute with the children had to be a copyright dispute.

Walinsky responded that the issue was whether Mary Cheever had full authority, as she had claimed she did in the contract, to make or enter the agreement to permit publication of these stories.

"Does the contract say that she has some form of assignment of rights from her children with respect to the contract?" Goettel asked.

Walinsky granted that there was nothing about that in the contract. He was clearly unsure about whether renewal copyrights were owned by Mrs. Cheever or Mrs. Cheever *and* her children. All he knew was that Mrs. Cheever had represented that she was the copyright owner when she signed the contract. It was obvious that he had not been given or had forgotten the information Paul had received from Pattishall: that the three stories for which copyright had been renewed since John Cheever's death automatically belonged to the children as well as to Mrs. Cheever, although Mrs. Cheever had the legal right to assign publishing rights to these stories as long as she shared the proceeds with the children.

"The will," Walinsky said. "I may say, Your Honor, I have a copy of the will. And I believe that Mary Cheever received all of his personal property, which would have, of course, included the copyrights. So when any purported assignments to the children may have taken place, I don't know. That would clearly be an issue in the action."*

The judge replied that Garbus had said that the children had inherited their rights through the will.

Walinsky said he didn't believe they had.

"I didn't say that, Your Honor," Garbus said.

"That was the impression you gave," the judge said.

"No, I didn't," Garbus said.

"That was certainly the impression you gave me," the judge said.

"No," Garbus said. "You asked me a different question. Mary Cheever got everything through the will."

Although Garbus had certainly said that the children had been left the copyrights "by will" and the judge had repeated "by will" after him, Goettel was willing to give Garbus a second chance. "And at some subsequent time," His Honor asked, "the children acquired rights from her?"

No, Garbus said. "I believe that—by virtue—that's what I was trying to describe before, that I believe by virtue of that, she and the children then are joint copyright holders."

At this point Maura Wogan rode to the rescue. "May I?" she asked modestly, then explained that "any copyright that is renewed after the author's death is automatically renewed in the wife's name and the children."

"Oh," the court said, "really?"

Fascinated, he asked how this affected the copyrights of Hemingway, for instance, who had "a series of wives and a bunch of children." Maura Wogan said that the law dictated the rights.

"Isn't that interesting!" Judge Goettel said. "I don't know, it seems to me that somebody like Academy, which apparently is in the publishing business, knowing that they're dealing with old stories . . . . is charged with the knowledge of this unique bit of Anglo-Saxon 'demesning' of interest to lawful heirs that apparently the copyright laws embody and would have looked into that aspect of it."†

---

*The "personal property" could include copyrights only for the original copyright periods. These "purported assignments" should not, really, have been an "issue" in the action.

†This is not Ango-Saxon law but is based on a U.S. Supreme Court decision in *Ballantine v. Da Sylva*.

In any case, he said, "the critical threshold hurdle is the question of the interest of the children, who are clearly not signatories to the agreement, and therefore are not bound by the forum selection."*

The forum selection clause, of course, dictated that all litigation stemming from the contract would have to be conducted in Chicago.

The judge was really intrigued with the "unique" copyright law. "It strikes me," he said, "it's a piece of legislation fraught with problems. Think about Hemingway with his various wives and various children.† I just don't understand how that thing works."

Adam said he would try to run down the facts. The judge said that made sense.

In the final moments of the hearing, the judge inquired about Franklin, who had been named in the Cheever's suit. "Can you tell me whose side Dennis is on here, Academy's or Cheever's?"

Tom Ferber, representing Franklin, responded, "At this stage of the litigation, there's no question, he's on Academy's side."

The judge said he was going to reserve decision on the matter and looked forward to receiving additional papers the following week.

When Paul told us about this hearing, we said it seemed to us that if the "children's interest" really was "the critical threshold hurdle," we could simply leap over it by dropping the three stories the children had a partial interest in, even though there was no way this partial interest could legally prevent Mary Cheever from granting us publishing rights to those stories. We knew the children's claim was specious, but it seemed to us that it might be wise to keep out of that courtroom in White Plains. We thought that three stories were a small price to pay.

But Paul was adamant. The children's copyright was a nonissue, he said; there was no reason why we should give up anything.

---

*I quote again from the Pattishall statement: Mary Cheever had the right to give exclusive publishing rights, but she was required to share the income with the children. The children were thus bound by the forum selection clause.

†Only the author's widow at the time of his death qualifies for these renewal rights.

14

"It Competes Directly with the Published Literature of John Cheever"

In the last week of May, Garbus amended his complaint. Franklin was dropped as a defendant, the Cheever children claimed interest in the three stories renewed since the author's death, and Mrs. Cheever claimed copyright in thirty-five stories instead of five.* Scott Donaldson had suggested in his introduction that some of the stories were sketches. Now, Garbus maintained that certain of the Cheever writings were not stories but sketches ("Hereinafter 'the Cheever Sketches'"). Academy had signed a contract for "Stories" and not for "Sketches," ergo, the publication of "Sketches" was copyright infringement. Then there were the Lanham Act charges, among which was the claim that the Work competed "directly with the published literature of John Cheever" and books written by "the Cheever children concerning the late John Cheever, including *Home Before Dark,* the *Letters* and the *Journals.*"

In an affidavit accompanying this interesting complaint, Garbus swore that as soon as the Cheevers learned of the contents of the book, they "moved quickly" to stop its publication.† Mrs. Cheever's intention in signing the contract, he said, was to signal that she "would at some later date create" a compilation. The title, *The Uncollected Stories of John Cheever*, Garbus said,

---

*Mrs. Cheever really owned forty-five stories, as Garbus himself had told Judge Goettel. Among the thirty-five listed in Garbus's amended complaint were two to which she did *not* hold copyright: "Expelled," held by *The New Republic*, and "Behold a Cloud in the West," held by the Estate of Horace Gregory. "Buffalo" was listed twice in the amended complaint—once as one of the stories owned by Mrs. Cheever and then again in another list as one she did *not* own.

†The reader is reminded that Mrs. Cheever was given the manuscript with the table of contents on December 12, 1987. Garbus's "cease and desist" letter to Academy was dated February 17, 1988.

was only "tentative," so it didn't mean anything. And the word "all" was not included in the contract, so Academy could not have meant *all* the uncollected stories.

Lots of people, he argued, publish "ten, fifteen or twenty stories." Look at Gabriel Garcia Marquez, look at *Goodbye Columbus*, look at *Dubliners*, look at Salinger's *Nine Stories*. Then there were Isaac Bashevis Singer, William Saroyan, Ferril Sams, Bernard MacLeventry, Francine Prose, Gordon Lish, Bernard Malamud, and Alexander Solzhenitsyn, whose books contained, respectively, nine stories, fewer than fifteen stories, thirteen stories, eight stories, nine stories, twelve stories, twenty-five stories, thirteen stories, and, in the case of Solzhenitsyn, six stories and twenty poems. (No mention was made of the number of pages in these collections.) The yardstick, Garbus averred, was not the number of stories in what he called *The Collected Stories of John Cheever*, published by Alfred A. Knopf, because "there were specific economic and professional reasons to have such a large collection published at the time. It was several years before Cheever's death. Those reasons do not exist here."

And even though Academy, "a publisher experienced with the Copyright Law," knew that Mrs. Cheever could not grant an "exclusive right" to those stories renewed since Cheever's death, he continued, "immediately after and as the agreement was being made, Academy attempted to learn which stories were and were not available." And Academy "went to these magazines and obtained permission to use some of the copyrighted stories." The permissions listed on the "book acknowledgement page" were proof that Academy had actually contacted these magazines!

Then there was the advance, which came to "approximately $33.00 a story." And Academy's intended distribution of the famous "fifty thousand" samplers, at what Garbus now called "the Memorial Day Book Fair," proved the value of the copyrights.

There followed an elaborate discussion of the difference between sketches and stories, using definitions culled from *A Handbook to Literature* and the *New Riverside Dictionary*. Included was one definition of a sketch as "a short often comical act in a revue or variety show."

Finally, the complaint accused Academy of copying the design of the dust jacket of Knopf's *Stories*; affixed to the document were Xeroxes of both designs, with the apparent intention of proving this point, although the Knopf book's type was rounded, ornate, and enclosed in a giant letter C while the Academy type was stark, rectangular, and not enclosed in anything.

So there it was. "The Academy book is an attempted theft and desecration of the literary reputation of one of America's best known and respected authors . . . . To say that the Cheevers sold assets (copyrights) worth many hundreds of thousands of dollars for one half of $1500 is to believe in the tooth fairy."

"There's nothing here, it's not a case. I just hope," Paul said, almost to himself, "that some lunatic judge doesn't decide there's something in it."

"Lunatic judge!" I cried, alarmed. "But that can't happen, can it? You said both judges were good. You said Kiley was one of the best judges in the system. And Goettel has a good reputation."

"Yes, yes," Paul said. "That's right."

At this point we had not yet read the transcript of the May 20 hearing in White Plains. Paul had told us only that Goettel wanted more information about "the children's copyright." So we were happy with our judges. In fact, we had a nasty moment when someone in Westchester County went berserk and shot a judge dead as he sat on his lawn. We saw this at home on the evening news; we couldn't remember our judge's name, but after the initial lurch of the stomach, we decided the victim wasn't our man. Bruce read about it the next day in the *New York Times* and phoned us in a panic.

"Something horrible has happened," he said. "Someone shot a judge in Westchester County . . . . Is that our judge?"

"No, no," I said. "It's awful, but it isn't our judge."

"Oh, thank God," Bruce said. "I mean, I thought, here we have this great judge, this fair judge, and it's just our luck that somebody shoots him."

I had to admit that it was just the kind of thing that could happen to us. But it hadn't.

"What a relief," Bruce said.

15

"I Want You to Publish This Book"

While the lawyers kept busy, we set off for the booksellers convention in Anaheim, armed with our tasteful black-and-white catalogs with their cover photograph of a drained and ailing John Cheever, our tasteful dark blue and orange samplers, and our rolls of stickers disavowing Cheever authorization. Paul said that it was a real coup for our side that the Cheevers had not tried to stop us from promoting the book at ABA. Signing that agreement had been a concession on the part of the Cheevers, which lent credibility to our project. "They've made a mistake," Paul said. "It will hurt them at trial."

We had an excellent spot in the convention hall. People we hadn't seen for years stopped by. We talked to reporters about the lawsuit and gave out samplers; everyone seemed to think that the sticker was our clever publicity gimmick. Garbus had been busy, too: the daily convention newspaper carried a story that Academy Chicago had reached an "interim agreement" with Mary Cheever in which Academy was "allowed" only two thousand samplers with the Cheever "disavowal" in red print. "The publisher," the story said, "had originally planned to distribute 50,000 samplers."[1] The *Los Angeles Times* mentioned "the vastly reduced number of sampler readers."[2]

On June 3, 1988, Judge Kiley took jurisdiction over our case in Chicago, dismissing Mrs. Cheever's objections.

Adam Walinsky sent Judge Goettel a response to Mrs. Cheever's various complaints, in which he reiterated his strong conviction that this was a contract case and did not belong in federal court in White Plains but in circuit court in Chicago. Walinsky explained the children's copyright status: the Copyright Act provides that when copyrights in works created before 1978 are renewed by a dead author's surviving spouse, the spouse takes the rights as a class with all the author's surviving children. Walinsky pointed out that under the law "where one of two joint owners grants a license, the other has no claim for infringement" but only for a proportion of the fees. The heirs, he wrote, do have the right to terminate existing publishing rights, but it is a limited right: it is not automatic and must be exercised, if at all, only during severe time restrictions. Since the three stories to which the Cheevers were laying claim had been first copyrighted in the 1950s, the Cheever children could not legally terminate publishing rights to them until the year 2013.

Walinsky provided a plethora of precedents to support his contention that Mrs. Cheever had the legal right to permit us to publish those three stories.

That certainly seemed to wipe out the children's copyright claim.

In the first week of June, Paul called to tell us, to our considerable surprise, that Garbus wanted us to go to New York for a settlement meeting on June 15. We had been so traumatized by the steady stream of insults and distortions in his court papers that we immediately became angry and suspicious—or at least suspicious; we were already angry. His offer was a trick, we said, and we wanted no part of it. Besides, we had to go to Montreal the week of June 15 to attend a feminist book fair, and we had no time for a visit to New York.

Paul was insistent that we go. He came to our offices with Cynthia Johnson, determined to pressure us into it. He would write out an agenda, he said, and prevent Garbus from pulling any tricks. And as to our feelings about Martin Garbus, Paul said solemnly, "Martin said to me, he told me, 'If I have said anything or written anything that has hurt anyone's feelings, I am really sorry. I apologize.' I told that to Bob Stein and he was amazed. He said, 'Martin Garbus actually *apologized?*'"

I said I didn't care what Martin Garbus did.

Paul said that Judge Kiley would insist on the meeting; he could *order* us to do it. If he heard that we had refused to meet, it would not look good for us.

Jordan, weakening, suggested that the Cheevers come to Chicago, after we came back from Montreal. And then, too, we had to give a talk at the Radcliffe publishing course on July 13—maybe we could meet in Boston then?

Paul waved all this aside. We must phone Mrs. Cheever at Garbus's office, he said; it was all arranged.

So the next day, June 7, Jordan phoned Garbus's office from home.

"Ah, Mr. Miller," Garbus said. "All the Cheevers are here—Mrs. Cheever,

Ben, Susan . . . . Mrs. Cheever will get on the line."

There were various shifting noises, and Mrs. Cheever came on. "I want you to publish this book," she said. "And I want it to be the best book possible. I don't want money."

What she wanted, she said, was a new introduction. A different introduction would be better; maybe it would make a better book. She thought William Maxwell might be willing to write it. She just wanted to say that we could resolve this problem: it was possible that if we changed our plans a little, we could have a better book. She objected to the introduction and to the way the stories were presented: she wanted a designation in the table of contents that the early stories—the ones written before 1941 or 1942—were *very* early stories. She wanted them grouped under the subheadings of the years they first appeared: "1930 to 1935" and so on. Perhaps, she said, she could see the galleys in time to make some annotations and still make it possible to keep to the September publication date. She could get the material to us by July 1. That was all she wanted, she said, and she had no objection to our publishing the book; she thought we could all have a book we could be proud of.

Jordan said he would get back to her. Paul was delighted with this offer; he immediately faxed Garbus a letter confirming these points.

"I have the feeling we can resolve this thing," Paul said to us. "The only problem . . . ." and here he touched on the central point, which had eluded us. "If the judge brings down some kind of decision—I mean if he dismisses the case or accepts it—the one who wins might get hard-nosed, and there goes our agreement. I asked Martin, I said, 'Let's go to Judge Goettel together and suggest he hold up his decision until after the settlement meeting,' but Martin said he already had had to amend his complaint and ask for special favors and he was too embarrassed to ask for anything else."

He kept referring to Garbus as "Martin." It was Maura who was difficult, Paul said, not "Martin."

We knew that Paul would negotiate in good faith, and if Goettel dismissed the case, we would still stand by our word. But we believed that if Goettel accepted the case, Garbus would find an excuse to back out of any agreement we made. In addition, I was convinced that Garbus would use anything said at the meeting against us in some way. Paul took this into account; he set an agenda for the meeting in which he stipulated that nothing said or done during the course of the meeting could be used in any manner by anyone in either the New York or Chicago litigations. Every-thing was to be confidential.

Reluctantly, we agreed to the meeting, but we refused to go into New York City. We insisted on a location near the airport. Paul and Garbus settled on the Royce Hotel, which was about three hundred yards from LaGuardia Airport. We would all meet there on June 15, a Wednesday, in the middle of the week we were spending in Montreal.

Paul's agenda, in addition to the confidentiality stipulation, provided that the Cheevers would "indicate the matters of importance to them," which Mrs. Cheever had said would be "the introduction, some possible additional material from the book and possible changes in a portion of the contents." The Cheevers would propose another introduction and some additions or changes to the text of the book, "but the proposals will be made in the form of suggestions, not ultimatums." The reference to addi-tional material stemmed from a remark Garbus made to Paul that Ben had some stories we didn't know about. Ben had hinted to me, too, in our phone conversation, that we didn't have all the stories. Neither Jordan nor I believed that.

Paul sent Garbus the agenda on Friday, June 10. Ironically, he discov-ered that afternoon that Goettel had accepted the case, thus effectively kill-ing all settlement discussions, although we were yet to realize that. Goettel's opinion stated that "the critical issue between the parties is whether Mrs. Cheever intended, in the publishing agreement, to convey her copyrights to the uncollected stories of John Cheever. Defendant argues that by agree-ing to a tentative title . . . Mrs. Cheever agreed to assign all copyrights which she owned. The plaintiffs respond that a tentative title in a publishing agree-ment does not define the contents of a book, much less the scope of a copyright license and that they can establish this through proof concerning the custom of the trade. That is an issue which cannot be resolved on a motion to dismiss."

I found this surprising. The judge himself had said in the May 20 hear-ing: "You don't have to assign the copyright. All you have to do is authorize the publication by the copyright owner."* And that is what Mrs. Cheever had done in the contract; she had authorized publication. This was clearly

---

*See p. 73.

a contract case. Surely Garbus himself had set the settlement meeting because he thought there was a good chance the judge would dismiss this suit.

Goettel went on to consider the issue of "the children's copyright," which, he said, made everything "even more complex. The defendant takes the position that it can obtain publishing rights from a person who holds interest jointly with others." He would not attempt to resolve that "at this time," he said, "but we would think that for such to be the case there would have to be a specific assignment of copyright rather than the general undertaking of the copyright agreement . . . . we must accept [the children's] well-pleaded claim to be joint copyright holders with their mother."

We all knew, as the lawyers at the copyright specialist firm had told us, that under the law the children had no basis for a claim against us. Goettel himself, in his final opinion in August, was to say this "issue" was "irrelevant."

The forum selection clause, the judge said, was Academy's strongest argument. Questions about "contractual rights" clearly belonged in Chicago. There really wasn't any reason, Goettel said, why we couldn't have two lawsuits going at the same time.

We did not care at all for the tone of this opinion; it seemed ominous to us. Our contract, the judge said, was "a form uniquely unsuited to the endeavor under discussion," with its eliminated paragraphs and "inked-in changes," although he granted that this was "so often unfortunately the case with literary matters." He referred to Franklin as "a go-between" and added a footnote complaining that Kronish, Lieb had misspelled "*per stirpes*": "For some reason, defendant's counsel uses the phrase '*per stripes*' not once but four times in their appendix to their memorandum in support of the motion to dismiss."

It seemed to me that Garbus, too, had merited a few slaps of this kind, but they had been reserved for us. Paul said that these were just some "cheap shots" that didn't mean a thing. I tried to go back and read the opinion with his eyes—after all, he had been practicing law for twenty-seven years—but every time I read it, my heart sank.

16

The Royce Hotel: "You Won't Sell as Many Books as Random House"

We flew to Montreal with Sarah Leslie of our office, set up our display in a large gymnasium on the University of Montreal campus, and spent a day sitting in our booth waiting for feminists to drift by. Then early the next morning, Jordan and I left for New York and the meeting at the Royce Hotel, scheduled for 10:00 or 11:00 A.M.

"Welcome home," said the official on the American side.

We emerged into the Air Canada lounge, where our sons Bruce and Eric were waiting for us. They had wanted to come, and we had wanted them with us, so we had insisted on their presence despite Paul's objection. When Paul arrived a few minutes later, we went out and piled into two taxis. It was a short drive from the airport to the Royce Hotel—so short, in fact, that Eric and Paul's driver threw a sort of fit: he argued heatedly with the dispatcher about losing his place in line, hopped frantically in and out of the cab, and stopped finally in the middle of the street several yards from the hotel, refusing to drive them any further. "I hate this city," Paul said.

Franklin's lawyer, Bob Stein, was waiting for us in the green-and-tan lobby, which had certainly seen better days. Franklin himself was not there because Susan had requested that he not come. We had arranged that he would go to the Air Canada lounge in the afternoon and wait there for us so that we could tell him what had happened.

We went to the Directors Room, where there was a large, rectangular table. Garbus was there, with Maura Wogan. After genial greetings—exchanged mostly between Garbus and Paul—we dispersed ourselves around the table. I faced the door with my back to the windows, and Eric sat three seats down from me on my right, with Bob Stein on his right. Jordan positioned himself at the head of the table; Maura was on his left facing the windows; and Bruce, Paul, and Garbus sat there, too, in a ragged row.

Once we were settled, the Cheevers made their entrance in a sort of jovial burst. They worked the room, shaking hands and chatting graciously. Susan was wearing a black cotton suit and brown loafers; Mrs. Cheever was sedate in a striped shirtwaist dress with a string of beads. After the amenities, Susan shared the head of the table on my left, next to Jordan. Mrs. Cheever sat down next to Maura, facing me. Ben, in a navy blue blazer and chinos, took a chair next to me, on my right.

The atmosphere was pleasant. Susan admired my dress. Mary Cheever told Paul that he looked like a young Saul Bellow.

Garbus stood up and said that lawyers pose and pontificate and if this was to be a truly fruitful meeting, no lawyers should be present. There were already, he said, people at the table who didn't belong there—a reference to Bruce and Eric—so he and Maura were going to withdraw in the hope that . . . etc., etc.

For some reason Paul did not like this; he pleaded with Garbus to stay. But Garbus was adamant. He stood at the table, a heavy man with a rather flat face with small curly features in the middle of it and very curly hair on top of it, and talked at some length about how lawyers talk too much. Then he and Maura withdrew, to Paul's apparent dismay.

I had decided to begin the discussion by going over Scott Donaldson's introduction line by line. Since I had been told that we were there to work out differences about the editorial content of the book, I thought we might be able to agree on the introduction if the Cheevers would point out the parts of it they objected to; these could be changed or dropped. We believed that we had an obligation to try to salvage the introduction because we had a commitment to Donaldson, who had been rewriting it ever since he had received Mrs. Cheever's letter of protest. It was obvious that he wanted to be on good terms with Mrs. Cheever and would make any changes she suggested, within reason. As I began to read the introduction aloud, Susan moved close to me to read chummily over my left shoulder.

The introduction began with the comment that these were uncollected stories, not unpublished ones. " 'John Cheever wrote them, sold them to magazines and saw them into print. They are part of his corpus, not drafts or false starts he thought better of and decided to abandon. The distinction is a crucial one in a time when the discarded dross of some authors is dug up, drastically reshaped and tricked out for presentation as, say, the legitimate work of Ernest Hemingway—' "

Susan interrupted. "I really resent that," she said mildly. "I deeply resent it. Some of my friends worked on that Hemingway material."

"That's right," Mrs. Cheever said. "That's certainly uncalled for."

I said I supposed we could delete that; I did not point out that Donaldson's comments on the Hemingway material in no way reflected an eccentric opinion. I went on: "'These are John Cheever stories and hence worth reading—'"

"I don't accept that," Susan said. Her tone was still friendly. "These are very early stories."

"That's right," Mrs. Cheever said, nodding emphatically. "John never wanted these stories published."

"'On the other hand,'" I read, "'these are also stories that Cheever (and his editors) chose not to print in book form.'"

"Some of them have been in books," Susan said.

Mary Cheever suddenly became agitated. She expressed great distaste for the Donaldson introduction. Raising both arms high in the air, she said it was not true that John Cheever had repudiated his formative years. Her face was contorted, her voice broke, her arms were trembling.

I set the pages of the introduction down on the table. "I can see there's not much use in going on with this," I said. "We're not going to come to an agreement about this introduction."

"Did you know I hated Scott Donaldson when you commissioned this?" Ben asked pleasantly.

"No," I said, "how would I know that?" I started to explain how our contact with Scott Donaldson came about. I said that he had very kindly sent us a copy of "Bayonne," a story we had not been able to find—

"Oh yes," Mrs. Cheever said. "A story about a *waitress* in a *diner*."

"Can't the thing be scrapped?" Ben asked, referring to the introduction.

It was obvious that that was the only answer. I decided to try a new tack. I suggested that Susan and Ben write the introduction.

Susan beamed at me. Ben said, "Maybe you could write it, Mummy."

"I suppose I could," Mrs. Cheever said, smiling. "I'd have to find the time. You and Susan could do it."

"I suppose we could do it," Susan said. "We'd have to call a press conference . . . . "

Jordan remarked that we would have to get Scott Donaldson's agreement to the scrapping of his introduction. "And we'd like to include 'Why

I Write Short Stories,'" he added, referring to Cheever's 1978 *Newsweek* essay. Franklin had a copy of it.

Ben said that would be fine.

I told Ben and Susan that if we were going to use "Why I Write Short Stories," theirs could be a sort of foreword; it wouldn't have to be long.

Susan said she could get it ready in three weeks. She looked at Ben. "Don't you think so?" she asked him.

"I suppose so," Ben said. "I'm not in the habit of writing without getting paid, but I suppose so."

The next item on the agenda was Mrs. Cheever's suggestion that in the table of contents, the stories be grouped under subheads by publication date.

I pointed out that the stories were arranged chronologically and the date of original publication appeared at the end of each story. But, I said, I certainly had no objection to grouping them under subheads in the table of contents.

We seemed to be making excellent progress. Garbus and Maura came back and took seats at the table, Maura next to Mary Cheever and Garbus next to Paul.

Mrs. Cheever said she would like the stories rearranged: the "strongest" ones should come first so that the reader would not be turned off at the outset. I told her that would destroy the chronological order that she herself wanted for the table of contents. And really, I added, chronological order would show the author's development.

Susan said that if reviewers read weak stories first, they might give up on the book. "You don't know what reviewers can be like," she said.

"Reviews are not something that will matter in the long run," I said. I tried to explain that this was an important book by a major writer; that it would be treated with respect. But in any case, I said, the book would take its rightful place in the Cheever canon.

"John was just a teenager when he wrote those stories," Mary Cheever said. She mentioned "Bock Beer and Bermuda Onions" as a particularly inept story. People who liked the 1978 Knopf collection, she said, would open the new book in the store, see an early story like "Bock Beer," and put the book back on the shelf. These stories should be put in the back of the book or dropped altogether, she said.

Susan said she thought they should be dropped altogether.

Jordan said he would have to hold firm on that point: "uncollected," he said, meant all those stories that had not appeared in any Cheever collection, and we really could not pick and choose among them. It would be irresponsible. There was certainly interest in Cheever's early work, just as there was in the early work of any major writer. In addition, he said, these stories were very interesting in their own right.

The Cheevers listened quietly. It appeared that they would be willing to accept the chronological arrangement and the subheads.

Paul, who was taking notes on a yellow legal pad, was pleased at the way the meeting was going. "So," he said, summing up, "we're agreed that Susan and Ben will provide a foreword in three weeks; 'Why I Write Short Stories' will be the introduction, and the stories will be listed under subheads in the table of contents."

"I'm going to need another galley," Susan said, taking mine, which was on the table in front of me. "What's going on with the paperback rights?" she asked me casually.

I told her the truth, which was that I didn't know: Scott Meredith was handling that, and we had had no communication with the agency for several weeks. "We should hear something soon," I said.

"It looks extremely good for us in court," Susan said. "Have you seen the judge's opinion?"

I told her I had.

"Don't you think it looks very good for us?" Susan asked. "I mean, if you've read that opinion?"

"Well," I said. "We still have the trial in Chicago."

"Oh," Susan said, "Chicago." She made a dismissive gesture.

The last item on the agenda was Franklin's editor's note.

Mrs. Cheever said she could not see why Franklin should have an editor's note.

I told her that Franklin had to explain the arrangement of the stories; tell the reader what stories had been omitted and why—we had omitted those stories that later became chapters of novels—and so on.

The Cheevers said that they would allow the note only if Franklin limited himself to strictly "technical" information and did not make "value judgments." This was apparently a reference to Franklin's calling some of the uncollected stories "one of American literature's best-kept secrets" because they dealt with "strike-busting, foreclosed mortgages, barracks life, apartment shortages or bleak boarding houses." We said we would take that up with Franklin; we were inclined to think that he would willingly cut his note. Bob Stein agreed.

It had been quite painless. Everything seemed settled.

Without warning, Mrs. Cheever whipped out her glasses, popped them onto her nose, and flipped open a folder. "Now," she said, with relish, "I'm going to talk about *money.*"

Somebody—I think it was Bob Stein—said, "That's not on the agenda."

There was no response. Paul sat silent. Mrs. Cheever began to read her demands. She wanted 100 percent of the royalties and all her legal fees paid. Or else she wanted 120 percent of the royalties.

After a brief, stunned silence, Paul rallied. He said he assumed this was an extreme position that was being taken for purposes of negotiation. Otherwise, why were we all there?

"Let's talk about the Mets," Ben said good-humoredly.

Susan said she was starving. Eric offered her a pear, and there was some banter about Snow White and the wicked Queen. It was now 12:30 and definitely time for lunch.

We adjourned to the coffee shop, where we split into two groups. The Cheever faction sat along a wall to the right, and our group found a table in the middle of the room. Conversation at our table was desultory. Bob Stein was telling us at length how shrewd Martin Garbus was, when suddenly there was Martin Garbus in the solid flesh hovering over us. He was waving a paper.

"I came to show you Judge Goettel's opinion," he said, "in case you didn't notice how strong it is for our side. My clients asked me to show it to you."

Paul shook his head. "Your clients are making a big mistake," he said. "A big mistake."

"Oh, get out of here, Marty," Bob Stein said.

"Tell your clients they're making a big mistake," Paul said.

Garbus continued to hover, holding the paper toward Paul.

"Marty, Marty," Paul said. He sighed.

"Get away, Marty," Bob Stein said. Garbus withdrew, taking the paper with him.

Paul kept shaking his head. "A big mistake," he said. "His clients are making a big mistake."

"I don't know," I said, toying with my lunch. "I thought that opinion did sound a little funny toward us."

"Oh, there were a couple of cheap shots about spelling," Paul said. "But that doesn't mean a thing. The judge is going to decide this case on its merits. He hasn't even heard it yet."

A copy of the opinion was on the table; I read it again because I didn't feel like eating. Rereading it reinforced my feeling that Susan was right. Things looked good for the Cheevers in White Plains.

We spent the rest of the lunch hour discussing Mrs. Cheever's demands. When we returned to the Directors Room, Paul made a little speech in which he expressed outrage that the agenda had been departed from and then, as a gesture of conciliation, offered to raise Mrs. Cheever's share of the paperback royalties. Garbus did not find this offer acceptable. "This is a million dollar contract," he said. "A million dollar contract. Granted you won't sell as many books as Random House, but it's still a million dollar contract." It was Franklin's share of the royalties that concerned him. "It's insane," he said. "It's insane! Why should he get all that money? For what?"

"It was his idea," Jordan said. "The project wouldn't exist without him."

"There are ten thousand Franklin Dennises walking the streets," said Garbus. "Give him ten thousand dollars. That's good enough pay for having lunch."

"All we have is the work my father left us," Susan explained. "And we have to milk that for all it's worth. I'm a greedy pig," she added playfully.

Jordan looked at her. "I can't believe you said that," he said.

"All my life I've wanted to be rich," Susan said to him. "Haven't you?"

"If I wanted to be rich, I certainly wouldn't have gone into publishing," Jordan said.

"Nothing here can be decided without my client's agreement," Bob Stein said.

"Yes, where *is* your client?" Mrs. Cheever asked. "Why isn't he here?"

"Well, he's not here," Bob Stein said evasively. None of us wanted to say that Franklin was waiting at the airport. We had a feeling that the Cheevers would make merry over it.

Garbus countered Paul's offer of a higher paperback percentage with a demand for 99.5 percent of the author's royalties. And the Cheevers wanted the right to preview and approve or disapprove of all advertising and promotional material for the book. We replied that getting their approval for advertising and promotion would be a cumbersome, time-consuming process. We didn't see the point of it anyway.

"Nothing can be decided here without my client," Bob Stein said.

"Well," Paul said, "maybe you should go and get him."

Bob said he thought he would. He stood up.

"Where is he?" Ben asked.

"He's in the Air Canada lounge at LaGuardia," Bob said.

Susan laughed heartily.

"*Where* is he?" Mrs. Cheever asked.

Susan told her that he was in the Air Canada lounge at LaGuardia.

"In the Air Canada lounge!" Mrs. Cheever said. She laughed heartily.

"I'm going to get him now," Bob announced.

Susan's mood shifted suddenly. She glared at Bob. "Yes, go on," she said loudly. "Go get him and don't come back!"

"That's very rude," I said to Susan. She looked at me blankly.

We chatted while Bob Stein was gone. Ben was very friendly. He said that he would hate to see this chance, this opportunity, go down the drain and he hoped there was something we could all do to ensure a positive outcome. He turned to me. "I think I handled that thing wrong with Franklin and Andrew," he said, in a confiding tone. "I think it was too abrupt."

"Well, it did come as a shock to him," I said. "Franklin is a very decent person."

"Oh, I know," Ben said. "We should have gone about it differently."

Susan asked Garbus whether the Millers had read Goettel's opinion again. Then she turned to me and commented with satisfaction that she thought Garbus was "smart." "That's why we hired him," she said happily. "Because he's *smart.*"

At about 3:15, Mrs. Cheever announced that she was leaving. Garbus had told us several times how fortunate we were to have her in our midst. The desired impression seemed to be that, at seventy, she was too old and frail to spend her time at meetings.

"We'll see you tonight, Mummy," Ben said.

"Is there a party?" Susan cried. "Am I invited?"

We were later to learn that there was, indeed, a gathering that evening at Ben's home. Andrew Wylie was a participant.

Mary Cheever walked over to me to shake hands and say good-bye.

I asked her whether she had driven herself there. I had a dim idea that we might use that against her if Garbus were to maintain that she was too fragile to leave the house under her own power. She said yes, she had driven down from Westchester.

After she had left and Garbus had looked at his watch several times, Bob Stein returned with Franklin. All eyes followed Franklin as he came in, looking as though he were trying to disappear under his hair, walked around the table, and sat down between Ben and Eric.

Ben gave him a friendly greeting and asked him for a cigarette.

Paul said that Academy needed to have a private meeting. He suggested that the Cheever faction wait in the restaurant.

After Paul had closed the door firmly behind them, a lively discussion ensued about how much of Franklin's share of the royalties could be given to the Cheevers. Bob Stein tried vigorously to protect what he saw as Franklin's interests; Franklin sat silent, looking miserable.

I knew that Franklin's primary interest had never been money. "My God," I said, "we've got to get this settled. If we give them eighty percent of your share, we can provide a little extra to you out of Academy's share, Franklin."

On the Academy side, we all believed that there was a possibility of a settlement coming from this meeting.

Bob was placated. There were bangings at the door, mingled with muffled protests from Garbus that time was passing.

Paul opened the door, and the Cheever group reentered. Ben sat down next to Franklin again and bummed another cigarette. Paul read our offer from his yellow legal pad. Franklin was willing to give up 30 percent of his share—in actual fact, he stood ready to give up 40 percent if that was the only way to settle the matter, but Paul wanted to reserve some room for negotiation. Academy Chicago would provide advance copies of all advertising and promotional material to the Cheevers and consider all suggestions, although the company could not give up control. That was our offer, Paul said, and we hoped it would resolve the conflict.

Garbus said they would think it over and he would call Paul around 10:00 the following morning (Thursday, June 16) and give him the decision. Paul was going to be in Cincinnati, where he was embroiled in an endless lawsuit over toxic shock and tampons.

We parted amicably, Susan carrying off two copies of our galleys. Ben started after her down the hall and then came back to the meeting room, where we were standing in the doorway. He looked very trim in his blue blazer and striped shirt and tie. I have the impression—I may be wrong— that he was carrying a tennis racket.

"I hope we can resolve this thing," he said warmly.

I said I hoped so, too, and I appreciated his goodwill. He said that he was embarking on a new career as a writer. I replied genially that we might consider publishing his first novel.

"You'll have to deal with Andrew!" he cried jovially and pushed off.

We trudged wearily out of the Royce Hotel: Franklin and Bob Stein to return to New York, Bruce to Chicago, Eric to Iowa where he had been working, Paul to Cincinnati, and Jordan and I to Montreal and the feminists. Paul remarked lightly that he wished we would stop using him as our lawyer.

"I don't like the people I meet through you," he said with a sad smile.

17

"As If This Were Dirty Laundry. . . . Gossip"

The next day, Thursday, Garbus did not call Paul as he had said he would. On Friday, Paul faxed a summary of the Royce Hotel meeting to him with a letter saying, in part, "At the time this letter is being sent (afternoon on Friday, June 17, 1988), I have not heard a word from you."

Late that afternoon Garbus responded by fax that the Cheevers had learned that while negotiations were going on, Academy was trying to sell the book, with all the stories and the Donaldson introduction, to a paperback reprinter—arranging for a sale, to close on July 1, of "the very book" under discussion. The Cheevers, Garbus said, believed that Academy was negotiating "in bad faith" and all the settlement negotiations were just a ploy "to delay discovery and the disposition of this case." He assured Paul that he had too much respect for him to believe that he was aware of this at the time. Academy was behaving in an "unheard of" way and by distributing bound galleys, was further violating the Cheevers' copyrights and demonstrating its "lack of sophistication in the publishing world." He expressed sorrow that Paul's client "did not see fit to mention while we were in the room that the galleys were being sent around with a preface that you know Mrs. Cheever objected to. It was silly. You must have known that we would know it within a few hours."

Paul wrote back, calling "both the tone and the content" of these accusations "nonsensical": the Cheevers, he pointed out, had been informed that a paperback auction was going to be held. "Indeed, you probably did not recall at the time you sent your letter that the Cheevers had given Academy Chicago written permission to conduct that auction."

On Monday Paul received another long letter from Garbus, telling him that "the entire publishing community" was aghast at our temerity; everyone thought that what Academy was doing was going to hurt "whoever publishes any future Cheever stories." Without explaining this mysterious comment, he went on to say that he had been through this "many, many times," and he knew that booksellers and distributors would demand "guarantees, warranties and indemnities" from Academy before they would take a book under this kind of cloud and that they would take the book "in extraordinarily reduced quantities" unless Academy was "prepared to make a substantial investment in that area." It might be, he said darkly, "that the largest booksellers will not take it at all."

This was the most errant nonsense. Orders were pouring in from distributors and from booksellers large and small; we were beginning to consider a print run of more than fifty thousand. We thought that Garbus might have been motivated to write this stuff to Paul out of fear that we would publish the book before the trial and the hearing: judges sometimes will accept the fait accompli of a published book, especially by a small press that cannot afford the destruction of a print run. Garbus had used that argument himself when he defended our publishing friends Carroll & Graf against a suit by Bantam over a book of Louis L'Amour stories in the public domain.* In any case, we had no intention of publishing the book until the courts upheld our contract; selling the paperback rights would be only a gesture if the book did not come out.

Since we honestly knew nothing about this auction, we called Ted Chichak at Scott Meredith, who told us that a paperback auction was set for June 29; Dell had placed a $100,000 floor bid on the book. Chichak told us he had received what he called a "cease and desist letter" from Garbus, threatening legal action unless Scott Meredith stopped attempts to sell rights to the Cheever stories. Chichak had replied that efforts to place the project with a reprinter would continue.

We asked Chichak whether it really was a good idea to hold this auction under these circumstances. It seemed rather pointless to us. Chichak said that if the auction were enjoined by a judge, no one would blame us, but that if we canceled it, the reprinters would be annoyed with us, which would hurt our dealings with them in the future. For some reason that escapes me now, we accepted this advice, and so did Paul, who also had a talk with Chichak.

We learned that Andrew Wylie had found out about the floor bid from Gerald Howard, a friend at Viking Penguin, and had told the Cheevers about it at the gathering at Ben's place on the night of the Royce Hotel meeting.

---

*The stories were in the public domain, but Bantam sued at the behest of Louis L'Amour, who was angry about this publication.

During all this uproar about the auction, Maura Wogan phoned Paul and asked him whether we would accept an offer from the Cheevers to buy the book from us. Paul suggested she name a figure. After a few hours she called back to offer $55,000, an offer we rejected. We thought it was probably as serious an offer as the offer to work out a settlement at the Royce Hotel.

I asked Jordan if he remembered reading somewhere that Kissinger and/or Nixon had evolved a "madman" theory of diplomacy: the use of erratic and unpredictable behavior to confuse and disorient the enemy. Jordan said he did remember reading that.

On June 23, Garbus filed in White Plains for an order enjoining the paperback auction, claiming, among other things, that the Cheevers' rights were being violated under the Lanham Act. Judge Goettel set a hearing on this motion for June 24 at 10:00 A.M. Meanwhile, Judge Kiley scheduled a hearing for Monday, June 27, to determine a date for the Chicago trial.

Paul had to take a 6:00 A.M. plane to White Plains, where Goettel denied Garbus's motion for a restraining order against the auction. He told Maura Wogan to take the matter up with Judge Kiley in Chicago. But, he said, if Kiley refused to act, Maura should come back to him with another motion in writing. He commented that the written permission the Cheevers had given us to sell subsidiary rights was "ambiguous."

On Monday, June 27—two days before the auction—Maura Wogan flew to Chicago for Judge Kiley's hearing. She filed an objection to Paul's request for an early trial date, arguing that the Chicago trial should wait until after the White Plains hearing. Kiley set a tentative trial date of August 8. Since Maura had not mentioned the auction, Paul told Judge Kiley that Judge Goettel had instructed her to ask in Chicago for a decision on the auction. Kiley said there was no motion before him for an injunction. Maura replied that she had no intention of asking Kiley for an injunction; she intended, she said, to get an injunction from Judge Goettel.

That same day, while Maura Wogan was in Chicago, Garbus filed anew in White Plains for the injunction against the auction and also for a restraining order against distribution of "reviewers' copies" of the book. Goettel refused once more to enjoin the auction. But he issued the restraining order, citing the Lanham Act claim that he had found so unconvincing in May. The restraining order was good for only ten days—long enough to put a damper on the auction. And in ten days another restraining order could be issued. We thought that Goettel would issue it.

Garbus wrote a letter to Dell, threatening to sue them for copyright infringement. On June 28, he was quoted in the Westchester Gannett paper as saying that the "result" of "making bids on a product that has a cloud over it . . . is you will get a book that gets a lower bidding price." He said, too, that the Cheevers intended to "file motions by the end of the week in U.S. District Court in White Plains to dismiss the court case in Chicago and move it to New York . . . . We want the case in New York."[1]

We knew that a judge in New York could not dismiss a case in another jurisdiction. Paul said that Garbus must have been misquoted.

Wednesday, June 29, was a pleasant, sunny day. While reprinters were having their morning coffee, they could read in Edwin MacDowell's publishing column in the *New York Times* that Judge Goettel had issued a ten-day preliminary injunction against publication of *The Uncollected Stories of John Cheever*. Garbus was quoted as saying "the auction's taking place is much less important than Judge Goettel's halt on publishing the collection."[2] Several bidders backed out.

Dell got the book at 5:00 P.M. for $225,000.

Scott Meredith told the press that it was unprecedented to get more than $200,000 for a collection of short stories.

We were relieved that it was over. Mrs. Cheever had gone to great lengths to choke off the bidding for paperback rights; if we won this case, she stood to be considerably out of pocket. But then, so did we; it had been our decision to go ahead with the auction. Basically the whole thing was, as Paul said in one of his rare comments to the press, "much ado about nothing." However, he complained to Judge Goettel in a letter about Garbus's behavior in this matter. It was improper, Paul said, for Garbus to "seek to intimidate" prospective bidders through letters and phone calls—we had evidence of such activities—and "to plant newspaper stories adverse to Academy, so that they would run the day of the auction." Paul said that this conduct was "an improper effort to simulate the injunction no court ordered" and it violated the American Bar Association's Canons of Professional Responsibility. "The Cheevers," Paul wrote, "do not come into this Court with clean hands."

Judge Goettel managed to handle Paul's outrage without going to pieces. He refused to postpone the date of the July 11 "evidentiary hearing," despite Paul's argument that Judge Kiley would be deciding on copyright when he decided on contract at our Chicago trial and so would make the White Plains hearing unnecessary. Paul quoted Garbus's statement to the Westchester paper that the Cheevers wanted the case moved to New York as evidence that they were trying to subvert Goettel's ruling that the contract question should be decided in Chicago. In addition, Paul pointed out that the July 11 date meant that depositions would have to be taken on July 5, 6, and 7, thus allowing for "only one day per deponent." Attempting to make use of Garbus's fantasy of Mrs. Cheever-as-feeble-old-invalid, Paul argued that "Cheevers' counsel had indicated that Mrs. Cheever might not be physically capable of answering more than a few hours of questions per day."

It did not surprise us that Goettel remained impervious to these arguments. What did surprise us was that Paul offered the alternative date of August 1, thus demonstrating a willingness to let Goettel hear this case before the August 8 Chicago trial date. We ourselves thought it might be worthwhile to put up some kind of fight to postpone the White Plains hearing until *after* the Chicago trial. But Paul did not agree with us. He kept saying that the purpose of the evidentiary hearing was to examine the "question of the children's copyright." He kept repeating this as though it was a perfectly sensible idea. We did not see how we—or any of the Cheevers for that matter—could contribute any information on the children's copyright. The law was the law, wasn't it? The Cheever children either had a copyright interest in this case or they didn't have one, and to us it seemed crystal clear that they didn't have one that could affect our contract. Paul himself had said this, the copyright experts at Pattishall had said this, and Adam Walinsky had researched it and come up with the same answer.

We were upset about this hearing for several reasons. One was that we had a long-standing commitment to speak at the Radcliffe publishing course in Cambridge on July 13, and if the hearing lasted for more than two days, we might not be able to fulfill that obligation. But Paul was adamant. Judge Goettel had set the hearing for July 11, and July 11 it had to be.

After some initial difficulty, Paul got a list from Maura Wogan of the Cheevers' expert witnesses: Ellis Levine, senior counsel for Random House; Robert Gottlieb, once head of Knopf, a division of Random House, and at that time editor of the *New Yorker*, owned by the owner of Random House; Rhoda Gamson of Viking Penguin's contracts department (Garbus often represents Viking Penguin in litigation); and Nancy Coffey, then an editor at St. Martin's Press. Wogan told Paul that these people would testify on publishing industry "custom and usage" in the matter of "tentative titles, delivery of manuscripts, assignment of copyrights [and] the meaning of different clauses which appear in the publishing agreement," on "publishing agreements in general," and on "the value of copyrights to publishers and authors." In addition to all this, Wogan said the Cheevers planned to call Alfred Kazin and Professor Gabriel Mottola, who, along with Robert Gottlieb, would testify about John Cheever's reputation, about the difference between a sketch and a story, and about "the significance of the Cheever literature."

It seemed to us that most of these witnesses were going to testify on contract, which Goettel had specifically relegated to the Chicago court. And John Cheever's reputation surely had nothing to do with copyright. What, we asked Paul, was going on? Paul kept saying that this was a hearing into the children's copyright. He said Garbus was simply confusing the issue by bringing in all these witnesses to testify on contract matters, and therefore we were not going to present any expert witnesses of our own to rebut Garbus's points because those points were clearly outside the scope of the federal hearing. And too, we might, Paul said, endanger our trial in Chicago if we put on a full-scale trial in White Plains. So he was going to wait and put on all our witnesses before Judge Kiley.

That made sense. But, we asked, while the Cheever witnesses were on parade, wouldn't we be sitting there looking kind of dumb?

Paul replied that this was a hearing into the children's copyright.

The press was showing a lively interest in the case. John Blades of the *Chicago Tribune* interviewed Mrs. Cheever,[3] who "complained about the 'insignificant advance,' . . . the magnitude of the collection and the unflattering implications about her late husband in the introduction by Scott Donaldson." She went on to say, "Academy Chicago is a small press, and my impression when I signed that terrible contract was that this would be a small edition for libraries, for students . . . . I had no idea they'd grabbed what they thought was a gold mine, which was their idea from the beginning."

Ben, too, talked to Blades. "We didn't want to sue them," he said. "We only wanted a chance for the input they promised us. This nice little book had turned into something bigger than we had in mind, and they were getting it for very little money. . . . So I had my agent call the Millers offering to buy the book back for twenty times what they'd paid. They said no. I had my lawyer call them and they still said no. Then I decided it was time for a personal talk. But when I called Anita Miller and offered to come to Chicago, she started screaming at me and we both lost our cool." Despite all this, Ben said, the family were still hoping to resolve things amicably until "an off-duty policeman came to my mother's house and served her a summons. Mummy was very upset."

Mary Cheever told Blades that what really got to her was Scott Donaldson setting up parallels between John Cheever's life and his stories and implying that the stories were suppressed because they revealed "something about John that he didn't want known. I just can't stand that kind of implication, as if this were dirty laundry. . . . gossip. The reason John didn't want them reprinted was because they were immature."

Ben said that money was not the principal reason for the family's "disaffection"—they only wanted to see the stories "published appropriately. But what Academy Chicago is trying to do, I think, because I really haven't had a rational conversation with them, is to get people to read these not-very-good stories because they think they're learning things about Daddy that he wanted hidden, and that's deeply offensive. Daddy made a profession of not hiding things."

18

Mary Cheever's Deposition: "I Would Like This Creep to Finish"

On July 5, 1988, Paul flew to New York to take the Cheevers' depositions. The first deponent was Mary Cheever; Garbus was at the Kronish, Leib offices to "defend" her deposition. At the outset, Paul was cheerful and composed. As the day wore on, he became increasingly frazzled. Ben, Susan, and Maura Wogan were in the room, commenting audibly on the proceedings. Garbus interrupted often and suggested answers to his client when her replies did not satisfy him.

As is routine in depositions, Paul asked about Mrs. Cheever's background. She was born May 4, 1918, earned a B.A. degree from Saint Lawrence College, and married John Cheever in 1941. Beginning in 1962, she taught composition and creative writing at various local schools and colleges.

Paul began by attempting to take her through the events encompassing the signing of the contract. She remembered getting the July 10, 1987, letter from Franklin, which she said came as a surprise to her: Ben had not mentioned the project to her beforehand. She put the letter in a drawer, and the next thing she remembered was that Maggie Curran told her that ICM thought very well of Academy Chicago. And when she got the contract, she sent it to Maggie, as Maggie had told her to do. She didn't remember discussing it with any of her children. She had not, she said, spoken to anyone at ICM since the contract was signed. It was always Maggie she did these things with, she said, and always on the phone. Maggie "always handled everything, all permissions, all contracts, all advances—foreign, you name it." She did not remember talking to Ben about this project at all. Or to either of her other children.

Paul showed her Franklin's first letter to Ben, dated June 15, 1987, which she said she had only recently seen and which mentioned Franklin's "tennis pal," Tom Glazer, and the fact that Franklin had lived over "Sally Swope's garage." Perhaps, Paul said, she could help him with some of the names in that letter. Who was Sally Swope? "She's a friend and neighbor of mine," Mrs. Cheever said. "A woman of some wealth and importance." She had had a conversation with Sally Swope about this project, and Mrs. Swope had told her that Franklin was good at tennis and golf.

When Paul began to ask questions about John Cheever's early story collections, Garbus said he would get that information, if Paul left "a space" in the deposition; he would get the information certainly by Friday. He was trying to spare Mrs. Cheever, whose "endurance" was not going to be "endless," and he wanted Paul to "get the best of Mrs. Cheever" while she was there.

Paul thanked him and said he would like to do things his way.

Who, Paul asked her, had published the collection *The Housebreaker of Shady Hill?* She hesitated. "Harper?" she asked. "Was it Harper?"* If she was asking Ben and Susan, she clearly got no answer. Garbus interrupted to say that this was not terribly relevant and was going to exhaust Mrs. Cheever, and he resented it. Other than Ben, he said, no one knew the answer to that question. Paul replied that he believed he was entitled to take Mrs. Cheever's deposition. Susan, Ben, and Maura added their own comments, and Mrs. Cheever forgot the question.

Paul went on to show her the title page of the Knopf omnibus and ask her to identify it. Garbus interrupted to observe that Paul might not know it but everyone else in the room knew that the Random House paperback line was not Knopf, but Vintage. The implication—often repeated—was that Garbus and his clients were "insiders" in a kind of publishing fraternity or fellowship and Paul was an "outsider."

Paul moved on to the subject of copyrights. Mrs. Cheever said she did not keep track of her husband's copyrights. She believed that ICM did some of it, and occasionally she got letters from the Curtis Brown agency and from "certain publishers, Random House . . . . Usually they take care of it." She had no copyright file at home. All she had were these letters she just mentioned, and she kept them in a drawer. The same drawer where she put the letter from Franklin.

Garbus requested a five-minute break, and when he came back, he announced that Mrs. Cheever had expressed a willingness to work through

---

*It was Harper.

lunch "because at the end of the day she may flag." Paul said he was assured a full day, starting at 10:30 A.M. at Mrs. Cheever's request, and Garbus was now just wasting time.

On questions about her agreement with ICM, Mary Cheever said that the agency would take 10 percent of the advance from Academy Chicago, but she couldn't remember whether they would take 10 percent of any royalties.

Paul showed her the publishing agreement with Academy. She said she had read it before she signed it, but not carefully.

"This can go to the judge on Friday," Garbus said. "There's no question that she signed the document. The judge laid out the legal issues here and the legal issues don't refer to whether or not she read every single clause."

"I suggest that you are wasting time and behaving in an improper manner," Paul said.

He asked Mary whether she had discussed any part of the publishing agreement with anyone before she signed it or whether she had discussed it with any of her children. She said she had not, and she had not kept a copy—she thought she might have given her copy to Ben—and she couldn't remember to whom she sent it after she signed it.

The next thing that happened, she said, was that Franklin came to see her. She believed it was in October.* He had phoned first. Paul asked her what Franklin had said about why he was coming to see her. She began, "He wanted to talk about—" and then broke off abruptly. "I don't remember the conversation at all," she said.

The thing she really wanted to talk about in connection with Franklin's visit was the "hostess gift" of five books that he had given her. She offered to itemize these, which she called "small, obscure books . . . . translations of poetry, reprints of 1917 correspondence between obscure professors."† Paul asked her to tell him about "what was said or done" during Franklin's visit.

But Garbus wanted her to talk about the "hostess gifts." "Did he tell you

---

*It was on December 12.

†This "correspondence," *The Lyttelton/Hart-Davis Letters*, was exchanged from 1955 to 1962 between George Lyttelton, a retired Eton don, and Rupert Hart-Davis, a well-known London publisher and writer. The first volume had received a full-page positive review in the *New York Times Book Review*.

about the books?" he asked. "Was there a dialogue concerning the books? Was there a dialogue concerning the project? 'This is the kind of book Academy does'?"

"I respectfully object," Paul said. "I know that is improper. I wish you would stop."

The only thing she remembered about the visit, she said, was that she had given Franklin a copy of "Behold a Cloud in the West." She did it, she said, to prove to him "that he had not finished his research." Paul asked her whether Franklin had returned the book to her. After she complained to Mr. Miller, she said, it was sent to her by registered mail. "And if you know the Ossining post office, that is a nasty thing, to be sent something by registered mail . . . . Because there is no parking and you have to stand in line. You have to hike to the post office and stand on line!"

Paul showed her the alphabetized list of stories—typed by Mary Dennis from Jordan's handwriting—that Franklin had given Ben in November. She had not seen this list before, she said, and every title was wrong. She became agitated. "It says the Art of the—I suppose that refers to a story that was entitled 'The Autobiography of a Drummer.' 'The Beautiful Mountains,' with an 's' on it. I never saw so many mistakes! The embarrassment of it—the embarrassing—He has—the embarrassment! I never saw anything so extraordinary! My God," she cried, "how can he have done this? He must have been drunk when he made this list."

Paul showed her Garbus's February 17 letter to Jordan, which had been copied to her. She said she had not seen it until she was shown it in Garbus's office in the early part of May.

She identified Andrew Wylie as a literary agent. She had met him for the first time at Ben's house on the evening of the Royce Hotel meeting. She had never spoken to him about anything before that, and she had never written to him.

Paul offered to show her a copy of the letter she had written to Donaldson, but she said she didn't need to see it. She began, with strong input from Ben and Susan, to detail her objections to the introduction. Great attention was paid, she said, to "some very, very early stories." She hoped she could eliminate these because they were immature; they were not good Cheever stories. It seemed to her that the introduction was "merchandising these very imperfect stories in terms of gossip," telling "the future reader" that the stories "will tell you some little-known, unpleasant facts about this author that you may have admired and enjoyed." And she was outraged by the table of contents because "they were printing everything they could have laid their hands on" and they had not asked her permission. They had put the collection together without consulting her about one thing.

Paul reminded her that in her May 3 letter to Donaldson, she had said that he made a false assumption when he said her husband selected the stories in the 1978 Knopf collection. "Did your husband have no role at all in the selection of these stories?"

"Very little," Mary Cheever said. "He was ill at the time. I believe he sent some manuscripts or some listing to Gottlieb, but he did very little."

This answer did not sit well with Garbus and the Cheever children. "He had the final approval," Garbus said.

"Mr. Garbus," Paul said, "I think you should tell your clients and Mrs. Cheever that this is not their deposition. It's not a time for them to be suggesting answers to Mrs. Cheever."

"They weren't suggesting an answer," Garbus said.

"Of course it's not time for you either," Paul said.

"Of course," Mrs. Cheever amended her answer, "he looked it over and approved of it before it was sent to press, but he had nothing to do with the selection." She added that there was no problem "because he and Gottlieb agreed about the literary quality of his stories."

Asked her opinion about individual stories, Mrs. Cheever said that "In Passing" was a very immature story but a very interesting one. "Expelled" was immature but not embarrassing. "Fall River," "Late Gathering," and "Bock Beer and Bermuda Onions" she found to be immature.

Garbus interjected that they could save time if they said that it was Mrs. Cheever's view that "anything before '47 ought not to be reprinted." And indeed, she had said earlier that John Cheever had told Robert Gottlieb that he did not think anything before the war, "anything before 1947," should be included because they were "embarrassing, immature and imitative."

But Mrs. Cheever would not accept Garbus's stricture. "I'll modify it," she said. If some of the early stories were reprinted with "intelligent editorial comment," they might be included. She said she thought "In Passing" and "The Happiest Days" were interesting stories. She also wanted to amend the date of 1947 to 1943. She thought that "Sergeant Limeburner" (1943) was not embarrassingly immature, and neither were "two or three of the war stories."

"So it's clear," Garbus said. "I think you and I understand each other. Our legal position is that she has a right to pick and choose any one of the stories for any one reason. That is her right under the contract. By going through embarrassing and immature, that might be one standard, but under her contract she's not responsible for any standard. She can decide to keep out a story or she can decide to print two stories or three stories solely at her discretion."

"I suggest you save your arguments for the court," Paul said.

"Otherwise," Garbus said, "we are going to be here all day."

After lunch, Mrs. Cheever said that when Franklin gave her the spiral-bound manuscript, she had the impression that "she was to read these stories and choose from them in due course."

Paul wanted to know what she meant by due course.

"No publication date had been set," she said. "No dates of any kind had been set. I had no idea that there was any hurry for me to do this, this selection, but I was convinced that it was for me and only me to select the stories."

"What led you to that conclusion?"

"Because they are my property," she said, becoming agitated again. "Those stories. They are my inheritance!"

She gave Franklin a copy of "Behold a Cloud in the West" out of the goodness of her heart, she said, and not so that it could be included in the book. She had never met Franklin before he came to her house, and she knew he had never met her husband. Paul showed her the title page of Franklin's copy of *The World of Apples,* inscribed to Franklin by John Cheever. She verified Cheever's signature, remarking that she did not know that Franklin had played a part in the publication of the book George Hunt had written about Cheever. "I didn't know that Franklin Dennis had anything to do with it," she said.

"It may have had something to do with the publicity," Garbus observed. "Do you know who the secretaries were, the copyright?"

Paul objected to these questions.

"This is getting silly," Garbus said.

Mrs. Cheever said that when she signed the contract, she believed that she would be asked to choose the stories because she owned them and because Franklin Dennis's "hostess gift" of five books had led her to believe that Academy was a small scholarly house.

"Wasn't that *after* the publishing agreement was signed?" Paul asked.

"I guess it was," she said. "Yes."

On the matter of the difference between a sketch and a story, she said that had never been established. It was sort of like arguing about "the number of angels standing on the head of a pin." She had not thought that the question of sketches would come up when she signed the contract. She said she had not thought about whether her children had an interest in any of the stories, but "it would have been no problem" because she and her children usually agreed about what they should do . . . Garbus cut her off and suggested an addendum to her reply: "And what should be done."

"Mr. Garbus," Paul said, "you know that is not proper."

"Mr. Freehling," Garbus said, "this is abusive."

When Paul introduced the subject of the Royce Hotel meeting, Garbus directed her not to answer on the ground that there was to be no disclosure of that meeting and also on the ground that it was now 3:30, and it was "absolutely clear" that Paul was "belaboring this woman." Paul should talk to Ben and Susan and consult "other documents."

A considerable disturbance arose, with several people talking at once. "I object to it," Garbus said, "and I direct the witness not to answer. I don't see why we go through it four times."

Paul turned to the court reporter. "Ms. Reporter," he said, "the atmosphere of this room, the conditions under which I'm being asked to take this deposition, make it impossible to continue. I am going to ask Mr. Garbus that both Ben Cheever and Susan Cheever leave the room if you want to continue."

"They're parties," Garbus said. "I can ask them both not to say anything, which I will now do."

"I think it's way past that," Paul said.

"A lot of your conduct is way past that," Garbus said.

"I'm asking you to please ask them to leave the room."

"I will not do it," Garbus said.

"Then I'm terminating the deposition at this point," Paul said. "We will resume upon application to the judge."

He was not, he said in response to Garbus's somewhat alarmed question, terminating all depositions. He would resume with Susan Cheever tomorrow.

"We'll start with Miss Cheever at ten A.M.," Garbus said. Then he thought of something. "I have a better idea," he said to Ben and Susan. "I'll ask you both now to step out of the room. Let's see where we go."

After a short break, Mary Cheever offered to amend her definition of the difference between a sketch and a story. Paul said dryly that she could wait until her own lawyer asked her that question.

Asked about royalty arrangements for the Knopf omnibus, she said that she did not know what these were; she didn't know how many copies had been sold; she did not know whether the same publisher had brought out the hardcover and the paperback; she did not know whether there were separate contracts for the hardcover and the paperback. She didn't know what royalties had been paid on the book.

Paul asked her what she had found objectionable in the advertising for the book. As she replied, Maura Wogan kept prompting her in whispers.

"Ms. Wogan," Paul said, "please stop."

"Aren't you able to help me?" Mary asked piteously.

"No," Paul said, "she's not supposed to help you while you're having your deposition taken."

"I'm just pointing out to her a document she should be reading," Maura Wogan said. "It's very clear from the testimony that went on before that a lot of the stories have been—all of the stories have been available."

"They're all available," the witness echoed dutifully.

"To say that they were previously unavailable is untrue," Maura Wogan observed.

Garbus asked Mrs. Cheever whether she wanted to stay until 5:00 or whether she wanted to quit.

"I would like this creep to finish," Mrs. Cheever said.

Paul said he wanted that on the record.

Garbus said that this was as abusive a deposition as he had ever seen and Mrs. Cheever was exhausted.

Shortly after that, Paul said he had no more questions.

19

Franklin Dennis's Deposition: "I'm Going to Ask the Witness Not to Speak with His Attorney"

Franklin was deposed on Thursday, July 6, at Garbus's offices. It was a day Franklin would never forget. Ben was there. Cynthia Johnson, who was in an advanced state of pregnancy, was defending Franklin because Paul was deposing Susan Cheever that same day at the Kronish, Lieb offices. Franklin had asked Bob Stein to help defend his deposition, but Bob had said that Franklin shouldn't spend the money; it wasn't necessary.

Franklin is mild-mannered and generally passive; he is not a combative personality. He fell back under attack. At the Royce Hotel, Garbus had said that there were "ten thousand Franklin Dennises" walking the streets, and in a June 20 letter to Paul, Garbus said he wanted to "highlight" the "issue" of Franklin. Had Academy researched his background? What *was* his background? What "transactions" had he been "involved in with Academy," and what did Academy have in its files "relating to Dennis?" Because to Garbus's "knowledge," Franklin knew "absolutely nothing about Cheever" except "what he learned through Ben Cheever and through his recent involvement with the uncollected stories."

When the deposition began, Garbus asked Franklin about that first meeting with Ben at the Chez Vong restaurant in New York. Franklin said that Tom Glazer was present.

"And Mr. Glazer heard everything that was said?" Garbus demanded. Franklin said that was true.

And did Franklin meet Susan Cheever at the Cheever house in Ossining? And did he have specific conversation with her on the "book project"?

"Nothing of substance," Franklin said. "It was just—it was, you know, 'nice to see you again.'"

"You don't recall specific discussion about the book project?"

Well, Franklin said, he thought Susan said that she saw he had a new business, becoming involved in book projects, and he said yes—

"Do you deny," Garbus asked, cutting him off, "that there was any conversation about this particular book project?"

Franklin said that there had been conversation between him and Mary Cheever. He was puzzled by these questions because he could not know that in her deposition, Susan was claiming that Franklin had told her friend Warren Hinckle that the book he was planning was really just a student guide, not a real book, and that it was going to be mimeographed and not typeset.

"I asked you," Garbus said, "whether or not you deny there was a conversation between you and Susan Cheever concerning this book project?"

He paced back and forth about the office, stopping often to lean close to Franklin as he questioned him, occasionally putting his hand on Franklin's shoulder. Cynthia kept objecting.

"Did you have any conversation with Warren Hinckle about this book project?"

"No," Franklin said.

"You deny that?" Garbus said, raising his voice.

Cynthia objected.

At this point, moving on to another topic, Garbus began to interject the word *some* into his questions: the result of this would be a tacit admission from Franklin, on the record, that the projected book was to consist of "some" rather than "all" the uncollected stories. This would negate the book's title. Franklin, concentrating on his answers, did not notice this, and neither did Cynthia.

"At the time you wrote to Mr. Cheever," Garbus said, "you were interested in publishing some of the short stories that did not appear in the omnibus?" Franklin said that was true. "Did you discuss with Mr. Miller the project was a collection of some previously uncollected stories?" Yes, Franklin said, he did. And so it went. "When you said 'some uncollected stories,' which were you then talking about? . . . And then you were going to take some uncollected stories and not others, is that right? . . . When you said to Mr. Miller, 'some uncollected stories,' he then wrote a letter . . . . When you said to him, 'some uncollected stories,' tell me the discussion you had." Frequently he cut off Franklin's answers to ask a fresh "some" question. "Let him finish his answer," Cynthia said, and then again, "Mr. Garbus, give him a chance to finish the question."

"Isn't it a fact," Garbus said, "that there is a difference between the December galleys and the bound galleys that are now being submitted—a difference in that there are some stories in the bound galleys that were not there in December and some stories in bound galleys in addition to those that were there in December? Isn't that fair?"

Cynthia asked Franklin whether he understood the question.

"He understands," Garbus said. "I'm going to ask the witness not to speak with his attorney."

"He can consult with his attorney at any point he wishes," Cynthia said.

"He cannot," said Garbus, "and your attorney was very clear yesterday that it's not the practice there and not here. He can state whatever he wants on the record."

"That's certainly not true," Cynthia said.

"It's certainly true with regard to New York practice," Garbus said.

"I don't care what New York practice is," Cynthia said.

"We'll get a ruling," Garbus said. He addressed Franklin. "Will you answer the question?"

"He's not answering the question until he speaks to me," Cynthia said.

While Franklin was conferring with Cynthia, Garbus said, "Let the record indicate that he is conferring with counsel. It's been going on a few minutes. It's over my objection and it's contrary to what Mr. Freehling said should happen with a deposition."

After some questions about "ring-bound galleys" and "photostatic copies," Garbus reverted to his "some" theme. "Now the first time you met, you used with Mr. Cheever the words you used with Mr. Miller, right, that you wanted to publish a volume of some previously uncollected stories? And you used those words when Mr. Glazer was present at the first lunch; is that right?"

"Why," Cynthia asked, breaking in, "don't you let him testify as to what he said, instead of you testifying?"

"We'll get into that," Garbus said, mysteriously.

"What I did say," Franklin said, "is that I had a very strong sense that there were many stories of John Cheever which had not been collected in a volume of John Cheever short stories that were worthy of research and consideration for a volume of short stories."

"You also knew that there were some stories that were thought to be bad uncollected stories, isn't that correct?"

"No," Franklin said.

"Never knew that?" Garbus said in apparent surprise.

"I did not know that, no." And in truth Franklin did not believe that John Cheever was capable of writing a bad story.

"You never read the Gottlieb introduction to the Knopf book?"

Here Garbus was referring to the preface to the 1978 omnibus, written not by Robert Gottlieb but by John Cheever, who wrote that the order of the stories was, to the best of his recollection, chronological, "and the most embarrassingly immature pieces have been dropped."

"Well, I certainly had," Franklin said, "but I wanted to see for myself."

"And you've seen for yourself in some of the publicity stuff and some of your editing notes, hadn't you yourself seen that some were inferior stories?"

"Well," Franklin said, "he was such an accomplished writer that what would appear to be less than good in comparison with some other writer, from him would be more than adequate."

Garbus asked Franklin whether he remembered telling Ben "in Mr. Glazer's presence" that Mrs. Cheever would have the right to decide what was in "the book."

Franklin said he didn't remember saying that specifically.

Garbus asked him whether he had told Ben in Glazer's presence at that first meeting that the Cheever family would have the "final decision with respect to the Cheever stories?"

Cynthia pointed out that this was basically the same question Franklin had just answered.

"Yes—" Franklin said hesitantly.

"Didn't you also," Garbus said, "tell him that—"

"Let him finish the answer," Cynthia said.

"He said yes," Garbus said.

"He was going on," Cynthia said.

"—and my recollection is," Franklin said, "that . . . the stories would be found, there would be a discussion and evaluation among the parties . . . the Cheevers and the publisher and myself."

Garbus asked him whether he had told Ben "in the presence of Mr. Glazer that the final decision about this book would be the Cheever family?"

"Yes—" Franklin said.

"He said yes!" Garbus cried.

"I—" Franklin said. "We're getting awfully specific and that meeting was an explor—"

"If you don't remember, say you don't remember," Cynthia said.

Well, Franklin said, he didn't remember being that specific. He certainly invited the Cheevers to be "intensely involved in the volume," and he was trying to "impart" that there would be "great consultation" and everybody would be involved and they would come up with a "mutually satisfactory compromise or package, whichever they would approve of—"

"Let me ask the question again," Garbus said, "in case you don't understand it. It's a very specific question and you said yes before."

"He didn't!" Cynthia said. "His testimony stands."

Garbus asked whether Franklin told Ben "in the presence of Mr. Glazer" that the Cheever family would have the final decision about the stories.

Cynthia objected that the question had been asked and answered. Franklin asked for a break so that he could leave the room with Cynthia.

"Just let the record indicate," Garbus said, "that after every question he refers to his counsel, that we are not getting anywhere in this deposition and that every question has been modified."

When Franklin came back, the question was read to him, and he said, "I don't recall saying those words. No."

"You don't recall one way or the other?" Garbus said. "Do you recall telling Mr. Jordan [*sic*] that the final decision with respect to the selection of stories was in the Cheever family? Back in August?"

Franklin said he couldn't recall that specifically.

But, Garbus said, however he worded it, Franklin told "Mr. Jordan" that the "final say-so" on the book's contents was "in the hands of the Cheevers." Wasn't that right?

Cynthia said that this mischaracterized prior testimony and also that the question had been asked and answered.

Franklin said that was certainly his intention, but he couldn't recall using those specific words.

"Well," Garbus said, "you are literate, you're a college graduate? . . . Were you able to express your intention to Mr. Jordan [*sic*] about this project?"

"You're asking me to recall a specific thing that I can't recall."

"Well, do you recall making that specifically clear to Mr. Cheever at the first meeting with him?"

Cynthia objected.

"Were you able to express your intention then?" Garbus asked.

"Mr. Garbus," Cynthia said, "you've asked the same question five times."

"It's a different question," Garbus said.

"It's the same question," Cynthia said.

"Mr. Dennis?" Garbus said.

"I'll just say," Franklin responded, "that I don't recall using those specific terms. I think that—"

"That's fine," Cynthia said. "You've answered the question."

"I'm entitled to an answer," Garbus said.

He continued to ask the question, and Franklin continued to say that there was going to be a process and he had wanted the Cheevers to be part of it.

After another five-minute break, Garbus moved to a new theme. From the papers we had lightheartedly sent him, he had gleaned the hardly startling information that Academy was squeezed for cash. Jordan had had to send Franklin postdated checks. Garbus mentioned a letter Franklin had written to Jordan suggesting that it might be a good idea, when the paperback rights were sold, to ask the paperback publisher to contribute to advertising for the hardcover book. "Absent the paperback monies, they didn't have enough money to advertise, print and distribute this hardcover book, isn't that correct?"

Cynthia objected. "Why don't you ask him what he knew instead of testifying for him?"

"Did you know?" Garbus asked. "Did you ever do a memo, Mr. Dennis, about the need for paperback monies?"

Franklin said he did write a memo "suggesting that we could do co-marketing or cooperative marketing with a paperback house, and that if the paperback rights were to be sold, that money could be used for the advertising of the hardcover book."

"And you knew at the time that the Academy didn't have the money?"

"That's not what he testified," Cynthia said, objecting.

"Did you know whether the Academy had the money?"

Franklin said he didn't know. But he wrote the memo because he didn't think "you ever have enough money to promote a book, so I was just encouraging." In response to a series of questions on this subject, Franklin kept saying that he could not recall any specific conversation about it, and

Garbus kept asking him whether he could recall it. Franklin said that "it's good to have as much money as you can to promote a book" and he saw this as a "legitimate way of increasing the promotional budget." He didn't explore it, he said; it was just an idea he thought the Millers should bring up with Scott Meredith.

What was Franklin's "intention" in going to see Mrs. Cheever in December? Had he used the words "some previously uncollected stories"? Franklin said he didn't think he used any terms at all; he said to her, "Here is the table of contents. This is as close as we can come to the work in progress, but there are these other stories we want to include." He had brought the copies primarily, he said, for Ben Cheever because Ben had said he wanted to read "a number of the stories," the "Townhouse" stories among them, and Franklin brought them to Mrs. Cheever because Ben was going to be visiting there that weekend, and because Franklin wanted to show Mary Cheever what had been done, to "elicit her help in finding some stories" that had been identified but not located, and to ask her whether the *Newsweek* essay could be used as a preface.

"You indicated before," Garbus observed, "that your intention that the Cheevers have final control over the selection of stories lasted until January."

"Objection," Cynthia said. "That completely mischaracterizes his prior testimony."

"Had you at that point," Garbus said, "read the Gottlieb introduction to the Knopf book [*sic*]? Had you ever learned that the Knopf book stopped at 1947?"

"What do you mean," Cynthia asked, "'stopped at 1947'?"

"He knows," Garbus said.

"Well," Franklin said, rising to the occasion, "it started in 1947."

"You knew that?" Garbus asked keenly.

Franklin said he did.

"And you knew that many of the stories you had given to Mrs. Cheever were pre-1947?"

Franklin said that was correct.

"And you knew, did you not, that Mrs. Cheever had never wanted to see that stuff published, the pre-1947?"

"No," Franklin said.

"You never knew that before today?"

Cynthia objected. "Asked and answered."

"No," Franklin said.

"When did you learn for the first time that the Cheevers did not want to see the stories prior to '47 published?"

"Objection," Cynthia said. "It assumed that he ever learned it."

"Maybe he never learned it," Garbus said.

Franklin said he had "surmised as much from pieces in the press in the last couple of months, but actually this morning is the first time I really heard someone say that."

Asked about the "next step" after his visit to Mrs. Cheever, Franklin said that he expected that Mrs. Cheever and other members of the family would "review" the galleys "and have a response and that would be part of the process." But, he said, he never got that response.

Here Garbus elicited some information about Franklin's background. He had worked as assistant editor and marketing assistant at two independent publishers and had reviewed fiction for *Publishers Weekly* for nine years. He had majored in English and political science. He had never done graduate work, and he had never done any "English teaching," as Garbus put it.

Returning to the subject of the famous December visit to Mrs. Cheever, Garbus asked whether Franklin had said to her, "We are interested in publishing some previously uncollected stories." Cynthia pointed out that this question had been asked and answered. Franklin thought this was a strange question: why would he bring Mrs. Cheever a virtually completed manuscript, for which he had a signed contract, and then tell her he was "interested" in publishing "some" stories?

Garbus asked whether Franklin's "intention" had changed from the summer until the time he met with Mrs. Cheever. Franklin replied that in late October or early November, he had told Ben that all the stories that had been identified as uncollected should be in the volume, "for a number of reasons."

"When did you tell him this?" Garbus asked.

"Tell him? Late October."

"Wasn't that the first time that you ever told anybody that Academy was interested in publishing all the uncollected stories?"

"The first time I told anybody?"

"Yes. Any of the Cheevers."

"Oh, well, that's true, because Ben was the only person I was really communicating with, as I said, by telephone."

"You never told him that you wanted to publish all the uncollected stories?"

"I just said I did," Franklin said. "As I said, somewhere between late October and probably mid-November."

"So," Garbus said, "the first time you told Ben you wanted to publish all the uncollected stories is in October or mid-November? . . . And it never crossed your mind up until that time that you were interested in publishing all the uncollected stories?"

"Objection," Cynthia said. "That's not what he testified."

"Is that fair?" Garbus asked.

"No," Franklin said. "That's not fair. It was always a possibility."

"But the first time you told the Cheevers about that possibility was in October or November?"

"Well, I thought that my letters were implicit that that was always a possibility and when I told Ben that, he said, well, that sounds like a good idea. That's what I recall."

Then there was the question of the number of stories. Nobody discussed whether the volume would contain one story, three stories, or one hundred stories, did they, at the outset? Franklin said he came away from that first meeting certain that they had been talking about a book, not two or three stories.

"Well," Garbus said, "a book of short stories could be ten stories, it could be fifteen stories, can't it?"

"That's true," Franklin said. "But we weren't talking about two or three."

"So," Garbus said, "you came away from that first meeting thinking that you were talking about a book of ten to fifteen stories?"

"Testifying for the witness," Cynthia said.

"So," Garbus said, "you didn't know whether it was two or three or ten or fifteen or more?"

"I knew it wasn't going to be two or three. There would be no point in doing a book of two or three stories. You would want to have as hefty a book as possible."

"You knew a book of Cheever stories could be a substantial book and could sell a substantial number of copies, isn't that right?"

"This is completely irrelevant," Cynthia said.

Well, Franklin said, since he himself was such an admirer of John Cheever, he was certain there were many other fanatics out there like himself, and he would think there was a great prospect of the book being successful.

"Even at ten to fifteen stories?" Garbus asked. "There's a Cheever audience out there that buys Cheever whether it be three or four stories or ten to fifteen stories, and you knew that."

Franklin agreed, while Cynthia objected to "this continuing line of questioning, talking about a book of ten to fifteen stories, which has no relevance to this litigation."

Franklin said that the book would have to have some range to it to be successful.

"It could have a range of ten stories," Garbus said helpfully.

Franklin agreed that that was certainly possible.

"When you spoke to Mrs. Cheever, you never told her, did you, that you were thinking of anything more than ten to fifteen stories?"

Cynthia objected. "Not only," she said, "has he testified over and over . . . Moreover, you're the one who keeps interjecting ten to fifteen stories—"

Garbus wanted to know whether Franklin had ever asked Mrs. Cheever to give the copyrights to the stories over to him.

"Well," Franklin said, "I thought that was what the contract was."

"I move to strike," Garbus said. "Did you ever ask her to assign any copyrights over to you or to Academy?"

Cynthia said he couldn't move to strike Franklin's answer simply because he didn't like it.

Did Franklin know the difference between a sketch and a story?

Franklin said he thought Scott Donaldson used the word "sketch" as "somewhat of a synonym for a short story."

There ensued a series of questions about Franklin's ability to make "a distinction with respect to Cheever material, what's a story and what's a sketch," as Garbus put it. Was Franklin a Cheever scholar? Did he consider himself "an expert in the English business between a sketch and a story?" Franklin said he thought he could come up with an "informed evaluation."

Then there was that troublesome title. "Why don't you use the title 'Some of the Previously Uncollected Stories,' which was the term you used with Miller?" Garbus asked. Cynthia said that was Garbus's title, not Franklin's. Franklin said that you could not call a book "Some of the Previously Uncollected Stories." He did not seem to think that was a snappy title.

"What are the other titles you could use for a book where you had some of the uncollected stories?"

Cynthia said this called for speculation and moreover, it was irrelevant.

"Come on, Mr. Dennis," Garbus said. "You're in the publishing business."

"This is ridiculous," Cynthia said. "You're wasting this time with Mr. Dennis. If you want to draw titles out of the air, be my guest."

Didn't titles change in "over three-quarters of the cases"? Wasn't it a fact that they changed more often than not? "Fifty percent, sixty percent, give me a number, Mr. Dennis. You've been in the business for a while." Couldn't the book have taken the title of one of the stories for the "overall" title? Didn't Franklin plan to discuss the title later with Mary Cheever? Wasn't that the normal process? Didn't Franklin remember Mr. Cheever objecting to the title? Specifically objecting?

No, Franklin didn't remember that.

"No discussion at all?"

"No."

"With Mr. Cheever?"

Garbus really wanted to get rid of that title. It was probably the way Henry II felt about Thomas Becket.

Was Academy a reprint house? Did they do much "original fiction"? "Isn't it a fact that if you compare them with the amount of original work they do is very small [*sic*] and is a very small percentage of their total publication?"

When Garbus left the room for a brief recess, Cynthia and Franklin sat alone with Ben. To fill the silence, Ben asked Cynthia pleasantly when her baby was due. Then he turned to Franklin and said calmly, "Franklin, you know my mother isn't a young woman. Why are you taking from her what's rightfully hers?"

Franklin sat, completely exhausted, in the corridor of Garbus's firm, waiting for Cynthia to come back from the restroom so that they could go to lunch. Garbus came down the hall and stopped next to him. He put his hand on Franklin's shoulder.

"This too shall pass away," Garbus said.

After lunch when the deposition resumed, Garbus asked Franklin if, since 1982, he had ever "received a nickel for editing a book." Had he ever "received a nickel as a pure editor"? And couldn't the book be delayed for six months? Weren't books often delayed? Aren't scheduling dates often tentative?

"He's not a publisher," Cynthia said.

"He keeps saying he is," Garbus said.

"*You* keep saying," Cynthia said.

"He's something," Garbus said. "He's a publisher, an editor, he's something. You're right, I have trouble finding out what it is. Let's go, Mr. Dennis . . . . You get four hundred dollars a month from Academy." Who were Franklin's other clients? Had he ever edited for any of them and gotten credit as an editor?

Franklin said he had evaluated manuscripts for them.

"Do you understand English?" Garbus shouted. "Do you know what the word 'edit' means?"

Cynthia said that if Garbus could not ask a civil question, Franklin was not going to answer.

If, Garbus asked, the Academy book earned $1 million for the author, wouldn't Franklin's share be "many times" his annual income? This was a big thing for Franklin, wasn't it? Franklin had a lot at stake here financially.

Franklin said it was a big project for everyone.

"But financially for you," Garbus said. "You would make more from this book than you make in three years, isn't that right? Four years, five years?"

Cynthia objected that there had been no testimony about Franklin's income. Garbus went on: " . . . if you were to make twenty-five percent on this book, you would make more than you made totally in the years 1982, '83, '84, '85, '86 and '87, isn't that correct?"

Franklin said he would have to check his income for those years. He repeated his statement that this book would be a substantial event for all concerned.

"Can I please have an answer to my question?" Garbus said. Would Franklin be making more money here than "let's say" he had in the last three years? "Certainly important for you financially, isn't it, Mr. Dennis?"

Cynthia objected.

"Isn't it?" Garbus said. "And you know that if this contract is broken, you will have nothing to do with any other Cheever publication, if there is one?"

Cynthia said that question was irrelevant.

Garbus asked why Franklin had "claimed" that some of these stories were "the best-kept secrets of American letters." Franklin explained that he meant that the subjects Cheever dealt with here were not his standard subjects "in the public common mind."

"Is it your story," Garbus said, "that the Cheevers were keeping these secrets?"

Cynthia said that Garbus was distorting Franklin's comment. She directed Franklin not to answer.

"Who was keeping this secret?" Garbus demanded.

"I don't know," Franklin said. "I don't know."

"You said it was a secret! Who's keeping that secret?"

Franklin said that all he knew was that "the public, the reading public, the many people who admire John Cheever, would be interested in reading these stories."

And wouldn't it titillate people to read something called "the best-kept secrets of American letters"? Franklin said "titillate" was the wrong word; a better word was "intrigue" or "excite." There was nothing perverse about it, Franklin said.

Garbus showed Franklin a letter Franklin had written in April to the Book-of-the-Month Club, in which he had mentioned "68 lost Cheever stories." Had Franklin referred to these stories as "lost" in letters to others or in conversation with others? Franklin said he couldn't remember; when he used the word "lost," he meant something that had been found—

"Can you tell me who lost them?" Garbus asked, cutting him off.

Cynthia objected.

"Mr. Dennis," Garbus cried, "who lost them?"

Cynthia objected again.

"Who lost them?" Garbus said.

Franklin said they were never lost in the physical sense.

The Cheevers, Garbus said, could have published these stories at any time, but they had not chosen to do it. Had Franklin ever asked the Cheevers why these stories were lost? They weren't lost to Dennis Coates, the compiler of the Cheever bibliography, were they? "So who were they lost to then, other than according to you?"

Cynthia objected.

"Mr. Dennis," Garbus said, "other than you in the entire United States, who has ever said that these stories were lost?"

Franklin said again that they weren't physically lost. They weren't available.

"Other than you," Garbus said, "who ever said that these stories were 'the best-kept secrets of American letters'?"

Franklin said he couldn't think of anyone else who said that.

"So!" Garbus cried, "Amongst all the Cheever scholars and academicians in the United States, the only person that ever said these stories were lost, or that they were the best-kept secret, is you, is that correct?"

Cynthia objected. Franklin said he didn't know every word that had been written by Cheever scholars, but he thought these words were probably exclusively his.

And had Franklin mentioned in his letter to Ben that these stories might have some effect on Cheever's reputation? Didn't that indicate that Franklin had "somehow had communicated" to him "information that the Cheevers didn't want to see this previous material published?"

Cynthia objected. Franklin said he had no such information. He just thought it was "an appropriate way to phrase the possibility of this project."

"Didn't you know," Garbus shouted, "from Swopes and Glazer and the other people that the reason the stuff hadn't been published prior to June fifteenth, the time you wrote that letter, was because the Cheevers didn't want it published?"

"That's not true," Franklin said. "No!"

"Didn't Glazer say that at the meeting you had with him and Cheever?"

Franklin said he didn't recall that.

Garbus came up to Franklin and leaned closely over him. "You're an intelligent man," he said. "These are stories written in '37, '38, '45. Why didn't you think they had been published?"

Cynthia pointed out that they *had* been published.

"Republished," Garbus said.

Franklin said it was an enigma. He thought "maybe it was the circumstances of events in John Cheever's career."

"What events? Be specific," Garbus urged. "What events could stop a man from republishing these stories other than the fact that his family didn't want them republished?"

Franklin said he didn't know. The Cheevers were "involved in other matters and these things take time. Circumstances change." He said it was very hard for him to answer that question.

Did Franklin know what the words "embarrassingly immature" meant? Did he ask Ben or Mrs. Cheever why another book of short stories had not come out after the Knopf book? Did he ask them if any of the stories offended them? Wasn't Franklin waiting in January to hear from Ben and Mary Cheever which of the stories offended them and which they thought were immature and didn't want published?

Cynthia objected. Franklin said he didn't think of himself as sitting around waiting; he viewed the thing as an ongoing evolution. He was expecting a reaction to the process of getting the book out.

What, Garbus asked, was the reaction Franklin expected when he gave stories to the Cheevers that he knew John Cheever had called "embarrassingly immature" and had chosen not to publish? Or republish?

Cynthia said she was objecting on so many grounds she didn't know where to begin.

Didn't Franklin know, Garbus said, that the Knopf stories "started in 1947? Were written in '47 and thereafter?" Didn't it say that on the cover? "The back cover, doesn't it say '47? You're a Cheever scholar, you've never seen the paperback?"*

Cynthia said that Franklin had not testified that he was a Cheever scholar. "He formerly was," Garbus said. "Before this deposition."

Had Franklin kept time sheets of his work? Wasn't that work "basically secretarial work . . . . a twenty-minute job?" How much time had Franklin spent on it?

Franklin said he didn't keep any record of the time. "It was an awful lot of time."

Garbus leaned over Franklin and demanded to know what "an awful lot" meant. Had he gone to the *New Yorker*? How was he involved in it? "You look at the Coates, you get the list, you have someone pick it up. What else is there?"

Cynthia said Garbus was testifying for the witness.

"No!" Garbus cried. "What else is there? What else is there? Tell me what you want to do for half a million dollars, Mr. Dennis!"

---

*The copy on the covers of the paperback edition of the 1978 collection does not mention 1947 or any other date.

Cynthia found this argumentative.

"Mr. Dennis!" Garbus cried, looming over Franklin. "Aren't you ashamed of yourself?"

Cynthia said they were going to stop now.

Garbus said he wanted an answer.

Cynthia said Franklin was not going to answer that ridiculous question.

Garbus said he didn't mean that last question about whether Franklin was ashamed of himself. He meant the question about what Franklin did.

The process finally ground to a halt, and Franklin crept out into the hall, where he encountered Susan, fresh from her own deposition.

"Oh," she cried happily, "there's Franklin! Hi, Franklin!"

20

Susan Cheever's Deposition: "They Are Essentially Package Engineers Rather Than Publishers"

While Franklin was being interrogated by Garbus, Paul was at the offices of Kronish, Lieb, taking Susan Cheever's deposition, which Maura Wogan was defending. The atmosphere in the room was not friendly.

Paul set about eliciting Susan's background. She had a 1965 B.A. from Brown University, had been a Westchester County newspaper reporter, and had edited the "Lifestyle" section at *Newsweek*. She left the magazine to write novels. In 1984, two years after her father's death, she published *Home Before Dark*, the book that revealed John Cheever's alcoholism and bisexuality.

Paul asked Susan what the "Lifestyle" section was. Maura interjected that it was a section that "deals with interesting facts about people's lives." Paul was not amused. He pointed out that during Mrs. Cheever's deposition the previous day, Maura and Garbus, and to some extent Susan and Ben, had "persisted in giving answers for the witness to many, many questions, and I think that is totally improper." If that happened today, he said, he would terminate the deposition. Maura replied that Paul had "mischaracterized" Mrs. Cheever's deposition and she was not going to allow Susan to answer "confusing questions."

After running through Susan's marital history, Paul asked her about her involvement in the present litigation. It all began, Susan said, when she went to call on her mother in Ossining with her friend Warren Hinckle in "early fall of '87 . . . . October, September, or November."* She was surprised to find Franklin Dennis—whom she knew from her days at

---

*It was, as we have seen, December 12.

Newsweek—"standing in the living room next to the dining room table." Although she was pleased to see him, he was "less than friendly" to her, and she wondered why. On the dining room table, Susan said, "was something which looked—it was a blue manuscript bound together with a plastic spiral binder . . . . Well, it was pages loosely bound together with blue plastic. I think also with a blue plastic cover. I'm not sure."

She said she introduced Franklin to Warren Hinckle. "We entered into the conversation and I—" She stopped, then began again. No, what happened first was that her mother was in the kitchen. Susan made that very clear. "She was not in the dining room with us. I went into the kitchen to say hello to her. Warren asked Franklin—and I overheard this, but I was not part of the conversation—what the binder was." Warren, she explained, was a newspaperman and "extremely interested in type, in the way books are made." So he looked through "the binder" and asked Franklin, "'What are you going to do with this? What is it? How is it going to work?' And, Franklin said, 'Well, it's like—' Franklin—I guess there was something on the title page that either said The Uncollected Stories of John Cheever or whatever. Anyway, Franklin said to Warren—well, I'm not sure—these are not Franklin's words, obviously. My recollection is not that perfect, but it was something like he was not sure if they would end up setting this up in type or whether they would re-xerox it. Warren was noticing that most of the Xeroxes or many of the Xeroxes were unreadable—"

Maura began to whisper in Susan's ear.

"I object to your interrupting," Paul said. "I object to your interrupting the witness's answer. I submit that this happened any number of times yesterday. It should not occur. Let the record show that Ms. Wogan has just interrupted the witness's answer to whisper to her. I presume now we will get a continuation of the answer."

"Where was I?" Susan asked. Oh yes, she remembered. "Warren and Franklin. Warren asked a lot of specific questions about how this was going to be printed. Franklin's answer was that he was not sure if they were going to set it in type or if they were going to have to re-xerox it or use facsimiles. Warren said, 'What's it going to be?' Franklin said, 'It's for students, Cheever volume. Volume of Cheever stories for students.' Warren's understanding was that it was going to be produced in that format. In other words, a spiral binding format as a college text aid or whatever, as is sometimes done. And Warren asked Franklin why he was leaving it. And Franklin told Warren—

and this is now—this is now—anyway, Franklin told Warren that he was leaving it so that Mrs. Cheever could read it and choose which stories should go in this so-called book."

Susan said she came out of the kitchen and joined in this conversation—a three-way conversation, she called it, making it very clear that her mother was "at no time . . . . a party to this." She repeated that Franklin seemed "profoundly uncomfortable" with her, something she "could not understand at that time." They talked about "the purpose of the binder" and whether it could be xeroxed or set in type—a subject she found uninteresting. Franklin, whom she characterized as "an extremely pleasant, friendly person," expressed the hope that her mother "would have time to read through it and see which stories she thought should be in it." Since some of the stories in "the binder" were "illegible," Susan said, "there was some discussion. In fact, I think there was a joke about how these stories probably would not be in it because she wouldn't be able to read them!"

Despite this affable, and even jolly, atmosphere, Susan noticed that Franklin appeared ill at ease and scuttled away. "Franklin left in a hurry. As I say, I was surprised at the time that he was not friendlier to me. I was just surprised. He left—he rushed out. I'm not sure he said good-bye to my mother." At the very least, she had hoped that he would sit down and have a cup of coffee with her so that they could talk about "old times." But no. After hanging around chatting about type and Xeroxes and "facsimiles" with her and Warren, Franklin suddenly rushed out.

Franklin had said that Fred Cheever had come to the house that day with Susan and Warren Hinckle. Paul asked Susan now whether anyone else had come with them. Susan said that no one else was there. And the material Franklin had left on the table: "Was it a binder or more than one binder?"

"A binder," Susan said.

"A binder?"

"A binder," Susan repeated.*

"Your brother Fred was there too, was he not?"

"I don't think so," Susan said. "Was he? . . . . No, wait a minute. I have no recollection of my brother Fred being there."

On the table in front of Susan was a set of the typeset preliminary galleys

---

*Franklin had brought the stories to Mrs. Cheever in *two* binders.

that Franklin had sent to some reviewers. Off the record, Susan asked Maura where those galleys came from.

"We got them from Mitgang," Maura said, off the record.

Paul brought this conversation into the record, "Am I to understand, Ms. Wogan, that those were provided to Mr. Garbus by Mr. Mitgang?"

Maura said she didn't know where those galleys came from. She knew that Garbus had gotten them "from someone and not from the Cheevers."

"Didn't you a moment ago tell Ms. Cheever that Mr. Garbus received them from Mr. Mitgang?"

"I speculated," Maura said. "Maybe from Mr. Mitgang. That speculation was purely speculation. That is not based upon any facts that I know."

Susan once again took up her story of that afternoon in Ossining. After Franklin left, she said, she and Mr. Hinckle and her mother went into the kitchen and discussed "the blue binder." While Mr. Hinckle flipped through "it," he and her mother talked about "Mr. Dennis's incompetence in xeroxing the stories and putting the holes in the binders right through the stories." And her mother commented on "the immature nature of some of the stories." It wasn't a long discussion, Susan said. Just a short one, during which Mrs. Cheever chuckled over "the incompetence of Mr. Dennis's research, saying she had provided him with an additional story." The project, Susan said, was believed to be "a small edition by an academic house with a few stories." Her mother was reluctant to choose them, and the conversation centered on Franklin's "indecisiveness and incompetence." But, Susan said, she thought to herself, Fine, "there had been previous small editions of my father's stories."

Maura interjected the remark that Mrs. Cheever was reluctant to read the stories because they were hard to read. Paul said that the record would reflect Ms. Wogan's "coaching of the witness." Susan was offended by this. "I already said that," she complained. "I don't like the idea of him saying that I'm being coached." This led to another off-the-record conference between Maura and her client. When she came back on the record, Maura explained that she had simply been discussing "with Ms. Cheever whether or not she was enjoying her coffee."

Susan then provided more background to her involvement in the case. One important factor was a conversation she had had with Robert Gottlieb, editor of the 1978 omnibus and former head of Knopf, who at the time of this deposition was editor of the *New Yorker*. At a dinner party in 1982, after her father's death, Susan was sitting at a round table with Gottlieb on her left, and Gottlieb said to her, "Your father did not want those stories published." The party was at Gardner Botsford's house, and no one else was in earshot. Susan and Gottlieb were talking about the "entire literary legacy," and when Susan mentioned the "stories and sketches," Gottlieb said they weren't worthy of publication, and she agreed with him. She said she knew that there were "about ninety of them." She and her mother had assumed that her father did not want them published.

After another conference with Maura Wogan, Susan embarked on the story of her actual involvement with this litigation. It began at another dinner party, this time at Ben's house in January or February of 1988. Maura began to whisper to her, and Susan said the party might have been in December 1987. She noticed that Ben was worried about "Franklin's ability to do what he needed to do and about Academy Chicago." She learned then for the first time that there was a contract, which led her to make inquiries and discover that Academy Chicago was "essentially package engineers rather than publishers." She went on at some length about that family dinner, which she characterized as "a confused social situation." She couldn't remember the conversation verbatim, she said modestly, she had no ability that way. All she remembered, really, and she wanted the record to reflect this, were her "impressions," not people's exact words. Every now and then a word would jump out, as the word "facsimile" had jumped out of the conversation she had overheard between Franklin and Warren. She did remember comments at that dinner about Franklin's "inability to distinguish between a collected and an uncollected story" and "disparaging comments about Franklin Dennis's literary judgment, inasmuch as he had such a thing."

"Which," Maura said, "he did not."

Susan said she wished she could remember who was at Ben's that night. Ben's wife, Janet,* might have been at the table, although she might have been in the kitchen. Mrs. Cheever might have been there. Susan's six-year-old daughter might have been there. Ben's two-year-old son might have been there. She remembered "a crowded dinner table," with her at one end and Ben at the other. "So there must have been people in the middle . . . Quite a few. Not twelve. But six."

---

*Janet Maslin, Ben's wife, reviews films for the daily *New York Times*.

"Including children," Maura said.

"Yes," Susan said, "it was a—"

"Family dinner," Maura said.

"An informal family-type dinner," Susan said. "Family and friends type dinner."

And then there was John Updike. Susan had talked to him, too, about her "literary legacy." Not a specific conversation. An indirect one. It might have taken place at her father's funeral, or it might have taken place on the telephone. She didn't think anyone else was present. It was a little confusing for her, she said, because the way she remembered it . . . .

Here Maura pointed out for the record that Paul had sighed "rather loudly."

"John Updike," Susan said, "mentioned that he was asked to write—this is why—" She fell into confusion.

"Would you like to consult with me for a second?" Maura asked.

"No," Susan said. "Yes. Just let me say—"

"No," Maura said sharply. "I want you to talk to me."

They left for another conference, and when they returned, Maura said for the record that she and Susan had taken a break "only because Ms. Cheever had some confusion about the scope of Mr. Freehling's question and wanted to discuss that with me." Susan, Maura said, was confused about the "timing" of the conversation with Updike; she had a "distinct recollection" of its happening at John Cheever's funeral, but "other facts" led her to believe that it could not have happened at the funeral, and that confused her. Now Susan was going to give her memory of the conversation, but she wanted it on record that she was just not sure whether it was at the funeral or not. Anyway, Updike had suggested that Susan might think of publishing some of her father's "old stories" from the *New Yorker*, although he didn't say that "in specific words." Susan told him they might do it, but she also told him that it was her father's wish not to publish them because he wanted to be known for "his current work," not "things he had done in the past." This, Susan said, was "a very short conversation. It was hardly a conversation."

Paul asked whether there were any references in the journals to the stories. Maura refused to allow Susan to answer on the grounds of relevancy. She left the room to consult with Garbus on this question, and when she returned she announced that she had been informed that Cynthia Johnson had "taken the position that she can speak to her client at any time and whisper in her client's ear at any time during the deposition and had had numerous breaks throughout the deposition . . . . To the extent," she concluded, "that Mr. Freehling has any objection to similar conduct which really, in the case of Ms. Cheever, has only been to clarify questions, is not appropriate and I would like the record to record that fact."

The last major conversation from Susan's memory bank was one allegedly held with Lynn Nesbit of ICM—the agency that had negotiated the disputed contract. Susan described Ms. Nesbit as a friend who had phoned her in New Hampshire because she had heard about "the case"—no, she corrected herself, not the case because there was no case yet—Ms. Nesbit had heard about the "problem" and wanted to discuss it.* By that time, Susan said, there was "concern" not only over Franklin's ability but over the dawning realization—which the Cheevers found hard to believe—that Academy was going to publish not "a small edition" of stories, as they had all "understood," but "were planning to take this contract and run with it, in spite of the fact that they had—"

"In other words," Maura said, "breach it."

Paul told Maura that if she did that once more, he was going to terminate the deposition. She said that was his right.

Susan took up her narrative once more. So Lynn Nesbit called her to voice "distress and concern about Academy Chicago's plans to publish what, at this point, began to look like a serious trade book and not a college textbook, aid or small edition for scholars at all." Susan said that Lynn Nesbit was "extremely concerned" and "extremely worried about the contract . . . . She felt badly that she had not written a more ironclad contract . . . . She said something to the effect of she was not there when it went through or she would have made sure that it was the kind of contract they had to comply with."

"Or indeed," interjected Maura, "a contract that had to be complied with."

"That's it," Paul said. "This deposition is terminated. And I will take the position in front of the court that we were not given an opportunity to take a deposition of Susan Cheever uninterrupted by her counsel repeatedly and absolutely without justification. And in my experience of twenty-seven years, without precedence—"

---

*The reader will recall that Jordan called Lynn Nesbit in January after Wylie called me. Ms. Nesbit said she had no idea what was going on and would phone Susan and ask her about it. See p. 33.

"I will agree to simply state my objections," Maura said. "I will make no gratuitous comments. If you wish to continue, I agree that I will simply raise my objections and nothing more."

Paul asked her sternly whether she would agree that what she had done in the last few minutes was "improper conduct by a lawyer."

She said no, she would not give him that much. But she would not do it any more. She said she thought she was "simply trying to correct what might have been something misunderstood." But she would raise her objections and not make gratuitous comments on the record.

Paul left the room to consult with Adam Walinsky and came back to agree to go on with the deposition, based on Maura's "representation" that she would not do that again.

Susan resumed her Lynn Nesbit story. In the phone conversation, Lynn Nesbit told her that Ben had consulted with Andrew Wylie about the contract. "One of the things that Lynn was saying to me was, 'Andrew can't help you with this contract. You need an attorney because it looks as if Academy Chicago is not going to honor this contract. This is not a matter for a literary agent. This is a matter for an attorney.'"

Paul asked whether Susan had discussed this litigation with Andrew Wylie. Maura interrupted to say she wanted to take a luncheon recess. She had "to do a few things." Paul responded that it was now 12:40, and they had agreed to go to 1:00. He wanted to go on with the deposition. Please.

"I said no," Maura said. She said they would be back at 2:15.

After lunch Paul returned to Susan's conversations with Andrew Wylie. Susan said she had talked to Wylie some time in January or February at lunch with Ben, at a restaurant called Les Pleiades. "It means The Swans,"* Susan said. Andrew had heard "through his professional grapevine" that "the Millers were planning a large edition of many stories, not at all what was in the contract, not at all what we expected."† Andrew advised them to see a lawyer. He said he thought they would like Martin Garbus. Wylie was her literary agent; she had hired him early in 1988. Before that, she had been represented by Literistic. She had never been with ICM.

Paul asked whether she had discussed this litigation with her brother

---

*In fact, it means "the Stars." "The Swans" would be "Les Cygnes."

†The "professional grapevine" was apparently Ben. See p. 143 and see also p. 192.

Fred. She said she had, in February or March or late January. On the telephone. And what had she said to Fred, and what had he said to her?

"You know," Susan said, "I don't remember."

"That's your answer," Maura said.

"I don't remember."

Paul brought up the allegation in the first complaint, that "the defendants have distorted and greatly diminished the value of the copyrights of the Cheever stories." In response, Susan read a prepared statement, in which she said that she and her family believed that these stories should not be published because they were of inferior quality, immature, were not good Cheever, and Academy's publication of them would "distort and greatly diminish" the value of the Cheever copyrights. At least a dozen of them were not stories at all, but sketches. She then named seventeen sketches: "Expelled"; "Late Gathering"; "The Autobiography of a Drummer"; "Play a March"; "In the Beginning"; "A Place of Great Historical Interest"; "Dear Lord, We Thank Thee for Thy Bounty"; "A Walk in the Park"; "Manila"; "The Journal of a Writer with a Hole in One Sock"; "The Habit"; "The Leaves, the Lion-Fish and the Bear"; "The President of the Argentine"; "The Night Mummy Got the Wrong Mink Coat"; "The Island"; "Brooklyn Rooming House"; and "Buffalo."*

Since Susan had signed the complaint, Paul asked her about the allegation that many of the uncollected stories had actually appeared in collections. In what collection, he asked her, did "Behold a Cloud in the West" appear?

Susan said that the previous day, during her mother's deposition, she had heard her say that it was in a book called "something like New Letters in America." That was all she knew about it.

And "National Pastime"?

She didn't know anything about it. She couldn't remember what her mother said the day before.

Maura whispered to her, and she went on to say that at the time she verified the complaint, she had asked her brother Ben if "National Pastime" was in another collection. He said yes.

---

*It is perhaps worth noting that six of these stories dated from the 1950s, 1960s, 1970s, and 1980s and that "The Island," which appeared in 1981, was probably John Cheever's last story. "The Habit" was included in the 1978 omnibus under another title.

Paul said that Maura had suggested that answer. Maura said she was not suggesting an answer; she was only reminding Susan of a conversation she had had with her brother. Paul said Maura had no right to remind Susan while Susan was having her deposition taken.

Paul asked whether she had read all the stories in the bound galleys before the amended complaint was filed. She said she didn't remember. Did she read "Buffalo"? She didn't remember. No—she amended that answer. She did read it. Of course she read it. She had read many of these stories "twenty or thirty years ago."

Paul asked Susan whether there was any relationship between Knopf and Ballantine Books? The question was prompted by the fact that Knopf had published the 1978 stories in hardcover, while Ballantine, a sister company, had produced the mass paperback edition. The trade paperback had been published by Vintage. Knopf, Ballantine, and Vintage were all divisions under the Random House umbrella.

Susan did not know whether there was any relationship between Knopf and Ballantine.

Paul was possibly still smarting from Garbus's assertion the previous day that "everyone in the room" except Paul knew that Vintage was Knopf's paperback imprint. Paul asked Susan what paperback trade name Knopf used.

She replied that she was embarrassed to say she didn't know.

Susan did not know whether there had been an auction for the paperback rights of the 1978 *Stories.* Like her mother, she knew nothing about the terms of publication or the royalty arrangements for the *Stories.*

The deposition ended at two minutes after five.

21

Ben Cheever's Deposition: "I Don't Know a Lot about What Is in This Xerox"

The first question that Paul asked Ben was when he was born. Ben gave a succinct answer: he was born on May 4, 1948; he was, he said, his mother's thirtieth birthday present. This was a promising start, but unfortunately it was the last succinct answer Ben gave. When Paul asked him when he first learned that Academy might publish any of the stories, Ben said he didn't have any of the stories in mind when he first talked to Franklin. Paul tried it again: when did Ben first hear from Franklin about this project?

Ben said he was approached all the time by people wanting to use Cheever work. He only returned Franklin's call because Franklin said he knew Tom Glazer, who had been a friend of Ben's father and had given Ben some letters to use in the book of letters he was getting together, which was probably going to be delayed because of this litigation. Simon & Schuster was upset and concerned about that. And so was Ben. He couldn't do the work he needed to do while he was sitting at a deposition.

Paul moved to strike this answer as unresponsive and asked the question a third time. This time Ben answered it and went on to say that he and Franklin had had a good talk at Chez Vong about John Cheever and whether the Cheevers thought there was anything—"any small overlooked work"— Academy could publish. Ben wasn't paying much attention because he thought Franklin worked for the University of Chicago Press, although at the time or maybe later he remembered being in the Pan Am Building elevator looking at a newspaper story about Academy Chicago and realizing that it was not the University of Chicago Press—here Garbus began to whisper to him, and Ben said that Academy was "a scholarly publisher." Paul objected to the whispering, and Garbus replied that Ben was finished with his answer when the whispering started.

Ben said he told his mother that Franklin represented "a small university press probably* and they were interested in publishing something by Daddy and did we have anything that press could publish?"

Paul asked whether he had seen letters from Franklin to Maggie Curran, and Ben said he didn't know. He talked at length about having gotten into hot water at the *Reader's Digest* for taking a three-month leave of absence to work on the letters; about having a year-old son; about desperately trying to finish the book of letters and show the people at the *Digest* that he was a "good citizen"; about how Franklin told him over and over that he wanted to please the Cheever family; and about how at Chez Vong he had told Franklin his "litany," which was that only his mother could give permission to publish anything and she would never do that until she had discussed it with his sister and him and his brother, too. It was complicated, it was difficult, it had caused trouble, but their method was to have their mother "in the driver's seat, consensusing" with them all, and she had done it for the last three years and it was "a long and messy and complicated process," and he had told Franklin that at least a dozen times.†

Paul asked Ben whether he had seen Franklin's first letter to Mrs. Cheever and if so, when.

Ben replied that Franklin had said that if they found some good stories and if the whole Cheever family agreed that it was a good idea to publish them, he, Franklin, was going to be listening to them at every point. And these were the same people who sued his seventy-year-old mother—she was sixty-nine at the time. She called Ben in tears because an off-duty policeman came down the drive and served papers on her. Here Franklin had said a million times that he wanted to help the Cheever family. "You sue them?" Ben cried. "Is that how you help them?"

Paul moved to strike that answer as unresponsive. Garbus objected. Paul asked Ben about a paragraph in Franklin's August 20, 1987, letter to Mary Cheever, mentioning John le Carré. Had Ben seen that? Ben wanted to know first if Paul was going to strike his answer because he was not going

---

*The University of Chicago Press publishes about 250 books a year and has a backlist of over 4,000 titles.

†The reader is reminded that in her deposition, Mrs. Cheever said that she knew nothing about Franklin's project until Franklin wrote her and that she discussed it only with Maggie Curran before she signed the contract. "Maggie," she said, "always handled everything." See p. 107. See also p. 186.

to spend a lot of time and energy crafting an answer if Paul was going to strike it because he didn't like it. He had to have a guarantee that Paul was not going to strike it. Paul explained carefully that the stricken answer did not leave the transcript. It remained there. It was not erased. It was to be left to a judge to decide the admissibility of the answer. But Paul had a right, he said, to ask Ben to confine his answers to the questions asked him.

Mollified, Ben said that he did not discourage Franklin from writing to Le Carré. He then went off on a commentary on Franklin's "character": Franklin had a way of exaggerating things, and Ben wondered whether Franklin really had lived over Sally Swope's garage. He didn't know, or he didn't think, that Franklin was "a scoundrel."

Asked about the January 1988 meeting with Franklin and Wylie at the Algonquin bar, Ben went off onto what he called "a bridge," talking about his suspicions and that the contract called for the book to be published at a mutually agreeable date and that the Cheevers could say, "Publish it in 2050," and that would end it. Franklin, he said, was basically a nice guy, but something had happened to him. Here Ben interposed a story about an automobile mechanic in Ossining who was incompetent. And Franklin had not gotten the introduction from Le Carré, and there was that list of stories with the typos and the "ring binder" of the stories with "two pages of one story and then a page missing from another." He went on at length about good Xerox copies, which were so important, and the *Chicago Tribune* story said that Ben was going to edit the journals and he didn't want the rest of his family to think that he was going around saying he was going to edit his father's journals all by himself.* And here was Franklin, who seemed "sloppy," and he wasn't going to abide by the contract, and there was that incompetent mechanic in Ossining who was at least, Ben thought, honest. So Franklin should be talked with, not unpleasantly, and Ben had lunch with Andrew Wylie, and Andrew said it sounded very bad.

Garbus asked Paul whether he was going to strike Ben's reply. "Just ask him questions and answer," Garbus said. Paul said the answer was for sure not responsive, but Ben had said he would feel comfortable supplying a

---

*Robert Gottlieb edited the *Journals*. John Blades, in the *Tribune* (January 3, 1988), did not write that Ben was going to edit the journals. He wrote, "In a few years, Ben Cheever hopes to bring out a selection of excerpts" from the journals.

"bridge" for his answer. Garbus said they should not be getting into this long discussion without cutting it short. "Tell him!" Garbus cried. "Instead of listening to him ten minutes and then making a motion to strike, as soon as you see him getting into areas that you don't like, make a motion. Otherwise we'll be here forever."

Paul said he was not going to make a motion to strike and he would like Mr. Cheever to answer the question.

Ben said he had called Franklin and told him there was somebody he would like him to meet, an agent named Andrew Wylie. The main bar was full, so they sat in the back bar. Here Ben said he was having a lot of trouble reconstructing what happened. He remembered that Franklin had the bound galleys of Updike's new book, and he seemed proud to have it, although "everybody" got bound galleys of a book like that; Ben's office was filled with bound galleys. But he couldn't reconstruct that conversation in the Algonquin bar. Garbus interrrupted to tell him not to do it. Ben said too much was said there, it was "too charged." He didn't know if he asked Franklin if he read all the stories; you couldn't read them all. "I said, 'I don't know a lot about what is in this Xerox, but I do know that some of the stories are in collections, so—'"

Garbus suddenly interrupted Ben to say that he needed a last morning break and when did Paul want to break for lunch?

"I want this on the record, " Paul said, stunned. "I never heard of breaking in in the middle of his answer."

Garbus said that Cynthia had done it all the time the day before and that Ben had to go to the bathroom.

After lunch, Ben was asked if he knew the significance of the parentheses around some titles in the table of contents. Ben said that his father did not leave a lot of money, but "believe me, if he was alive, none of you dear people would have done this, you would have changed your name, had plastic surgery and gone to South America because he would have killed you." One of the things that mattered to John Cheever, he said, was that stories should be neatly typed and double-spaced. Money, he said, had corrupted "these people"; it was really despicable, it was theft. He hoped they were paying Paul a lot of money because he wouldn't want to represent them. They were "just creeps." Franklin had taken the contract and said, "'What the hell, I'll publish every fucking story I can get my hands on, do a shoddy job—who cares? I'll be rich and famous. Forget John Cheever . . . .

What does it matter if his lousy stories come out and they are not so good? My name will be associated with it, Franklin Dennis edited these stories'— which should say that Franklin Dennis swindled Mary Cheever! That would be more appropriate! What," he asked, presumably of Paul, "is your explanation of what is going on here?"

With some difficulty, Paul elicited some biographical facts from Ben: he had a B.A. degree from Antioch College and had been an editor at *Reader's Digest* for twelve years.

Garbus would not allow Ben to answer any questions about the dates the letters encompassed or whether any of the letters referred to any of the stories under discussion. Ben said, "I will say, that it is my intention in the book of letters to—"

Garbus cut him off. "Your intention is not interesting," he said. "This is question and answer."

Paul asked if there were any stories mentioned in the journals. After a consultation with Garbus, Ben said that the journals were not "clear." Had Ben's father said he wanted his journals published? "As a matter of fact," Ben began, and Garbus cut him off, directing him not to answer because the question was more complicated than he was making it. Ben tried again to talk about the journals, and again Garbus cut him off, saying it wasn't relevant.

On the subject of the Cheevers' expert witnesses, Ben said he had met with Robert Gottlieb in Garbus's offices. Had they discussed what questions Mr. Gottlieb might be asked if he was a witness in the hearing? Ben didn't remember. "Mr. Gottlieb," he said, "is a literary eminence. You don't move him around like that. We were interested in what his opinion was."

In a discussion about sketches, Paul pointed out a story in the Knopf omnibus entitled "A Miscellany of Characters That Will Not Appear." Were these sketches or stories? There seemed, Paul said, to be a dozen or more subparts to this piece.

"But," Ben said, "there is a reason they are all under one title."

"What is the reason?"

"I presume there is a reason why they are under one title," Ben said. He had not read "A Miscellany of Characters," but he said he would guess that they "refracted" against each other. The story worked, he said, as a whole. It wasn't "a random collection of knick-knacks." It was, in fact, "a single story." That, he said, was his guess.

Was every one of the "writings" in the Knopf book a story rather than a sketch?

Ben said he had reread them a couple of years ago. He had not reread them since this case began. He guessed that they were all stories. In response to a final question, Ben said that the contents of every one of his father's other books of stories "were all stories."

22

Andrew Wylie's Deposition: "What Was the Man's Name?"

Andrew Wylie was deposed on Friday, July 8, at the Kronish, Lieb offices. At the outset, Garbus read a prepared statement announcing that he did not represent Wylie in any matter. He wanted to make it clear that Wylie was not his client, "other than for the purpose of this deposition."

After Wylie was sworn, a wrangle developed over documents bolstering the Cheever children's claim to ownership of copyright. Paul had asked for these repeatedly, and now he asked for them again. Garbus suggested that Paul get copyright certificates from Washington. They cost, he thought, a dollar apiece.

The deposition began. Wylie could remember very little about his involvement in the case, an involvement in which Paul was interested because he thought that Wylie, along with Ben and Garbus, might have been guilty of tortious interference with a contract. Wylie could remember seeing the publishing contract for the first time in "the first two months of 1988," but he didn't remember the circumstances of his seeing it, although he thought Ben Cheever had shown it to him; he couldn't remember where. He couldn't remember when he had heard of Academy Chicago Publishers for the first time.

At this point Garbus interrupted to say he had a phone call from Maura Wogan stating that she had given Paul "a lot" of the alleged documents attesting to the children's copyright claims. Paul ignored this.

In response to Paul's question about when Wylie and Ben had discussed the publishing agreement for the first time, Wylie said, "Ben expressed concern about Academy's intentions in regard to this book." But he couldn't remember what Ben had said or his own answer. Then there was a page of Wylie's handwritten notes torn from a spiral binder. The date written on it was January 19, 1988. Wylie said it reflected phone calls from a "variety of people," Ben Cheever among them. Garbus objected to this line of questioning. "Can't we just get to the case?" he asked. "Isn't this just irrelevant and beating a horse [*sic*]?"

Wylie said he knew "generally" what the litigation was about. His understanding, he said, was that "the Cheevers don't want this book published. Academy Chicago wants to publish it." He didn't know how many conversations he had had with Ben Cheever on this matter. His best recollection was that he had had a few. Paul asked him what he meant by "a few." "I mean a few," Wylie said.

"Is a few more than two?"

"Yes."

"Is it more than five?"

"I don't know."

"Is it more than ten?"

"I think it is."

"Tell me what your best recollection is."

"I just have."

Garbus directed the witness not to answer.

"More than two and less than ten, is that right?" Paul asked. Wylie said that was his best recollection. Not every conversation had been in person. He thought he had had "two, three" conversations with Ben in person on this matter. When was the last time Wylie had a "face-to-face" conversation with Ben?

"Conversation concerning the flight of sparrows or this case?" Wylie asked. On being informed that it was this case, he replied, "Peripherally at a dinner with Ben and his wife and Susan and Mary." He thought it was about a month ago. He didn't know what was said. "My memory is not accurate as to the details of conversations transpiring a month ago." But he did recall that the three Cheevers were concerned and displeased by the attitudes of Academy Chicago, and he thought he expressed his opinion that "Academy Chicago's behavior was inappropriate." He had not, he said, reviewed any correspondence between any of the litigants, between the *New Yorker* and Mrs. Cheever, or with ICM. Paul asked him if any of that would be relevant to the issue of whether Academy Chicago's behavior was inappropriate. Wylie said that a contract was a contract. He based his opinion on what the Cheevers told him, and he did not ask to see the correspondence because "I had nothing to do with this."

"What do you mean," Paul asked, "you have nothing to do with this?"

"He's not a lawyer," Garbus said. "He's not an agent that deals with the book."

"What do you have to do with this?" Paul asked. "Where do you fall into this drama?"

"That's what I would like to know," Wylie said.

"You fail to understand that he doesn't," Garbus said. This deposition, in his opinion, was simply a way of abusing somebody who happened to be a friend of the Cheevers. "He had nothing to do with this in any way prior to hearing for the first time of the Cheever disgruntlement. Is that a fair statement?" he asked, appealing to Wylie. Wylie agreed that it was.

Paul objected. "You have plenty of time to ask the witness questions," he said. "We all know, despite your posturing, that Mr. Wylie's name appears on more than a few documents in this case. I want to know why."

Garbus said he was going to apply for sanctions. This was an abusive deposition.

Paul asked Wylie about the meeting with Franklin and Ben in the Algonquin bar. Wylie said he didn't know when it was. He didn't know whether he had a diary for that date. Here Garbus interrupted to take another phone call from Maura Wogan about Paul's request for copyright documents. Garbus said he wanted that call on the record. Ms. Wogan, he told Paul, said that all the documents had been turned over to Mr. Freehling.* He resumed his conversation with Maura and, after he hung up, pointed out that it was now two-and-a-half minutes to eleven and that "we spoke from five minutes to eleven to two-and-a-half minutes to eleven about the specific request that Mr. Freehling had made."

"Directing your attention," Paul said to Wylie.

"If people have a reason to disrespect lawyers," Garbus observed, "we are certainly showing it in this room."

Paul directed Wylie's attention back to the meeting in the Algonquin bar.

"Ben was quite upset," Wylie said, "and expressed his displeasure with the fact that—what was the man's name?"

"Mr. Dennis?" Paul said.

---

*There are no documents that show the children's "interest" in the copyrights.

Yes, that was the name. "—that Dennis was going ahead with Academy Chicago to publish a book of his father's without seeking the approval of the Cheever family . . . . " Ben, he recalled, "did go on a bit with Dennis, asking him to stop attempting to get this project through without the Cheevers' input." Wylie said he asked "Dennis if he knew a lot about John Cheever's work. He said yes. But in the course of the conversation he revealed that he believed that John Cheever's work had always been published by Knopf, and anyone who knew anything about John Cheever's work would know that this was not the case. His first two books were published by Harper and Row.*That did not impress me."

And then there were the Xeroxes. Wylie pointed out to Franklin, he said, that "his reading must have been at best casual if that was the source of his text.† I recall that I was alarmed by this . . . . I was quite alarmed by this, because the man was claiming to have read the work and a good part of it was illegible. This seemed to me especially careless and disrespectful."

He could not recall that there was any discussion at the meeting about whether "some alternative should be pursued to Academy Chicago publishing the book." In connection with possible writers of an introduction, Wylie said that he laughed at the suggestions of John le Carré and Raymond Carver. He considered them both "inappropriate" choices. John le Carré wrote thrillers, and Wylie felt that "his comments on the nature of John Cheever's work were at best of no interest." Raymond Carver was a "moderately young writer with a moderate reputation. I felt that his reputation was perhaps greater than it ought to be and it was disrespectful to Mr. Cheever to have his work associated with a writer of that calibre." He had suggested Updike or William Maxwell. No one had mentioned Scott Donaldson.

He could not remember what Dennis had said about the Xeroxes, which were "a mess, illegible, sloppy . . . . he maybe stammered or something. I had pointed out to him that he could not possibly have read the stories carefully since a good part of them were illegible. That is an embarrassing

---

*John Cheever's first two books were published by Random House and Funk & Wagnalls, respectively. Franklin recalls no discussion of Cheever's publishing history at the meeting in the Algonquin bar.

†The "source of the text" was, of course, the original Xeroxes of the stories from the magazines. There are no other sources.

situation for a man presenting himself as an editor."

"Let's keep the answers shorter," Garbus said. "We won't have to be here forever."

Wylie said that he had not met Garbus before he introduced him to the Cheevers. He knew him by reputation only.

Had he ever represented that Garbus was his lawyer?

"No," said Wylie.

"I'm not his lawyer today," Garbus said. "I'm here solely for the purpose of this deposition."

Wylie said that he had introduced the Cheevers to Garbus by telephone. There was a subsequent meeting, but all he remembered about it was the way Garbus's office looked; he remembered nothing that was said. "My position in it was to bow out once I made the introduction." And he might have talked to Garbus once or twice before yesterday; he might have said, "What is happening," or something cursory like that. "I have always seen myself as not having any relationship to this ordeal." He had spoken to Maura Wogan about an "attempt to get me to appear or something like that." It was on the telephone. "I was in Venice and I was brusque . . . . I said, 'I'm in Venice. I have no intention of listening to this. Goodbye.' I hung up . . . . She said there was some question of a deposition, and I said essentially, 'Thank you. I'm in Venice. I'm not interested in discussing things. Goodbye.'" He had not discussed the matter with anyone else that he could recall. An editor had called him from Viking Penguin to ask him whether he was aware that Academy Chicago was conducting a paperback auction "based on bound galleys of the alleged book."

Once more the deposition was interrupted by a call from Maura Wogan. Garbus said she was offering Paul "other documents . . . . limited edition books" as a "courtesy." Paul said he did not wish to waste Wylie's time talking about documents that had nothing to do with his motion. Garbus said they had reached "a level of psychosis."

Paul returned to the conversation Wylie had had with the Viking Penguin editor. A man, Wylie said, named Gerald Howard.

Had he spoken to anyone else about this Academy Chicago matter?

Wylie believed he had spoken to someone at Doubleday, "a paperback woman who had gone to Avon . . . . I asked her if she had gotten the material and she said yes . . . . The materials submitted by Scott Meredith in the paperback auction."

"Why were you asking the question?"

"I wanted to see if the materials had been sent to more than one house."

"Why did you want to know that?"

"I was interested," Wylie said,

"Why?"

"I was interested . . . . to see whether an auction was being conducted with more than one house."

"Why did you want to know that?"

Garbus offered a suggestion. "Curiosity?"

"Yes," Wylie said. "Curiosity."

"Just idle curiosity?" Paul asked.

"I'm never idle," Wylie said.

Garbus said that every publishing house in New York was talking about the auction. "Everybody was amazed at it. There were phone calls going around." It was an extraordinary event. "And if you want to conclude from that . . . . Mr. Wylie has malevolent—my language is very bad—involvement in this thing, it's absurd."

Garbus's remarks, Paul said, were "inappropriate posturing."

"We're sitting here since ten o'clock at a deposition with a man who has nothing to do with this prior to February of '88," Garbus said. "All you are doing is abusing a friend of the Cheevers."

Paul asked again why Wylie would be curious about the paperback auction. Wylie, echoing Garbus, said that it was "unprecedented to conduct an auction in the middle of litigation." Paul said he didn't understand why that would concern Wylie.

Wylie said that when planes were shot out of the sky, he watched the news. When publishers sold paperback rights during litigation, he tried to find out about it. It was the area he was involved in. He had "a natural curiosity" in keeping informed about his business. He believed he spoke to Gerald Howard and the Doubleday person on the day that the "material" was sent from Scott Meredith.

Paul showed Wylie copies of three letters that had been blind-copied to him by Garbus: one was Garbus's February 17 ultimatum letter to Academy; the second was a June 17 letter to Paul; and the third, also dated June 17, was a letter to Scott Meredith.

Wylie said he did not remember getting any of these letters. On June 17, he had called Garbus's office and left a message with an assistant that the auction was taking place. He might have gotten the letters from "Marty as a courtesy and threw them out" because they did not relate to his business. He could not remember when the conversations with Gerald Howard and the Doubleday woman took place. "You are driving me crazy asking me the same question," he said.

Had he spoken to Mary Cheever? Didn't his notes on the page from the spiral notebook indicate a telephone conversation with Mary Cheever? Why was Mary Cheever's name on that sheet?

"I have no idea. It says 'executor equals Mary.' I assume that means I am making a note. The purpose of the retention of this page, quite clearly, since it's surrounded with red lines, is to make a note of where Franklin Dennis had disappeared to. He disappeared," Wylie said, "behind the walls of Pryor, Cashman, Sherman and Flynn."

Further, as the lawyers put it, deponent saith not.

23

Evidentiary Hearing, White Plains, Day 1, A.M.: "Is That the One They Made into a Movie?"

We flew into White Plains on Sunday, July 10, and checked into the White Plains Hotel, a gloomy, fiftyish pile. We were the first of our party to arrive. Paul and Cynthia were expected that evening. Our sons Mark and Bruce and Mark's wife, the novelist Jean McGarry, were arriving later that day in Montrose to stay with Franklin and Mary. We unpacked and, feeling rather restless, set out to see if we could find a copy of the local paper; Franklin had said there was a story in it about the case.

It was an extremely hot, humid day. We walked through town: all the shops were closed, and the streets were deserted. A feeling of malaise enveloped us. We could not find a copy of the paper anywhere, so we returned to the hotel in the stifling heat and phoned Franklin, who read us the story. The bulk of it, written by Ellie Volstad, consisted of statements from the Cheevers saying that the stories were immature and statements from us saying they were worth reading. Ms. Volstad quoted two scholars: Andrew Delbanco and George Stade, both English professors at Columbia University. Professor Delbanco said the collection was not "particularly important," it was "really just a convenience," but for the serious student of modern American fiction, "it would be a good thing to have." Professor Stade said the writer had the right to do what he wanted with his work. As long as the spouse didn't revise or alter the work, it would be, he said, "legitimate to expect her to have control."

Anne Tyler, the novelist, said, "It's pretty clear-cut. You could say about anybody's horrible work that it shows the writer's development. But he should have some control, or his family should have some control. To say the public is owed the stories is saying they own the writer, and that's not true. I'm sure there were paragraphs he threw out when he was writing the stories. The public doesn't deserve to see those just because he wrote them."[1]

After a very good dinner in the deserted hotel dining room, we sat in the lobby watching people. Our depression did not lift. When Paul and Cynthia arrived, we met with them in our room and went through our depositions, checking for errors. The transcript of Jordan's deposition was bulky; the session had lasted nearly all day. Maura Wogan had not been abusive, although she had been insistent. My deposition had been very brief. There were questions about the "tentative title" that Garbus found so troublesome and one odd question to me about Warren Hinckle's dog. The only notable moment in the depositions occurred in the afternoon, when Maura Wogan suddenly went off the record and offered us a copublishing deal with Knopf for the book. This threw all of us, including M. Leslie Kite, into a tizzy. We suggested that Maura put something on the table. That was the last we heard of it.

The next morning we all assembled in the dining room for breakfast and then set out, a ragged crew, for the courthouse, Paul and Cynthia hauling suitcases of documents on little traveling carts. It was a long, hot walk. The courthouse was a dull office building; Judge Goettel's courtroom was on an upper floor. As we approached the large double doors to enter the courtroom, two slight men in seersucker suits passed each other, one going in, one coming out.

"Hi, Bob," said Seersucker I. "Have a good time over the weekend?"

"Marvelous," said Bob, Seersucker II.

"That was Bob Gottlieb," Jordan said. The other, it developed, was Ellis Levine, Random House senior counsel.

There was no central aisle in the courtroom: the only aisle was on the left; it opened out on the right to several rows of long benches. Everyone who sat on the far right had to walk past everyone sitting on the left near the aisle in order to get in or out. We sank into the front bench near the aisle. Franklin and Mary sat with us; Mark, Bruce, and Jean took seats in the elevated last rows, also on the left, near the door. There were several people sitting near Susan and Mary Cheever to the extreme right of us, behind the table for the plaintiffs' lawyers. I felt noticeably submerged, as though I were at the bottom of a well.

Paul and Cynthia went to their left-hand table; Adam Walinsky and Tab Rosenfeld from Kronish, Lieb were already there. Also present in the room were Martin Garbus, Maura Wogan, and a tall person with an unusual haircut who was later identified as Russell Smith from Garbus's office. A number of Garbus's assistants, all women, bustled about with papers. As we settled down, Garbus walked up and handed something to Walinsky, who suddenly slammed his fist onto the table. "Damn it, Marty," he said loudly, "is that your idea of courtesy? I've been in this room for an hour, and at five minutes to ten, you hand me these papers!" With what proved to be a characteristic gesture at moments like these, Garbus, who had turned away, shrugged without looking back.

Ben came in wearing a backpack and edged past us to get to his contingent.

When the judge entered, Garbus's assistants settled comfortably into the jury box. Walinsky, after introducing Cynthia to the judge, announced that he himself was withdrawing and that Paul would conduct the case.

Garbus embarked upon his opening statement, in which he said, among other things, that once the defendants realized that Franklin's deposition testimony "ended the case, they tried to change that testimony." He said that if the testimony changed "further" that day, "I think you have a situation that requires a recommendation for a perjury indictment." He then talked about the tentative title and Academy's "extreme financial problems. They can't pay their bills." So, he asked, what did they do? "Before they have a book, they contact Scott Meredith." They "try to raise money, which you see then is a plan developing which is to be a theft of the copyrights of Mrs. Cheever. So while the Cheevers believe they're working on a small book, they're going to an agent and they're trying to raise a fortune in order to sell this book." Franklin, he said, is a "packager, a promotion person . . . . and the reason he gets to have his name affixed to something like the Cheever property is because of the swindle that they were trying to perform on the Cheever estate, namely take these copyrights for a few bucks."

Paul objected. "This is supposed to be an opening statement, not a closing argument."

The judge agreed, and Garbus announced that he wanted to call Franklin.

Paul, in his opening statement, said that this hearing was about a copyright issue because the judge had said that the contract dispute should be settled in Chicago. "Now if, for reasons that I don't understand, Your Honor wants to hear about the contract, I would like to address how the contract came about. But I don't believe that this is an appropriate issue for argument by Mr. Garbus or for testimony by the witnesses. I think the only issue before Your Honor is the issue of whether the children have copyright interest. And that is what I hope we'll address."

Franklin was sworn in. Garbus, about to mark documents for exhibit, could not find a copy of the bound galleys. He said he believed the court had a copy; he had delivered it "at their last meeting in late June." The judge cheerfully announced that the galleys were "misplaced." He thought one of "the student law clerks" had taken them to read. He said he didn't think he needed the galleys, except for the table of contents, and he still had the sampler. He had read that.

Garbus began his examination of Franklin: "By the way," he said, "you're a college graduate?" Upon being assured that this was the case, he said, "You understand the English language?"

Paul objected. The judge sustained it.

Hovering over Franklin, holding his deposition transcript open, Garbus began to read parts of it to him loudly. Franklin leaned back in his chair until he was nearly horizontal; his aim appeared to be to get as far away as possible from Garbus. In doing this, he also got as far away as possible from the microphone. We could see his lips moving, so we knew he was responding. This went on for some time. A few people from the Cheever side squeezed past us to get to the aisle and freedom. One was a matronly woman with a bouffant hairdo, a large pearl ring, and a benevolent expression. I took her to be a friend of Mary Cheever, there for moral support, but she was actually Rhoda Gamson from the contracts department of Viking Penguin, a frequent client of Garbus's.

Paul finally objected to Garbus's reading to Franklin from his deposition: "The only purpose a deposition transcript can be used for is to impeach the witness or show some change in his testimony. The witness hasn't been given an opportunity to testify from the witness stand. This is not proper examination."

"With a hostile witness," the judge said, "I'll allow it."

The examination may not have been improper, but it was certainly boring. After another half hour, the judge called a recess.

We went out into the narrow, carpeted hallway where there were a few seats and a public telephone. Russell Smith immediately took possession of the telephone; he was to spend most recess time on it, saying loudly, "Yes, it's going great! Just great!"

Jordan, Bruce, and I gathered around our lawyers at the far end of the hall. I stood next to Adam Walinsky.

"Franklin is a terrible witness," he said. "Just terrible. Awful."

All Franklin had done so far was murmur inaudible responses to readings from his deposition.

"The judge is going to grant this injunction," Walinsky said.

"But we can appeal that, can't we?" I cried, from the greenish depths.

"No," Walinsky said. "No appeal."

"Paul!" I cried. He was talking to Walinsky's assistant, Tab Rosenfeld. "Can't we appeal an injunction?"

"Yes," Paul said.

"You can't," Walinsky said.

"Absolutely we can," Paul said. "It's an appealable ruling."

"I'm too expensive to stay here," Walinsky said. "I'd better leave. You don't need me."

We all shook hands and said good-bye. It was time to return to the courtroom. On our way we passed Russell Smith, still on the phone.

When the session began again, Garbus resumed reading to Franklin for a considerable period. Then he asked him how far behind Academy was in its payments to him. Paul objected. "I don't see what this has to do with the matter before the court," he said.

"I don't either," the judge said. "But apparently it's being used for some form of bias or impeachment purpose. So I'll allow it, in hopes of moving things along."

The judge frequently interjected questions. At one point he interrupted to ask Franklin whether he had ever contemplated publishing "every single one" of the stories he found. Franklin said yes, he did. The judge then observed, "That would then be 'The Complete Uncollected Stories of John Cheever.'"

That was certainly a mistaken observation, since we could not call a collection "complete" unless we knew for sure that there were no other uncollected stories in existence, and we could not know that. It was an indescribable sensation, sitting in that courtroom with Garbus's people in the jury box and Garbus bending over a nearly prone Franklin while the judge looked on. It reminded me of old movies I had seen about the Deep South.

Garbus then read a large portion of Franklin's deposition that, he said, "talked about the use of the word 'some.'" That naturally went on for quite a while.

The judge fidgeted and finally said the examination was "extremely tedious . . . . If you're not going to question the witness, if you're going to assume you have to read his answers from the deposition in every instance, you would be better off just reading the transcript, such portions as you wish to. On the other hand, if you're going to question the witness, ask the questions directly. Let him answer them and only when his answer differs, go to the transcript."

Garbus said he would cut his examination in half and put the transcript into the record. The judge told him to condense those portions he wanted him to read.

When the subject of the "tentative title" came up once more, the judge fell into a speculative mood. "It's not a very imaginative title," he said, referring to the one we had chosen, "and it doesn't tell you an awful lot about the book. But we never really resolved what sort of book you were going to put out here. As a general proposition, there are two types of anthologies of short stories of an author whose short stories have in part been published and in part not."

The judge loved to talk about Literature. Here he was developing a marginally interesting viewpoint that had nothing to do with the case at hand, since all the stories under discussion had previously been published.

"One type," the judge went on, "would be the best of the unpublished stories and clearly not all of them. That would be a book directed toward the general reading public. Another type would be more directed toward students of literature, professors and what-have-you, and it would be an attempt to demonstrate the development of the art of the author. That's very rarely done, and it's only for authors who have already achieved an enormous stature, and in whom literature courses would have an interest in seeing the early stories, the rough stories, the gradual development, and so on. Which of these two types were you and the Cheevers talking about publishing, if either?"

"I don't think we got that specific," Franklin said. "We just knew—I knew, and I assume the Cheevers knew, that there was a body of work that was unavailable in book form to the American reading public, and that it was worthy, that this material was worthy, of investigation and publishing."

"One problem that you have to deal with," the judge said, "is that there had already been a volume of collected stories published, correct? . . . . And at least *prima facie*, all the best stories were in there. There might be some gems that had been missed, and it may have been a few weak ones, but by and large you were competing against a published volume of probably the best of his stories, right? . . . . So, you couldn't really do a work that would show the author's development as an author, because unless you were going to attempt to use some of those stories, you were going to be leaving out the best of his work, correct?"

"Uh-huh," Franklin said.

"Incidentally," the judge said, "was there any talk about using some of those stories in this book?"

By "this book" he was referring to our book of uncollected stories; by "those stories" he meant the Knopf book. He was asking whether we had considered putting any of the stories from the Knopf collection into our book of *uncollected* stories.

"No," Franklin said slowly, feeling like Alice in Wonderland, "that was the point of this book—that these stories had never been collected in any Cheever volume—exclusively John Cheever stories—in the past."

"All right," the judge said. "You're left then with just two options: to pick out those most worthy of collection, which hadn't been previously published or to throw everything that was available in. In other words, 'The Complete Uncollected Unpublished Stories of John Cheever.'"

Franklin said that all the stories had been published in magazines.

This was news to the judge. "There were no totally unpublished stories?" he asked. "Or if there were, you didn't have access to them."

No, Franklin said. The Cheevers said there were none.

"So," said the judge, "your only alternative then is to take all of them or some of them, and you indicate that this was a continually unresolved issue, albeit in talking with the Cheevers, you used the word 'some.'"

Franklin, who had said repeatedly that he did not remember using the word "some" in this connection, pointed out, for what it was worth—and it should have been worth a lot—that he had told Ben in late October or early November that Academy was going to publish *all* the stories and that Ben had said fine.

The judge remarked that Cheever and Gottlieb, presumably, had probably "collected the universe of his stories up to that point, which is to say they would have all of them together and be looking at them in terms of selection."

Franklin said that the Knopf editor did not have all of the stories together because some were in magazines that he did not see.

"You had stories," the judge said, "that hadn't been included in the collected stories. Now I think we can assume that a lot of them were not included because Mr. Cheever did not think they were worth publishing at that time . . . . So you're really confronted with stories in three categories: post-publication stories, stories the author didn't think were up to the quality of the others that were published. And then everything pre-1947, which he apparently decided were immature and not worthy of publication, albeit," he added graciously, "he may have been overcritical about them."

Paul tried, with respect, to point out that Cheever had not said that everything he wrote before 1947 was embarrassingly immature.

As the judge continued his discussion, it developed that he was unaware that John Cheever had published six collections of stories before 1947. "That's a lot of stories," he said when this was pointed out to him. "Incidentally," he added, "I should tell you that some of my limited knowledge of these facts comes from reading the *New York Times* book review yesterday of the recent biography by Scott Donaldson . . . . It was a typical *New York Times* book review. It's more of the reviewer than it is of the book being reviewed." He looked out over the courtroom and chuckled. "But it was a lukewarm review," he said.

The Cheever faction chuckled back appreciatively.

The judge began to leaf through the Knopf collection. "I see the short story 'The Swimmer' is in this book," he said. "Is that the one they made into a movie?"

Garbus went on examining Franklin for a while until the judge entered the examination once more. "John Cheever was something unusual as a writer of fiction in modern day, was he not," he said, apparently to Franklin, "in that he seems to be more a writer of short stories than novels . . . . How many novels did he write?" Franklin "counted in his head" and said five.

"There have been famous writers in the past who were primarily short story writers," observed the judge, "like de Maupassant and O. Henry, I think his name was Porter. But if you're talking post–World War II, I can't think of an important author who is thought of primarily for his short stories, other than Cheever. Can you think of anybody else?"

Franklin suggested Updike.

The judge said he thought Updike was primarily a novelist.

Franklin said he had published short story collections, too.

That ended, for the moment, Literary Notes from the Chimney Corner with Judge Goettel. Garbus resumed his questioning, until the judge interrupted again to ask Franklin to speculate. "Suppose," he said, "they [the Cheevers] had come back to you and said, 'These twenty stories, we think they're no good, we don't want them included'—what would have happened next?"

"Your Honor," Paul said, "I guess for the record I should object to the hypothetical nature of the question. But I'll sit down."

"I'm trying to find out what his mind-set was at the time," the judge explained. He repeated the question.

"Well, first off," Franklin said, "my understanding up to that point was—from Ben was—that all the stories should be in, because of the idea of being all-inclusive."

Ah, but, the judge said, Mary Cheever had not "affirmatively adopted" that "notion." Ever. Franklin said that was true. The judge repeated the question. What if Mrs. Cheever had complained about twenty stories? What would Franklin have done?

Franklin said he would have given serious consideration to that, spoken to the publisher, and he thought that "we would have come up with a solution that would have pleased the Cheevers."

And what if those twenty were in the public domain?

No, Franklin said, "my feeling was that we wanted to do a book which the Cheevers approved." He said he had no knowledge of "which copyrights she owned or anything. I just assumed that if we had a signed contract from her, she was giving us . . . . the rights and permissions to go ahead with the project." He was not, he said, aware of the "legal ramifications."

"You assumed," the judge went on, "since she had signed the contract—which was a contract, really, of the type you use with an author creating a new book, who obviously must be signing the contract agreeing to copyright terms—that if she agreed to the publication of the works, editorially, she was already committed to the copyright assignment."

Franklin said that was right.

"Where did you get that concept from?" the judge inquired.

Franklin, who was, of course, not a lawyer, resorted to an answer based on common sense and the normal practice of the publishing industry. "Well," he said, "I assumed that it—she—I think I followed your question; it would only be my lack of experience that I didn't—is, that, you know, why would she then sign a contract? I mean, why would they want to have this book? You know, it was an idea which I had, and I asked them about it. I wrote them, I met them, and they sounded enthusiastic about it."

"What you're saying," the judge said, "is that, since they didn't raise copyright questions in the beginning, you assumed that the copyrights *qua* copyrights were not going to be a problem."

Franklin said that was it.

"But," said the judge, "you were aware that there might be editorial problems, in terms of selections of stories, preface, so on and so forth?"

"Sure," Franklin said. "It was a process."

The judge asked Franklin how many books "of this sort" he had been involved in in the past: that is, "collections of short stories of a deceased author, all of which have been published in magazine form earlier." Franklin's answer, of course, was "None." The judge asked whether "Mr. Miller" had ever been involved in such a process before. Franklin said he didn't think so, but the judge would have to ask Mr. Miller.

Garbus was allowed to ask Franklin some questions about his letters and the contract, and then the judge returned to the fray. He asked Franklin detailed questions about the contract: who crossed out this, who crossed out that, when was it crossed out, who wrote in this, who typed in that, and "Did it occur to you that this particular publishing agreement was almost totally unsuited for the kind of work you were dealing with?"

Franklin said he had to confess it didn't.

"Well, for example," the judge said, "referring to Mary W. Cheever as the author was totally inapplicable, right?"

Paul said that at the outset the contract had referred to Mary W. Cheever and Franklin Dennis as the author.

"All right," the judge said. "That's even worse."

Paul said he wasn't sure about that. "We're dealing with editing an anthology."

"You call it an editor," Garbus observed, "which they do, which he isn't."

The judge then read aloud the clause that stated that the author would deliver to the publisher, on a mutually agreeable date, one copy of the manuscript, and so forth. "Now," he said, "that's a standard thing for a new work being created by an author. But it had no relationship to what you and Mrs. Cheever were attempting to do, did it?"

"Doesn't seem so now," Franklin said.

The judge called a recess for lunch.

Chicago Tribune

Anita and
Jordan Miller
stand behind
Franklin
Dennis

Cynthia Johnson,
Paul Freehling's assistant

Mary Cheever at her Ossining home with her Labrador, Cocoa

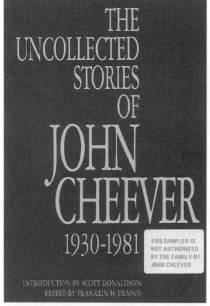

Sampler with the required sticker

John Cheever

Ben Cheever in the library under a painting of young John Cheever

Susan Cheever with her daughter and Mary Cheever

© Faye Ellman

Martin Garbus (right)

Robert Gottlieb, former Knopf
and *New Yorker* editor, and his
beloved plastic handbags (below)

Theo Westenberger

Paul Freehling

Tom Leavens

Marina Garnier

Andrew Wylie

Federal Judge Gerard Goettel puts on his judicial robes

Justice James Heiple of the
Illinois Supreme Court

Chancery Court
Judge Richard Kiley

24

Evidentiary Hearing, White Plains, Day 1, P.M.: "Which President Were You Speaking Of?"

We trooped out into the midday heat to seek a restaurant suitable for the ten of us: Jordan, me, Paul, Cynthia, Tab Rosenfeld from Walinsky's office, Franklin, Mary, Mark, Jean, and Bruce. I followed along, enveloped in my packet of woe like a goldfish in a Baggie. After pausing at several places that were vetoed by various members of our group, we finally found a pleasantly dark, acceptable restaurant. As we waited to be seated, I looked out the glass door and saw, across the way, Garbus leading his considerable procession down the street like the Pied Piper, single file: Ben, Mary, Susan, Maura, Gottlieb, Ellis Levine, Rhoda Gamson, Russell Smith, the very tall woman with a lot of hair, and some clerical assistants. Apparently they, too, had difficulty finding sustenance because after we were settled, Paul, who was facing the door, said, "Here they come."

There was a certain amount of commotion while they were being seated behind us, and Paul cautioned all of us to lower our voices. At one point Paul and Franklin left the room to phone Tom Glazer and ask him whether he was willing to come to court and testify to the conversation at the Chez Vong lunch. Paul would not issue a subpoena for him; he wanted Tom to come of his own volition. Tom said he would rather not get involved; Paul left it at that.

When court resumed at two o'clock, Franklin was temporarily excused from the stand so that Robert Gottlieb could testify. Garbus said this testimony would take only fifteen minutes; Gottlieb was, after all, a busy man who had to get back to New York. Paul reminded the judge that he had set aside two days for this hearing; what if after the two days were up, the defense had not had a chance to put on witnesses? What would happen? The judge said they would talk about that when they got there.

Garbus questioned Gottlieb about his career. He had joined Simon &
Schuster in 1955, become editor in chief there, and left in 1968 to become
editor in chief and then president of Knopf. In 1987, he left Knopf
to become editor in chief of the *New Yorker*. He had edited the work of
John le Carré, Barbara Tuchman, John Cheever, of course, Robert Stone,
Richard Adams, Antonia Frasier, Robert Massie, Toni Morrison, just "doz-
ens upon dozens." He oversaw the whole *New Yorker*, but he himself edited
John Updike and V. S. Naipul.

Garbus asked Gottlieb how the editorial process had worked with the
Knopf collection.

Gottlieb said he had proposed the collection to Cheever, who didn't
think it was a good idea because his best stories had already appeared in
small collections; why would anyone now want a large collection? But
Gottlieb felt very strongly that the world needed such a book and that it
would be a success. So he persuaded Cheever to let him draw up "a tentative table of contents for him to examine."

Gottlieb's next step, he said, was to borrow "the complete bound issues
of the *New Yorker* from a friend" and read "chronologically" every Cheever
story that had appeared in that magazine. Then he asked Cheever and
Cheever's agent for any "extra material" that had not appeared in the *New
Yorker* or in earlier story collections, and from them he got "x" number of
tearsheets and copies of manuscripts,* all of which he duly read. Then he
made "more or less" the table of contents and explained the "theory" of his
"choosing" to John Cheever.† Several excellent stories were left out, he said,
because they were "too much like other stories included." He had ruled out
the stories from Cheever's first collection, *The Way Some People Live,* because Cheever was ashamed of the book; he thought Cheever "probably"
used the word "sketchy" or "sketches" in connection with it. "I mean, really," he said, "my impression of those pieces and why they shouldn't be
in—and that would have been true of all his earlier material, most of which

---

*We had been told by Ben that Cheever had not kept any manuscripts; that was why we
had had to xerox from the magazines and could not check any originals.

†Gottlieb had chosen only two stories that had not been included in earlier collections:
"Common Day" and "Another Story," both from the *New Yorker*. The rest of the 1978
omnibus consisted of the complete contents of the five previous Cheever collections and
three stories from a 1956 collection called *Stories,* which included stories by William
Maxwell, Jean Stafford, and Daniel Fuchs as well as by Cheever.

or all of which had been found or assembled for this book called *The Uncollected Stories . . . .* "

"You spoke of sketches," the judge said. "Would you define what you mean when you say 'sketches'?"

This, Gottlieb said, was "a thorny issue, because everyone could define them differently." But he "felt" that a sketch was "more of an impression" and lacked "narrative development." Newspaper people, he observed, wrote "sketches." The judge commented that it was hard to use the word "plot" in connection with a short story, but would Gottlieb say that a sketch lacked plot? Yes, Gottlieb said, but even more, you could get "fakey plots" into short stories, but what you could not get into a sketch was "development of a narrative or development of character."

"A sketch," the judge said, "is more likely to be shorter than a short story. But is the length of it definitive in determining whether something is a sketch or not?"

Gottlieb said the judge was absolutely right. The length was not definitive, and yet a sketch was certainly more likely to be shorter than a short story, although there were short short stories.

The *New Yorker,* the judge observed, runs a lot of reasonably long pieces, which he would call sketches rather than short stories. Gottlieb said he didn't know; he would have to know which ones. All right, the judge said. Let's look at the sampler.

Garbus appeared to be tiring of this literary discussion. In order to save time, he said, he should say that he did not intend to use Gottlieb as an expert witness. He was only going to ask him about the "Cheever testimony," whatever that was.

The judge was reluctant to relinquish Mr. Gottlieb, "I'm almost done," he said.

In that event, Paul said, he would move to strike Gottlieb's testimony. It was all hearsay, and its only conceivable basis could have been to qualify Gottlieb as an expert.

"Why did you bother with all the things he read," the judge said with some irritation, "if you weren't going to use him as an expert?" Garbus said he was only trying to show Gottlieb's "familiarity with the litigation." He just wanted to get "his conversation" because the judge had asked about it that morning "concerning Mr. Cheever."

But the judge seemed to want to go on discussing stories and sketches.

He asked Gottlieb if he was familiar with the three stories in the sampler. The witness said it was very hard to remember "which stories I read I didn't publish ten years ago." But he "certainly read" the "Town House" stories. He remembered them. "The last one," the judge said, "if you read it, you certainly wouldn't forget it. It's just about somebody who gives up smoking and everything he sees thereafter reminds him of cigarettes." "That sounds more like a sketch than a story," Gottlieb observed.

He was right on the mark there. That story was called "The Habit" in our book; it had appeared in the *New Yorker* under that title in March 1964, and it was a sketch by anybody's standard. Funnily enough, we were to discover later in the year that Gottlieb had included it in the Knopf collection as one of four sketches under the title "Metamorphosis": it had been included under that title in the Cheever collection *The Brigadier and the Golf Widow and Other Stories,* published by Harper & Row in 1964.

The judge said "The Habit" was decidedly a sketch, and so was "Bayonne," the first story in the sampler, although he thought "Bayonne" was a very good sketch. "Town House," he found, was "almost your usual *New Yorker* short story." Gottlieb agreed and added that it was one of a series of six that were "all interrelated and together," the kind of thing for which there had been a vogue in the late thirties and early forties—things like *I Remember Mama* and *Meet Me in St. Louis . . .* "Semi-sketches, semi-stories . . . "*

"I think I would have no questions of this witness other than that," Garbus said.

The judge asked Gottlieb what percentage of the 1978 Knopf omnibus was taken from other collections. Quite a few, Gottlieb said, a large number. More than half? "Oh, yes," Gottlieb said, at least half.† And the early five volumes [there were actually six] were all fairly short? Yes, Gottlieb said, "you would assume eight, ten, twelve stories would be in such a volume."‡

---

*John Updike was later to express more enthusiasm for the "Town House" stories than Gottlieb evinced here. See the *New Yorker*, May 30, 1994, p. 110.

†Since only 5 stories out of 61 had *not* been taken from earlier Cheever collections, the percentage was considerably more than half.

‡Cheever's first collection *The Way Some People Live*, contains 29 stories (256 pages); *The Brigadier and the Golf Widow* has 16 stories (275 pages). There are 14 stories (237 pages) in *The Enormous Radio*.

Garbus was determined to put a stop to this. "If you're going to go beyond the purpose I called this witness, namely the Cheever-Gottlieb conversations, I would object to it."

The judge then went off the record so that he could go on chatting about literature with Robert Gottlieb.

Paul wanted that exchange on the record, as he made clear when he began his examination of Gottlieb. The judge, Paul said, had asked Gottlieb to name some of the outstanding American short story writers. Would Gottlieb mind repeating some of the names he had given off the record? Hemingway, Gottlieb said, Faulkner, Updike, and Raymond Carver. He did not include Nathaniel Hawthorne or O. Henry, whose real name, the judge had informed us, was Porter. Asked whether there were any sketches in the Knopf collection, Gottlieb said he would have to reread the entire book to tell Paul that. The judge suggested that Paul show the witness a few possible sketches and let him respond. Accordingly, Paul asked Gottlieb to read "A Miscellany of Characters That Will Not Appear" in the Knopf hardcover. Ben had been asked about this "piece" during his deposition and had been unable to deliver a "definitive judgment" on it.

This "Miscellany," which was included in the Cheever collection *Some People, Places and Things That Will Not Appear in My Next Novel* (1961), consists of a sort of list of subjects numbered from one to seven. Number one is a paragraph describing the "pretty girl at the Princeton-Dartmouth Rugby game" who wanders out "of the pages of my novel because I never saw her again." Number two reads in its entirety: "All parts for Marlon Brando." Number three is a paragraph about "all scornful descriptions of American landscapes with ruined tenements, automobile dumps, polluted rivers," and so on. Number four consists of two sentences rejecting "all explicit descriptions of sexual commerce." Number five, three very long paragraphs, begins "All lushes" and describes two events in the life of a middle-aged alcoholic called X, with a wife, three children, and two dogs. Number six, beginning, "Out go all those homosexuals who have taken such a dominating position in recent fiction," deals for a page and a half with a beautiful boy whose father neglects him and whose mother hangs a pearl necklace around his neck. The final sketch is about a mediocre writer whose work contains all the material in the foregoing list, including "fat parts for Marlon Brando," and who dies babbling about the plot for a rotten new novel—dying, Cheever says, like "a generation of story tellers" who cannot "hope to celebrate a world that lies spread out around us like a bewildering and stupendous dream."

The question, the judge said, was would Gottlieb call that a sketch?

Gottlieb said he would not call that a sketch. "This is an attempt," he said, "which you may or may not feel successful, to—if there is a literary device involved here—these numbers and specific things—that when they're brought together are meant to give a literary impression—a composite impression—a complicated meaning. I don't know that I'm equipped to say what it is, but it does not proceed in the way I would say a sketch proceeds . . . . I would not call it a conventional short story. It's not attempting to be that."

Paul handed the book to the judge, while the witness commented, "That book is worth its weight in gold." The judge read the selection and agreed that it wasn't a sketch. "But it's not a short story either," he said. "Sort of hard to say what it is."*

Gottlieb was excused, and Paul called Franklin back to the stand to lead him through the circumstances preceding his letter to Ben and his resultant phone conversation with him. The judge interrupted to ask about misspellings in Franklin's letters. "You have an interesting spelling in here of 'enterprise,'" he said, "e-n-t-e-r-p-r-i-z-e. Was that intentional, or just a slip?"

Franklin said it wasn't intentional.

"And you didn't mean to put the 'w' in 'copywrite' in the next line either, I guess," Judge Goettel said.

Franklin said he didn't mean to.

"Actually," the judge said, "'enterprise' with a 'z' sort of has a ring to it, you know. It connotes something worth doing."

These sallies were greeted with appreciation by the Cheever faction sitting to the right of us. Ellis Levine, of Random House, was sitting next to Garbus at the plaintiff's table, whispering to him from time to time.

Franklin testified that his December 12, 1987, meeting with Mrs. Cheever ended at about 3:00 in the afternoon when Susan, Susan's friend Warren Hinckle, and Fred had arrived. Franklin said he said hello to Susan, whom he knew "in passing"; Fred introduced himself, and Franklin introduced

---

*Although I am not a literary eminence, I feel equipped to say that this "miscellany" is a satirical commentary on what Cheever considered the state of the fiction of his day.

himself to Hinckle. Then, since he and Mrs. Cheever had concluded their business—he had delivered the Xeroxes to her so that she could give them to Ben, he had gone through the table of contents with her, and she had given him a copy of "Behold a Cloud in the West"—he thought "the most diplomatic thing would be to thank her and leave." Which he did. A week or so later, he spoke to Ben, who said he had been reading the manuscript: he found the "Town House" stories very amusing and talked about the associations "Sergeant Limeburner" had for him. "That story," Franklin said, "is about a very seemingly sadistic Army sergeant who, you know, is a great help to his men, because he whips them into shape. But he is a cruel figure."

"That's a cliché character," the judge said.

"It doesn't show in the story," Garbus interjected. "But the way Mr. Dennis is reviewing it—"

Franklin said the denouement of the story was not cliché "because he sacrifices himself for his men, but not in combat." Ben, he said, had told him that John Cheever used to tell his children that Sergeant Limeburner would get them if they didn't behave. In that same conversation, Franklin said, Ben complained about the xeroxing, for which Franklin apologized. Around Christmas time, Franklin left a message for Ben that the *Chicago Tribune* writer John Blades wanted to do a story about the three Cheever books being planned for release in 1988. Then the next time Franklin saw Ben was on January 15, in the Algonquin bar, where Ben had invited him to meet Andrew Wylie. This, Franklin said, was "a shocking encounter for me because I was totally unprepared. And Ben had said that he'd like me to meet a literary agent, and he didn't say why, and that was the day before . . . . So we met at the Algonquin Hotel. But I hope," he said, addressing Goettel, "that's not cliché."

"Yes, it is," the judge said. "Quite a few people have written some stories about the Algonquin as a meeting place."

"It was shocking," Franklin said, "because I was totally unprepared for what happened. And Ben said some words—started off very pleasantly, and then Andrew Wylie came in and—who is not known for his subtle ways, and I found that out very soon. He looked me square in the eye and said, 'How big is this project? How many stories are going to be in this volume? This is going to be a big project.' And I said, 'Well, we anticipate approximately sixty-eight stories.' And it was very soon after that, that he said,

'Well, it's ridiculous to have Academy Chicago Publishers do this book. It's totally inappropriate. These Xeroxes which I've seen are completely unacceptable. They indicate the shabby job that's being done. This project has been terribly handled.' And he said that the advance that Academy Chicago had given Mrs. Cheever was a crime, that within ten minutes he could go out and get a hundred thousand dollar advance. He said with great glee that 'none of my authors ever earned back their advances.' And it was a pathetic situation for me," Franklin said with strong emotion, "because I could not grapple with this man, who is an obstreperous figure. But also Mr. Cheever was there and seemingly Andrew Wylie was speaking for him too, and I did not want to—you know—get into a big fight. I remember saying, 'This reminds me of the day the president was shot.' And everybody laughed. But as it turns out, maybe I wasn't so wrong—I mean my experience."

"Which president were you speaking of?" Judge Goettel asked.

"Any one in my lifetime," Franklin said. "But anyway, I mean, we went down the whole list. It was really outrageous. 'Can't do a thing right. Scott Meredith is an order taker. Nobody can sell the book at Academy Chicago.'" Franklin said he did not believe that it was the project itself that was disturbing Wylie "and presumably—well, very obviously"—Ben. It was the fact that it was Academy Chicago that was doing this book of sixty-eight stories. "And there was almost nothing I could do, and I didn't want to get into an argument. And Andrew Wylie said, 'Well, John le Carré, that's not appropriate. Raymond Carver isn't appropriate. Saul Bellow is appropriate.'"

That, Franklin said, was what he could recall about the Algonquin meeting. Paul then released him. We were surprised that Franklin had not gone on to say that Wylie had offered him 25 percent of the Cheevers' royalties in a new contract and instructed him to come to his office on the following Monday. Ben had mentioned in his deposition that Franklin was supposed to go to Wylie's office. When we asked Franklin about this later, he said he had expected Paul to ask him about that, but to his surprise, Paul had ended the cross-examination without asking him. Of course, it wouldn't have mattered anyway.

In Garbus's redirect examination, Franklin was asked again and again the things that Garbus had asked him the first time: didn't he know the Cheevers didn't want these stories published, didn't he know Ben had offered to come to Chicago, hadn't Franklin tried to find out about copyrights from Maggie Curran, didn't Franklin contact Scott Meredith in September, didn't Franklin know that Jordan contacted them? Until the judge finally put a stop to it, Garbus forced Franklin to read aloud the errors from the alphabetical list of stories he had given Ben.

Garbus's next witness, Mary W. Cheever, as she called herself, testified that Franklin "came by" and gave her two packets in blue binders, which she put on the dining room table. She didn't remember if Franklin had told her who he worked for, but she said he came to see her because "he thought of getting some stories together to be published."* He must have mentioned a publisher, but she probably did not pay much attention.

"Did he mention any university presses, do you remember?" Garbus asked.

Paul objected. The judge said, "Well, she doesn't seem to remember, so he can attempt to refresh her recollection."

"He said 'Academy Chicago,'" Mrs. Cheever said, remembering. "And that sounded to me like a university press, in my ignorance."

Paul said that the memory of what Franklin said was admissible but how she interpreted what he said was not admissible. He moved to strike.

"Oh," the judge said, "I disagree with you." Her understanding of what Franklin said had some "pertinence" to all of this. "He said he was from Academy Chicago and that to her sounds educational. Correct?" he asked the witness, beaming at her.

"Correct, Your Honor," she said, beaming back.

Garbus asked her about the famous five books that Franklin had brought her as a gift. Two, she said, were from Academy Chicago. "One was of some volumes of letters between some nineteenth-century Englishmen. I haven't read it," she said, with obvious truth, since the letters cover the years 1955 to 1962. "Another," she said, referring to *Ramage in South Italy*, "was impressions of Italy, also reprinted from something that had first been printed at least a hundred years ago." And then there were three books from "the Marlboro Press, Marlboro Vermont": one was a translation from the Catalan of poems, a poet whose name she had forgotten; the other was another travel book—Mediterranean places, she believed, she didn't remember precisely, she was sorry. But was she allowed, she asked, looking up at the judge

---

*The reader is reminded that Franklin went to see Mrs. Cheever in December, about four months after the contract was signed, and he brought her a manuscript.

with a smile, was she allowed to say that her "overall impression" was that "they were small press editions, small editions from small presses? My impression was this was obscure material, not what we call trade books." She added that after Franklin left, she thought to herself that it was going to be very hard to read those poor Xeroxes.

"Well," the judge said, "the major problem is the *New Yorker* has that funny skinny little type and it doesn't reproduce very well."

"Not very well," the witness echoed, beaming and bobbing her head at him.

"The copies from the other magazines are very legible," the judge observed.

"Especially when the ring binder goes right through a column of type," Mrs. Cheever said, apparently misunderstanding him. "And it isn't even straight on the page in some cases." She looked at them, she said; she had been told she should look at them, or it had been suggested that she should look at them and pass them on to Ben. "That would be something we could both study." And she had indeed passed them on to Ben very soon afterward, she said.

Garbus showed her her letter to Scott Donaldson and asked her to tell the court how she believed that Donaldson's introduction defamed her husband and why she objected to it.

Paul said he didn't see what that had to do with the copyright issue.

When it evolved that a second page of Mrs. Cheever's letter was missing—no one had it but Paul, who couldn't offer it because he had made notes on it—Garbus suggested that Mrs. Cheever go through the Donaldson introduction and tell the court her objections.

The judge reminded Garbus that Paul had an objection to this line of questioning: "The battle over the introduction is a matter of the contract and not a matter of the copyright." Garbus responded that it was a Lanham Act claim, "namely, that they are passing this work off as something other than what it is. You heard from Mr. Gottlieb. He didn't use the term in court, he used it with me, 'the worst of Cheever' or 'left-over Cheever.' And she discusses that. She also discusses the interpretation that Donaldson puts on the material and which you will also ultimately find. And that's behind the previous exhibit in the way they sell this book as the best of Cheever."

Judge Goettel said he didn't see that this letter from Mrs. Cheever to Scott Donaldson had much to do with any Lanham Act claim. But he added that Mrs. Cheever was saying that Donaldson was not paying any attention to her views on the introduction, despite the fact that she held the copyrights. Garbus said he would move on; he would not ask any questions about that letter to Donaldson. But he read aloud from it.

Paul had only a few questions for Mrs. Cheever, about the contract and some letters from ICM. He whispered to us after she left the stand that he did not want to get into a "pissing contest" with her.

Susan was the next witness. She was dressed as she had been at the Royce Hotel—barelegged, in a black cotton suit and brown loafers. She gave a truncated version of her deposition testimony. She came with a "friend" to visit her mother; in the house she found Franklin, who didn't seem pleased to see her; her mother was in the kitchen or upstairs "and on the dining room table was this blue binder." Susan was still talking about one binder, although her mother had just testified in her presence that the xeroxed stories were in *two* binders. When she asked Franklin "what the purpose of the blue binder was," Susan discovered that Franklin was collecting together all the uncollected stories. "I understood what he was doing," she said, and then quickly corrected herself. "I can't say I understood, right?" she asked, presumably of Garbus. "How can I put this?" She couldn't remember Franklin's words, she said, but it was "certainly clear that he was gathering all these stories together, either for our selection or for our approval." She repeated her deposition story that Franklin had said he might do "a facsimile edition, ... something for scholars or even students." And then "he left in a hurry."

Garbus asked her what Gottlieb had told her about her father's desire not to have these stories published. On Paul's objection, Goettel said that what Gottlieb told her would not be admissible. Garbus tried it another way. Did she know of her father's desire not to have these stories published? Paul said that what John Cheever told his daughter was not an issue in this case. "Probably not," the judge said, "because it more likely goes to the contract issues. But since I'm not sure where it's going at the moment, I'll allow it."

Susan said she had had a conversation with John Updike at her father's funeral. Paul objected, and the judge told her that she couldn't tell the court what Mr. Updike told her but she could tell the court what she said to him. Susan said okay and told the court that she had told Mr. Updike that she did not think her father wanted those stories published and that, indeed, her father had been opposed to the red book.

"It won a Pulitzer," the judge said. "Did your father change his mind?"

No, no, Susan said, never. He was "adamant about not going back to the past . . . . I mean, he felt very strongly that he did not want to have mementos dredged up and presented to his audience."

After a discussion about sketches (Susan said it was "like a poem must not mean but be"), Garbus asked her whether her father was on a payroll from 1930 to 1943. Paul objected. Judge Goettel said he didn't know Susan was alive at that time; he asked her when she was born. She replied that she was born in 1943. Garbus asked her whether it was fair to say that her father had no other income than the money he made as a writer. "Except," the judge added, "when he was in the service." Garbus said, "He wasn't an academic. He wasn't a journalist. He didn't work for an insurance company and write at night." Susan said that was true.

Paul said this had nothing to do with the issues.

"Yes," Garbus said, "to getting out material to make a dollar that he realized later on that he didn't want to use as a standard for himself." Garbus seemed very comfortable in that courtroom. He strode about, up and down, back and forth, gesturing broadly, speaking loudly. Paul, thin and sharp-featured, sat tightly at his table.

When Paul rose to examine the witness, he attacked her strongly because she had signed the verified complaint swearing to her joint ownership of stories to which she had no claim whatever. Susan said she had relied on her lawyers; she had not done her own copyright work, okay? The judge pointed out to her that the story "Emma Boynton," to which she had laid claim, had been renewed during her father's lifetime and could not come under "the statute." Garbus interposed that they had dropped "Emma Boynton" in the amended complaint because they had done "more copyright work."

Paul said he viewed the allegations in the complaint of the children's copyright interest "as an absolute sham and a fraud on the court, because they have no interest." At the appropriate time, he said, he wanted to bring to the court's attention the fact that in arguing the case for the children's copyrights, Garbus had quoted a "part of Nimmer on copyrights, deliberately omitting the next paragraph, which explains why the law that Garbus purports to have cited here is not the law and is not applicable."*

---

*Both Paul and the Kronish, Lieb lawyers were taken aback at Garbus's use of the Nimmer quotation. It is worth noting that Judge Goettel was to use this very citation of Garbus's, with the selective omission, in August.

Susan was released, and Garbus remarked that it was growing late. The judge asked Paul how many witnesses he planned to call. Paul said that at that point he hadn't heard much evidence bearing on the children's copyrights, so he was not clear how many witnesses to call. The judge said that the Cheevers had the burden and if they didn't present anything, Paul wouldn't need any witnesses. But how many witnesses did Paul have on the other issue that the judge framed in his opinion—whether or not Mrs. Cheever was transferring copyright when she signed the contract? Paul said the only evidence was the contract itself, which did not assign copyrights but granted publishing rights to Academy Chicago. He didn't believe he would present any witnesses on that "issue."

"The long and short of it is," the judge said briskly, "you won't take up much time."

Sitting dimly in my pew, moving aside occasionally to make room for Cheever witnesses to perambulate, I wondered whether there was any "copyright issue" at all here, since in standard publishing contracts the author always retains the copyright and grants the publisher only publishing rights. It was clear that the famous "children's copyright issue" did not exist. Why then were we there?

Garbus announced that he was going to put Mrs. Cheever on the stand in the morning "for two questions I forgot to ask her."

Court recessed for the evening.

25

Evidentiary Hearing, Day 2, A.M.: "Who Is the Beggar?"

True to his word, the next morning Garbus recalled Mary Cheever to the stand. He asked her whether she had intended to assign any "copyright interests" when she signed the agreement (No); whether she knew at the time that her husband did not want his early works published (Yes); whether she and the family had agreed among themselves not to publish those stories (In general, yes); had she ever delivered a manuscript (No); and had she agreed to publish at any particular date (No). The judge asked her whether she intended to deliver a manuscript on some subsequent date. She said she had taken "delivery" to mean that she would "make a selection, perhaps deliver a table of contents with some suggestions about . . . . arrangement and editorial comment." After that, the judge said, did she intend to "assign those copyrights?" She said she would, "so to speak."

She said that she had thought that since it was a small press, "it would be a small book and a small edition." The Cheevers had published other "small books": four of her husband's stories had come out as "single storybooks in very small, elegant, editions." She understood "the so-called editor, Franklin Dennis" was going to do the research, which involved finding the stories. Since Franklin had obviously done that, the judge did a little probing. Was it a question of "simply locating stories that weren't readily available?" Yes, but she thought he might do more than that. He might find out about "some of the circumstances surrounding the writing of the stories." There was a great deal an editor could do that was not done in this case.* The judge asked for more details: "You envisioned then some annotation about the origins of the stories and the circumstances of the author when he wrote them?"

---

*In none of John Cheever's story collections, including the 1978 omnibus edited by Gottlieb, is there any detailing of circumstances surrounding the writing of the stories. There is not even any attempt to give publication history or the dates of the stories themselves.

"Yes, I did," she said, ducking her head and smiling up at him. "On the literary quality too."

The literary quality was, she said, "very poor, mostly these stories are very poor. They were written under duress to make enough money even just to eat and my husband was not ashamed that he had to make his way exclusively as a writer." He had no job, except for a couple of years when he worked for the WPA. The judge then engaged in some biographical research. Was John Cheever in the service during World War II? Oh, yes—for four years. And in what branch? Well, first the infantry and then the Signal Corps, and "he worked in Astoria writing."

"Astoria, Oregon, or Astoria, Queens?" asked the judge. Upon being told that it was Astoria, Queens, he wanted to know what Cheever's rank was in the service. She said she believed he was a technical sergeant.

Garbus asked her what magazines her husband had written for before the war. All she could remember, she said, were the *New Yorker, New Republic, Collier's, Mademoiselle,* the *Atlantic,* and maybe *Cosmopolitan.*

"*Liberty* and *Saturday Evening Post* were the two best-paying at that time," observed the judge, traveling down Memory Lane. "Did he get any stories in them?"

"No," Mrs. Cheever said. "He never did."

"They were more popular sort of literature," the judge said.

"Yes. *Collier's* was very popular."

The judge agreed that *Collier's* was popular.

Garbus, taking back the reins, asked her about her December meeting with Franklin. Did she remember that in her deposition she had said it was October instead of December? Yes, she said, but "we have since determined that it was a very warm day. It was still chrysanthemums in the garden. We remembered it as October or November, but actually it was December." And what happened on that day? "It was a very brief meeting. He put down the Xeroxes. I glanced at them. Then I said, 'I bet I have a story you haven't found,' which to my mind meant, Your research is not finished."

"Your Honor," Paul said, "this is the same question that was asked of the witness yesterday."

The judge agreed that they were now going back over yesterday.

"She didn't fully testify as to that meeting," Garbus protested.

"She apparently didn't remember," Paul said, "and now Mr. Garbus has put some ideas in her head, but this is not proper questioning."

Garbus was outraged at this insulting accusation. "I object," he said. "I think she did mention going to get a story—" His Honor said. "But now she's going to go through the rest of it," Garbus said. "—in another book," the judge said. He sustained Paul's objection and told Garbus to put another question. Garbus asked her whether she was able to read the Xeroxes. She said she wasn't; she didn't try very hard. "I thought I'd wait until they get something I can read without too much trouble." The meeting with Franklin, she said, lasted for no more than twenty minutes. "Then my daughter and her friend came in."

Franklin had said that Fred Cheever had been there, too, but his mother—like his sister—had apparently forgotten him.

Paul rose for cross-examination. Now that Garbus had brought her back, Paul had decided to ask her some probing questions, which he had not done the day before. He asked her about the contract. Why did she call Maggie Curran? "Because," Mrs. Cheever responded with some hauteur, "the estate employs a literary agent because they're supposed to have some expertise about contracts and I thought I should avail myself of that."

Did she contact her son Ben and talk to him about it?

"Talk to him about the contract?" she said. "No, I didn't talk to Ben about the contract."

How about Susan? No, she didn't talk to Susan. And her son Federico?

"Well," she said, "that would have been more logical, since he's a lawyer. But he doesn't live on the east coast, so it wouldn't have been so easy." Anyway, she did not contact Federico and discuss the contract with him. She trusted her agency, she said. She relied on them for this sort of work.

And after she got the contract back from Maggie Curran and before she signed it, did she contact Ben to talk to him about it? She didn't remember. Did she contact Susan? She didn't think so. Why not? "I must explain that I see a great many contracts," she said. And she signed a great many contracts. And she did not read them very carefully. She relied on her literary agency.

Paul asked her what all these contracts were that she received.

"Well," she said frostily, "you don't know very much about the literary world, do you, Mr. Freehling?" They were contracts for taping stories, for televising and filming them, for anthologizing them, for translating them.

Did Franklin's job include locating stories? And was that complicated? Didn't she know where all the stories were? "Some of them were in magazines that had been out of print for a long time," she said.

The judge entered the discussion. "A number of these stories were written before you ever met your husband?"

"Oh, long before," she said, bobbing her head and smiling at him. "When he was a boy of eighteen."

"Did he keep a running file—keeping a copy of everything he wrote?" the judge asked.

"He kept no files," Mrs. Cheever said, still smiling. "No correspondence, no letters, nothing."

"Not very businesslike," the judge observed.

"Not at all," she responded.

"Like most authors," he said indulgently.

"That's right," she responded.

Paul reminded her that she had said that part of Franklin's job was to "ascertain the circumstances under which the various stories were written."

"I believe," she said coldly, all smiles stopped together, "I said I imagined that might be one of the functions of an editor."

"And just how did you expect Mr. Dennis to go about doing that?"

"Well, you know, lots of people do that kind of research. I didn't realize that Mr. Dennis is less than competent and had been bothering my son to find out what stories there were."

"Well, wouldn't your son be an appropriate source—"

"No!"

"—for the information as to what the circumstances were of writing the stories?"

At this point Mrs. Cheever delivered a little speech: when she was a teacher she taught something called "The Research Paper," and she learned all the sources there were for locating the works of any particular author. If Mr. Dennis had been a student of hers and brought her those "ring binders," she said, she would have given him perhaps a C-plus for effort: "the research was incomplete, the product was sloppy, and he had no thesis whatever, no ideas about how to arrange or select those stories, no thesis whatever."

"How were the stories arranged?" Paul asked gently. "Chronologically?"

"Yes," she said.

And did Mr. Dennis have access to John Cheever's letters and journals?

"He certainly did not," she said indignantly.

"Now," Paul said, "you also said that one of the jobs of an editor like Mr. Dennis would be to determine the literary quality of the stories, is that right?"

"I thought he might consider the literary quality of the stories. But evidently no such idea entered his head."

"Do you think it possible, Mrs. Cheever, that he found these stories all to have literary quality?" Garbus said he would object to what Mr. Dennis thought was possible, and Paul withdrew the question.

"That's too speculative," the witness said to the judge with a smile.

"Yes, it is," the judge said, beaming down at her. "Sustained."

Paul asked whether there were stories in the table of contents that she believed had no literary quality whatsoever.

"Well," she said, "you have to have a definition of 'literary quality.'"

"Yes, that's a little too vague," the judge said. "But would you say that some of the stories in there are not worthy of republication?" She said she certainly would. And were some of them worthy of publication? Yes, she said, some were. "And how," Paul said, taking over again, "will we go about determining which are which, Mrs. Cheever?"

"Well, presumably," she replied, smiling up at the judge, "some of us have some taste and knowledge about these matters."

Paul asked her whether she had ever expressed herself to either Mr. Dennis or Academy Chicago "as to specifically which stories you consider are not worthy of republication."

"I was never asked," she said, frowning. "I was never consulted, never! I was waiting to be consulted."

"Did it occur to you, Mrs. Cheever," Paul said, "that they were waiting to hear from you as to which of the stories you thought did not . . . . "

His voice trailed off as a remarkable change came over Mrs. Cheever. Her face twisted with rage. *"Who is the beggar?"* she cried harshly. "You know, they should call me, not I call them!"

A hush fell over the room. The buzzing of the Cheever group ceased.

"I'm sorry," Paul said, after a moment. "'Who is the beggar?'"

"Who is the—what's the more polite word for beggar?" She was still glaring at him. "Who is asking and who is giving? They're asking, I'm giving. They should call *me.*"

Paul rallied visibly. "But they brought you, didn't they, a set of notebooks that had stories in them? Isn't that right?"

"You mean the binders of the Xeroxes?" She was still in a rage. "Yes, they did, they did! So what was I supposed to do? I thought I should wait until they asked me what I thought about them. They never did!"

"Didn't you understand, Mrs. Cheever," Paul said in a reasonable tone, "when they gave you those binders, that they were asking you to tell them which of these stories you felt shouldn't be published?"

She sat huddled together. "I did not understand what was required of me," she said. "Nothing was said to me. The only thing that was perfectly clear was that they wanted any help I could give them, and I found that very brazen, that they should ask me to go through letters and journals to find out about stories they couldn't find out about themselves. I found that so annoying!"

"Well," Judge Goettel said, "I should think looking through the letters for references to stories and where they were to appear or had appeared would be almost like looking for a needle in a haystack."

This was, of course, exactly what I had done in compiling my massive bibliography of Arnold Bennett's journalism. There is no other way to do it.

Garbus agreed with the judge. "That's true," he said. "Also a lot of these letters are in libraries. In other words, the Cheevers had some letters. But most of the letters were to be found in libraries. Mr. Dennis could have found it. They were asking for specific letters that the Cheevers were working on for future book publication in Simon and Schuster."

"I would have thought," the court said, "that certainly for the things she had copyright to, her copyright papers would be the best source for information like that."

"Oh, Your Honor," Paul said, rowing against the tide, "you'll hear that Academy Chicago went and got all the copyright papers. Mrs. Cheever apparently felt that there was some obligation on the part of the editor to do more than look at the public record, but to get into the private records of John Cheever, which they requested the opportunity to do. But unfortunately or fortunately, they didn't ask the Cheevers to do it for them—they asked for an opportunity, and they were denied that opportunity. So be it."

"She did not say she wanted them to go through the private papers," the judge said, "because they were already being prepared for publication and to disclose them might impair that publication."

Paul asked Mrs. Cheever whether she had told Franklin when he came to her house that she would give him a C-plus for effort and a lower grade for results. During the interim she had composed herself somewhat. "I was not uncivil to this young man," she said.

"Well," Paul said, "did you ever tell Mr. Dennis that you were unhappy with the quality of the product that he delivered to your home in the middle of December, 1987?"

"No," she said.

And what had happened between December 12, when Franklin came to her with the stories, and the middle of February, when Garbus sent his letter to Academy Chicago—what had happened to sour the relationship between the Cheevers and Franklin and Academy Chicago?

"We were getting very nervous about what they were doing. We were getting all sorts of mixed signals about what they planned to do. It began to look as though they were planning to publish all of his stories without consulting me or Ben or anybody."

"And you did not want all of the stories published, Mrs. Cheever?"

"I certainly did not."

"Had you decided which of the stories you wanted published?"

She hadn't been asked to decide, she said. She added that she would "not dignify this within the term 'relationship,' what I had with Academy Chicago." Or with Franklin, she added, whom she had seen only once in her life.

The judge intervened here once more, to ask some questions about Andrew Wylie. Between the December meeting with Franklin and the phone call two months later, did Ben talk to her about Wylie or did she talk to Wylie directly? Her reply was no. Yes, she had spoken with Ben, but no, Ben did not give her Wylie's opinion. He didn't? the judge asked again. Did he mention Wylie at all? Yes, in connection with Ben's "career as a self-employed writer." Did Ben mention Wylie in connection with this particular work? No, she responded. The judge threw in the towel on Wylie and fell back on Ben. "Did Ben give you as his opinion the fact that the project that Academy was contemplating was not in conformance with what you and he had originally envisioned it [*sic*]?"

"Yes," she said, "yes, he did. He had gotten the impression from Mr. Dennis who had—perhaps in an unguarded moment—sort of clapped his hands and said, 'Oh, we're going to make a lot of money' to my son Ben."

The judge reminded her that she didn't really have to rely on what Mr. Dennis said; he had left her those two spiral notebooks containing, he would guess, forty or fifty stories.

"But I had no idea they contemplated publishing them all," she said. "It never occurred to me."

"In other words," the court said, "you simply, when he left them with you, viewed them as his collection of stories from which a selection would be made."

"That's correct."

"And then," the court went on, "Ben told you that he was getting the impression that they were going to publish every story they could lay their hands on."

"That's right," she said.

"I understand," the judge said. "And that is not what you had originally thought this was all about."

"No," she said.

Paul asked her whether she had met with Wylie about this book. Yes, she said, would Paul like to know when?

"Don't keep me hanging," the judge said roguishly. "When did you?"

She had met him on the evening of the Royce Hotel meeting, she said, and she had never spoken to him before that. And, Paul asked her, had she heard that Wylie had been consulted about this matter before she met him that evening? "Well," she replied coldly, "why would I be interested in the opinion of my son's literary agent? I knew myself what the danger was here."

"Incidentally," the court asked, "is he connected with one of the larger agencies?"

No, she believed he had his own agency.

Paul asked her opinion of the Scott Donaldson introduction. It was, she said, "the most degrading, absolutely uncalled-for group of assertions . . . . No holds were barred here." The judge broke in to tell Paul that he was doing exactly what he had objected to Garbus doing—"namely, going into contract issues."

"I'm sure that may well be true, Your Honor," Paul said. "I have a very difficult time separating out in my mind the contract issues from the copyright issues. But," he added quickly, "I think you're probably correct."

"I can separate them in my mind," the judge said, "but factually they have a tremendous area of interplay because, in Mrs. Cheever's view of the contract, she had a veto over what would be published. And if she has that over the contract, she has *de facto* control over the copyrights. So the two things do interrelate."

Ben was the next witness. Asked by Garbus about his meeting in January with Wylie and Franklin, Ben talked and talked. His primary concern was that the work being done on the book "was a little shy, the Xeroxes were bad . . . . " He got lists and notes from Dennis with mistakes in them. But he wanted to be friendly, and he didn't want to say to Franklin, "Look, you're giving me things I can't read. You're not listening to what I say. You seem to be violating our understanding." He thought that if Andrew and he got in the room and got to talking in a friendly way, they could find a way to resolve the issue so that Ben would be happy and Franklin would hear what he had to say. "He hadn't—he hadn't been hearing what I had to say," Ben said again. And again. Because he had said to Franklin maybe fifteen times that he didn't have the final vote and they were a long way from making the final decision. He would pass on what Franklin said and then "we'll all sit down and make a decision that makes everyone happy— " Garbus interrupted. Had Ben learned prior to this meeting that they intended to publish this book in the fall?

Ben said that was interesting because he didn't have any idea when the publication date would be. One of the dates they were considering, he said, was the fall. And he read in the *Chicago Tribune* story—a copy of which he had had to ask Franklin for—that they were considering fall publication, and it also said that Ben was editing the journals alone, his father's journals, and that might offend his sister and brother, and they were very careful about not offending each other about that. So he had lunch with Andrew about his own business—Ben was very apprehensive about whether he could make it without a job—and Andrew was trying to reassure him, and Ben told Andrew about what was going on with Academy Chicago and that he, Ben, didn't like the job Franklin was doing and he didn't want to make Franklin sore, but maybe they could have a meeting and find some way to let him hear that. Maybe he would hear it from Andrew, and then they could proceed. So they had this meeting.

The judge wanted to know who selected the Algonquin. Ben, who had heard Goettel call it a cliché choice, promptly responded, "Franklin Dennis. And in fact I said, 'Isn't that a little corny?'" The main bar, where "the great ones" sat, was full, so they had to sit in the back part. But they had a lot of peanuts. And at the end—Garbus interrupted to ask what Ben had said at the meeting. Ben replied that he didn't run down a bill of particulars, "in the same way my mother didn't give him a C-plus. You don't say things that are going to hurt people's feelings, unless there is a real benefit," and he didn't see any benefit in that, so he thought maybe the best thing to do would be "just to somehow find a way to end this relationship, polite and friendly and, you know, if a book of some of my father's stories came out, we would find a way to involve Franklin in it, and everybody would be happy." So they "kind of asked around that," and Wylie kept saying, "'How big is this project?'" for two reasons, one being his and Ben's suspicion that Franklin and Academy weren't in a position to handle the subject properly, and the other question was "how many stories were going to be in this." And one of the responses Ben remembered Franklin making, which kind of surprised him but in a way pleased him, Franklin said to Andrew, "'I'd like to meet with you again.'" And Andrew said, "'With Ben or without Ben?'" And Franklin said, "'I'd like to meet with you alone.'"* And Ben thought, "Well . . . . "

Ben said that his understanding about the Academy book was that it was going to be a book that pleased him, his mother, his sister, and Academy, composed of, "if we could arrive at them, a few stories that weren't readily available for people that would be made readily available in a limited edition." At Garbus's request, Ben produced his diary and noted the entry for July 16, 1987: it said, "University of Chicago, Franklin Dennis," and what Ben "assumed" was Franklin's telephone number.

Asked about his phone call to Chicago, Ben said he called because Garbus had sent a letter, in January or February. . . . and Ben had a friend who was a lawyer, whom he "ran with," and he "said to me a thing I didn't really know: if you ever want to settle something important, you have to meet in person, without lawyers." So he thought he would call the Millers; he wouldn't say anything nasty. He would just suggest. Incidentally, he was very busy on his own book of letters, a book of his father's letters, "probably not going to come out till January, maybe even February, on account of all this legal stuff. Instead of going over my book, I've been doing this." The phone call was one attempt; the meeting with Wylie was another. Because

---

*Franklin Dennis remembers vividly a strong desire never to see Andrew Wylie again.

he still understood the thing that Franklin said to him over and over was that, you know, he wanted to please the Cheever family. And his mother remembered signing a lot of contracts. They'd had a lot of very, very pleasant relationships with small publishers—

"This is beginning to sound like a stream of consciousness," the judge said. "Let's go back to when you first met Franklin Dennis." Ben said he first met him at a restaurant named Chez Vong on the East Side, and Ben went there—

"That's where, not when," the judge said.

Ben said it was on July 28, and Ben met him because Franklin was a friend of a friend of his father's. Ben thought that Academy Chicago was the University of Chicago. Franklin wanted to know if there were any manuscripts, any Cheever work they could publish, and Ben didn't know, he thought Daddy threw out all his manuscripts and then Franklin asked if there were stories that were not in the Knopf collection, and Ben said yes, there were, and in fact Ben had been reading them, and Franklin asked who owned the copyrights—

Garbus asked when Ben first learned that Franklin wanted to publish them all, if he did.

"Late in October or early November," Ben said. "Late in October or early November . . . . he said that Academy Chicago was considering the possibility of publishing all the stories that had not been in any other collections. And he said, you know, that would be—people would be interested in them and maybe that was a good idea. I wasn't sure I liked the idea, but I just—" He said he reminded Franklin again to find the stories, they would look at them, Franklin would talk to his mother, they'd have a "family powwow," and then they would decide.

When, the judge asked, did Ben first see the publishing agreement that his mother signed in August?

Ben said that he was sent a copy shortly after she signed it. But he had to confess—and he didn't think it was uncommon for writers—he didn't know whether he'd be a writer—but like people who make their living on their contracts—he didn't read it carefully. But he did read the letter that came with it . . . . so he thought, All right, they had put his mother on notice, that was good . . . . So he had this conversation with his mother, telling her that they were a small publisher and he would be surprised if they even were capable, you know, of printing . . . . And he told Franklin his mother didn't think some of the stories were so good, "but we'll get them and locate them," and you know he wasn't holding a gun to Franklin's head . . . .

"We seem to be running on again," the judge said.

It was time for a recess.

We walked out into the hall, where Russell Smith was already on the telephone. "Yeah," he was saying enthusiastically, "it's going great!"

We were having a desultory conversation with our son Mark and his wife Jean McGarry, when Bruce came up to us. His face was bright red. He had had an encounter with Ben in the men's room. Just before Ben exited, he had said to Bruce, "I hope you're proud of your parents." Bruce, bristling, had followed him out. "Yes," he had said, "I'm very proud of my parents!" Ben, glowering, had turned and advanced toward him, and Bruce had braced for a physical attack. Garbus had hurried up, made soothing noises, and led Ben away.

When we returned to court, Paul began his cross-examination of Ben, trying to find out what exactly had upset Ben so that he arranged the meeting in the Algonquin bar. Was it the quality of the Xeroxes? Well, Ben said, he was grasping for the concrete to explain his feeling, his growing uneasiness. No, it wasn't just that the Xeroxes were shoddy. Communication was only working one way—Franklin didn't seem to be hearing what he was saying.

Communication about the shoddiness?

No, Ben said, about the size of the book.

So Ben's principal concern was the size of the book?

Ben said he had a number of concerns. He supposed a lawyer would have been more astute. But he was concerned, he wasn't hysterical. He meant, he wasn't as upset as he should have been.

But, Paul persisted, what he was trying to find out was what concerned Ben. Was it the size of the book? Well, Ben said, this was a process, as Franklin put it. It was Ben's understanding that nothing had been decided about the size of the book. But he began to suspect that Franklin wasn't hearing what he was saying.

"About what, Mr. Cheever? About the size of the book or about something else?"

Ben said that one of the things that he was very concerned about was that Franklin hadn't heard—although he had said it to him repeatedly—that his mother owned the copyrights. Any decision that was going to be made was going to have to be made by his mother, any decision about a specific story. No specific story was mentioned in the contract. Every time Franklin came to him with a proposal, Ben would say, "'Ask my mother. You know my mother is listed in the phone book.'" Franklin finally did call her and visit her. But Ben was afraid that Franklin just wasn't getting this. It wasn't clear to Franklin, and Ben thought this meeting with Wylie might make it clear to him.

This one instance Ben was talking about, Paul said, did it concern Franklin's request to use the *Newsweek* essay?

Ben said that was right. "You're learning quite a bit about publishing, Mr. Freehling."

And Franklin went to her and "asked for permission and she gave permission, wasn't that right?"

Yes, Ben said, but Franklin never went to her and asked for permission to publish any of the stories in the bound galley, never once.

And was it Ben's concern at the Algonquin Hotel that Franklin had not communicated enough with Ben's mother?

Ben said that he had a number of concerns. One was that he didn't like the way the project was proceeding. It seemed—there were indications—that this project was proceeding without his mother being asked for her opinion and that it was proceeding sloppily.

How sloppily?

Well, Franklin had originally asked Ben to edit the book and Ben was too busy. But Ben immediately thought of the things he would do if he were to edit the book, and it seemed to Ben that Franklin wasn't doing them.

"Did you tell him what those things were, or were they just in your head?"

Ben said it was difficult to remember now, but he wanted "this problem solved with the least possible unpleasantness." So he didn't . . . . his mother had given Franklin a C-plus . . . .

Paul repeated the question. Did he tell Franklin what those tasks were that an editor should perform, or were they simply tasks in Ben's head?

Well, at that point, Ben said, he thought they were a long way from the final determination—from any final decision. "So that the court was still out on what Franklin was to do or not to do." But it looked to Ben that he was not doing it . . . .

Paul repeated the question for the third time. Garbus objected.

"Well," Judge Goettel said, "he's not answering the questions very succinctly." He proceeded to provide a little assistance. "I take it you didn't tell him—you didn't criticize his editing at that point, because you felt it was premature."

"I think that's accurate," the witness said.

Paul asked whether the meeting at the Algonquin was the first time that Ben had criticized Franklin about what he felt was his shoddy performance as an editor.

No, Ben said, he had expressed concerns to Franklin before. About the John Blades story in the *Tribune,* for instance. The Xeroxes, for instance. Franklin acknowledged that they were sloppy, but he said neater things would be done . . . .

Approximately how many times had Ben spoken to Franklin on the telephone before the meeting at the Algonquin?

"You're assuming that I gave this whole project a great deal more seriousness than I did," Ben said.

"Are you telling me that you did not treat this project seriously?"

"I'm telling you that this was very preliminary, as far as I was concerned, and that it was going to be, as far as I was concerned, a small book of a few stories, over which we were to have the final say and that I wasn't even going to be the one who was going to have the final say. My mother was, in consultation with me, my sister and my brother . . . . There were a number of such projects going on during the same period of time."

"I believe that you said your goal at the Algonquin Hotel meeting was to end the relationship between the Cheevers and Academy Chicago and Mr. Dennis. Is that right?"

"I don't think I said that. If I did—I don't think I said that. That was certainly—I didn't know what was going to happen . . . . "

"So the purpose of the Algonquin meeting was to allow Mr. Dennis to speak?"

"And to allow me to speak."

"Had you decided at the time of the Algonquin Hotel meeting that you felt this project could be handled better by another publisher?"

"I have to say," Ben said, "you know, that—No, I hadn't decided that. I thought that one of the painless ways of getting out of what appeared to be a messy situation would be to have it handled by another publisher. I certainly hadn't come to the decision that that was—I didn't have my heart set on that. That was one of the things we would discuss and we did discuss it."

"Have you ever talked to Mr. Wylie about having another publisher handle this project?"

"Yes," Ben said.

"What other publisher?"

"It wasn't that specific."

Perhaps it is appropriate at this time to note that Ellis Levine, senior counsel of Random House, still sat at the plaintiff's table with Garbus, frequently whispering to him. Garbus objected to "the form of the question, when he says 'this project.' It's clear we're talking about two different things."

"Well," the judge said, "I take it we're talking about the uncollected stories of John Cheever."

"That's what the witness didn't understand," Garbus said.

"Let's be sure the witness does understand," Paul said. He turned back to Ben and asked him whether he had ever talked to Wylie about taking the stories to another publisher. "All or any of the stories?"

Yes, Ben said, but he couldn't tell Paul whether he talked to Wylie about that before January.

And did he talk to Wylie about a specific publisher that he might take all or some of the stories to?

"I don't have any recollection of talking to him about that," Ben said.

Had he talked to his sister Susan about taking these uncollected stories to another publisher?

Garbus objected: "He keeps putting his question 'all or some' which are totally different. He's answering yes and now he's talking about taking this particular collection, the uncollected stories. I object to the form of the question."

The judge apparently understood the objection; he asked Ben if he understood the question.

Ben appeared to be rather agitated. He kept shifting in his seat and fiddling with the microphone. "If you're saying—the trouble—you know, I think my difficulty is understanding that this contract refers to something called *The Uncollected Stories of John Cheever*. Could be one uncollected story, could be nine uncollected stories. Could be—and certainly in my mind, and I believe I probably told Franklin, it could be that we would look at all these stories, my mother would read all these stories and she wouldn't want any of them published. So whether we would bring—you know, we're too far in speculation."

"But the question, Mr. Cheever," Paul said, "was, did you ever talk to your sister Susan about utilizing some publisher other than Academy Chicago for some or all of the uncollected stories?"

"Did I ever?" Ben asked.

"Yes."

"In my whole life?" He pulled at the microphone and shifted in his seat.

"Some or all again," Garbus observed.

The judge tried to help. "Once it became apparent that—other than a small publication of limited stories—that they were definitely contemplating a large publication of a lot of stories, did you ever discuss with your sister or anyone else taking the project to a different publisher?"

Ben's agitation appeared to increase; he pulled at his microphone, and it flew off its stand and dangled limply before him. Gales of laughter rose from Susan and Mary and their entourage.

"I seem to have broken my microphone," Ben said wretchedly. His face was flushed. "What we were trying—It seemed to me the problem—"

"They're *laughing* at him," I whispered to Franklin, who was sitting next to me. "His own sister."

"Yes, they are," Franklin said.

"I can't help feeling sorry for him," I said. "Don't you feel sorry for him?"

"No," Franklin said.

Ben finally answered the question, which was whether he had ever discussed with his sister or anyone else, taking the project to a different publisher.

"Yes," he said, "I did."

"With whom?" the judge asked.

"At some point," Ben said. "I can't remember having a discussion of it with my sister, as a matter of fact. Ask me a specific—another specific question."

"'With whom?' is a specific question," the judge said.

"With whom? I must have said it to Andrew at some point. You know, the thing is, that we have been talking about this a lot recently within the last month. And so I can't remember what was said—" The judge said that he was really only interested in those events that occurred more than a month or two ago. "All right," Ben said. "More than a month or two back, I don't believe there was any discussion about bringing it to another publisher."

Paul moved on to Ben's statement that he had confused Academy Chicago with the University of Chicago Press. In the summer of 1987, Franklin had given Ben Academy's catalog and some newspaper articles about Academy. Did Ben read them? Ben said he looked at them; he didn't read them.* And why, Paul asked, did Ben think Franklin had given his mother copies of the spiral notebooks?

There was a very good reason for that, Ben said. He had been "reading some of the—some of these stories for the letters and Franklin and I talked about them and I was eager to read them. And she was going to look at them. And it turned out that she couldn't read all of these and I couldn't either. But she passed them on to me so I could read them—not with the idea that they would be a book, but with the idea that I would find them interesting."

"So Mr. Dennis provided you with spiral notebooks because he thought you—provided your mother with the spiral notebooks because he thought you might find them interesting?"

"That was the research that was being done preliminary to the decision that was to be made about the possible publication of my father's uncollected stories. A thing I made very clear to Mr. Dennis is that final decision time was going to come. The first thing to do, he seemed to think, and I agreed, was to find the stories. So these were the stories that he found. The idea that this would become a book, well . . . . "

"Mr. Cheever," Paul said, "having found the stories, was it then time to make the selection?"

"He hadn't found them all," Ben said. "And I think you know that before you decide whether you're going to use a story or not, you've got to read it. Maybe that's a novel idea for a lawyer, but in publishing, people

---

*In his deposition Ben said he read an article about Academy in the *Washington Post* while he was riding in the elevator in the Pan Am Building. The reader is reminded, too, that at the Chez Vong luncheon, Franklin specifically rejected the suggestion that he take the stories to the Princeton University Press because the project was too commercial for a university press.

ordinarily read things before they decide whether they're going to publish them."

"Was it then time—" Paul began, clearly closing in on the crucial question: why hadn't the Cheevers made a selection?

Ben interrupted, saying, "You couldn't read all these stories—"

At this point the judge cut in. "This is not getting us anywhere," he said. "Let's change the subject for a moment." He began to question Ben about whether he was living at home with his parents in 1978; did he know anything about the "process that was gone through" with the Knopf book? Ben repeated everything that Gottlieb had said about borrowing volumes of the *New Yorker* from a friend and so on. But no, he himself didn't know anything about the way the work was put together in the 1970s. The judge asked whether just his mother would make editorial decisions or would it be a family decision?* Ben repeated that they would all end by agreeing, they would all come to something that would make them happy, and so forth. The judge asked whether it might not be worthwhile to study the "poorer and earlier works" of accomplished artists for "cultural understanding purposes as opposed to intrinsic merit?" Ben said these stories weren't impossible to get; he had copies of some of them himself. Had Ben, the judge asked, thought the stories would be annotated "with editorial comment and descriptive background" by Academy? Yes, Ben thought that would have been a good idea. "Did Franklin Dennis," the judge asked, "strike you as having adequate editorial abilities and depth of publishing background to accomplish that sort of work?"

Ben said that one thing about Franklin was that he wanted to be accommodating. So Ben thought if it got to that point—to the point where they had six or eight stories that Mummy thought was going to make a nice book—then if they thought it could be annotated, someone else could have come up to annotate it. But no, Ben didn't think Franklin could accomplish it. Toward the end of December, Ben was beginning to suspect that no, Franklin wouldn't. Not that he was incapable of it, but that he wouldn't do it and wouldn't think of doing it.

The judge asked Ben whether he had ever done any editing. And would

---

*Mrs. Cheever had already testified that morning that she did not consult her children about these things; she relied on her literary agency.

Ben agree that "the worst thing that an editor can be to his author is accommodating?" Ben said that an editor has to be both firm and accommodating, to which the judge responded that it was tough to be both at once, and Ben said that you have to be both: "if you're too firm you'll never have any authors, and if you're too accommodating, they'll never have any success."

When Paul proceeded with the examination after this exchange, he did not take up again the line of questioning about when Ben intended to make his selection of the stories. He asked instead about the introduction. Had Ben objected to the choice of Le Carré or Raymond Carver? The judge interrupted again. "By the way," he said to Ben, "do people get paid for writing introductions? .... Any time I do a foreword to an attorney's legal book, all I get is a free copy of the book."

"Your Honor," Garbus said, "I'm prepared to represent you."

Everybody was having a swell time, except all of us and possibly Ben, who was now allowed to step down so that Garbus could begin his parade of expert witnesses—all expert in contract, which the judge had said should be decided in Chicago.

First came Ellis Levine, who had been in the Random House legal department since 1975. He interpreted the contract to read that Mary Cheever should select the stories. The first paragraph of the contract did not, he said, convey Mrs. Cheever's copyrights, however: it constituted "a transfer of ownership to the exclusive rights in the work which the author delivers under paragraph one and which the publisher finds satisfactory in form and content." In response to a question from the judge, Levine said that he didn't know about what work Gottlieb and Cheever did together, but he knew that frequently when an editor is working with an author with whom he's worked before, they had lengthy discussions about what was going to be in the book before they finally came to terms on a contract and had a contract prepared.

"Well," said His Honor, "that sort of stands in stark contrast to the publishing agreement at issue, where they entered into an agreement without selecting stories."

When Paul began to question the witness, he took care to put a few things on the record. He and Ellis Levine, he said, had been classmates at Harvard Law School.

"What a coincidence," the court said.

And, Paul continued, he and Mr. Levine had had a conversation outside the court that morning before the door was unlocked: Paul had asked Mr. Levine what he expected to testify about, and Mr. Levine had refused to tell him, wasn't that true?

Yes, Mr. Levine said. Mr. Garbus had asked him not to tell him.

And, Paul said, he had told Mr. Levine that if he was coming here as someone independent and unbiased, he would talk to Paul and tell him what his testimony was going to be. But Mr. Levine had refused to do that. And Mr. Levine had sat through the entire hearing, hadn't he?

Yes, Levine said, yesterday and thus far that morning. He had, as noted, sat at the plaintiff's table and consulted frequently with Garbus.

"You did that," Paul asked, "at the request of Mr. Garbus? . . . . Is there any attorney-client relationship between Mr. Garbus and Random House?" Levine said there wasn't any. "Why," Paul asked, "have you sat here through the entire hearing?"

Because Garbus asked him to, Levine said.

The judge asked Levine if he was being paid and, upon receiving an affirmative reply, remarked that that was a good reason for him to be there. Paul asked the witness whether, in the hundreds of contracts for anthologies that he had reviewed at Random House, "any of them involved the writings of a single author who was deceased at the time the publishing agreement was entered into?"

Levine didn't recall.

After a discussion of copyright, in which Paul attempted to demonstrate that Mrs. Cheever had not "conveyed" any copyrights to Academy Chicago, but had granted publishing rights only, the judge entered the scene again. What, he asked, did "term of copyright" refer to in this contract—did it refer to the rights that existed when the stories were first published? Ellis Levine said he thought it did, but the judge said he thought it didn't. This, he said, was "a particular hitch in all of this," and there was "an additional aspect which seems to cloud the situation": this was the clause that required the author to deliver the manuscript as finally arranged by the editor. "Who," the judge added, "in this instance is Franklin Dennis . . . . Have you ever seen something like that stuck into an anthology publishing agreement?"

"Not in those words," the witness replied cautiously.

"If all the editor has to do is select which stories are going to be published and line them up in a row," the judge said, "and if the author is determining what should be in the manuscript, what is the editor's role in this type of publishing agreement?"

Levine said he wasn't certain, beyond the editor doing the arranging.

"What does 'arranging' mean?" the court demanded.

Levine said it was ambiguous "to my mind." But what was not ambiguous, he added, was that the author was supposed to deliver the manuscript.

Shortly thereafter, it was time for lunch.

26

Evidentiary Hearing, Day 2, P.M.: "Do You Contend That She Knew What She Was Doing When She Did That?"

After trailing through the hot, muggy streets for a protracted period, we finally ate lunch in a hospital cafeteria—the only public eating place where Paul felt safe from Garbus's group.

At 2:10, we were back in court, Levine still on the stand. After some discussion about whether the contract gave Academy control of anthology rights—Paul said it didn't, Levine said it did, and the judge agreed with Levine—the witness was dismissed to resume his seat at the plaintiff's table, and Jordan was called to the stand. Garbus asked him, among other things, whether he thought the stories were a gold mine and whether Franklin had talked to him about "some" uncollected stories. Then the judge entered the fray.

"If," he said, "the work were to contain all the uncollected stories, and if Mr. Dennis were going to arrange them, what function would Mrs. Cheever as the author have to play?"

Jordan said she was to give Academy her approval, "in the sense of permission to publish the work as a whole. That's implicit, it seems to me."

"Well," the court said, "what do you mean, 'publish the work as a whole'? Suppose she said, 'I like these twenty-five stories and I don't want these twenty-five stories.'"

"We actually tried to elicit that kind of response," Jordan said. "And our contention is that by keeping in constant touch with Ben and/or Mrs. Cheever, by delivering these blue spiral-bound volumes, that we were saying, 'This is what we've turned up. This is what we hope to publish. What do you think of these?' And we never had from Mrs. Cheever any written or verbal response to that gesture."

"Well," the court observed, "the reviewers will tell you what they think of a book but generally the author writes the book."

Jordan replied that Mrs. Cheever was not the author of the book.

The judge said it seemed to him that whether "the denomination of 'author' is correct or incorrect, it certainly connotes some greater function in putting out the work than you are now saying she was supposed to have." Jordan said it was clear to all of us that she was not meant to trot out to the local library and to spend four or five months getting material through Inter-Library Loan. The judge said everybody agreed about that. "That being the case," Jordan said, "the burden really was on us, on Franklin and Academy, to ferret out the material which, in fact, is what we did."

The judge said Mrs. Cheever would probably not disagree with that. He launched into a litany of quotes from Mrs. Cheever: she says that locating the stories was one of Mr. Dennis's functions . . . . She says that part of her function as an author was to select stories and decide on what was going to be published . . . . She says the blue volumes were just left with her . . . . She found them virtually illegible, and she thought it was a report, a report on what had been found to date.

Jordan replied that the blue volumes had been sent to her to elicit a response and she had never said to us that they were illegible. The judge observed that Jordan and Mrs. Cheever had spoken only "on one occasion." When Jordan finished recounting the two phone conversations he had had with Mrs. Cheever, the judge said, "The Cheevers take the position that the works of John Cheever are markedly better in the post–World War II period than the pre–World War II period. When did you first become aware of that critical distinction in his works which they place [*sic*] . . . . When did you first become aware that they take the position that most or all of the pre–World War II stories would not be reprinted?"

Jordan said, "To this day, no one has said to us, 'We don't like this story, we don't like this story, we don't like this story' either in a letter or verbally." The only contact we had from the Cheever family or its agents, he said, involved termination of the agreement: "not negotiation, not elimination of certain stories—but termination of the agreement."

"Well," the court said, "we're not really getting at what I'm getting at."

The Cheever children seemed irritated by Jordan's testimony. Garbus was sitting at the plaintiff's table, leaving the questioning to the judge. Susan kicked Garbus's chair several times and whispered to him loudly that she thought he should object. Garbus ignored her. Finally, with considerable bustle, Susan and Ben gathered their things, pushed past us to the aisle, and left the courtroom.

The judge asked whether Jordan thought the early stories were "artistically as strong"—presumably he meant as strong as the later stories. Jordan said he thought some of them were; they were vastly different. As a matter of fact, he said, he found some of the very early stories quite brilliant; others weren't brilliant but still showed the genesis of Cheever's artistic development. Jordan quoted Donaldson, who had said that even the weakest of the stories had some flashes of brilliance or scraps of interesting dialogue. Cheever was there, Jordan said, and you could see his development, which is why we had decided to arrange the stories chronologically.

"That's a different answer than the question I asked," the judge said. "Are the earlier stories artistically of the same merit as the older stories?" Presumably by "older" Goettel meant "later." Jordan said he thought some were, yes. "What percentage?" the judge asked. Jordan said it was pretty hard to put something like that in percentages. He guessed that twenty to twenty-five out of fifty were on a par with vintage Cheever.

When it was Paul's turn to cross-examine, the judge interrupted with a second invitation to Jordan to speculate. What if Mrs. Cheever refused to let Academy publish the stories she held copyright to? What if she took out every story she owned the copyright to? And what if, when Jordan called her—as he said he would do, in that case—she said, "'Well, I don't want to give away my copyrights. I don't mind giving away those that are in the public domain or those that are owned by somebody else, but you're not getting mine for three hundred and thirty-seven dollars.'"

Jordan said it would have been awfully late for her to do something like that, and it didn't happen, of course, but if it did happen, in theory it would be something we would want to negotiate. The court said the way Jordan was describing it now, she was never meant to deliver any manuscript at all; Mr. Dennis was to "get up" a manuscript, and she was to approve it. Jordan said that since she was not required to deliver the manuscript, her approval was what was left for her, yes. The judge said he didn't understand what Jordan meant when he said she was not required to deliver a manuscript. He read out paragraph 2 of the contract, which, thanks to me, said, "The author will deliver . . . . " "That certainly sounds like the standard delivery of a manuscript by an author," he said.

Jordan said that Franklin Dennis's function in getting the material and presenting it to her was probably not far removed from what Robert Gottlieb did with John Cheever. "But," the judge said, "they didn't go to contract until after the two of them had agreed on what was going to be published, at which point they denominated the work and they entered into a contract."

To me, sitting woebegone in my Baggie, this exchange between the judge and Jordan was beginning to sound very much like an argument. I was not, of course, a lawyer, but it sounded like an argument to me. I remembered miserably the day Jordan was fashioning the contract and his asking me, "Shall I say 'will deliver' or 'has delivered'?" and my pedantic response that we had not yet put a manuscript together, so why not say "will deliver"? If we had said "has delivered," Mrs. Cheever would have signed the contract anyway because she never had any intention of "delivering" a manuscript herself. So I had made a stupid decision and provided a convenient loophole to create a noose that could be—and now clearly was being—put around our necks.

Jordan pointed out that unlike the Knopf situation, we didn't know what was out there when we drew up the contract, so it had to be done that way. and the judge said that what Jordan was really saying was that the language in the contract didn't mean what it said and the editor was to "get up a manuscript and, at most, run it by Mrs. Cheever." Jordan replied that the understanding was implicit among all of us that Mrs. Cheever was not expected to put together a manuscript; that was part of our function, "to get it and show it to her, which in fact was what we did."

"Why doesn't the publishing agreement say that?" the judge demanded.

Jordan said that publishing agreements, like most human beings, are fallible, and that we had altered our standard agreement as best we could to suit the circumstance. The judge's reply to that was that Jordan's "earlier testimony" had indicated that he "didn't do any altering at all," that he sent it out "almost in its unrevised printed form and that the alterations were made by the Cheevers' agent, Creative Management, Incorporated [*sic*]." Paul interrupted here to point out that the judge had asked *Franklin,* not Jordan, about these alterations,—Jordan had not given any "earlier testimony," of course—and he suggested that the judge ask Jordan about these alterations now. Jordan accordingly explained who had crossed out what and written in what.

When Paul asked what steps had been taken to find copyright information on the stories, the judge cut in to ask Jordan if he knew what happened to copyrights when the holder "becomes defunct. Assume it's a publishing company, a magazine company, and it goes out of existence."

Jordan said he thought it reverted to the original copyright holder, "if it's a magazine, let's say." "Assume that the copyright holder is dead," the judge said. "Then what?"

Jordan said that he supposed if the copyright holder died intestate, there was a problem. He could leave that part of his estate to relatives. "Not according to the plaintiffs' counsel," the judge said. "They say it goes by operation of law."

This was a reference to the situation that ensued when copyright was renewed after the death of the author and the heirs shared, by law, rights in those renewed copyrights. Jordan did not see a connection between this and the rather complicated defunct magazine question, so he said he wasn't equipped to answer the question. "Some of these magazines that published the earlier Cheever stories have ceased to exist," the judge said.*

Paul, taking the reins again, asked Jordan specifically, "just to be sure there is no confusion," whether he thought Mrs. Cheever was assigning any of her copyrights to him or whether any member of the Cheever family was assigning any copyrights of any kind. Jordan's answer was no. "All you were receiving," Paul said, "was the right to publish?" Jordan said that was correct.

When Jordan was finally released and Garbus began to call his other witnesses, Susan and Ben returned to the courtroom.

Garbus's next witness was Rhoda Gamson, who had been a "director of contracts" for twenty-eight years at various New York publishing houses. Her position was that our contract was so amorphous that it didn't convey anything to us at all. On cross-examination, Paul asked her whether if the book was called "The Complete Uncollected Stories of John Cheever"—a

---

*There can be many complications when magazines hold the copyright to stories. If the magazine assigns the rights to the author, there is one situation; if the magazine does not assign rights and does not renew copyright, that constitutes another situation. A third situation arises when a magazine renews the copyright for one issue of the magazine but not for the individual stories and does not assign rights in those stories to the author. Some of these situations raise questions that have never been resolved by the courts.

title supplied by Judge Goettel—that title in a contract would be an amorphous description of a body of writing. "Well," the expert responded, "it's amorphous to the extent that the author hasn't delivered the manuscript yet. You have no idea what the author is going to do with all of these stories."

"Moreover," the judge added, "it's only a tentative title . . . . "

Ms. Gamson told Paul there was no difference between transfer of a copyright and a license to publish; she was not a lawyer, however. She had been a music major at college.

Paul objected to the third expert witness, Nancy Coffey, who was going to say the same things that the other experts had said. The judge sustained the objection. Maura Wogan then read into the record several pages of Jordan's deposition in which he explained the publishing process and why the book had to come out in September. This was an extremely tedious procedure, and the reason for it was unclear to us.

There ensued a discussion between Paul and Judge Goettel, during which Paul took the position that nothing that had come into the evidentiary hearing could justify the issuance of a preliminary injunction. The judge responded with some of Mrs. Cheever's arguments. Reminded by Paul that we had a tentative trial date in three weeks, Goettel said there was "a chicken and egg situation between the contract agreements and the copyrights." Paul said that we were not contending that Mrs. Cheever had assigned any copyrights to Academy Chicago; we were claiming that she gave us "permission to publish certain stories."

"Which stories?" the judge asked.

"The uncollected stories of John Cheever," Paul said, "every last one of them, provided, however, that there was an understanding that there would be a selection process."

"Even some she didn't know existed?" the judge asked.

Paul said that was right: "It was a finite body of literature which couldn't be expanded because unfortunately her husband was deceased. And within that finite body, there was to be—there was, by understanding, not by contract but by understanding—there was to be a selection process. But she conveyed her rights, such as she had, to publish whatever stories worked their way into the final selection process, absolutely."

"Do you contend that she knew what she was doing when she did that?" the judge asked.

Paul said he thought that ICM knew exactly what it was doing. The judge said that he "somehow got the impression that at some point or other Andrew Wylie supplanted ICM as the Cheevers' literary agent with respect to this work."

Paul was surprised at this. "Never," he said, "did Mrs. Cheever suggest for a minute that Andrew Wylie had replaced ICM. I believe she said she never met or spoke to Andrew Wylie at any time until mid-June."

"Yeah, but that's the point," the judge said. "When you had these settlement discussions in mid-June and you were talking business aspects, instead of ICM being there, Andrew Wylie was there."

"Oh, no sir," Paul said. "No, sir."

"Wylie wasn't there?" the judge asked, surprised.

"No, sir," Paul said emphatically.

Garbus entered the discussion. "They tried to create Wylie as this Satan, why he's all over the place. He spoke to Mrs. Cheever once, he met her in the house once. He had nothing to do with the settlement, was never involved in the settlement. The reason the Court believes he's all over the place is they have tried to make him the provocation for all of this."

The judge dropped the subject and said he would reserve his decision on Paul's motion on the lack of evidence for a preliminary injunction. Paul wanted to know whether the "sketch-versus-story issue" was still in the case. The court responded that it was in the case but as "a very subsidiary issue." The "threshold issue," he said, was whether Mary Cheever was going to be given the power to select the stories. If she was going to be given that power and she didn't like sketches, she could drop them. If she wasn't going to be given that power, he didn't see anything in the contract that said you couldn't publish sketches. His own feeling, he said, was that there "is a distinction, but it's not a distinction that is easily demarked. It's like a question of how high is up." In some instances, he said, the sketches "have greater literary merit than a full-blown short story." So he was suggesting, he went on, that it wasn't worth pursuing this distinction "at the moment. If it ever becomes of any critical nature—and I don't think it's going to— I'll let you know."

I found this whole line of reasoning baffling. It seemed to me that Mrs. Cheever had always had the power to select the stories and had never exercised that power. We had never taken it from her. As Jordan had pointed

out, none of the Cheevers had ever said they didn't like any particular stories. I couldn't understand why this was not an important point. And I
didn't see how the sketch "issue" could "become critical."

Paul asked the judge whether he would reserve his ruling until Judge
Kiley resolved the contract issue. "No," Goettel said, he would work on the
case during the last week in July. The only thing he was expecting from
Paul was legal papers on the "issue" of the children's copyright. He added
that "if somebody could come up with a case that involved an anthology
contract by someone who hadn't written the works and who was to be the
author but didn't apparently have much control over what was going to be
published, I would be interested in seeing that case."

"I'll write one tonight, Judge," Garbus said.

We ourselves took the suggestion seriously, and in the next weeks compiled, with the help of our son Mark and the Scott Meredith Agency, a
collection of contracts between publishing houses and the heirs of dead
authors.

Paul asked permission to attempt to locate Maggie Curran, who had
retired from ICM and was off someplace apparently writing a book. The
judge said that if Paul "popped up" with Maggie Curran and she had something "vitally important to reveal on the facts" and if he hadn't decided the
case, and if he wasn't on trial with something else, he might listen to her.

Garbus asked that the temporary restraining order (TRO) be extended.
"Well," the judge said, "they obviously can't publish before September. But
that doesn't mean they won't take some pertinent steps in that direction in
the interim."

Paul said that the TRO was very broad and "handcuffed" Academy because it prevented the company from giving the bound galleys to book
reviewers or writers who might give advance notices. The judge said Academy had given out galleys already to "the more potent reviewers like the
Washington Post and the *New York Times*." Paul agreed that the *Times* had a
galley. Garbus said most of the media had galleys already. Paul said that
that wasn't true and Garbus knew it. The court remarked that "most of the
media doesn't have it. But the influential ones do." Paul said that the most
influential were *Publishers Weekly* and the library periodicals. Garbus observed that there were "very few reviewers that don't have Xerox copies."

The judge said he would continue the restraining order for ten days,
with one exception: "You can give one of the blue bound copies to *Publish-*

ers Weekly. If they haven't already borrowed somebody else's, it will be quite a convenience for them." Paul thanked him twice. The judge said he was going on vacation and wouldn't be back until a week from Monday.

"Your Honor," Garbus said, "have a good vacation."

"Your Honor," Paul said sincerely, "may I say on behalf of all of us—I'm sure I speak for Mr. Garbus as well—I don't know that I've ever had an evidentiary hearing in front of a judge who listened as attentively and participated as vigorously as Your Honor did, and we appreciate that."

"Well," the court said with a shy smile, "it's very nice of you to say that. I ask too many questions. Good day."

27

Interlude between Courtrooms: "The Second Thing They Do, Is They Come before You in a Judge Bash"

We went off to Boston in a propeller plane to give our lecture at Radcliffe. We were, of course, glad that the hearing was over, but it had not left us with good feelings. As we were leaving the courtroom, Paul warned us not to speak to the press: this was "right on the edge," he said; it could go either way, and he didn't want the judge reading something that might affect his decision. We ourselves were not convinced that things could go either way, but we turned down an interview with a woman from the local Gannett paper. I remained enclosed in my dismal Baggie.

While Jordan and I sat tensely glum in our wavering aircraft, with an occasional spurt of water falling on me from the light fixture, Mark, Jean, and Bruce were in Montrose with Franklin and Mary. To work off their frustration, they put on a series of playlets based on the recent hearing, taping them for our later amusement. Mark played Mary Cheever, Franklin was the judge as straight man, while Bruce was both Garbus and the famous off-duty policeman who had dared to deliver the summons to Mary Cheever, despite her age. There was a heartrending scene in which she, in the garden among the chrysanthemums, at first mistaking the officer for a menial, directed him to the back door, and then, when the true significance of his mission was borne in upon her, gave a piercing shriek of horror. In a third role, Bruce, employing a prep school accent, delivered a rambling monologue à la Ben Cheever. And Mark, risking serious injury to his throat, read aloud, in his Mary Cheever voice, a hostile poem, apparently addressed to her husband, from her poetry collection, *The Need for Chocolate and Other Poems.*

All this naturally occasioned great hilarity in the Dennis household, and made everybody there feel better. We, however, remained mired in depression, despite our heartening reception by the Radcliffe students, who seemed fascinated by our distinctive approach to publishing and even more by our recounting of the main facts of the Cheever case. We were not cheered even by a call to our Boston hotel room from Paul, who was feeling very optimistic. He told us that an ICM person by the name of Herb Cheyette wanted to be deposed because he had a tale to tell, and this could be a significant break. Paul was pleased because the judge had not immediately granted a permanent injunction and had allowed us to send a review copy to *Publishers Weekly.* He didn't understand, he said, why we were so depressed; hadn't we seen Garbus slink off after the hearing with his tail between his legs? If he were the judge in Chicago, Paul said, he would give Mrs. Cheever a specific time period in which to name those stories that she felt should not be published and tell her that she would have to give good reasons why each story had to be dropped. Then he would order the book published without those stories, but he would not allow her to drop more than, say, fifteen stories.

On our return to Chicago, we learned that Garbus was trying to get our case there dismissed on the ground that a sufficient hearing had already been held in White Plains. In her brief, Maura Wogan said, first, that a continuation of the action in Illinois would be "a complete waste of judicial resources and an unjustified imposition upon all concerned." Academy could not obtain relief from Kiley's court, she said, because jurisdiction over copyright is exclusively federal. Second, the Chicago court had "no jurisdiction whatever" over the Cheever children. Third, Goettel's court— the United States District Court for the Southern District of New York— was capable of resolving all issues, including the contract claim. Fourth, a Chicago hearing would simply duplicate the New York hearing. Fifth, all the witnesses lived and worked in New York and were planning to testify in the federal action. Sixth, Mary Cheever and Franklin Dennis lived in New York. Lastly, several key witnesses were not subject to subpoena in Illinois and would be unwilling or unlikely to appear. And not only were there no appropriate witnesses available to Mrs. Cheever "in Chicago or any other city besides New York," but there were also "no major publishers with headquarters outside of New York City, aside from university presses and specialty houses."

A good deal of paper accumulated in connection with this Cheever motion for dismissal. Paul said Mrs. Cheever spoke "with forked tongue," and Russell Smith accused Academy of employing "the big lie technique." Apart from hyperbole, I found these Cheever arguments disquieting. Judge Goettel had certainly heard great hunks of the contract case in New York, although it had been Paul's understanding that he was not going to do that. Garbus had announced early on that he was going to get the Chicago case dismissed and moved to New York. Jordan and I felt that a trial in White Plains would be a catastrophe for us.

While the lawyers filed briefs, our son Mark took literally Goettel's statement that he would like to see examples of cases involving "an anthology contract by someone who hadn't written the work and who was to be the author but didn't apparently have much control over what was going to be published." Mark busied himself finding examples of contracts for such anthologies (although these contracts, of course, did not necessarily evolve— or degenerate—into "cases"). He came up with the names of posthumous collections by Eli Bishop, Vladimir Nabokov, Wallace Stevens, Robert Lowell, Flannery O'Connor, William Faulkner, James Agee, F. Scott Fitzgerald, Eugene O'Neill, Ernest Hemingway, Robert Frost, Thomas Merton, Carson McCullers, Thomas Wolfe, Gertrude Stein, and John Crowe Ransom.

Scott Meredith supplied us with some copies of contracts. In one, the contract for *The Short Stories of Philip K. Dick*, the Estate of Philip Dick, "hereinafter called the Author, licenses the publisher to publish said stories in the English language." One could assume that the Estate of Philip Dick was not going to run around selecting stories and breathing heavily down the neck of Martin Greenberg, the editor—especially since the contract specifically stated that Mr. Greenberg would select the stories.

In another Scott Meredith contract, the Author is the "Colonial Bank as Trustee" under the will of Manfred B. Lee and the estate of Frederic Dannay. Here the Author agrees to deliver to the publisher three finally revised copies of the manuscript. I would guess that no one expected the Colonial Bank to burn the midnight oil collecting and revising the manuscript for *The Best of Ellery Queen*.

Jordan and I went to the library and spent some time examining short story collections. We were struck by Joseph Blotner's introduction to *The Uncollected Stories of William Faulkner*, published in 1981 by Vintage Books (a division of Random House). Mr. Blotner comments that some of the stories "are clearly apprentice work, but . . . display qualities to be found in the best fiction . . . . Taken together, these stories present a view of Faulkner's developing art over a span of more than thirty years." Faulkner wrote some of these stories, Mr. Blotner says, because "he was a craftsman who depended exclusively on his pen for his livelihood and very often had to write what he thought would sell rather than what he wanted to write." The stories in this Vintage collection are printed "in the order in which they appeared in the magazines." Among the many people whose help Mr. Blotner acknowledges there are no relatives of William Faulkner, although many of the copyrights are held by Jill Faulkner Summers and Estelle Faulkner, who apparently did not fear that the publication of "apprentice work" would damage William Faulkner's reputation.

In addition to providing Paul with the names of various posthumously published collections, Mark tracked down Maggie Curran, who was working part-time as a maid at a summer hotel on Block Island. Both ICM and Garbus had said they did not know where she was. Paul wanted to depose her and, now that she had been found, Garbus wanted to depose her, too. Garbus wanted to depose a lot of people: the Scott Meredith Agency; Dell and other bidders in the paperback auction, including Harper & Row; Bill Rickman, vice president of the Chicago bookselling chain Kroch's and Brentano's; and Carl Kroch, the venerable son of the founder of that firm.

One person Garbus apparently did not want to depose was Herb Cheyette of ICM—he whose deposition Paul saw as a possible breakthrough, since Mr. Cheyette had let it be known that he wanted to be deposed because he had some things to say. The lawyer for ICM was Sidney H. Stein of Stein, Zauderer, Ellenhorn, Frischer & Sharp. Mr. Stein arranged for Maggie Curran to be deposed in his offices, but there seemed to be some confusion over when Mr. Cheyette could be available. He might, Mr. Stein said, have to go to California. Garbus wrote to Sidney Stein to suggest that Mr. Cheyette's deposition be postponed to the end of August or the beginning of September. Paul protested to Sidney Stein that he had issued a subpoena and Stein had agreed that Cheyette would appear in the offices of Stein, Zauderer, Ellenhorn, Frischer & Sharp at 10:00 A.M. on August 3.

Mr. Cheyette was not present in those offices for a deposition on August 3, and on August 26, Garbus asked Judge Goettel to quash Paul's deposition subpoena directed to Cheyette on the grounds of "relevance." Judge Goettel said he thought it would be a good idea to postpone Garbus's motion until after the Chicago trial. Paul agreed to this, reminding Stein that "the subpoena to Mr. Cheyette remains outstanding" and a new deposition date would be set. In the end, there was no date, as far as I know, and Mr. Cheyette was never deposed. Whatever he had to say, Mr. Cheyette will go to his Maker with it unsaid—at least in court.

On July 27, Maggie Curran was deposed in Sidney Stein's offices; Stein said it "made most sense" for the deposition to take place there so that neither of the contesting parties would "obtain any presumed edge" by having it in a Cheever or Academy law office. The implication seemed to be that ICM was neutral in this affair.

Maggie Curran's testimony lacked a certain spark; in fact, it verged on the robotic. It also lacked some consistency. Asked by Garbus whether she had "put in that word editor" next to Franklin's name, she replied, "I did not write that Franklin Dennis description." Asked if she had crossed out "co-author" and written in "editor," she replied, "No." But somewhat later, she said, "I deleted the word 'author' and substituted the word 'editor.'" At one point Paul suggested that Garbus stop shaking his head "no" at her when he wanted a negative reply. She answered Garbus woodenly: Mary Cheever was the author; Mary Cheever controlled the book; Mr. Miller never told her that Academy intended to publish all the uncollected stories.

She had been, she said, at ICM since 1973 and had retired at the end of October 1987. From January through April 1988, she worked three days a week for the Atlantic Liberty Savings Bank in Brooklyn, and she was presently on the housekeeping staff of the Surf Hotel in Block Island. In June or early July 1988, she had had a conference call from Garbus's office and talked to Maura Wogan and Herb Cheyette.* She had had several conversations with Cheyette; he had called to tell her that she had been subpoenaed and that Mr. Stein was her lawyer. She had met Garbus for the first time the previous day, in Mr. Stein's office, where Garbus "went over the contract" with her.

She said she had never discussed the contract with Lynn Nesbit until Nesbit asked her about it in January or February, so Ms. Nesbit found out about the publishing agreement only "when there was an attempt to break the contract." What, Paul asked, did she mean by "an attempt to break the

---

*The reader will note that Garbus did not seem to know where Maggie Curran was when Paul raised the question in court on July 12.

contract?" Well, Maggie replied, that was what she was told; she couldn't remember who told her. It was during her visit to the office in early 1988. Paul asked her whether she had any "understanding that this was to be a trade book of short stories sold in bookstores." Garbus objected, and Sidney Stein joined in the objection. Paul asked her whether she had any understanding at all "as to what the purpose was in publishing this book." She said she objected to the word "understanding." Paul tried again, asking her if she had "any knowledge or information as to what the parties anticipated with regard to the purpose of this book." Over Garbus's objection, Maggie said, "No."

Asked about her ICM telephone logs, she said she stored them in a cupboard. Paul asked Stein to check those logs; none had been produced for Academy. "What particular information in the telephone logs were you looking for?" Stein asked. "What are you requesting?" Paul said he was requesting "any reference to any telephone call, be it incoming or outgoing, that pertains in any way to the matters that are in litigation here." "In Maggie Curran's telephone logs," Stein said. Paul responded, "Or anyone else if there was someone else who had telephone conversations." That included, he said, Lynn Nesbit, Herb Cheyette, or Lew Grimes.

"Your request," Sidney Stein said, "is certainly taken under advisement."

After the deposition, Paul wrote a letter to Stein officially requesting the logs. It is probably unnecessary to say that the logs were never produced. Paul asked Garbus for his notes taken in his talks with Maggie Curran. Garbus refused to give them to him.

On the same day that Maggie was deposed, Garbus deposed Ted Chichak of the Scott Meredith Agency. Paul was present but only to represent Academy. Garbus asked Chichak whether he had told various people the case was settled. How many times had Chichak spoken to Paul? Did Chichak know that process servers were looking for him on Wednesday, Thursday, and Friday? What days in the previous week had Chichak been out of the office? Was he sick on Thursday? Had he gotten any phone calls from anyone in his office on Tuesday, Wednesday, Thursday, and Friday? Was Bill Haas—the foreign rights agent—in the office on those days? How far physically did Bill Haas sit from Chichak? Had Chichak talked to Bill Haas before he came in today? Had Chichak read articles in the *New York Times* about this case? Had he discussed those articles with anyone in publishing or at Academy? If the Cheevers won, had Chichak asked Academy whether they would stand behind him financially? Did he get an indemnity from them?

Chichak denied repeatedly that he had told anyone, or anyone had told him, that the case was settled or that he had been in his office Wednesday, Thursday, and Friday. He replied to the "indemnity" question by saying that Academy's assurances that they were entitled to go ahead with the book were enough, and Scott Meredith had agreed. "We were hired to do a job and we did it."

On Friday, July 29, Garbus fired off two consecutive faxes to Paul. In the first, he responded to Paul's request for the letters and journals by saying that Judge Goettel had said they should not be turned over to Academy unless there was "an adverse ruling by a court."* In the second fax, he demanded to know "the fee relationship" among Academy, Franklin, and Paul's firm Pope, Ballard. What were the legal fees, were they on an hourly basis, or were they on some kind of contingency? He said he found it "incredible, given Academy's financial condition" that it could afford to pay "the very substantial legal fees involved if the payments were made on a straight hourly basis." If, he wrote, Pope, Ballard had a contingency arrangement or financial interest in the book, they could "conceivably be considered a vicarious copyright infringer." If the Cheevers were successful before Judge Goettel, they intended to add other parties as copyright infringers, including Scott Meredith (presumably the agency), Academy's printer, and the Millers personally. He believed there were "over 12,000 separate acts of infringement and the Cheevers would receive a substantial judgment." He was asking for the name of the printer because the Cheevers did not believe that Academy could pay that judgment. If "neither Academy, Jordan Miller, Franklin Dennis nor Anita" would give him information about attorneys' fees, he would subpoena Pope, Ballard. If there were "vicarious liability," Pope, Ballard might have a claim against Academy, "posing potential conflict problems."

July 29 was also the day of Judge Kiley's hearing on the Cheevers' motion to dismiss the case. Garbus flew into Chicago for the hearing. M. Leslie Kite was, of course, present, and so were Jordan and I, although we had almost been afraid to come because we thought the judge might very well dismiss the case. It seemed crucially important to us that it be heard in Chicago and not in White Plains.

---

*When Judge Goettel could have said this was a mystery to us.

Judge Kiley began by saying that he had no view on whether the case should go forward on August 8, the tentative trial date, or whether it should be dismissed. Did Garbus have anything new to say?

Garbus had a great deal to say. All the issues before Judge Kiley, he said, "had each been discussed and some of them decided in a variety of ways before Judge Goettel." One issue was the date of publication; the judge heard "a great deal of testimony" on that. He speculated at length about what Judge Goettel—for whom he appeared to have great respect, bordering on reverence—would do: "I anticipate that he will, after having heard from them as to why they have to publish this book immediately and now it has to be set for publication and knowing that twice [*sic*] and you'll find out, and the testimony that we took yesterday and the documents that I'm going to hand up to you—there is no reason why this book can't be published a year, two years from now." The book, he said, was years off, even if the Cheevers lost the case. "The second thing they do," he said, "is they come before you in a judge bash and tell you without a transcript and—"

"They do what?" asked Judge Kiley.

"Judge bash," Garbus said. "In other words, they criticize Judge Goettel—without giving you a copy of the transcript and without telling you the particular ruling that he entered."* Goettel's remarks, he said, were "taken out of context and an old argument, long before he held a hearing and long before he rendered his decision, I think you will see Judge Goettel at that point had the benefit." Out of the White Plains hearing would come issues that would "collaterally estop parties and have a res judicata effect."†

"Was that a trial?" asked the judge, referring to the White Plains hearing.

"No," Garbus said, "a preliminary hearing."

"You're not going to get any res judicata or collateral estoppel coming out of a ruling on a preliminary injunction," Kiley said, "are you?"

"Of course you will," Garbus said. "I believe you will."

This statement led to an argument of considerable length between Garbus

---

*The transcript of the evidentiary hearing was not yet ready, and no ruling had been entered.

†*Res judicata* means "a thing decided." Both this and *collateral estoppel* are terms meaning that when a qualified court brings down a decision after a full, fair trial, neither party can litigate the course of action again in another court.

and the judge. Finally Kiley said that he and Garbus had a fundamental disagreement about findings of fact or conclusions of law that come out of preliminary hearings in the District Court of New York; he also had a disagreement with Garbus on res judicata. It was an "abstract interest" and really, he said, made no difference for these purposes. He noted that it was now 1:30, and he could give the lawyers only ten more minutes.

Paul said he hoped the judge would give him a chance to respond: "Very little of what Mr. Garbus said is true." He went on to point out that Goettel had stated over and over again that the contract issues were not before him, and Judge Kiley had similarly ruled that the contract issue belonged in Chicago. The hearing in White Plains, Paul said, concerned only the issue of the children's copyright. The Cheever children were not parties to the Chicago suit, and in any case only three stories were in question on that issue. "The only issue Judge Goettel is going to decide at this time," said Paul, looking into a decidedly cloudy crystal ball, "is whether the children are entitled to an injunction."

The judge asked what would happen if Academy prevailed on its contract claim in Chicago and Mrs. Cheever prevailed on the copyright claim in New York.

Paul said that in that case, three of the sixty-eight stories would have to be removed from the book. He said it was conceivable, although he had trouble imagining it, that if Kiley found the contract valid, Goettel could still rule that Mrs. Cheever had not licensed her copyrights to Academy. He didn't want to say categorically that that couldn't happen. He repeated that the most that could happen, however, was that "if Judge Goettel were to rule as far as he could for the Cheevers, three stories would have to be removed." It was important for the judge to know, Paul said, that if he were to dismiss this case, Academy and Franklin would be without any forum to bring their case. Paul said he knew of no case in the annals of Illinois jurisprudence where an action with a forum selection clause of Illinois was dismissed on any grounds and the case moved to another state. And there would be no federal jurisdiction because there was no diversity of citizenship—both Mrs. Cheever and Franklin were citizens of New York.* Academy would thus be left with no remedy for its contract case unless it filed in still another court—

---

*Diversity of citizenship is not required in a copyright case before a federal court. Copyright claims can be brought only in federal court.

presumably New York State or New York Supreme Court. And the whole process would have to start all over again.

Garbus responded that the critical issue between the parties was whether Mary Cheever had intended in the publishing agreement to convey her copyrights. Everything Paul had said was "utter nonsense." He turned to Paul, who was sitting at the plaintiff's table, and announced, raising his voice, that he was going to read Goettel's opinion accepting the case "and you tell me if I'm reading it wrong!" He lunged at Paul and thrust a fistful of papers almost under his nose, with a stabbing motion. "This is Judge Goettel's decision!" he shouted. "This is the hearing!"

"Counsel," the judge said, "we're not before a jury. You don't have to do something like that."

Garbus retreated and said that everything Paul had said about the Goettel hearing was "misrepresentation." "I'm not making this up," he said, brandishing his papers. The contract does not convey publishing rights, he said, because the contract says that she will deliver a manuscript and she never delivered a manuscript. She was never asked to deliver a manuscript. Academy claimed at the hearing that they had the right to deliver a manuscript. "One of us is living in fantasyland . . . . What the judge told Mr. Freehling," Garbus added, "he said, 'Why do you keep arguing about the children's issue? You have an issue here with respect to Mrs. Cheever.' He refused to deal with it." Addressing Kiley's question of, as he put it, "What happens if the two courts do this and the two courts do that?" Garbus said it was a simple issue. "The contract may be valid, and that's what Judge Goettel said, but valid for what?" His crystal ball at this point was clearer than Paul's.

Garbus said that when Paul called it "a permission question, Judge Goettel laughed him out of court. I'm not making this up." He then began to quote what he said was a statement from Judge Goettel. It quickly became evident that he was not reading a statement from Judge Goettel, but the truncated quotation from Nimmer that he had used, evoking Adam Walinsky's strenuous objections, in a brief for Goettel. As Garbus read from it, he said, "This is the hearing." Finally he interrupted himself to say, "I'm sorry—I'm now quoting—I've done something and I apologize—I'm now quoting from Nimmer which is not Judge Goettel. I thought it was, notwithstanding—in other words, to make it clear, the first paragraph I quoted to you was from Judge Goettel—" (which it wasn't; it was from Nimmer)

"—I am now quoting from Nimmer." But he was in fact repeating the "first paragraph," which he had just said was from Judge Goettel.

Judge Kiley cut this short by saying that he had decided to wait until he got the transcript of the White Plains hearing before deciding whether to dismiss the case. He remarked, with some asperity, that he was not concerned about "the private interests of the litigants." The forum selection clause had been determined to be enforceable and not unreasonable. But what he found "absolutely, fundamentally relevant" was "the question of the public interest." This was apparent to him, he said, as he was sure it was to Judge Goettel. "It makes absolutely no sense," he said, "from a public, judicial, administrative point of view, that two courts conduct two hearings that overlap, that are so substantially related to one another that in essence the same witnesses will be testifying in two different courts largely about the same subject area." He wasn't going to "cast the stone" about which party was abusing the process: "This is obviously a dispute carrying deeply felt feelings." What was important to him were the resources of two courts overburdened by litigants "both here and there whipsawing back and forth in their private stratagem to gain advantage or disadvantage." There was no question in his mind, he said, "that this dispute should be in one place. There is absolutely no question about it. And I can't imagine a judge, anywhere in this country, state or federal, who would say otherwise."

We certainly agreed with him. But why he couldn't imagine any judge saying otherwise was baffling, since Judge Goettel had said otherwise when he had accepted this case, knowing that it was already set for trial in Chicago. However, we have since learned that Paul could have tried to get the federal case removed to the federal court in Chicago and then consolidated with the circuit court. He had had a reasonable chance of doing that, apparently.

Kiley went on to say that he couldn't decide whether there was a real potential for inconsistent decisions between the two courts because Garbus and Paul had given him "about the most conflicting versions of what is going on in New York that in my short and limited experience I've ever seen." So he intended to wait until he got the transcripts and then he would decide "the public interest question." He would read the transcripts, read their briefs, and then call them in and tell them how he was going to rule on this. But in the meantime he suggested that both parties forget their differences for the moment and get together and see if the case couldn't be tried in New York to save a colossal waste of time and money. Of course, he said, Academy would have to sacrifice its forum selection clause.

Garbus said he would certainly agree to that. The judge acknowledged dryly that that was to be expected. Paul said he needed twenty-four hours to think about it.

We were not happy with this hearing. We were upset because we thought the judge was angry with us and would decide that the public interest dictated a dismissal. Paul, who admired Kiley for what he perceived to be his breadth of vision, said it was still possible the judge would take the case after he read the transcript because Goettel had clearly stated that the contract should be tried in Chicago. But, he added, if Kiley did decide to dismiss, it wouldn't be the end of the world.

"You can get a fair trial either here or in New York," Paul said earnestly. "Either judge will give you a fair trial."

28

Goettel's Opinion: "All Plaintiffs Will Prevail"

On Wednesday afternoon, August 3, Paul phoned in great excitement to tell us that Goettel's opinion had come down and that he had issued a preliminary injunction against the book. Paul had not yet been able to get hold of a copy of the opinion; he had found out about it only when Herbert Mitgang of the *New York Times* had called him for comment. Paul was away from his desk when the call came, and his secretary had told Mitgang that Paul knew nothing about the opinion. Paul phoned Adam Walinsky and told him to try to get a copy. Just as Paul hung up, Mitgang called back.

"What do you make of it?" Mitgang asked.

How, Paul wanted to know, had Mitgang been able to see the opinion so quickly? Mitgang's answer was that the *New York Times* had representatives at the court in Manhattan. Paul pointed out that Goettel's court was in White Plains. "They check through everything," Mitgang said. Paul commented that this injunction would hold only until there was a trial in Chicago.

"Show me where it says anything about a trial," Mitgang said.

"I can't show you anything," Paul said. "You've got the opinion."

Mitgang hung up.

The Westchester Gannett reporter called and told me that Judge Goettel said that even if the contract was found valid in Chicago, he did not intend to dismiss the case. I was surprised by this because I did not see how, if we had a valid contract, we could be accused of copyright violation. When we received the opinion, faxed to us by Paul, we found it to be a carefully crafted basic acceptance of Garbus's case, which would probably influence the judge in Chicago if he were to read it. It began with a brief retrospective of John Cheever's fifty-year career, describing him as "a major American literary figure." Mrs. Cheever was identified as "his literary executor." Franklin was called "a literary promoter and editor" who did "much" of his work for Academy Chicago, which, in its turn, was "a small publishing house in Chicago specializing in literary works of limited popular appeal but of purported cultural value." "Dennis," the judge wrote, having "obtained an introduction to Benjamin Cheever described Academy Chicago to him in such a way that the younger Cheever thought it was a university press associated with Chicago University [*sic*]."

The judge said that Mary Cheever had "envisioned" a "modest work" with a small printing over which she would have control because she knew her husband considered his early works inferior and didn't want his reputation "sullied by their collective publication." But Academy Chicago had "developed a different perspective" because "Dennis, as intermediary, was interested primarily in keeping both parties satisfied rather than in perfect harmony." And Academy Chicago believed that it "had found a gold mine in both the literary and financial sense." The judge even mentioned the "hostess gifts" that Mrs. Cheever had been so eager to describe in her testimony; those five books, the judge said, "purportedly of cultural value but not for mass publication . . . confirmed Mary Cheever's view that Academy Chicago was engaged in a limited project which was far from completion." Goettel made this statement despite the fact that Mrs. Cheever was given the books four months after she signed the standard commercial contract, and given them in conjunction with a nearly completed manuscript that she accepted without question.

Judge Goettel rejected the tentative title as meaningless, repeating his conviction that the book should have been called "The Complete Uncollected Stories of John Cheever." (No one, it is true, had been called upon to point out that you can't call something "complete" unless you know that it really is complete.) The publishing agreement was, he said, "ambiguous" and had to be construed against the defendant who prepared it. He contrasted it with the Knopf agreement with Cheever whereby, he said, Cheever himself put together the stories and delivered two copies to the publisher—this despite the testimony of Gottlieb and Mrs. Cheever that it was Gottlieb who chose the stories and put the omnibus volume together.

The Lanham Act claims did not, he said, require "a preliminary injunction at this time." The children's copyright "issue" he decided not to "resolve"; that wasn't necessary "for present purposes." In a footnote he mentioned the possibility that "the more altruistic arguments" about Cheever's reputation were "secondary to plaintiffs' interest in securing a larger share of what may be substantial sums of money." Garbus, he noted, believed that "hard- and soft-cover" sales of the book "will run into the millions of dollars." But that, he added, did "not detract from the validity of the Cheevers' claims."

He granted the strength of the forum selection clause in the contract, but he said that if he were to rule on the contract issue, Mary Cheever would "have a substantial likelihood of succeeding." If Judge Kiley should rule the contract valid, then "the issue of copyright violation would come to the fore." It was "simply unreasonable" to conclude that the contract's "intent" was that "Mrs. Cheever would license all of the uncollected stories of John Cheever to the defendant for publication." Consequently, even if Academy won in Chicago, "it would seem likely that one (Mrs. Cheever) or all plaintiffs will prevail on the copyright infringement claim" in White Plains. As a further tap on the arm to Judge Kiley and to us, Goettel remarked that "the copyright issues need never be reached if Mary Cheever prevails on the contract issue in Chicago."

The effect of this opinion upon us can be imagined. Paul was devastated. He had honestly believed that Judge Goettel would render a decision based on the evidence. And perhaps all U.S. citizens internalize some trust in the good faith of judges, especially federal judges. So we were deeply upset when we saw Garbus's flimsy case enshrined in this official form. We felt as though someone had died. The pleasure drained out of our work; we seriously considered closing down the press. Our legal bills were very high, and now there was the question of an appeal. We had thirty days to file one.

It had now become crucial that Kiley take this case; there was no longer any question, even in Paul's mind, about what would happen if there were a trial in White Plains.

Russell Smith wrote Goettel a letter telling him that Judge Kiley had "indefinitely postponed the August trial" and had reserved decision on Mrs. Cheever's motion to dismiss until he could read the transcript of the White Plains hearings. Smith told Goettel that Kiley had taken "a strong position against the maintenance of two separate actions in this dispute," and asked for permission to file a motion in White Plains for partial summary judgment.*

---

*A summary judgment is a preverdict judgment given in response to a plaintiff's motion, when only questions of law are in dispute or when the court's decision must be the same whether the court accepts the plaintiff's or the defendant's version of events. It removes the necessity for a trial.

On August 10, Judge Goettel wrote back to Smith (sending a copy, of course, to Paul and Walinsky):

> Dear Mr. Smith:
> In response to your letter of August 4th, it may be that Judge Kiley and I are playing Alphonse and Gaston with each other. However, his decision to postpone the Chicago trial was made before he had seen my recent opinion. I suggest that, if it has not already been done, Judge Kiley be sent a copy of my opinion and he then indicate whether that has changed his decision not to proceed with the Chicago trial. Obviously, if he does not change his position, you are free to proceed in whatever fashion you believe to be correct in this district.
>
> Very truly yours,
> Gerard L. Goettel

Judge Goettel's opinion received a good deal of press coverage. Mary Cheever was widely quoted as claiming that her husband would have been "horrified" by the book in question because it included "early work that was not up to his later standards." Adam Walinsky commented that he did not believe there could be any basis for a copyright infringement trial if the contract were upheld in Chicago.[1] Franklin called to tell us that in the report on the decision in the Gannett Westchester paper, Susan Cheever was quoted as saying, "the family might be forced to publish some of the stories after the case was resolved, to pay legal fees .... We don't want to suppress the stories, but they would have to be presented in a different way—in a way that shows this was an apprenticeship,' she said. 'Those stories are available now (in the original magazines) to anybody who wants to read them. Maybe some of them should be published again. We don't know yet.'"[2]

Franklin thought this statement was remarkable, since the family's case in White Plains had seemed to hinge on their conviction that these stories would damage Cheever's reputation. "This proves that they simply wanted a bigger publisher," Franklin said. "It should help a lot in this case in Chicago." We agreed with him. Jordan called Paul and, in considerable excitement, read him the quote from Susan. Paul said he didn't think it meant anything. He was not in a very good mood.

We spoke to Paul again on Saturday, August 6. Three days had passed since Goettel's opinion had come down, and we all still felt awful. Jordan asked Paul if he was still depressed. "Of course," Paul said. He was very tense and in a state of shock. He found it difficult to believe that the judge had swallowed Garbus's argument whole, so to speak. It was as if we had presented no case at all. "Evidently," Paul said, "he believed Ben and he did not believe Franklin."

Kiley was holding a hearing at 9:30 on Monday morning, August 8. Paul was expecting the worst. He was becoming rather angry and was prepared, he said, to appeal in order to force Kiley to take the case. He no longer admired Kiley's position on "the public interest" versus our "narrow" concerns: his feeling about that was now similar to one expressed by a lawyer married to one of our staff, who had said, when he was told about Kiley's cavils on that score, "What kind of horseshit is that?"

29

"It Looks Like It's Going to Be Relatively Easy"

The Monday morning hearing before Kiley turned out to be less horrible than Paul had expected. The judge did not dismiss the case but, keeping hope alive, announced that he was going to give a decision two days later, on Wednesday, August 10, at 1:00 in the afternoon. And, despite the fact that he made clear his displeasure both at our insistence on maintaining our forum selection clause and with the behavior of everybody in the case in general, he set a tentative trial date of September 12, subject to his Wednesday announcement. He said he would not be influenced by Goettel's opinion because Goettel had not held a full trial; he said, too, that Goettel would not be influenced by *his* opinion. Paul said he felt a lot better leaving the courtroom than he had entering it. And he told us that Kite came up to him after the hearing and said he thought the Cheevers had suffered a great defeat.

Nevertheless, we were extremely nervous on Wednesday as we went to court in a pouring rain. Our middle son, Bruce, joined us in the courtroom. Russell Smith was there with M. Leslie Kite and his associate Jerome Brozak; both Garbus and Maura were on vacation. With the three Cheever lawyers and Paul and Cynthia standing before the bench, Kiley proceeded to read his handwritten opinion for about twenty minutes. Paul said later that he died a thousand deaths during the reading.

Our hearts sank when the judge said he was primarily concerned about "the public interest question of efficient use of judicial resources and the avoidance of potential conflicting decisions in dual litigation." If it weren't for these concerns, he said, he would deny Mrs. Cheever's motion to dismiss "without hesitation" because she had agreed to the forum selection clause when she signed the contract. There was no question in his mind, he said, that the contract issues raised in Chicago were "part and parcel" of the copyright and Lanham Act claims raised in New York: all these claims were clearly interrelated and couldn't be divided for resolution. "The resolution of these questions before Judge Goettel depends in large part on how the contract dispute brought before me is decided." If Kiley ruled in favor of Mrs. Cheever, then both disputes would end, he said; if he ruled in favor of Academy, the dispute would continue, and its end would be decided in New York, not Chicago.

He blamed this "bedeviling problem" squarely on "both parties and their lawyers . . . . Both of you spend precious judicial resources while you serve your narrow, private interests," not able to "rise above trial strategy," preferring to "run back and forth between Chicago and New York and to hire two sets of attorneys in each place seeking advantage from court rulings." He said he had decided "to end this endless procedural maneuvering." Although he wanted to make it clear that he was disappointed with the parties and their lawyers and that he had misgivings about "wasting judicial resources," he was denying Mrs. Cheever's motion to dismiss.

Our relief was almost palpable: Jordan and I and Bruce had been convinced as we listened to him that the judge was moving in the opposite direction.

Russell Smith said gallantly that the Cheevers "were not going to lie on the tracks," but they would like it to be "the shortest trial possible . . . much as we love Chicago." They wanted to streamline the hearing by using the White Plains transcripts instead of witnesses. Kiley said that if there was "a hotly contested credibility question," he would like to see witnesses. But Russell Smith said the transcripts might be "perfect" for impeaching credibility.

The judge said he thought the case could be tried "in a couple of days." Russell Smith responded that he couldn't imagine it being longer than two days, and he expected it to be less than a day. "This doesn't jump out to me as being a particularly complicated case," Kiley observed. "It looks like it's going to be relatively easy." He reserved the weeks of September 13 and September 20 for trial.

At last we had won something.

Now we needed at least two expert witnesses, and there was the question of an appeal from Goettel's opinion. There had been some talk of an accelerated appeal, but this appeared to have evaporated. Now Paul said the appeal would have to be filed by September 3, the first brief would be due by October 3, and the second brief by November 3. There might be an oral argument. It would cost between $10,000 and $15,000. Paul said he was going to think it over because of the expense, but his feeling was that we should appeal. Franklin called to tell us that the lawyers at Pryor, Cashman—Bob Stein and Paul's friend Sandy Goldman, the senior litigator there—counseled that we should conserve our resources and let the appeal go. If we won in Chicago, they said, and Goettel zapped us, we could appeal then. If we appealed now and then won in Chicago, Goettel could say that he wasn't able to lift the injunction because we had taken it out of his hands. Theoretically, the injunction would be lifted if we won in Chicago, and there was always the chance that Goettel would *not* zap us after that. Although Paul now held Judge Goettel in what has been called minimum high regard, he was swayed by this argument.

A lull ensued. Garbus was on vacation in the Sierras until August 22. It was blessedly quiet.

The press was taking up the cudgels. In the "People/Books" column in the August *Vogue*, Tracy Young questioned whether Mrs. Cheever was "primarily concerned with defending her husband's upscale reputation or merely trying to maintain the Cheever industry as a family business . . . . But by ruling out stories that portray a grubbier milieu—and that show an apprentice writer struggling to find his voice—Mrs. Cheever is shortchanging her husband's admirers, who are more than willing to read him, warts, walk-ups and all."[1]

Jonathan Yardley, who had not spoken to us but had obviously been given a copy of Judge Goettel's opinion, took an opposing view in the *Washington Post.* "The chances that the book will ever see the light of day are not unduly bright," he wrote: he did not consider this bad news, except for Cheever collectors and "for those who hope to make a profit off such bits of literary remains as the collection would contain." The book "as envisioned by its publisher and editor, is essentially a literary scavenger job." He quoted liberally from Judge Goettel's opinion, noting, for example, that Goettel had said that Mary Cheever had "envisioned a rather modest work." The dead, said Mr. Yardley, are surely entitled to as much protection as anyone else. He said that Mary Cheever cared more for her husband's reputation than for money. Not, he added, that Academy Chicago acted "in bad faith . . . . but as often happens things get out of hand and a small publisher found itself with the unlikely and irresistible prospect of something approaching a blockbuster." Mary Cheever was "to be applauded for trying, however belatedly, to honor her husband's wishes."[2]

Mrs. Cheever did, however, have passing thoughts about money. "I sometimes think," she told David Streitfeld, "that any amount of money, like the million we all got for [rights to the] Journals, I think that people smell it. Know what I mean? I think they smell it, and say, 'There's money in Cheever stuff.'"[3]

In order to escape from this situation, which we found inexpressibly painful, we tried to work. It was difficult to concentrate. Jordan began to clean out his files, and I turned to an unusual project on which I had been working off and on in my spare time for some years. This was an historical novel by a Dutch writer named Hella Haasse, which had been brought to us in 1982 or so by Kalman Kaplan, a psychologist. His father Louis, an American-born employee of the U.S. Post Office in Chicago, had spent five years attempting to translate this novel, using Dutch-English dictionaries and grammars, and had died in 1958 shortly after producing a first draft. Louis Kaplan's widow had shut the manuscript away in a closet, and there it remained until her apartment caught fire in the late 1970s, when Kalman Kaplan discovered it while helping his mother mop up the mess left by firemen. The title page was missing, but after some difficulty, he identified the work—first published in Holland in 1949—and got permission from Mrs. Haasse to act as her agent for it in the United States. He called the book *The Forest of Expectations*, a rough literal translation of the Dutch title.

After a few rejections from other publishers, Kalman Kaplan saw an article about us in the *Chicago Tribune*, phoned me, and brought us the manuscript in a large cardboard box. I read the first ten pages or so and felt that the book, despite some stylistic difficulties, was a work that merited serious consideration. Kalman Kaplan had retyped the earlier chapters, but the bulk of the manuscript was in very rough condition: lines were blacked out, verbs and adjectives were typed with an assortment of synonyms enclosed in parentheses, and the writing style was awkward. Kalman Kaplan was aware of these shortcomings; he and I agreed that I would put the work into "literary" English. I assumed at the time that the translation was accurate.

I began to rewrite the book at home, at night, a few pages at a time. I took it with me on business trips and worked on it on airplanes and in hotel rooms. Gradually I accumulated a couple of handwritten notebooks. Now, in the slough of despond, so to speak, I was happy to escape into the

Middle Ages, and I began to work on the book full-time in the office. It was a great relief to me to have this pleasant and decidedly challenging distraction. Some of the text struck me as lacking clarity. Hella Haasse, to whom I had sent portions of my edited work, had reacted with amusement to parts of the translation. Throwing myself into this project, I bought a Dutch-English dictionary and tried some translating myself. *The Forest of Expectations* we found to be a clumsy title; Mark suggested we call the novel *In A Dark Wood Wandering*—a phrase that certainly expressed our psychological state at the time.

I could have no idea, of course, that this book was going to be a lifesaver for the company.

30

"You Don't See a Moral Issue Here?"

On August 23, Paul received evidence of Martin Garbus's return in the form of a subpoena: the law firm of Pope, Ballard was to be deposed on the subject of its "interest in or control over the book tentatively titled *The Uncollected Stories of John Cheever*, if any." The deposition was to begin on August 30 at 2:00 P.M. at Kite's offices and continue "from day to day until completed."

Paul had to go into federal court to get this subpoena quashed on the basis that the subject matter could lead to no admissible evidence and that this was an invasion of the attorney-client relationship and an obvious attempt to harass Academy's counsel on the eve of trial. A couple of days later Russell Smith adjourned the deposition "until after the Chicago trial" and asked Paul to withdraw the motion to quash.

Paul said he found this subpoena to be an almost unheard-of maneuver; it was also unwelcome because he was very busy. He had issued a demand that the Cheevers produce all publishing agreements they had signed for books of John Cheever's stories. What he wanted was a copy of the contract Mrs. Cheever had signed with the firm of Sylvester & Orphanos for a limited edition of the story "Expelled." ICM had negotiated this contract, and we knew that it was a dramatically different contract from ours. We wanted to disprove the Cheever lawyers' continual insistence that Academy Chicago was the same kind of press as Sylvester & Orphanos, which published only a few hundred signed, numbered copies of a single story in a fine binding, expressly for collectors and not for bookstores or libraries. Mrs. Cheever said she had lost her copy of the contract, and by a strange coincidence, ICM said that they had lost their copy, too! Sylvester & Orphanos said they had a copy, but unfortunately it was in storage somewhere; they would go and look for it when they had time.

Paul was working, too, on our list of expert witnesses. Franklin had suggested a couple of names: one was Bob Markel, former head of Grosset & Dunlap and editor at Macmillan; the other was Father George Hunt, editor of the Jesuit weekly *America* and the author of a critical study of Cheever's fiction, with whom Franklin had developed a friendship through their mutual admiration for the writer's work. Another possible expert was Estelle Stearn, in the contracts department of the University of Chicago Press, who had written us a letter saying that many publishers are creative in their interpretation of "author" and "similarly elastic with regard to 'delivery.'" Delivery, she said, simply means that the material should be available for use on an approximate date. Ms. Stearn was reluctant to testify in court, and Paul did not want to put a reluctant witness on the stand.

Father Hunt, by contrast, agreed to testify for us. He told Paul that something about this case did not "smell right" to him; he had read half the stories and felt that this book should be published. The stories, he said, were almost impossible to find. Paul was deeply impressed by George Hunt; he told us that he thought it was a tribute to Franklin that a man like that was willing to testify for us.

On August 29, Judge Kiley held the final pretrial conference. He said he would consider only one question: "Did Mrs. Cheever deliver, and if she did not, what are the consequences?" In the course of the conference, he asked Garbus whether Mrs. Cheever would consider removing the "objectionable stories" and letting Academy publish the others. Garbus said that the Cheevers would give us about five stories, if we printed only seven thousand copies and agreed to pay the Cheevers' legal bills. Kiley replied that Mrs. Cheever had an obligation under the contract to do something; certainly, he said, she could not satisfy the contract by delivering one story. Russell Smith must have looked amused because Judge Kiley added, "I assume from the way your associate Mr. Smith is smirking at me that he does not take this as seriously as I do."

Garbus announced that the Cheevers would not attend the trial and would present no expert witnesses. The judge said that if there was a question of "credibility," he would want to see witnesses. "When you hear the plaintiffs testify," Garbus said, "you won't worry about the defendants' credibility." He remarked that the Royce Hotel settlement meeting had failed because Paul demanded $2.5 million.*

*The reader will recall that the Royce Hotel settlement failed, in our opinion, because Judge Goettel had accepted the case a few days before. Garbus said at the time that it failed because the Cheevers learned that Scott Meredith was proceeding with the paperback auction. Paul never "demanded" money at any time.

The day after Paul submitted the names of our expert witnesses, George Hunt reported that he had heard from the Cheevers. Mrs. Cheever had left a message. Susan had talked to him on the phone; she was very sweet, he said. She told him that Franklin was a wonderful person who had been duped by Academy Chicago, that her mother had had to take out a second mortgage on her house to pay her legal bills, and that it was an act of hostility toward the Cheever family for George Hunt to testify for Academy. He replied to her that, on the contrary, he was trying to help John Cheever because he thought the stories were excellent and should be published. Susan told him that at the Royce Hotel meeting: (1) Academy refused to drop the Donaldson introduction; (2) Academy refused to alter the table of contents; (3) Academy refused to rearrange the stories (there was some truth in this allegation); (4) Academy was given a list of the stories the Cheevers wanted to drop, and Academy refused to drop them; and (5) Academy had asked for $2.5 million.*

Father Hunt remarked to Paul that he found it odd that Federico had not called him; he knew and liked Federico.

Cynthia flew to New York to defend the depositions of our two expert witnesses. She was impressed with both men. She thought that Bob Markel had bested Garbus by saying in the course of his deposition that Franklin had a dual role as coauthor and editor and that in Markel's opinion Franklin could deliver the manuscript and in fact did deliver it to Mrs. Cheever, whose silence had given assent to it. Garbus asked him if he had ever dealt with a publishing agreement where the author disapproved of the manuscript or a portion of it. Yes, he had, Markel said, and the book came out under those circumstances.

Before his deposition started, Father Hunt told Cynthia that he had had a call from Ben, who had asked for five minutes of his time and characteristically talked for an hour. Unlike Susan, Ben spoke bitterly about Franklin. Like Susan, Ben said his mother had had to take out a second mortgage on her home; he asked George Hunt whether he wanted to cause an old lady to suffer. Hunt replied that he hardly knew Ben's mother, that the stories had not been available, and the book was an important one and should be published. When it was obvious that Father Hunt was going to stand firm, Ben said that if he testified, Ben's lawyer and his agent would make it "difficult"

---

*As I have said, all these points were untrue, with the exception of (3).

for Hunt "to function in the publishing world." Father Hunt told Ben that sounded like a threat, and Ben hung up.

During the deposition, Garbus asked Father Hunt whether he had had any discussions with John Cheever about "the selection process for the Knopf book." Yes, Father Hunt said, he had in fact asked Cheever why he had not included at least two and possibly three of the uncollected stories: "The President of the Argentine," "The National Pastime," and "The Temptations of Emma Boynton." John Cheever had replied that he didn't include them because he forgot about them. Hunt told Garbus that he had the impression from Cheever that the editor of the Knopf book had drawn a "line of demarcation" with the publication of *The Enormous Radio and Other Stories*, which came out in 1951. All but three of the Knopf stories had been included in previous Cheever collections, Father Hunt said. He believed that the selection of stories for the Knopf book was out of Cheever's hands.

He told Garbus that he had never heard that John Cheever did not want these uncollected stories published. Garbus said that Mrs. Cheever did not want these stories published: "So, with respect to the moral issue, you being a Father, do you not believe that she has a moral right, putting aside contracts and otherwise, to not have these stories published if she doesn't want them published?" Father Hunt said he could not answer that question; he was only there to give testimony about the quality of the stories.

"I presume," Garbus said, "as a Father you deal with moral aspects in every aspect of your life?"

Father Hunt said he hoped so.

"Why are you here?" Garbus asked. Mrs. Cheever, he went on, was the literary executor, her husband had told her he didn't want these stories published, and Mr. Gottlieb, his editor, had testified in court that Mr. Cheever did not want these stories published. "You don't see a moral issue here?" Father Hunt responded that he did not want to answer that speculative question. He had not seen or heard Mary Cheever's testimony, and he didn't know how well it was documented or who the witnesses were. It was not his area of competence, and he didn't know either Mrs. Cheever or Mr. Gottlieb.

Garbus brought up the subject of Franklin, whom George Hunt had known since 1981. Did he know that if the book was published, his friend Mr. Dennis would make about $1.5 million? Did he know that Franklin received monies from Academy, that he had been on their payroll since 1982, and that because of Academy's financial condition, Franklin had not been paid in about a year? No, Father Hunt said, he did not know any of that.

George Hunt disappointed Garbus by stating that there were sketches in the Knopf collection, but he gratified him by testifying at length to the shortcomings of Scott Donaldson's introduction, which he thought placed too much emphasis on biographical elements of the stories, often without sufficient basis. We heard later that Garbus was so gratified by this that after the deposition was over he told Father Charles Whelan of Fordham University, a lawyer who had accompanied Father Hunt, that if he had known how Hunt felt about the introduction he would have asked him to be a witness for the Cheevers. If Academy won this case, Garbus said, it would be because of Father Hunt. Father Whelan remarked that Garbus should not have suggested that because George Hunt was a Catholic priest, he should support Mrs. Cheever "morally." Garbus took this criticism graciously, and the two priests departed.

As the trial date approached, Paul was inundated by demands from Garbus. One demand concerned Father Hunt: Garbus wanted copies of the contract for and reviews of his book *John Cheever: The Hobgoblin Company of Love*; contracts for any other books about Cheever he might have written; copies of all his articles and "any other writings" he may have produced. Then there was Robert Markel, our other expert witness. Garbus wanted copies of all contracts Mr. Markel was involved with at Grosset & Dunlap—this would cover the period 1978 to 1982—and all contracts issued by Grosset & Dunlap in the six years since Markel left them.

There were requests for copies of documents describing "assets and liabilities" of Academy, including accounts payable and accounts receivable; copies of all schedules of payments made by Academy to Franklin Dennis "or any third parties with respect to the work" or "documents referring to such payments or delays in payment"; copies of any "dunning correspondence from any third party to Academy in 1987 or 1988 regarding payments, complaints or inquiries"; and documents "referring to arrangement of financing for any step in the development, production or promotion of the work or connected with any problems in connection with such financing."

In addition, Garbus wanted copies of "all advertisements, promotional materials, press releases and all communication between either of the plaintiffs and the press in connection with the work"; all correspondence "or other communications between plaintiffs and third parties with respect to the work together with enclosures"; and "all newspaper and magazine articles quoting Academy representatives on the subject of the work or the dispute." Also requested were "all documents pertaining to subsidiary rights, including but not limited to either of the plaintiffs or Dell publishing," as well as all publishing contracts entered into by either plaintiff, all drafts of the August 15, 1987, contract, all pertinent pages of "Anita Miller's diary," and "all documents pertaining to or included in any lawsuits against either of the plaintiffs in any way relating to delivery or non-delivery of a manuscript."

I gave Paul my diary, and he xeroxed a couple of pages with notes about phone calls from Wylie and Ben. The rest of the stuff Garbus requested, Paul said, was either clearly inappropriate or did not exist.

31

Chicago Trial, Days 1 and 2: "They Could Be Bad, They Could Be Good, That Is Not the Issue"

September 15, Thursday, the day of the trial, finally arrived. We had spent the previous day and part of the evening in Paul's offices with Franklin and Mary, who had arrived on Tuesday. Paul was particularly exercised about a letter we had received from a librarian who had noticed that "The Habit," included in our book, was the fourth in a series of vignettes (or sketches) published in the Knopf edition under the title "Metamorphoses." Franklin had in fact discovered this a week or so before the letter arrived. Paul felt strongly that a copy of this letter must go to Garbus. But we didn't have it: I had sent it to Franklin without keeping a copy, and Franklin had left it at home in Montrose. Paul spent some time exploring the possibility that a neighbor who had the key to Franklin's house could go in, retrieve the letter, and overnight it to Paul. Franklin was not sure where the letter was, and it developed that the neighbor with the key was not available. Mary finally put an end to the subject by saying that she suddenly remembered that she had thrown the letter out. After that we talked a lot about the words "some" and "embarrassingly immature" and "final" decisions.

September 15 was a cool day; the walk to the courthouse was shorter and more pleasant than the walk to court in White Plains. Our sons Bruce and Eric were there, along with some of our office staff: our bookkeeper Elma Pador, Jane Kohn Winter, and Mary Jo Reilly.

Paul set up placards on an easel for his opening remarks. Garbus attempted to dispense with opening remarks by stating that the judge had decreed there were to be none. This was news to the judge and to us: Paul was thus able to point to these placards, which highlighted the sequence of important letters, including those from Joy Weiner telling Mrs. Cheever as early as November 1987 that thirty-eight *New Yorker* stories were to be included in the book. When his turn came, Garbus roamed about the court-room, intermittently pointing an accusatory finger at us and saying, among other things, that the judge should forget about royalties: all Mrs. Cheever was ever going to get from Academy was $337. This remark elicited gasps and other sounds from the Academy contingent in the audience. Judge Kiley then read us a very stern lecture about noise in the gallery. Paul was extremely upset by this.

Jordan went on the stand first and testified at length about the back-ground to the case and the contract. He took care to point out that our royalty arrangements were standard. Garbus objected, saying, "I happen to know for a fact that they are totally different." When Jordan tried to testify about his late May or early June conversation with Mary Cheever, in which she had requested the Royce Hotel meeting, Garbus objected again, saying that this phone conversation had been ruled "inappropriate" by Judge Goettel (it hadn't); later he stated that he, Garbus, had offered to name the objectionable stories to Paul, but Paul had refused a settlement conference, and "by February" it was too late (he hadn't, Paul hadn't, and it wasn't); that in January and February the Cheevers tried to change the stories, but Acad-emy said the book was "typecast" and wouldn't change them (the Cheevers hadn't tried); Mrs. Cheever was "over seventy years old" (she had turned seventy in May); it was difficult for her to come to Chicago, she "couldn't even come to Westchester and stay the first day of testimony, she had to leave early"; the "preface" called Mrs. Cheever's husband a homosexual, a Communist; Academy had printed "50,000 copies of the preface of the Donaldson's preface," and the Cheevers had to go "into federal court three different times" to get the "preface" withdrawn.

The judge asked Paul the point of Jordan's testifying about his con-versation with Mrs. Cheever. Paul carefully explained that in that relatively recent conversation, Mrs. Cheever had said that she wanted us to publish the book and had made no mention of fraud, or too many stories, or offen-sive stories. The judge said that he didn't see any "evidentiary value" in a conversation by parties in the middle of a lawsuit trying to "find a way around their problems." He sustained Garbus's objection.

On the second day, September 16, Father Hunt was slated to testify. Garbus began to back off from the Cheever position that the uncollected stories were "inferior." "A literary debate," he said, was not relevant to the "issues" in the case. Mrs. Cheever's "husband didn't want these stories printed. He could have been right, he could have been wrong, they could be bad, they could be good, that is not the issue." The judge said, "Let me get to the point, at least my perception of it. As far as you are concerned, even if all of these stories are of the highest literary quality, or have great literary quality from a number of different perspectives, it doesn't make any difference for the purposes of this case?"

"Right," Garbus said. The testimony before Judge Goettel, he went on, was that "Mr. Cheever and Mr. Gottlieb" decided to "exclude all stories prior to '47 . . . . It was Mr. Cheever's judgment, it was Mr. Gottlieb's judgment—as between Mr. Hunt and Mr. Cheever I don't know who is correct and incorrect." Garbus said he was not going to put Father Hunt "as against Mr. Cheever and he is going to say the stories are good and Mr. Cheever is going to say the stories are bad. What does that have to do with this? We can argue all day long about whether Mr. Cheever's judgment about leaving those stories out is correct or incorrect. That has nothing to do with this case."

Paul said that "if Mr. Garbus will concede for purposes of this case that the sixty-eight stories are all of high literary quality, then we'll need to reconsider whether Father Hunt is needed to tell Your Honor just that."

"Your Honor," Garbus said, "any story that Mr. Cheever runs and I thought I was very clear about this, is of higher literary quality than any story that Martin Garbus writes, or most other people write."

The judge said he thought Garbus was saying that Mrs. Cheever did not decide on the stories, she made no decision, she had no chance to make a decision, "so the literary quality or the integrity of the collection, whether it be large or small, to convey that quality, is irrelevant because she never made any choices. So if she made no choices it makes no difference whether she made them on the basis of literary quality or not because she hadn't made it then."

Paul said that the judge would hear from Franklin that both Ben and Mary Cheever had said they wanted all sixty-eight stories in the book. And during the course of the litigation, "we have been told over and over again that the Cheevers do not want this book published because the stories lack literary quality, because the stories are embarrassingly immature, and the like." Now if Mrs. Cheever was changing her position and conceding the literary quality of the stories, then Paul said that he thought he and Ms.

Johnson needed to rethink whether Father Hunt had to be a witness.

The judge said the question was whether the concession was necessary because the way he understood it from the two opening statements and from what little he had learned so far, "Academy Chicago made the choice."

"No sir," Paul said, "I'm sorry."

"I'm not stating a finding," the judge said. "I'm stating the perception of the defense." He then repeated that Mrs. Cheever made no choice; Academy Chicago made the choice, Mrs. Cheever had not exercised her right to make a choice. He repeated that a few times. His question, he said, was whether Mrs. Cheever had even exercised her rights "under the contract" to make a choice and, if she hadn't, whether she had given up those rights. "What," he asked, "has that got to do with the literary quality of the collection" in the plaintiff's galleys?

Paul said that sixty of the sixty-eight stories had been delivered to her in photocopy form and she had admitted in her deposition that she knew when these were delivered that it was time to make a choice. "Now what Your Honor may have to decide is whether by her silence she made a choice—"

The judge agreed, he said. Had she made a choice by her silence, or had she given up her right to make a choice because of her conduct—that, he said, was Paul's position. Or maybe she had not had the chance to make a choice "on either of those three issues. The quality of the choices already made don't become, at least from my perspective, apparently relevant."

Paul said that unless we misunderstood, and he didn't think we did, the Cheever lawyers had said both orally and in writing that these stories must not be published because they lacked literary merit. Even if she did have to make a choice, Paul said, she would choose no stories because she said they lacked literary merit. He was entitled to refute that, he said, by showing that the stories did have literary merit, unless the other side conceded the point.

"Your Honor," Garbus said, "Mr. Cheever could not write a story that does not have literary merit." Paul, he said, had misunderstood the Cheever position. "Not once did any of the Cheevers come in and say we don't like this story because it's not good or it's bad or whatever. What they said is, 'We never had a choice.'"

While we were digesting this amazing statement, the judge said that he was very happy not to have to decide whether the stories were good or bad:

he wanted to avoid making that decision. All he wanted to decide was whether Mary Cheever made a choice, didn't make a choice, or gave up her right to make a choice. If she hadn't made a choice and hadn't given up her right to make a choice, he said ominously, then the plaintiff's bound galleys were going nowhere because Academy Chicago could not make the decision. He himself was a former college English major, and he would love to hear from experts on both sides on these writings, and he would love to read them, but he just didn't see that it was relevant.

Paul said that he would have to confer with Cynthia about whether Father Hunt should be called, and the judge declared a short recess. We went out into the hall. The question now was how to get Father Hunt on the stand so that he could testify that Ben had threatened him. Paul had planned to bring this out on redirect examination, after Garbus evoked Hunt's dislike of the Donaldson introduction. But there could be no redirect if Father Hunt did not take the stand. I suggested Father Hunt testify about the difficulty of finding the stories, since the previous day Garbus had said that finding them was a simple, routine task. Cynthia said that there was an Illinois law stating that attempts at intimidation of a witness are an admission that the intimidator has a weak case.

We returned to court, and Paul asked that Father Hunt be called. He was sworn in. Garbus said he was entitled to know what Father Hunt was going to testify about. Paul said one of the subjects was the difficulty of locating the stories because Garbus had demeaned the research work. The other subject was "communications from the Cheever children to Father Hunt threatening him with retaliation if he came out here to testify."

On the subject of research, Garbus said he would stipulate "to this stuff." There were two bibliographies, and Franklin, he said, would testify that he was given that information by Ben Cheever.* "Once you get these two bibliographies, you can get the stories. And then there is some additional research, there's no dispute about that at all."

The judge asked whether the subject of research had come up in Father Hunt's deposition. If Garbus had had a chance to ask him about that, there would be no problem with his testifying. Garbus couldn't remember; he didn't think he asked him about it. It was a hundred-page deposition, he

---

*Franklin found a reference to the Coates bibliography as he was browsing in a San Francisco bookshop.

said; he might have "thrown out a bad sentence here or there," but he didn't think so.

"That probably wouldn't be possible, right?" asked the judge.

Paul asked Father Hunt whether he recalled being asked about the difficulty of getting the stories; he said he hadn't been asked. That left the question of the Cheevers' effort to intimidate him. The relevance of this testimony, Paul said, lay in the presumption under Illinois law that efforts to keep a witness from the courtroom was admission of the weakness of the case of those making the efforts. The judge said he would let him testify to that, and then he would take a look at the law.

Garbus said he knew that Susan and Benjamin Cheever had spoken to Father Hunt; he knew there was a relationship between Mary Cheever and Father Hunt or there had been one; he knew Father Hunt had been at John Cheever's funeral. He really didn't want to get into this "unpleasantness" unless Father Hunt wanted to. He just thought it was demeaning to everybody.

The judge said it was up to Paul, not to Father Hunt, and Paul said Father Hunt was willing to testify to it.

Garbus said, "In any event, the whole question of stopping him from coming here to testify, he is not testifying. So assuming—I'm just trying to think this out—assuming they were trying to interfere with a material witness, he is not a material witness."

The judge said he didn't think that would fit.

So George Hunt went on the stand and testified that Susan and Ben and Mary Cheever had all called him and left messages in early September. He never spoke to Mrs. Cheever. But the conversation with Ben, he said, "ended this way. Ben said to me, 'George, I want to warn you that our lawyer can make it very difficult for you and so too can the Cheever family.' And I said to him, 'Ben, that was not wise for you to say that.' And he reacted, 'What?' I said, 'Ben, that was not wise for you to say that. That sounds to me like an implicit threat.' And he said something like, 'Well—' and then he said goodbye and hung up."

Garbus gave a loud, short laugh and said, "Is *that* all!"

Susan Cheever, Father Hunt said, had spoken with him for about an hour, trying to persuade him not to testify. "She was very calm. She felt that I would be a hostile witness. I said, 'Well, maybe in a legal sense possibly, but certainly not in the emotional or moral sense.' She was trying to dissuade me because she felt that my appearance would upset the family, and especially her mother."

Paul released the witness. Garbus had "a few questions." Had Susan told him about "financial pressure the family was under as a result of these law-suits"? Father Hunt said Susan had said that her mother might be taking a second mortgage on the house. She didn't give him "any specific informa-tion" about the costs. And she said her mother was "'an older woman and she's been driven to distraction' or some phrase like that."

"Think about it," Garbus said. "She spoke to you about an hour. By the way, she's a woman in her early forties and up until this time you have been a friend of the family?"

"No," Father Hunt said.

"You had been to the funeral of Mr. Cheever?"

"Yes. I didn't know the family at all."

"Do you know why Susan said your presence, your presence having been at the funeral of Mr. Cheever and now testifying in the courtroom would be harmful or why Mrs. Cheever was upset by it?"

"I couldn't understand why," Father Hunt said unhelpfully. "I didn't know them personally."

"You never met Mrs. Cheever?"

"Yes, just to say hello. I don't think I exchanged—in four meetings, I don't suspect, more than twenty words." He did, he said, consider himself a friend of John Cheever.

"And when Susan asked you as a friend of John Cheever not to come to court and testify against the family, did that have any meaning to you?"

"No. What I was being asked to do was talk about the quality of John Cheever's work. I thought I was defending John Cheever."

Had Ben mentioned the "money pressures they were under"?

"He was very inexact about everything he spoke to me about . . . sort of reiterating what Susan had said, but not in even so definite a fashion."

Had Ben and Susan said, "'This whole thing is a tragedy. We never wanted to be involved in this kind of litigation'?" Father Hunt said they might have; he didn't recall. Had they said "'This is the first time anything like this has ever happened to the Cheever family'?" No, he didn't remember their saying that. Did Father Hunt know whether the Cheever family had ever been involved before "in litigation concerning any books?"

"The Cheever family as a family, no," George Hunt said.

Franklin went back on the stand after that and testified, as he had in White Plains—and Ben had verified it—that he had told Ben in late October or early November that Academy wanted to publish all the uncollected stories and Ben said that was a fine idea. The judge interrupted here to ask Franklin, "You say that you told Ben Cheever in late October or early November of '87 . . . . that Academy of Chicago [*sic*] decided that the best way to do this project was to do all of the uncollected stories?" Franklin repeated that this was what he had told Ben and Ben thought it was a good idea.

The judge's question was interesting because later, in the course of delivering his opinion, he was to say that he did not believe Franklin was telling the truth when he said this. It should be noted that Ben was not in Chicago to deny it, and Garbus made no attempt to question Franklin about it because Ben had admitted in White Plains that it was true.

When his turn came, Garbus kept Franklin on the stand for four hours, once more reading him sections of his deposition ostensibly in order to impugn his testimony. Paul objected that there was nothing in the deposition to impeach Franklin's testimony on the stand and therefore Garbus was using the deposition improperly. Judge Kiley said that he knew "there was a basis for it way back when he first started reading those [depositions]" so he was going to allow it. He did tell Garbus to stop yelling in Franklin's face and to show him the deposition. Garbus said he would lower his voice "if I can."

The air-conditioning went off at 5:00. Judge Kiley stopped taking notes and shifted restlessly in his seat. Finally, at 6:35, Franklin was released. We all—Eric, Bruce, Bruce's friend Julia Anderson, Mary, Franklin, Father Hunt, Cynthia, and her husband, Matt—went off to a delicious dinner at the Standard Club as guests of Paul and his wife, Sue. Cynthia, who was sitting next to me at the table, said she thought the judge would either give us the entire book or declare the contract null because Mrs. Cheever had not been sufficiently consulted. Paul said that he found it incredible that Garbus had thrown out half his case by stipulating that all the stories had literary merit. Now, he said, Mrs. Cheever can only say that she capriciously and arbitrarily wants to cut the stories, since there is no more question about their literary value.

He told us then what he had known for a week: that on September 30, Garbus was going to go before Goettel to add Jordan, Bruce, and me to the lawsuit so that we would personally be accused of copyright infringement. Paul attempted to soften this blow by telling us that it is difficult to pierce the corporate veil, and, he said, if we had done any infringing, it was a small, technical violation. He said he had not told us earlier because he thought Garbus was doing it mainly to unnerve us before the trial.

Paul did not agree with Cynthia about Judge Kiley's possible decision. He said he was pretty sure we would get a book of some kind.

32

Chicago Trial, Day 3: "Welcome to Our Fair City"

The trial resumed on Tuesday, September 20. Our second expert witness, Robert Markel, was slated to testify on publishing industry practices. He had been vice president and editor in chief of the trade division of Macmillan from 1961 to 1970, when he left to become senior vice president and editorial director at Grosset & Dunlap. In 1982, he resigned to form his own literary agency and packaging company. We met Mr. Markel for the first time before proceedings began. Our conversation was somewhat limited, since he said he could not discuss the particulars of the case with us at this time. He did tell us that his house on Grand Cayman Island had been hit by Hurricane Gilbert.

Garbus objected to allowing Markel to testify, on the ground that he had been slated to discuss the literary value of the stories, which was now a moot question, and to testify that Mary Cheever was not the sole author but rather the coauthor with Franklin, a question that was already inadmissible because Kiley had ruled that Mary was the sole author. After a considerable wrangle with Garbus ("what you are really seeing here, and I will use the word, you are seeing kind of a flimflam . . . . "), Markel was allowed to testify on the question of delivery of a manuscript.

Garbus held, at some length, that Mrs. Cheever had not delivered. Paul argued that she in fact had: she did not hand a manuscript to the publisher, but she acquiesced in the delivery because a manuscript was provided to her, she was asked if she had problems with it, and she never responded that she did. And Paul wanted Markel to testify on the meaning of the word "manuscript"—that it was not a final printed galley like our galley (now called Exhibit 36) but a set of photocopies with a table of contents like the set given to Mrs. Cheever on December 12 by Franklin Dennis. "Mrs. Cheever," Paul said, "having raised no objections to that manuscript, it was then delivered to the publisher and that is what is intended in the publishing industry." She did not, he said, deliver the bound galley, Exhibit No. 36; she did not see it until June because it was not printed until June. Mr. Markel, Paul announced, would describe how "delivery is handled in the publishing world." Accordingly, Paul asked Markel to tell the court how he understood delivery was to be accomplished under that publishing agreement, based on his experience in the publishing world. Garbus objected because, he said, expert testimony could not give meaning to a simple English word like "delivery." The judge said that Markel could tell him what "delivery" means in the industry, but he, the judge, would decide what "delivery" meant in the context of the plaintiff's "elements."

In response to Paul's question, Markel said his understanding of delivery was that the author "either physically delivers or causes to be delivered material in the form of usually typewritten or xeroxed materials, the manuscript which is described in the publishing agreement." To make things clearer, he added that delivery is accomplished by UPS or hand delivery "or whatever."

On the basis of pretrial conversations with the witness, Paul had expected an answer somewhat more helpful to us. After all, Estelle Stearn of the University of Chicago Press had said that "delivery" is an elastic term, which simply means that the material should be available for use on an approximate date. Garbus was happy with the witness's testimony. He announced that he agreed with it and would have stipulated to it.

"Counsel," the judge said, "please."

Paul tried again. When the publishing agreement says the author will deliver, is terminating the agreement an acceptable response? Could the publisher deem the manuscript to be delivered if the author was given a copy of the manuscript and made no response within a reasonable time? Garbus objected and was sustained. The judge said these nearly rhetorical questions were entering into his territory; *he* would decide "whether it was acceptable for Mary Cheever and others to terminate the contract."

Garbus, when his turn came, asked Markel whether it was understood from letters sent by Dennis that Mary Cheever had control over which stories were to be included. The judge sustained Paul's objection twice. Garbus said that he had prepared a "lengthy cross" based on this question and now he could not pursue that line of questioning. He did elicit from Markel the admission that he had never seen, as Garbus put it, "any document in this case which goes from the Academy to Mrs. Cheever which says, 'we have your manuscript, we accept it.'" Markel agreed that it was "common practice in the industry" to communicate an acceptance. "As a rule."

Paul approached the witness again. When the author of an anthology delivered a manuscript containing 90 percent of the stories, along with a table of contents of all the stories, did that constitute delivery of a manuscript? "It might," our witness said. It would depend on how the remaining 10 percent was and "how close to the definitions that the contract stipulated in terms of word length, or other aspects of it, the ninety percent was."

Of course, we had not specified "word length" in our contract.

Was it common for the publishing agreement not to define specifically the length of a book? Paul asked, walking into it.

Markel said it was not common.

Paul said perhaps he had too many negatives in his question. He asked Markel what was common in his experience "with regard to the definition of a book in a publishing agreement."

"It is common," Markel said, "to have a specific word length or some form of limitation of material in the contract." He wasn't crazy about our title either. "Generally," he said, "it's better defined than that."

Apparently undaunted, Paul asked whether there was a difference in the way a publisher would communicate with a living author creating a manuscript, as opposed to a literary executor for an author whose works are being collected in an anthology. Was there a difference in the document or communication that went out?

"There might be," our witness said. "It would depend on the individual circumstance."

Determined to win something for our side, Paul asked the witness whether he had come there that day because of the $750 and expenses he was receiving? No, Markel said, he was there "because I feel that the contract I have been shown should be looked upon in this case within the context of normal publishing practices, and I felt that it was a good and valid contract."

This was the best Paul could get, and it wasn't bad, since Garbus was maintaining that the contract was not valid. Markel stepped down. "Welcome to our fair city," the judge said to him. "Welcome to Chicago."

After lunch—Paul had laid out a tempting buffet at the Pope, Ballard offices—we returned to the courtroom to find Garbus setting up a blackboard on an easel. My brother was there, too, with a new vibrating beeper. The judge had thrown him out of court the first day because he had beeped three times. Fortunately he had not been sitting near us, so we hoped the judge would think he was with the Cheevers.

On the blackboard, Garbus was making a chart. He explained that it would detail all the things Academy had done after February first: printing catalogs, holding a sales conference, selling paperback rights, preparing galleys, talking to the Book-of-the-Month Club, talking to the Literary Guild,* designing a book jacket, and so on. He intended, he said, to ask Franklin on each of these points whether he knew at the time that Mrs. Cheever objected to the contract.

Paul said that all this was irrelevant, and the judge tended to agree with him. In response to this Garbus commented that "the Cheever stories average about ten stories," by which he presumably meant that the early collections "averaged" about ten stories, which was, of course, untrue. "Nine point four," Garbus said, "is the exact number. We submit a manuscript. We give them five stories, six stories, number ten, we do an introduction, they come back and they say that's not satisfactory, and we are here next month. I want to avoid that, and I think—"

"You wouldn't be here next month under any circumstances," said the judge, whose crystal ball was considerably murkier than Garbus's.

Paul said he was willing to stipulate to what was done prior to February and after January, to avoid taking up a lot of time with questions and answers. The judge said he did not see any dispute about the things listed in Garbus's left-hand column, and he was not asking for more information. Garbus said he had "a whole afternoon of Mr. Dennis, irrespective. Why don't we go ahead with Mr. Dennis and see if I run out . . . . it may well be that you have seen the last of us this afternoon."

"God help us," the judge said. He wanted Wednesday and Thursday to prepare his opinion, which he was set to read on Friday.

Franklin went back on the stand, and Garbus asked him various questions. Why hadn't he offered Mrs. Cheever more money when he realized the book was valuable, and did Robert Gottlieb's name appear anywhere on the Knopf collection, and did anyone ever tell Franklin that he had the copyrights that permitted the distribution of the bound galleys? This latter

---

*Franklin had talked to the book clubs in fall of 1987.

question sparked a lively discussion with the judge, in the course of which Garbus told him that this action should have been in federal court because the judge had to decide whether there was a violation of copyright. The judge replied that he was going to discuss copyright in terms of the contract. "If I decide that the contract is enforceable, then the copyright issue is going to come to the fore," he said. Judge Goettel would then take care of it; "he can do what he will."

After that came closing arguments.

Paul devoted himself to arguing against the Cheever affirmative defenses, which claimed that Academy had breached the contract by preparing a manuscript without Mrs. Cheever's participation or knowledge and that Mrs. Cheever was defrauded in the inducement to sign the contract because Academy and Franklin never intended to consult with her. Paul pointed out that Mary and Ben Cheever were informed of every significant detail involving the book until problems arose in January. "There were meetings. There were telephone calls. There were letters, meetings between Franklin Dennis and Ben Cheever, one meeting between Franklin Dennis and Mary Cheever. There were phone calls between Franklin Dennis and Ben Cheever. There were phone calls between Maggie Curran and Jordan Miller, letters between Jordan Miller and Maggie Curran. There were even . . . letters between the *New Yorker* magazine and Mrs. Cheever . . . . "

"There certainly was a meeting of the minds that this was going to be a book of the stories of John Cheever," he continued, "and as it developed . . . the precise identification of the stories and number of stories was discussed and agreed upon, agreed upon in the form of first an alphabetical list provided to Ben Cheever by Franklin Dennis and then a chronological list with sixty of the sixty-eight stories photocopied when Mr. Dennis provided these spiral binders to Mary Cheever."

It was Mrs. Cheever who breached the contract, Paul said. She announced that the contract was terminated through Andrew Wylie, through Franklin Dennis, through Ben Cheever, and finally through Martin Garbus in a letter. "The only equitable result for Your Honor to reach on our case, is to permit the publication of the sixty-eight stories that appear in the table of contents of the bound galleys, but surely it is not to allow Mrs. Cheever to walk away from this contract with the return of three hundred thirty-seven dollars and fifty cents."

He added that Mrs. Cheever was to get full royalties and that if she had wanted a larger advance, she had had the right to ask for it. Probably, he said, she accepted the small advance because it was not a typical case in which the author has to live off the advance while producing the manuscript.

The judge wanted to discuss all this with Paul. Let's assume, Kiley said, that no delivery has been made, and taking Paul's proposition that there were no unclean hands to justify a termination of the contract by Mary Cheever—Paul was asking him to declare that Academy could go ahead with Plaintiff's 36. What if he decided that that couldn't happen because she hadn't made a decision about what stories would go into the book and at the same time he decided that she failed at least up to the point where relations broke off? "What now?" the judge asked. "What is the remedy? How do you fashion a remedy? You are asking for a declaration that Plaintiff's 36 is the manuscript that Academy can go ahead and publish, and under my hypothetical here, I couldn't do that. So what's the alternative? And at the same time Mary Cheever can't walk away from her obligations."

Paul said Mary Cheever did make a choice; she testified that she knew it was time to make a choice. She made a choice either by not objecting to the sixty-eight stories or, by declaring the contract null and void, deciding that there would be zero stories, no reason given. Well, the judge said, the second part, from Paul's perspective, was unacceptable under the contract. "Okay. So what now? What's the remedy, apart from giving you Plaintiff's 68—or 36, I'm sorry."

Paul suggested that the judge could hold back the eight stories that had not been included in the manuscript Franklin had given Mary Cheever. Under Illinois law, Paul went on, she couldn't sit back and refuse to perform a task that had been assigned to her. The court must deem her to have performed that task, and if there were in fact some stories that for some reason she thought shouldn't be in the book, she had had more than ample time to express herself. "She has never expressed herself," he added.

"Once the lawsuit started," the judge said, "you know, you were—there was too much time running between New York and Chicago."

Paul said that when Mrs. Cheever instructed her lawyer to write a letter saying the contract was null and void that was a selection, that was a choice. "Your Honor I think must decide whether that was a legitimate position."

"If it was not?" asked the judge.

"If it was not a legitimate position, I think Your Honor must decide that she has had more than ample time to choose and has therefore lost her chance to her right to select from these stories." She lost her chance from December 12, when Franklin delivered the manuscript to her, until today, Paul went on, because she never made a selection.

"What good does it do talking about choices people should have made once the lawsuit is filed?" Judge Kiley asked.

Well, Paul said, there were two and a half months from December 12 to February 29, when the lawsuit was filed. And then even after February 29, there was a period when the Cheevers approached Academy and Academy agreed to resolve the dispute, even though the lawsuit was on file. She could have made her choice then. She never did it. Paul offered another solution: "Your Honor could say to Mrs. Cheever's lawyer, 'I am going out of town, I will be back on October eleven or whatever the date is, make your choice, but don't come back in here and tell us that you are choosing six or seven or twelve stories. If there's some of those 68 stories that for some reason, with good reason, exercising good faith and fair dealing, you think shouldn't be in the book, tell us by October eleventh.'"

"Okay," the judge said. "Then we have another lawsuit—put it another way—another hearing on whether her choices are consistent with the contract obligation to make choices in good faith." Paul agreed that that was within the realm of the possible. But he hoped that in that case, Mrs. Cheever would abide by Illinois law but she had had more than enough time and that the judge was fully justified in deeming the choice to have been made constructively.

"All right," the judge said. "Academy was making choices itself during the same period of time and I mean, I guess I'm having very serious problems with the idea that no choice means Plaintiff's 36. And on the other hand, I have very serious problems with the position that the contract is null and void. Now," said the judge, with some emotion, "between those two oceans, where does justice fall?"

33

Judge Kiley's Decision: "Most of the Dispute Has Been Decided"

Judge Kiley arrived in his courtroom at ten minutes past four on Friday, September 23, to read his decision. Garbus and Russell Smith were noticeably absent. Possibly they had deduced which way the wind was blowing when Kiley had said that Mrs. Cheever could not walk away from her obligations.

The good news was that the judge found our contract valid and enforceable: no fraud or misrepresentation, a meeting of the minds, and no unclean hands.

The bad news was that Kiley had decided that Mrs. Cheever had not made her "choice" and had not forfeited her "right to choose." She "may decide," he said, "to exercise her right generously or sparingly." In order to avoid "the jeopardy of bad faith and unfair dealing," Mrs. Cheever must give Academy no fewer than "approximately ten to fifteen stories." He based this figure, the judge said, on "the size and accomplishments of Academy Chicago and the size of previous John Cheever anthologies."

He had possibly been convinced by Garbus's dramatic presentation: "Mrs. Cheever," Garbus had said, holding his hands close together to symbolize a slim volume; "Mr. Miller," Garbus said, holding his hands wide apart to symbolize a fat volume. This pantomime was something any judge could understand. In addition, there was the probable influence of Goettel's opinion, which had been entered into the record over Paul's objection. Academy, Kiley said, picking up the words already picked up by Garbus and Goettel from the Westchester newspaper, saw a "treasure trove" and a "literary gold mine" in the stories, and began soon after the contract was signed in August 1987 to act with Franklin Dennis "unfortunately and inexplicably" on the "unjustified assumption" that they had a right to publish the uncollected stories of John Cheever and to select the stories.

Kiley said that he recognized the fact that the contract gave Academy the right to control the design and format of the work, but he wanted to emphasize that Franklin had written a letter pledging Academy's cooperation with Mary Cheever on all matters of publication.

"Now that I have decided the issues," the judge said, "it looks like most of the dispute at this level anyway has been decided." He added that he, personally, would like to see Mrs. Cheever make her choices in good faith, considering "the honest input of Academy and Mr. Dennis," since Academy was "perfectly capable of publishing a high quality work" like an anthology of "some" of John Cheever's uncollected stories. "For us consumers of high quality literary works," he said, "we ask you both to step aside of your deeply felt differences and think of us and do the work."

The judge did not seem to be aware that his decision raised as many issues as it "settled." He had mandated a number of stories, but he said nothing about the number of pages: the Cheevers could choose ten stories of a few pages each and provide us with a forty-page book. He had said nothing about the size of the pages: the thing could look like a thin, oversized catalog or one of the Big Little Books Jordan and I had read as children. By giving Mrs. Cheever the right to decide on design and format, he had taken that crucial control out of the hands of the publisher—where he acknowledged the contract had put it—and turned it over to someone who was hostile to the idea of our having any book at all. And he had given Mrs. Cheever no deadline for providing these "approximately ten to fifteen" stories to us.

On top of all that, he ignored the question of the quality of the stories she had to provide. Several of the uncollected stories had won prizes. Was she required to give us these? We had a subtitle: "1930–1981." Was she required to give us a story from each decade? And what about those stories that had fallen into the public domain? Could she give us ten of these, which anyone could publish? And could she then hold us to the terms of the contract requiring us to pay her a substantial royalty, despite the fact that she did not own the stories she was giving us? Finally, the judge had said nothing about whether Mrs. Cheever could sell the remaining fifty-eight stories to another publisher.

Thus we were not only upset and angry, we were also confused. Paul seemed stricken: he had had considerable respect for Judge Kiley; he had once referred to him as "a great man." Now the great man had come down with what our son Eric delicately referred to as "this lamebrain decision."

After we returned to our office that afternoon, Paul phoned to say that he was convinced that Kiley would not allow Mrs. Cheever to sell the stories elsewhere. And if Ben and Susan could not go elsewhere, surely they would settle this thing with us? even though that settlement would leave Andrew Wylie—who, Garbus insisted, was not his client—out in the cold?

While we were brooding over all this, Garbus and Russell Smith, back in New York, were busy having a letter hand-delivered to all the magazines that had granted us permissions to reprint the stories. The letter said that Academy had "induced" editors to grant permission by falsely claiming that it had a contract with Mrs. Cheever, who had sued Academy in New York for fraud, among other things. Garbus requested that the editors *immediately* (his emphasis) withhold or rescind these permissions; otherwise Academy might *immediately* rush this volume into print, ignoring Mrs. Cheever's objections. A copy of Goettel's opinion was included with the letter. Needless to say, no mention was made of Kiley's declaration that there had been no fraud and that the contract was valid and enforceable.

This missive prompted letters to us that cast some reflections on our integrity. Jerry S. Birenz, an attorney for Condé Nast Publications, publisher of *Mademoiselle*—and a sister company of Random House—withdrew permissions and added that Condé Nast had granted permission in December 1987 because Academy had "represented" that Mrs. Cheever approved; he understood that this was no longer the case—"if," he apparently could not resist adding, "it ever was."

Mary E. Ryan of W. W. Norton, which had not been able to grant us permission because it held no rights to "Behold a Cloud in the West," sent us a Federal Express letter "formally" asking that we remove their name from our acknowledgments. They had requested that we give them a "courtesy" line because the story had appeared in the collection *New Letters in America*, published by them. This was the book Mrs. Cheever had given to Franklin during his famous visit to her.

The "Editorial Counsel" for the *New Yorker* wrote us a letter that we found barely comprehensible: the gist of it seemed to be that the *New Yorker* had never given us any permission in the first place. His position appeared to be that Joy Weiner had simply asked that we credit the *New Yorker* for original publication and nothing more.

Paul found the Condé Nast letter particularly depressing. "They'll never stop," he said. "Do you want to go on with this? These are the most horrible people in the world. They're maniacs."

"You don't want to quit, do you?" I asked, horrified.

"No," he said, "of course not. But—they're going to fight these stories every step of the way." The book was worth it, I said. Not for money. For vindication. And surely this thing was coming to an end now? Paul said that he thought they were going to fight over every margin, every word on a page, everything. Because Kiley, despite the contract, had given them control over design and format.

Some letters from editors were friendly. *Harper's* magazine informed us, sympathetically, that they never rescinded permissions. Stephanie Poller of *Good Housekeeping* withdrew permission but graciously expressed the hope that Academy and "the estate" would "amicably work out" our differences "regarding this and other Cheever writings." We were grateful to *Harper's* and *Good Housekeeping* for their editors' kind words, and to Betty Klarnet of *Harper's Bazaar* for sending along a copy of Garbus's letter with her rescission. Garbus had not sent Paul a copy. For some reason reading Garbus's letter cheered Paul up; he said he thought it was "marvelous." He wanted Kiley to see it.

Paul received a drumfire of demands from Garbus for the delivery of the galleys and samplers to the Cheevers. Paul responded that since Academy did not intend to sell or distribute these, there was no justification for Garbus's "several demands" for delivery.

Then there was a letter from Garbus confirming a "conversation" that Paul told us had never taken place, in which Paul allegedly told Garbus that Academy was going to publish a book of fifty-five stories in accordance with Kiley's ruling, and that Academy would not allow Mrs. Cheever to see stories that had been excluded from the galleys so that she could consider them as part of her "selection." Garbus went on to say that he presumed that Paul's recollection of this "conversation" would "differ" from his, so in the future it would be best if he and Paul communicated only by letter; they had had "too many misunderstandings in the past."

Paul found this letter shocking. "They're acting stung," he said. "Evidently they think they lost."

In his next letter, Garbus asked Paul "in the spirit of cooperation" to tell everyone who had given us permission that these permissions were "no longer appropriate." In this same cooperative spirit, he asked again for the galleys and samplers to be delivered to the Cheevers. And he said he had seen Paul's "recent public statements," similar to statements made to him, that Academy intended to publish "all or nearly all of the sixty-eight stories." Could Paul please advise him whether Academy intended to publish these stories?

Paul said he thought that Garbus was laying some kind of trail to present to Kiley. He wrote a careful letter telling Garbus that he had not made any statements, public or private, that Academy intended to publish all or nearly all of the stories and further that Academy had no intention of publishing any stories controlled by Mrs. Cheever without her consent and would work with her to produce "expeditiously" a book "of the highest quality."

A meeting with Goettel was scheduled for the end of the month. A few days before the meeting, Maura called Paul to tell him that Goettel had phoned Garbus's office and wanted all the lawyers to meet in his chambers and sit around a table and talk. This struck Paul as odd, and with good reason, because the meeting with Goettel proved to be a hearing in his courtroom; nobody sat around a table and talked. There was no court reporter. Franklin and Mary took notes.

Judge Goettel began by announcing that he had read Judge Kiley's decision and that Kiley had obliged Mrs. Cheever to deliver a manuscript and had found that Academy had breached the contract by not consulting with her. "With all due respect," Paul pointed out, Judge Kiley had not used the term "breach of contract" in reference to Academy's actions.

"Well, that's my interpretation," said Judge Goettel.

There was some discussion of Garbus's amended complaint in which he asked that liability for copyright infringement be extended from the company to include Jordan, me, and our son Bruce, personally. Who, Goettel asked, is Bruce Miller? Was he heavily involved in the project? Garbus said he couldn't go into it in detail but Bruce Miller was present at the settlement meeting. Paul said he had no knowledge that Bruce was involved in the Cheever project.

Garbus requested a summary judgment (that is, a judgment on the law when the facts of a case are undisputed) or an expedited trial; he said that "the press" had reported "by implication" that Academy was selling the galleys and samplers "on the black market." He added that tensions between the parties had risen to the point that the case had become "matrimonial." Goettel responded that there was no possibility of an expedited trial. The issue was not pressing, he said; Garbus had delayed action himself by including more parties. Now the Millers needed time to answer the amended complaint; and, too, the Chicago case was still *sub judice,* and the Millers might decide to appeal it. So an expedited trial was out.

Garbus asked again for a summary judgment: Mrs. Cheever, he said, had to recover her legal fees; she was entitled to damages. Goettel replied that the case was not going to lead to much recovery because the alleged copyright violation was not "egregious." No big bucks there, he said, a magistrate could set the amount. He was willing to do it; it wouldn't be difficult.

Garbus moved to the subject of the galleys, asking Goettel for an order that all of them be "returned" to the Cheevers. Otherwise Academy could sell them for big money. Paul commented that Garbus kept talking about the galleys being "returned," but the Cheevers had never had them in the first place. Goettel did not rule on this, but he suggested it would be "wise" to "sequester" the galleys somewhere. He went on to observe that he agreed with Judge Kiley: Mrs. Cheever must, in good faith, select good stories. He had read in the papers that Mrs. Cheever hoped to sell the book to another publisher. But, he said, until she selected stories in good faith, she was not free to negotiate elsewhere. Garbus said that he did not agree. The judge responded that Mrs. Cheever could not give Academy "the dregs." She was boxed in, he said, because at the hearing she had contended that the prewar stories were no good. Garbus said that she should choose a "thematic" book: the "army years," the "depression years." Judge Goettel commented that some collections were unified by a theme; some were not. Some of the "sketches" in the collection, he volunteered, were in his opinion better than many of the stories.

This case, he told Garbus, cried out for settlement. "The ice is melting," he said. By this he apparently meant that interest in the book may have peaked. "What's the problem?" he asked. "Is it a personality problem between the lawyers?" Garbus said plaintively that he found his relationship with Paul to be very unpleasant and that he could not trust Paul or his clients. He repeated his request for the galleys and samplers and his accusation that Academy was selling them "on the black market." Paul said that that was the first time in thirty years that anyone had said anything like that about him. He had tried repeatedly, he said, to deal fairly with the other side.

Goettel granted Garbus's motion to add parties to the suit. Paul said he would serve it to Jordan and Anita Miller but he did not represent Bruce

Miller. Garbus ended with the complaint that he could not find out the name of the printer who was going to print the book. Goettel noted that Academy was "reluctant to cough up this information" and suggested that Garbus send Academy an interrogatory.*

With business more or less out of the way, Garbus and Goettel exchanged a little *ex parte* talk about a case coming up before Goettel in which Garbus represented one of the parties. "That's another one that cries out to be settled," the judge observed. Garbus said that one was like the Iran-Iraq war.

On the way out Paul, in the spirit of compromise, approached Garbus, who turned away irritably and said he would have to think about talking to Paul. They all rode down in the elevator together, Garbus silent and looking very angry. Downstairs in the hallway Maura asked Paul if they could have a meeting some time in October; Garbus stalked off, in the wrong direction, as it happened. Paul, bemused by what he thought was a "good guy-bad guy" routine of some kind, left the subject open and went on his way while Maura went to retrieve Garbus.

We were rather bucked up when Franklin and Mary told us all this on the phone: we liked hearing that the judge had said that there wouldn't be much money in the copyright infringement suit, that the case cried out for settlement, and that Mrs. Cheever couldn't give us dregs. But when we talked to Paul, our spirits drooped again. He was very upset with Judge Goettel. The thing to do, Paul said, was find another lawyer, preferably one from White Plains, to tell Goettel he should recuse himself. That would make him angry, of course, Paul said; every time this happens, the judge hotly denies the motion and then says, "I wasn't biased, but I am now and I'm disqualifying myself." This idea upset us; we did not think Goettel would recuse himself.

Paul was angry that Goettel had said that Kiley had accused us of breaching the contract and particularly outraged because of the *ex parte* discussion with Garbus about a pending trial. As it happened, Paul knew the lawyer on the opposing side; he was a Chicago attorney who had told Paul he was facing Garbus and had wanted to know what Garbus was like. Paul intended to tell his friend about it; he said the friend had a short fuse.

Mary Dennis wondered why Mrs. Cheever would want to spend $50,000

---

*No arrangements had been made for printing this book, so there was no printer.

or so on a trial to get back a pittance in damages. In any case, Mary was inspired by this hearing to imagine, after a talk with Bruce, a segment from what she called "a future Garbus memoir" entitled *A Backward Glance*:

> I first came up against Academy before they were the publishing giant they are today. Even then they were shrewd and ruthless: formidable rivals. But the moment I looked into the steel-grey eyes of their Harvard-trained attorney, I knew I was in for some low legal blows.
>
> My biggest setback came when I discovered that Academy's barracuda press agent was represented by a lawyer whom I had come up against before—Bob Stein, whose sheer bulk was enough to intimidate most adversaries.
>
> The discovery process had been a harrowing one for the relatively naive and sheltered Cheever family. Mrs. Cheever, a frail, ethereal woman, had to be hospitalized after her first day of interrogation. We were terrified that the tasteless Freehling would bring up potentially upsetting themes the family had fought so long and hard to keep secret. I learned early on that with the Cheevers, privacy was almost an obsession.

34

"A Literary Gold Mine"

Paul set to work on a Motion for Clarification, which he believed would help to sort out the mess Kiley's decision had created. I set to work on Hella Haasse's medieval novel, immersing myself in the fifteenth century because I found the present rather painful. Twelve of our most salable titles were out of print, we could not afford to reprint them, and we had not published anything worth mentioning in 1988. We were slowly sinking. Through rents in the clouds that covered us, we glimpsed the presidential campaign, which certainly did not cheer us up. Someone talked us into going to a Democratic rally in a suburb. The mayor welcomed us, saying, "I appreciate your asking myself to be here tonight." We listened to interminable speeches in a large, freezing room.

There were certain parallels between Michael Dukakis's situation and our own. As Bob Schieffer and Gary Paul Gates were to put it, "From a tactical standpoint, it was Dukakis's failure to understand the value of repetition that was the most serious flaw in his approach to rebutting Bush's criticism." Dukakis, they wrote, did respond to Bush's charges, but he failed to repeat his response. He felt that his response took care of the matter and that was the end of it. But the Bush team behaved differently. "When Dukakis responded to a charge, the Bush campaign simply repeated the accusation, and kept repeating it, refusing even to acknowledge that Dukakis had tried to rebut it."[1]

To help Paul with his motion, Jordan drew up a chart listing each story, the number of its pages in our galley, whether it was in the public domain, and whether it had received any awards or special recognition. Paul was fascinated to see that seventeen of the stories had received some sign of recognition by winning an award, being included in a general anthology, or serving as the basis for a Broadway play. In his motion, Paul pointed this out to Judge Kiley, noting also that twenty-three of the sixty-eight stories were less than six pages long, so it was possible that Mrs. Cheever could give us a book of ten stories that totaled fewer than sixty pages, since the judge had not mandated a page count.

For the rest, Paul pointed out that the Cheever lawyers had not cooperated in moving toward publication. And he ran once more through the obvious facts: there was no evidence that the parties had agreed to a small book; Jordan's and Franklin's letters attested to the expectation that it would be a big book, as did Joy Weiner's October 1987 letter to Mary Cheever announcing that thirty-eight *New Yorker* stories would be included in the collection. And only the 1978 omnibus, of all previous Cheever collections, could be considered comparable to *Uncollected Stories*, since it, too, provided a retrospective of Cheever's work. Paul asked for clarification on the question, which the court had not addressed, of whether Mrs. Cheever could negotiate with another publisher for stories she withheld from Academy. And then there were the still open questions of the size of the book Mrs. Cheever was to provide and the date of its publication, which, Paul said, should be no later than the spring of 1989, to avoid loss of momentum. He included the information, which he was sure would shock Kiley, that on the day the judge announced his decision that the contract was valid and had not been obtained by fraud, the Cheever lawyers had written to people who had granted permissions, implying that the contract was invalid and had been fraudulently procured. Paul attached a copy of Garbus's letter to that effect.

At the hearing that ensued, Judge Kiley promptly denied Paul's motion. He said that he was certainly not going to start reconsidering his conclusions; he felt satisfied that those conclusions were correct. He did explain that the reason he mandated the number of stories was to prevent "any expectation on Mrs. Cheever's part that she could pick one or two stories or make a decision that none at all would be chosen"—although he certainly did not agree and was not persuaded that the parties had contemplated a large book when the deal was struck in August 1987. And he was not going to deal with the question of when Mrs. Cheever should produce her selection, since loss of momentum was a business risk Academy took when it went to law.

The question of whether Mary Cheever could submit to other publishers stories she did not give to Academy had not, the judge said, come up before. That was probably, he said, rubbing it in, because Academy was operating on the strong conviction that it would get almost all of the sixty-eight stories in question. "I suppose," he said, with a noticeable lack of enthusiasm, "if the parties want to talk about that, they can submit additional arguments to me on that."

On November 2, 1988, Judge Kiley read his official ruling. He called Academy's behavior "inexplicable" and implied that Franklin was a liar: "I am not persuaded that Mr. Dennis told Ben Cheever in late November that the best way to do the work was to publish all the stories." We found this outrageous. Ben had admitted in testimony in White Plains that Franklin had told him that at the time, and Garbus had not questioned that assertion. We had assumed that Paul had submitted at least that part of Ben's White Plains testimony as an exhibit in Chicago. We learned later that Paul had not submitted it.

For the rest, the judge seemed to be following Goettel's scenario: Academy had discovered a "literary gold mine"; the Cheevers did not realize it; the Cheevers wanted to see "the research product" before they made their "selection"; Mrs. Cheever could not read the "Xeroxing" given her on December 12, and it was "unreasonable" to expect the family to make their "choice" from "Xerox copies of this quality." It was all a question of what Mrs. Cheever thought and what Ben thought. It was not significant that "a literary giant" had been sought to write the introduction; that said nothing about the projected size of the book. The title didn't mean anything either because "tentative titles do not define the work."

However, the judge said, he did not want to send the parties on their way without "guidance." So he gave an "advisory declaration to avoid the cost of further litigation and to further a complete resolution of this dispute." Mary Cheever, he said, would avoid implicating her obligations of good faith and fair dealing if she chose at least ten to fifteen stories of the size of the "stereotypical" John Cheever work: "All of his other collections of short stories included about ten to fifteen stories and ran anywhere from approximately 140 to 260 pages." He seemed to mean "prototypical" rather than "stereotypical." He added the comment that Academy's galleys, Plaintiff's Exhibit 36, went "considerably beyond the stereotyped perceptions of John Cheever's work." This reference to "stereotyped perceptions" seemed to imply that he had confused statements that the galleys offered new insights into Cheever's work with the *size* of pre-1978 Cheever collections.

Kiley also seemed to confuse the contract with Franklin's precontract letters promising cooperation with Mrs. Cheever "in all matters of publication": the judge declared that Academy must cooperate with her in all matters of design, format, and subsidiary rights. Letters Mrs. Cheever had received from Academy and from the *New Yorker,* he dismissed as merely evidence that Academy was trying to create an "atmosphere" in which it could publish the big book—an orchestrated attempt, in other words, to outwit Mrs. Cheever. Thus the judge turned that evidence on its head.

Mrs. Cheever could not, he said, negotiate or contract for the stories with another publisher until she satisfied her obligation to deliver the work to Academy and agreed on a date for publication of it. After that she was free to permit another company to publish the remaining uncollected stories as long as she did not bind herself to the promotion and publication of those stories simultaneously with Academy's stories.

Paul was most upset by this decision. That afternoon he messengered a letter to Kiley pointing out that the judge had erred in setting the standard for the smaller Cheever volumes at "140 to 260 pages." With the letter Paul included a chart showing the range of pages in the pre-1978 collections to be 174 to 275 (*The Way Some People Live*: 256; *The Enormous Radio*: 237; *The Housebreaker of Shady Hill*: 185; *Some People, Places and Things*: 175; *Brigadier & the Golf Widow*: 275; *The World of Apples*: 175). He asked for a correction and announced that he was calling M. Leslie Kite that afternoon to try to arrange a conference call with Kiley to discuss the correction.

M. Leslie Kite responded that he would not join the conference because he had no authority to do it. Russell Smith wrote to Judge Kiley, complaining that Paul's letter was inappropriate and that he had left out of his chart what Smith called "the small hardcover books produced by the antiquarian booksellers Sylvester & Orphanos."* Academy should really, he said, compare itself to these antiquarian booksellers rather than to "major houses with larger advances and wider audiences." Ignoring the fact that our contract set escalation clauses for sales above fifteen thousand copies and gave Mrs. Cheever no control over the size of the print run or the size of the book itself, Smith told Judge Kiley that "Academy is a small press which paid a small advance for a small book which was envisioned to be for a

---

*These were, as I have noted, editions of single stories done in runs of 150 copies, each signed and numbered, for collectors. As I have also noted, copies of the contract for "Expelled," the most recent story published by Sylvester & Orphanos, were "lost" by both Mrs. Cheever and ICM and unavailable from Sylvester & Orphanos.

small audience, the size of which was to be controlled by Mrs. Cheever."

It was now November 3. Ever since September 23, Smith wrote, Mrs. Cheever and her family had been analyzing and collecting the stories. They did not intend to merely slap together a bunch of disparate stories, as Dennis and Academy had done. They were going to create a book with a "unifying theme." If a minimum number of pages were imposed on Mrs. Cheever, she would be forced to include stories "merely for the sake of size" and thus sacrifice "the integrity of the work." He asked for a hearing on this. A couple of days later Smith called Paul, ostensibly to ask whether there had been any word from Kiley. Paul explained that the judge would never respond to a letter but only to a motion. Smith replied that there was no reason for Paul to submit a motion; by the end of November, Mrs. Cheever was going to give us *more* than 175 pages.

To my considerable surprise, Paul seemed to believe this. Maybe, he said, we shouldn't present the motion, maybe it isn't necessary. Jane Winter and Mary Jo Reilly of our office were delighted; they said they were sure that the Cheevers were really going to give us 175 pages. And Jane's husband, Art Winter, agreed. After all, he said, Mrs. Cheever was going to have to live with this book, so why wouldn't she want to make it an appealing volume? Impressed as always with a lot of people telling us something, we decided it must be true. If so, there had to be something wrong with it. We leaped to the conclusion that if the Cheevers really were going to give us a substantial book, they must be planning to include all the chapters from novels that we had decided not to use because they were actually already collected, in a manner of speaking. There were ten of these, and they were very long. The Cheevers had asked us several times for copies of these stories; we did not consider them stories but chapters. We managed to upset ourselves considerably over this and communicated our uneasiness to Paul. He said that it was possible that Kiley may not have mandated that Mrs. Cheever choose stories from the galleys—Plaintiff's Exhibit 36 (PE 36). Thus the judge had left another gray area. Paul said that he thought he had better write a confirming letter after all and he had better go ahead and prepare the motion. "You have said," he wrote to Russell Smith, "that you will deliver in excess of 175 pages by the end of this month. Please confirm that these stories are from PE 36."

Russell Smith responded by fax that he had not stated the manuscript would exceed 175 pages and that he had not said that Mrs. Cheever would deliver it by the end of November. Paul's letter, he said, confirmed the experience that M. Leslie Kite, Maura Wogan, and Martin Garbus had had with Paul. None of them wanted to have any more telephone conversations with him. And Paul was instructed not to communicate any further with M. Leslie Kite.

This missive threw us into a black rage. This is the end of all communication, we said; don't ever call them again. Paul said that was nonsense. He had to call them; attorneys can't work that way. He submitted the motion, in which he requested that the judge raise his minimum requirement to 174 pages because the 140-page minimum was based on error, and he requested also that the judge mandate that Mrs. Cheever's selections be taken from PE 36.

The result of this motion was that the judge called a hearing, restricted to Chicago lawyers, at which he displayed a degree of annoyance. He announced that he was unhappy with all the parties in the case and especially with Paul for writing a letter about the number of pages—on the *very day* that he, Kiley, gave his final decision! That, he said, was inappropriate. He would receive no more letters, no more briefs, no more motions. He wanted an order written, if the parties could agree on one, and then nothing more.

If people had any more arguments, he said, they could take them to an appeals court.

35

"John Was the King of Hades"

In late October, excerpts from John Cheever's *Letters* appeared in *Esquire* magazine: the cover of the November issue carried the legend, "The Intimate Letters of John Cheever." Inside could be found an introduction by Ben, in which he informed the reader that his father was occasionally a "cold-blooded" hypocrite and a "boorish snob" whose female lover had described him as "the horniest man" she had ever known. John Cheever told Ben to destroy the letters; Ben, usually obedient, had not done it. When one moved on to the letters themselves, one found that many had been written to male lovers: they were replete with references to "hard, wet cocks," "nice asses," and "soft balls."[1]

At about this same time, Mrs. Cheever complained to the press about the destructive appetite for scandal that had swept into the world of literature. "[John] wasn't a movie star. He was a writer. The only reputation he wanted was someone who wrote stories that people enjoyed."[2]

Also at this time Mrs. Cheever was interviewed by Andrea Chambers of *People* magazine, who quoted her as saying that she had given Ben permission to publish the letters partly to help him "work out his grief" but that she would have preferred that if they were published, it would be after her death. Although she had known that her husband had "emotional attachments—or disturbances or whatever you call them—with men as well as women," she had learned from the letters that his sexual activity was more frequent than she had thought. Mrs. Cheever confessed to Ms. Chambers that when her husband was infatuated with someone, "he would wonder why he was married to me, and he could be very brutal. He would get drunk and accuse me of having affairs with men, which I wasn't."

She said that in the 1960s, he had falsely accused her of having a lesbian affair with one of her students whom she had invited to live at the Cheever house because the student was having family problems. "John was horrible to her. He told me that if I didn't tell her to go away, he would rape her. Once he came down the stairs stark naked. I think he was trying to horrify us and force her to go." Often he got dressed up, making it obvious that he was going into the city to meet a lover. But "he always came home to dinner."

Ben, in his segment of the revelatory *People* interview, claimed that he was not exploiting his father's writing: on the contrary, he thought that his father might have been using him "to get his essence out to the world" because John Cheever was "committed to a kind of public exposure," having written *Falconer* about a man with homosexual leanings in an unhappy marriage. Ben said that he had "an implied contract" with his readers not to delete portions of his father's letters based on his own priggishness. He went on to say that there was an implication in Cheever's journals that John Cheever had his "first homosexual experience with his own brother as a teenager." And although he was bisexual all his life, Cheever nevertheless inveighed against "faggots" and frequently criticized Ben "for being effeminate."

Ben said that John Cheever confessed his bisexuality to him some days before his death but that Ben had known about it for years, ever since one of his father's male lovers had attempted to seduce him. "Mom always knew that too," Ben said. "She once told me that when he was on the telephone with a man, he was always holding the phone with one hand and rubbing his behind with the other." As a sort of climax to this interview, Ben volunteered that he had wondered whether it was possible that Daddy might have looked at him as "physically desirable" and part of him thought that would be terrible, but another part kept thinking, "How neat."[3]

Jordan and I contributed a few choice words to the article, much to Paul's annoyance. Andrea Chambers had flown out to Chicago to interview us.

Ben gave other interviews. He told Dick Polman of the Knight-Ridder News Service that twenty years earlier, his father had gotten drunk at a suburban party and begun to chase a woman "half his age" around the room. When he failed to catch her, he dropped his pants in front of the other guests and resumed the chase until Ben "intervened." If Ben brought a girl home and slept with her, it "would make Daddy feel competitive. Then he would sleep with my mother." In this interview Ben revised his story about the attempted seduction that had opened his eyes to his father's sexual proclivities. Now he said that it was not until June 1982 that John Cheever, as he lay dying, told Ben the truth. Then "in retrospect" Ben realized he had had unconscious knowledge. "'I don't mind, Daddy, if you don't mind,' Ben whispered, feeling bewildered."[4] Ben stayed with this version in an interview with Ruth Pollack Coughlin: "I think I was a fool before not to understand," he said. "My level of self-delusion was world-class. There were a lot of homosexual characters in his early stories, and look at *Falconer*. And his behavior was so homophobic."[5]

The *Letters* received, for the most part, serious attention from reviewers, who considered any work by John Cheever to be important. What began to creep in here and there was a note of disparagement—not of John Cheever, but of his family. Dick Polman commented that anyone wondering whether public figures have any rights to privacy "need only look at the Cheever family's ongoing campaign to acquaint Americans with the fact of the late author's boozing and sexual byplay, his insecurities, his self-destructive impulses."[6] Andrea Chambers echoed this: "The just-published letters are quite enough to rekindle the literary controversy about a writer's right to privacy—dead or alive."[7] Anne Hulbert in the *New Republic* mentioned "parent abuse." She was particularly struck by what she called Ben's "nonchalant" dropping of a comment by a male lover that John Cheever's orgasms were always accompanied by a vision of sunshine or flowers. "I wonder," Ms. Hulbert wrote, "how Cheever's son thinks this revelation compares with the republication of some sub-par stories."[8]

Ben defended himself against this criticism. "People feel we're the bad, wicked Cheevers," he said. "Should I have burned those letters? . . . . When you hide something like that . . . you distort the world. The only hope is absolute candor. If I'd read them and burned [the letters], people would have had a desperate misunderstanding about John Cheever."[9]

Certainly there was no suggestion that these letters should have been burned. Generally scholars expect that immediate family members will not publish material like this during their lifetimes but will seal it for future examination. Obviously we could not have cared less about the reputations of the surviving Cheevers, but it seemed to us that these revelations, coming so soon after his death, would begin to hurt the literary reputation of Cheever himself. I thought that surely someone, perhaps Robert Gottlieb, Ben's "literary eminence" (who had garnered some publicity of his own that November by publishing a coffee-table book of color photographs of his large collection of plastic handbags),[10] would attempt to explain to the Cheevers that a literary reputation is not immutable. One of the purposes of our press was to attempt to revive interest in authors like George Sand, Robert Graves, and J. P. Marquand, to say nothing of Arnold Bennett. I was particularly aware, of course, of what had happened to Bennett's reputation: attacks on him by Virginia Woolf and Ezra Pound, among others—many of them personal—had created a false image of him that was constantly conjured up by critics only superficially familiar with his work. Stories about him spread by dubious sources—his wife and mistress among them—were accepted as truth and crept into biographies and general literary histories.

Mrs. Cheever and Ben were now telling journalists that John Cheever threatened to rape schoolgirls, that he dropped his pants at parties, that he may have had a sexual relationship with his brother, and that he even possibly lusted after his own son. This kind of revelation was to be ratcheted up several notches a couple of years later when Susan published *Treetops*, ostensibly a "tribute" to her mother, and again when Robert Gottlieb produced the long-awaited *Journals*. This last publication evoked considerable negative press comment.

In connection with the publication of *Treetops*, the March 1991 issue of *Mirabella* carried an interview with Mrs. Cheever and Susan. The cover of the magazine bore the legend, "The Marriage from Hell: A Hair-Raising Visit with Mrs. Cheever." The theme of the interview was that Mrs. Cheever was an abused wife, flaky but talented, who was overshadowed by a nasty, childish husband. There was, for instance, John Cheever's refusal to accompany Mary to her father's house in the summer and his demand that she cook and freeze dinners for him for each night of the three weeks she would be away. This frozen dinner story was to be repeated again and again in reviews of *Treetops*. Another of Susan's complaints about life with John Cheever that received great attention and that we found particularly striking was that her father cannibalized actual family events in his fiction, to the distress of his wife and children. Details of the family's lives and the lives of their neighbors, Susan said, turned up in "the public pages" of the *New Yorker*. The story "The Hartleys" was, she said, "a clear account of a Cheever family ski trip." Apparently some fiction *was* "crypto-autobiography."

There were other revelations in *Treetops*: Mrs. Cheever had a "brief, wrenching affair" with a writer while her husband was alive—thus negating her statement to Andrea Chambers that John's suspicions about her were unfounded—and she flirted with Susan's boyfriends, while John made embarrassing passes at her brothers' girlfriends. In a crypto-autobiographical insight, Susan said that her father's anger against her mother in his work stemmed from resentments against his own mother. Speaking of mothers, Susan complained that Mary did not love her, and Mrs. Cheever told *Mirabella* that *her* mother didn't love *her*—not her stepmother, she and Susan explained. Her own mother.[11]

We hoped that critics and literary scholars would approach the revelations in *Treetops* with caution. There were some obvious errors in chapter 18, dealing with the lawsuit. Mrs. Cheever, Susan says, signed the contract because Jordan and Franklin seemed "gentlemanly and friendly, if a bit incompetent" and that Mrs. Cheever's understanding, based on conversations with "gentlemanly" Jordan Miller, was that Academy planned "a small book of five to seven stories." As we know, Mrs. Cheever had never met Jordan or Franklin before she signed the contract and had no conversations with either of them. It was with Maggie Curran of ICM that Jordan spoke, and Franklin wrote Mrs. Cheever one letter in which he mentioned two hundred stories and a volume or volumes. Then, too, there was the October letter to Mrs. Cheever from the *New Yorker*, telling her that Academy was using thirty-eight stories from that magazine alone. Susan said also in this chapter that "the Illinois Appeal Court" rejected Academy's appeal. This, as will develop, was not the case.

Susan had some harsh words for Paul, too. He was a tall man, she said, in "an ill-fitting suit" who angrily interrupted the judge. Paul, who is of medium height and an almost fanatically neat dresser, would probably have died before he interrupted a judge, even politely. She also called him a maniac.

"Oh," Paul said when I told him this, "who cares what Susan says."

Some things in *Treetops* certainly had the ring of truth. Judge Goettel, Susan says, "had no more use for Jordan and Anita Miller" than the Cheevers had. The judge and Mary Cheever "seem to come from the same genteel world. He will not betray her assumptions." Whether Federico called his father's work "vindictive" may be questionable, but Ben's comments on his work sound very much like Ben: "Language is a pistol," he is quoted as saying, "you shoot your little son and daughter with it . . . you cut your son and daughter in half."[12] Compare this with Ben's remarks about Academy Chicago in *Chicago* magazine: "The analogy that comes to mind? Someone knocks on your door and asks if they can use your phone, and then they rob you and pull out a gun and they say, 'Well, now I'm going to rape you. If you let me rape you, I won't hurt you,' and they rape you and then they shoot you in the head."[13]

The thesis of *Treetops*—in line with today's feminist consciousness—seems to be that Mary Cheever had "focused her energy on the development of her husband's gifts" at the expense of her own. Her passionate devotion to her husband led her to sacrifice her golden years to "fight" for him—or, at least, "to fight to protect her part of the inheritance left by [his] talent."[14]

36

"Paul Is Named Jack and Mani Is Amy"

While we waited for the Cheevers to bring forth their opus, we discussed—and discussed and discussed—possibilities. Since Judge Kiley's opinion was like a Swiss cheese, there were a lot of possibilities. Jordan and I assumed that the 140 pages that the judge had given us were 140 pages of our galley. We thought the Cheevers would choose stories from the galley, count all the pages, and send us a list. We thought this might not be so bad because our galley page was a large one—approximately 6" × 9"—and if we reformatted these pages into a book of a smaller size, we could get at least the 175 pages that we considered reasonable for a trade book. But Paul raised the possibility that the 140 pages might not come from our galley: the Cheevers might give us a typescript with ten lines on a page. That had not occurred to us; it was not a happy thought.

Then there was the question of the public domain stories. There were at least thirteen of these. Since the judge had said nothing about this, we thought it entirely possible that we would get a public domain manuscript over which Mrs. Cheever would claim control—and royalties.

Finally, on the last day of November, we received a letter from Mrs. Cheever. She explained that it was a cover letter for a manuscript that was being "delivered" to us "pursuant to our contract." That made clear—not only that her letter had been written by a lawyer—but that a packet was being sent us; if it was a packet, then it had to be a typescript, because otherwise they could simply have mailed or faxed us a list of the stories they had chosen.

Mrs. Cheever wrote that she had made a careful selection in order to provide a good book and she would welcome our comments, which she would carefully consider. She had several "proposals" for us: (1) given the book's "unifying theme," it should be called *Depression Stories by John Cheever: The Apprenticeship Years, 1931–1945*; (2) she did not want this book to be "advertised and promoted in the manner in which you attempted to market the last one"—she did not consider this "a mass market book,"* so she would "prefer that it not be promoted or advertised in the mass market media"; (3) the book should be published as soon as possible. She would "prefer to see it published no later than the summer of 1989"; and (4) after we reached "agreement with respect to the manuscript," she proposed that we "discuss the appropriate number of copies to be printed."

She wanted to make it very clear that she would not authorize publication "until we reach agreement upon all of the items discussed in this letter." She was sure that we would both agree on one point: "that the Cheevers and Academy have both suffered as a result" of the litigation. She hoped that we could "now move forward together to publish a book of quality."

The packet arrived the next day: 245 pages of typescript, neatly bound. As we had expected, the typescript had huge margins and triple—sometimes quadruple—spacing. There were fifteen stories, nine of them in the public domain. The "Table of Contents" listed, first of all, "Foreword by John Cheever; Introduction by Susan Cheever; Annotations by Mary Cheever."

The "Foreword" was "Why I Write Short Stories"—or half of it, anyway; it was suddenly interrupted by the first two pages of Susan's introduction, with no break in the pagination (C– as a grade for this?). Susan had obviously labored mightily over this introduction. She pointed out that her father had made it clear that he didn't want these uneven works republished, and she asked the reader to keep in mind that this book was "the result of a lawsuit and almost a year of litigation." These stories, she said lyrically, were apprenticeship work, "the first tentative notes, some mistaken, some off key, some pre-shadowing, of a full symphony . . . the first difficult chords in a music that will finally fill the hall."

Although the title gave the years covered as "1931–1945," the actual dates of the stories did not fit neatly into that classification. There were two stories from 1931, one from 1932, two from 1935, four from 1936, one

---

*The Cheevers and Garbus often talked about "mass market books." Technically a mass market book is a 4¼" × 7" paperback, printed on groundwood stock, selling for around $6 and distributed by IDs—independent distributors—to drugstores, supermarkets, magazine outlets, and bookstores. The covers can be stripped and returned to the publishers for credit while the text is pulped. These books are completely different from trade books, which are sold to bookstores by the publishers or by library and bookstore distributors. Covers cannot be stripped. Our Cheever book—as are all our books—was to be a trade book.

from 1937, one from 1939, two from 1940, one from 1942, and one from 1945. Not included from 1937 were the famous "Behold a Cloud in the West" and "Homage to Shakespeare," which had merited a collector's edition by Sylvester & Orphanos and had been anthologized in *Story Jubilee.* Also excluded were "Frère Jacques," one of the *Best American Short Stories of 1939*, and "I'm Going to Asia," which had received an O. Henry Memorial Award in 1941, a year that had been left out entirely in the material sent us, although two uncollected stories had been published that year. Mrs. Cheever also snubbed 1943, despite the fact that six uncollected stories had appeared that year, including "Sergeant Limeburner." Ditto 1944 and its four uncollected stories. At one point we asked Maura Wogan why "Homage to Shakespeare" had been omitted; she replied that Mrs. Cheever liked that story.

The year 1930 was not represented, even though Cheever had published his first story then: "Expelled" had to be an apprentice work if anything was. What *were* represented were stories Mrs. Cheever had called "embarrassingly immature": "Fall River" and "Late Gathering" (both 1931) and "Bock Beer and Bermuda Onions" (1932), which Ben had said that he particularly disliked. The bulk of Mrs. Cheever's manuscript had been called "sketches" by Susan.

Most of these stories had a "headnote" written by Mary Cheever, a contribution that she ostensibly believed constituted "intelligent editorial comment." These headnotes appeared with triple spacing and margins that made them look like laundry lists. Her note for "Late Gathering" told us that the farm in that story was a summer house where John and his brother Fred were weekend guests and that "Paul is named Jack and Mani is Amy." To compound the confusion she added that the names of the people who inspired Paul, Jack, Mani, and Amy were, she believed, "Ralph and Hazel." Commenting on "Bayonne," the story about a waitress in a diner, Mrs. Cheever informed the world that "writing is solitary work, for John it was often also hungry work. He watched and listened, and the way his observations worked on his imagination is illustrated in these two stories, 'Buffalo' and 'Bayonne.'"

By the time she got to "Play a March" (1936, and one of Susan's "sketches"), Mrs. Cheever appeared to be flagging. This, she said, "is story [*sic*] about an artist who is hungry." ("Play a March" is about a musician and his wife who dream of owning their own home.) But she forged ahead with "The Princess" (1936), revealing that "In Boston John and his brother Fred made friends with two sisters, Ginny and Teeny, who were the daughters, I believe, of a professor." Teeny was a dancer who acquainted John with the fascinating "world of professional dance . . . . He used this knowledge about dancers in the Depression in . . . The Princess' and 'The Teaser,' stories about obsession and despair."

Her headnote for "A Present for Louisa"(1940) informed us that John always wrote about what he cared about and "in 1940 John wanted to marry a girl (me) who had lost her first paying job and could not soon find another. He did not offer me marriage as a job. Would he have done so if he had plenty of money? As a surprise, a *fait accompli,* in the presence of many friends? Coercion! I believe he would have known better. What he did was to imagine a different sort of girl and man in a similar fix. And he wrote the story and the story was sold. Times have changed."

Finally came "Family Dinner" (1942), a rather harrowing story about two people on the verge of divorce who clearly hate each other and spend a dreadful evening with the wife's dull, pathetic parents. In her headnote here, Mrs. Cheever, probably not foreseeing Susan's revelations in *Treetops* about Cheever's antipathy to his wife's family, told us that her husband "enjoyed and admired my father and stepmother and they loved him. He imagined how they would feel if our marriage broke up. He wrote this story."

Torn between annoyance and laughter, we sent this "manuscript" to Paul and Tom Leavens, an intellectual property lawyer who had represented us in the past. Tom said he thought the contract had been breached by Mrs. Cheever's letter and her manuscript. He said it appeared that she was trying to prevent us from making money. Nine public domain stories out of fifteen was not good-faith dealing. He was particularly incensed by the format of the typescript: anyone who saw the spacing and margins could see it was a breach of good faith, he said. And it hadn't even been proofread. Paul's reaction was different: he was not happy with our unhappiness with this submission. He reminded me that I had offered Susan the opportunity to write an introduction. That was true, I said, but that was at the Royce Hotel. In any case both Tom and Paul agreed that we should write Mrs. Cheever a letter outlining our objections.

This letter required some painstaking work and consultations with Franklin and Mary, our sons, and the two lawyers. While we were tinkering with it, Russell Smith wrote to Paul expressing his annoyance that six days had gone by and Mrs. Cheever had not yet had a response from us. We commented that they suddenly seemed to be in a big hurry. It had taken them three months to choose these fifteen stories.

We finally sent our letter to Mrs. Cheever on December 13 by overnight UPS. We pointed out that her title was not suitable because "inclusive years in a title (1931–1945) are just that: inclusive" and she had not included all the uncollected stories published in that fourteen-year span. Also, the Depression did not last until 1945; World War II had ended it. This "apprenticeship" seemed rather long. In addition, she had excluded some rather major efforts, like "Homage to Shakespeare" and the "Town House" stories. "In other words," we said, "your title suggests a comprehensiveness which the manuscript does not approach."

We said, too, that we contemplated advertising and promoting this book just as we would any trade book and that questions of publication date, advertising, promotion and sales, and print run would be addressed by us when the editorial process was complete. We reminded her that our contract had an escalation clause based on the book's print run and that it required that we make all reasonable efforts to create a commercial success.

We went on to complain about the size of the book, the spacing and margins, the number of typos and errors—we could not resist this after having suffered through all the complaints about bad Xeroxes and sloppy typing. We complained about the number of public domain stories, which were 20 percent of the galleys and 60 percent of this typescript. We complained about the introduction and Susan's denigration of the stories and about Mrs. Cheever's headnotes. We were doing this for Mrs. Cheever's sake, we said: Susan's denigration would raise the inevitable question of why Mrs. Cheever had chosen these stories when she had said repeatedly that she preferred later stories, which were fully available to her for this manuscript. We reminded her that she had not selected any prize-winning stories or those chosen for limited editions.

We had come up with what we thought might be a formula for saving the book. We suggested that Mrs. Cheever select for our volume all the uncollected stories that had appeared from 1930 to 1944. Then we thought she could discuss a subsequent volume covering the years 1945 to 1981. We did not add that this second volume could be done by another publisher—most likely Random House—but that was what we meant. Thus the two volumes could preserve the complete, chronological compilation of Cheever's uncollected stories.

Garbus wrote Judge Goettel that the Cheevers had now delivered a fifteen-story, 243-page manuscript to Academy, with an introduction by Susan Cheever and annotations by Mary Cheever. The Cheevers had now "more than fulfilled their contracutal [*sic*] obligation as defined by Judge Kiley." If Academy decided to publish this, there must be "further discussions with the Cheevers concerning the print-run, advertising, format and design and other issues." He added that as soon as he heard from Academy, he would be "in a better position to evaluate the effect of that publication on the litigation" before Goettel. This was clearly intended to put us on notice that he would drop the litigation if we played ball. Paul responded with his own letter to Goettel, talking about the large margins, the twelve lines of text on some pages, Susan's "denigratory" essay, and Mrs. Cheever's severe limits on print run and advertising.

On December 27, we received Mrs. Cheever's reply, along with a long letter from Garbus. Continuing this exercise in futility, Mrs. Cheever said she, too, was pleased that the editorial process had begun and hoped we would soon agree on the contents of this small volume. She apologized for the manuscript contents being "in any way scrambled or imperfectly proof-read" but they knew that as publishers we were "well equipped to take care of these matters" so they didn't "hold up delivery of the manuscript for extensive editing." This was a gratifying change of attitude toward us. For the rest, she said, the title "'Depression Stories' need not indicate *all* Depression stories." She pointed out that they had omitted "one other Depression story, 'A Bird in the Hand,'" because it "seemed to us not to meet the standard set by the group we did select, which we consider very strong, both singly and as a group." And "A Trip to the Moon," although it was "published in 19845"—a definite D in proofreading here—was "inarguably" a Depression story, so they put the closing date up to 1945. If we considered the date more important than the content, we might prefer to omit this story. Or we could omit the dates from the title. "Expelled" and "Homage to Shakespeare" had not been included because these were *not* Depression stories.

She added that both her name and Susan's were valuable and Susan would be willing perhaps to "modify" phrases that seemed to us to "denigrate" the stories. She had reviewed the contract and couldn't find any mention in it of public domain stories. And certainly a story's public domain status was "no indication of its quality or lack of it." She did find these stories immature, but "some of them" she liked very much. In a dreary foreshadowing of what was to come, she said she had counted the words "per page in all John's collections of stories" and found that there were 300 to 350 words per page in all but the 1978 omnibus and our galleys contained "almost 100 more per page."

Garbus's letter was an argumentative, three-and-a-half-page demand for an end to arguments, in which he brought up not only Ben's belief that we were the University of Chicago Press but also Franklin's famous "hostess gifts" and our denigration in *People* of Ben's book of letters.

I escaped into the Middle Ages, working feverishly on Hella Haasse's novel. I was now not simply rewriting the English translation but rechecking the translation, painstakingly, line by line, with the help of a dictionary and Hella Haasse herself, whose English was fluent but not professional. She had agreed to come to Chicago in March or April 1989 to go over the manuscript with me. I had to finish the book before she came. It had to come out in the fall of 1989: our whole company was riding on it, so to speak. Things had come to a pretty pass; we were sinking below the horizon. We had been litigating instead of publishing, and almost all our money was going to lawyers—and not enough of it to keep the lawyers happy. It seemed to us that this book, the title of which was still not chosen—*Forest of Longing?*—was important enough to save us. Something had to.

37

"It Becomes Like a Garbage Can of Stories"

On January 3, Paul phoned. "Did you expect everything to be easy in '89?" he asked cheerfully. Oh-oh, we said, now what? "Judge Kiley resigned today," Paul said. "He's gone."

The judge had not signed the judgment order that was to wrap up the trial because Paul and Garbus had given him different orders. Paul's order called for 140 pages to be taken from our Exhibit 36; Garbus's called for 140 pages with no specification for their provenance. Now no one knew what to do. On January 5, Garbus notified Paul that it had been such a long time since he had heard from us that he considered that we had rejected Mrs. Cheever's manuscript and she was now free to go elsewhere. That she did indeed intend to go elsewhere seemed to be indicated by a comment she made to Bill Goldstein in *Newsday*: she said that she did not object to seeing in print those stories she had not sent us if they appeared "in the right context, with the right notes. They are not prime Cheever, but there are good things in them."[1]

Russell Smith informed Paul that they were going to go before Kiley if they could find him—Kite was reportedly trying to track him down—or his replacement if they couldn't find him, to have an order signed, and they were also going to ask for a declaratory judgment that Mrs. Cheever had now satisfied her obligations to us. Paul was pleased to hear this. If it was true that they wanted a declaratory judgment, he said jovially, they would have to submit a complaint, and there would have to be a trial. "We can oblige them," he said with a chuckle.

On January 12, Paul received a fax from Russell Smith: "As you know, there will be a hearing before Judge Kiley on January 24." Paul did not know. Included was an order to Kiley from the head of the chancery division, mandating the January 24 hearing, with copies to Kite, Paul, and Kiley's replacement, Judge Reynolds. The declaratory judgment plea seemed to have gone the way of all flesh. Paul said happily that he was going to ask Kiley to sign the order asking for 140 pages from our galley; there was no chance of even bringing up the question of the public domain stories. I commented that maybe this thing was finally coming to a head, "like a pimple." Paul thought this was pretty funny. He had been in a terrific mood ever since he heard that Kiley was leaving.

On January 24, Garbus appeared alone at the hearing for Mrs. Cheever; Paul was there with Cynthia, who had had her baby, and Tom Leavens. In his opening remarks, Garbus told the judge that he should be aware of "our attempt to resolve the dispute so that we wouldn't have this dispute. For example, one of the things that they have said in the way they try and use the language, is that we should only pick stories from the uncollected stories." He "reminded" the judge that there were two "bodies" of uncollected stories: one that Academy had never seen (this was the first anyone had heard of this) and one that was "segregated out" by the "editorial counsel" (these were the chapters from novels that had run in the *New Yorker*). The Cheevers had attempted to be conciliatory, Garbus said, and had agreed not to use any of the stories Academy had not seen (this was news to us) or any of the "segregated" stories (this was true; they had not used the chapters, possibly because these actually *had* been collected in Cheever novels). He offered to work out any problems Academy might have with the title of the book, the introduction, the headnotes. Susan was willing to alter her introduction; some of the headnotes could be dropped.

What they would like to do finally, he said, was "somehow to end this particular litigation." Unless it ended now, unless that order was signed, the judge would realize from seeing some of the letters—presumably our letter to Mrs. Cheever—that it "can fundamentally go on forever." Basically, we had the same feeling, and it was not an enticing prospect. Goettel had been right when he said this was a case that cried out for settlement. But there was no sign of compromise. The stories Mrs. Cheever had given us, Garbus said, were "wonderful, wonderful stories." In other words, he said, "what you have here is fifteen John Cheever stories, plus short stories [*sic*]." Then there were the headnotes. Then there were Mrs. Cheever's comments. (These *were* the headnotes.) He knew of "no such other book." He begged the court "to end the pain that's been going on with these letters, with these accusations, for it to stop." They had done everything they could do. Paul, in his turn, said that we were convinced that when the judge mandated 140 pages and ten or fifteen stories, he had meant that these should come from the bound galleys.

Kiley replied that he wished Paul were right, and he wished that he had had the galleys "in his mind's eye" when he made his decision. But the issue of pages came up after he announced his decision. "I can tell you frankly," he said, "that the issues that have come up now—whether there should be 300 words on a page or 400 words on a page or whether the margins should be one inch or one-and-a-half inches or two inches, whether there should be four spaces or two spaces between paragraphs, are questions that did not enter my mind." He was thinking about "past collections of previously uncollected John Cheever works" and not Exhibit 36. "So there you have it straight from the horse's mouth."

He granted that that did not answer the problem Paul had raised. He had to "refresh" himself on the testimony—particularly Franklin's testimony about the "page lengths" of previous Cheever collections. He didn't have the actual exhibits—well, maybe he did—but he had the table of contents. So no, he had not fully thrashed out before him the question of "the page length." If it had been an issue in the case, he would have addressed it. Paul pointed out that Garbus had provided the judge with the title pages and table of contents from each Cheever collection except the Knopf omnibus. Kiley had been given that book itself, along with the bound galleys.

Kiley said that it was not "clear" to him that "that was the entirety of the previous collections." And "it was to a certain extent inconsistent" with the Dennis testimony concerning page length. (And small wonder, since Franklin had clearly been guessing at the "page lengths.") "I dealt with the evidence I had," the judge went on. "I couldn't read anything into it." Paul had come back before he "even sat down on the bench," saying that he was "off 36 pages on my estimation." He could have said 180 pages, Kiley said, he could have said 230. What he was trying to do was to fix what he thought "was a fair refinement on a difficult concept," intending that the "parties wouldn't use it as a device to incorporate in their adversarial positions, but would actually use it to solve the problem." It might be correct that "one set of exhibits shows that the 140 figure is not the figure," but Franklin or maybe Jordan had given a different set of figures. He had to look at "the entirety of the evidence" that he had.

Paul reminded him that Garbus had asked Franklin to "state from memory" the number of pages in earlier collections, and Paul had objected at the time, and the judge had said that Garbus was entitled to "test Mr. Dennis's memory." Paul said he thought that was unfair because the number of pages of those books was in evidence before the judge in "the form of the table of contents pages." The actual number of pages was right there in the record. No book had as few as 140 pages. The judge said he chose a low number purposely because he was "speaking in terms of minimums." He didn't expect, he said, that "the parties were going to come in and try to strike for the low number rather than some other number." But he wanted to "set a bottom to it."

He agreed with Paul that if somebody typed out 140 pages with one word on a page, that wouldn't make any sense at all. But when Paul then suggested that the bound galleys were the "manuscript" arranged by Franklin Dennis that the contract called for, the judge became agitated. He disagreed completely, he said, he absolutely disagreed. Exhibit 36 was "irrelevant," he said: it was "predicated on a false premise" that "Academy of Chicago" [sic] could decide for itself what was going to be in the work, once the contract was signed. That was the "fundamental flaw" with PE 36. He made no bones about it: he hated the bound galleys. Academy went on its way "under a false premise." Mrs. Cheever should have had submitted to her "the fruits of the research," but she didn't, because the two binders she saw were "xeroxed copies of old magazine articles"; the bound galleys had certain other stories in them, and the parties certainly did not intend to deal with binders containing material that wasn't typed, that were just these Xeroxes of old "articles."

It just wouldn't be fair, he said, to "put Mrs. Cheever to the task of taking something that Academy of Chicago [*sic*] put together with Mr. Dennis without her and tell her to choose from that." Even the research and identification in PE 36 was faulty, he said, because stories were left out—those that ultimately were used for novels and other stories "that were not found were left out." Mrs. Cheever had to go up and get one of her own books—

At this point, Paul, striving mightily to extricate something from this muddle, objected strongly. He tried to explain that all the uncollected stories were identified in the table of contents, but his clients "didn't have the texts of about seven of the stories, one of which was the one that Mrs. Cheever provided to them." "But," the court said, "for purposes of the issue that we're talking about here, that would be important to have the text."

Paul reminded him that he had said that the format he, the judge, had in mind was the other Cheever books. If that was true, Paul said, then the judge must tell them "just what the format is, how we derive that format. Do we derive it by counting pages or counting words on the page? Do we take some sort of average?" We needed His Honor's help and guidance. "That's what you get for bringing that page issue in," the judge said. "See what you've done. What you should have done was to bring in to really solve this dispute the marketing angle, the format angle, the design angle, because that's going to be in this case possibly when people start going off on their own directions on those things, which just looking through those letters—"

Paul interrupted to implore the judge to tell us what the format was. And here Kiley allowed Garbus to hold forth. "I think," Garbus said, "this whole question of number of pages, I think it's a problem with the number of stories because I think a book has to have a coherent sentence. And what they did—and when he talks about a few words on a page, you have fifteen stories, you have endings of pages. You have things half off. But if you squished it together, even at this you would have 220 pages, and on a word count, it's 150 to 155 pages and the stories—"

"Word count based on what," the judge inquired, "number of words?"

Garbus said that "if you took this book and tried to make it the same size" as "a Random House Cheever book, it would be about 155 to 160 pages." He had asked the court not "to get involved in this kind of stuff," and now the judge had done it. "It has never happened before." He talked about the value of Mrs. Cheever's submission, commenting that the Cheevers had since found another ten stories "that they"—presumably Academy— "never even came up with." This was a coherent book, he said. "You can't just take fifteen stories and throw them up against the wall. They have to have some coherent sense." He wanted the judge "to decide whether or not this is the satisfaction of Mrs. Cheever's obligation."

The judge asked Paul how many words were on the page. What was the range of the "previously uncollected, but then collected stories of Cheever?" Paul referred him to the chart Jordan had drawn up. Garbus commented that Mrs. Cheever had said that there were "300 to 350 words per page in all but the mass market stories [*sic*]." He reminded the judge that these books had gotten "hundreds of thousands of dollars in advances." And here she was getting $337.

The judge asked how many words per page were in Mrs. Cheever's manuscript. Garbus said he didn't know. Paul said we didn't count every page but took pages at random and counted and there were great variations. Some pages had as few as 120 words on them, some had as many as 200. That was the most he found.

Garbus said if you get "into the whole question of pages, you are then taking control away from Mrs. Cheever as to what's to be in the book." He repeated that "you just can't take stories and throw them up against the wall." He begged the judge not to get into it because he didn't know "how you add pages to a book without losing the context of it and it becomes like a garbage can of stories." Paul pointed out that the judge had not mandated a book of Depression stories but simply a book "of certain dimensions." And we had, he said, to have the third dimension—what the judge meant when he said "pages, format of those pages, so that we can, I hope, forever stop this fighting and get a book out and make everybody a lot of money."

The judge accepted Garbus's order for 140 pages without specification about what kind of pages these were to be. He may not have defined it, Kiley said, but he did not and would not define it in terms of Plaintiff's Exhibit 36.

Paul asked him to define it now.

The judge said for purposes of this order, he was telling them what he decided, not what he was going to decide later. He then made emendations—correction of typos and grammatical errors—to his decision of November 2. Petty changes, he said, and the only reason he was making these changes was "that if it's ever appealed and some judge writes an opinion and quotes from my words, I don't want to see the word 'sic' in there."

He couldn't further define the 140 pages without further information, he said.

The judge cut off a lengthy protest from Garbus because he didn't have any more time. He had to leave. But he would take up the question of whether he should "make any further definition"—whether, that is, "I should modify the judgment order that I've signed here today." He was going off the bench "effective February 9th, so at the end of the day on February 9th I won't be able to answer the question." He needed to find out from Garbus what the "per page word is in your manuscript at 243 pages, how that would be affected by making it a 140-page manuscript in terms of the per page words." He also wanted copies of the six "John Cheever story collections." Every page couldn't have 420 words on it, so he wanted the range broken down for him. He wanted "to know the range, no less than, no more than, and the average."

Paul asked whether the judge wanted Garbus to give him this information only about the stories or about the introduction and headnotes and John Cheever essay as well.

Garbus said he just begged the court not to follow this path.

The judge said he hadn't decided; he was going to follow the path to decide whether he "should answer it or not. I may decide not to do it." His tendency, his experience, had been that each time he decided something further, it bred further fights, and so his instinct was to leave it the way it was. But he wanted to take a look at it. He didn't want a lot of "briefs and things" from Garbus—Garbus had already given him a seven-page brief when the judge had said he didn't want any; all he wanted was one sheet showing him "the range" of "words a page." And he needed a breakdown from Paul, too. And he wanted the copies of Cheever books sent to his temporary office on LaSalle Street.

Tom Leavens was very bucked up by the hearing. He thought Kiley was relaxed and pleasant, and he was optimistic that the judge would give us more stories. Paul's response was less enthusiastic. He was relieved, he said, that the judge had not decided to declare the contract invalid; for a moment there Paul had thought he was going to do just that. He no longer seemed to think of Kiley as "a caring person," as he had in October when Kiley had expressed concern over Paul looking tired at the Cheever trial. Word had gotten around that Kiley had not yet signed other orders besides ours. The judge, Paul said, had been under some stress as he left the bench.

Whatever condition he was in, the "caring person" had just arranged for us to put in a hell of a lot of work. Possibly he thought we deserved it because we were so evil.

38

"Enforcing a Contract for Mary Cheever"

Before we could immerse ourselves in a morass of word counting, we had to get copies of all the Cheever collections. His first, *The Way Some People Live*, is a rare volume. Franklin had a Xerox of it; luckily he and Mary had just returned from Puerto Rico, so we called him and told him to rush us a copy—carefully xeroxed, of course. We found the four Cheever collections we still needed at the Wilmette Public Library, where the rule was that you could take out only two books at a time if you didn't live in Wilmette. Since Jordan and I both had library cards, we were able to overcome that hurdle.

We began to count words the night of January 24, a Tuesday, and continued on Wednesday at the office. I interrupted my count of the words of *The Brigadier and the Golf Widow* to give a talk at the Chicago Women's Club, once run by Bertha Palmer and Ellen Henrotin. I addressed twenty-five ladies in hats, including one who fell asleep suddenly as if she were poleaxed. Before we sat down to lunch—beet salad and stuffed cabbage, and we were told to save our forks for the cake—I was introduced to somebody as "Dr. Cheever." Then back to the office and the counting, which continued throughout Thursday and Friday—all of us, Jordan, me, Sarah Leslie Welsch, Jane Winter, and Mary Jo, counting. We had arranged to send our charts to Cynthia on Monday morning, which could give Jordan and me the weekend to finish up, if we needed it.

Since Garbus's task was less onerous than ours, he was able to write to the judge on Thursday, January 26. Ignoring Kiley's injunction to put it all on one sheet of paper, Garbus wrote four pages, saying that the Cheever manuscript had a low of 77 words on a page, a high of 254 words, and an average of 222 words. Even, he said, without Susan's introduction and Mrs. Cheever's "prefatory notes"—the omission of which would be "an insult to the Cheever family and a disservice to the Public"—the average would be 354 words per page "in the form of a 140-page book." Garbus informed the judge that in addition to being avaricious and obsessive, we were comparable in size to Sylvester & Orphanos and also that you could not tell anything from looking at early Cheever collections because fifteen and twenty years ago, books were "a different size" from books today.

We finished counting and adding on Friday afternoon, and on Monday Cynthia messengered a letter to the judge, unfortunately addressing him as Richard J. Kiley—confusing him with the actor. She attached a chart showing that the six Cheever collections each averaged a total of 67,590 words, with an average of 311 words on a page. The Cheever manuscript, of which every word had been counted, excluding the introduction and headnotes, contained 37,460 words, averaging 169 words on a page. (None of the published Cheever collections had any prefatory material.) If the contents of the manuscript were compressed (or, as Garbus put it, "squished together") into 140 pages, the result would be 267 words on a page. "As a whole," Cynthia wrote, "the Cheever short story collections provide 80.5% more words than the manuscript provided by Mrs. Cheever." Academy therefore requested a modification of the order, suggesting that a manuscript of 67,590 words would be "a fair guideline."

We were dimly aware that all this counting and page turning was an exercise in futility, but we were optimistic by nature, and none of us, Paul included, wanted to think that the judge would put us through all this tedious work without being sincerely interested in the result. When, on February 10, Kiley issued his decision, it revealed that he had done his own page count of three of the earlier collections (the three shortest collections, incidentally): *World of Apples, Some People Places and Things,* and *The Housebreaker of Shady Hill.* He agreed with Academy's count on *People* (42,875 total, 245 per page) but disagreed with our count for *Housebreaker* (Academy: 57,905 total, 313 per page; Kiley: 52,725 total, 285 per page) and for *Apples* (Academy: 58,116 total, 334 per page; Kiley: 47,502 total, 273 per page). He did not count the words in Mrs. Cheever's manuscript. Even taking Kiley's figures rather than ours, the Cheever manuscript was short by 14 percent (*People*), 27 percent (*Apples*), and 41 percent (*Housebreaker*).

The judge agreed with Mrs. Cheever that any further "quantification of the good faith and fair dealing obligation, at least in the form suggested by plaintiffs, would undermine the publishing agreement which makes Mrs. Cheever the author of the work and gives her control over which stories will be included in the work." Mrs. Cheever's manuscript, he decreed, "comes close, *relatively speaking* [italics mine] to the other John Cheever collections nearest the minimum page number set by the judgment order." His decision was thus a self-fulfilling prophecy: that providing material for a 140-page book (a figure derived from what was clearly a guess by Franklin, to which Paul had objected) constituted good faith and fair dealing. Kiley remained unswayed by the added fact that 60 percent of the Cheever manuscript was in the public domain and could be published by anyone. So he denied our application for a further definition of Mrs. Cheever's obligation under the contract.

Herbert Mitgang reported in the *Times* that Mrs. Cheever was now free to edit her own "major collection."[1] This did not surprise us. We had known since January that the Cheevers wanted to take our collection to another publisher. Wylie had said so. At the end of June 1988, Mrs. Cheever had been quoted as saying, "The happiest outcome would be that we could either [*sic*] buy the book away from them and sell it to someone else who could do a better job of putting it together and promoting it."[2]

We were kept busy scurrying, or staggering, to the typewriter to produce clarifications. In the January 1989 issue of *American Lawyer* was a lovely photograph of Martin Garbus perched on a corner of his book-strewn desk, the illustration for an article headed "Enforcing a Contract for Mary Cheever." The gist of it was that Martin Garbus had won for Mrs. Cheever "the contract she had originally signed," not the one "fraudulently obtained" by Academy Chicago. This was a new wrinkle, as they say: we had been under the impression that Garbus had wanted the contract—and there had, after all, been only one contract—declared invalid. Paul's comment was that we should forget about this; he had let his *American Lawyer* subscription lapse because it was just a gossip sheet. But we wrote to the *Lawyer* anyway because we didn't like being accused of committing fraud and because we had great respect for the power of the press, gossip sheet or not.[3] Not so Paul: the *Lawyer* reporter told Mary Jo, to our great surprise, that she had spoken to Paul. Or tried to.

All this was very wearing. We knew that much of it was ridiculous, but it was also expensive and frustrating (and probably defamatory), so we were hard put to see the humor in it.

Mary Dennis rose above the anger and frustration to suggest possible Cheever titles for future collections:

John Cheever: The Korean Years
" " The Vietnam Years
" " The Kennedy-Johnson Era
" " and the Truman Doctrine
" " and the New Frontier
" " in Woodstock
When Cheever Slept: The Eisenhower Years
Baghdad on the Hudson: Cheever in Gotham
Up the River: The Ossining Years
Cheever Agonistes: The Drinking Years

Hilarious as this whole thing was, we decided to appeal.

39

"Mrs. Cheever Loves Those Stories"

The decision to appeal plunged us into more work that would not result in books being published. We produced a thirty-five-page analysis for Tom Leavens, which we called "Errors and Contradictions in Kiley's Opinion." It contained forty-seven points on which we believed the judge was vulnerable. We pointed out that Kiley made sweeping statements on points that did not exist in the contract. For instance, Kiley said that Franklin had "agreed to act as editor, do research and locate the stories and arrange them for publication once Mary Cheever had made her selection." But there was nothing in the contract about "research and location" or "selection," and the letters Franklin wrote did not mention this. We also told Tom that Kiley, like Goettel, constantly questioned Academy's intentions but never questioned Mrs. Cheever's intentions. Did she, when she signed the contract, intend to let Academy publish this book, or did she sign the contract intending to let Academy do the research and locate the stories so that she could then take the resulting manuscript somewhere else for a big advance? Then there was Kiley's statement that Academy had not "cooperated" with Mrs. Cheever, despite the fact that both Franklin and Jordan had written her and she had not replied. She had asked for nothing, even in Franklin's December 12 meeting with her, so how could we have failed to "cooperate"? Then there was the judge's litany of complaints that Academy applied to magazines for permissions to reprint and contacted Scott Meredith without specific permission from Mrs. Cheever. This showed, at best, a lamentable level of ignorance about publishing practices and the purpose of a contract between publisher and author. Indeed, the judge ignored the contract completely when he said that Academy had to exercise control of the design and format of the book "in cooperation with Mrs. Cheever."

On February 23, 1989, Tom Leavens filed the appeal asking for a reversal of Kiley's opinion. Tom was not an appeals lawyer, but he undertook the appeal, and Paul pledged Pope, Ballard's complete cooperation. We hoped that this appeal, pursued with the aid of an appeals lawyer in Tom's firm,

Marc Fogelberg, would convince the Cheevers to come to some sort of rapprochement with us. Our big book was undoubtedly dead, but we wanted to preserve a semblance of thematic consistency with enough stories to fill a book of reasonable size. If we couldn't get the Cheevers to agree to that, we would take the chance that a sensible appeals court would give us relief.

There were a flurry of phone calls between Tom and Maura Wogan, during which she held out a somewhat withered olive branch: they were willing to back off their strictures on the book's production and promotion. That was encouraging. Now all we had to decide were the number of stories. A "decade collection" seemed the obvious answer: Mrs. Cheever had given us eleven stories from the 1930s. There were twenty-one 1930s stories in our galleys. We told Tom to ask Maura if the Cheevers would substitute four of those 1930s stories for the four 1940s stories we had been given and then give us the six 1930s stories left in the galleys so that we could have a complete collection of twenty-one uncollected stories for the decade.

Maura took this under advisement and called back a few days later to say that Mrs. Cheever was willing to give us "Expelled" (1930), "Frère Jacques" (1938), "Treat" (1939), and maybe one more. We certainly wanted "Expelled" and "Frère Jacques," but we weren't crazy about "Treat," which ran a page and a half in our galleys and was basically a luncheon conversation between two New York City ladies, one of whom was terribly upset because her husband had lost his job and they had had to fire the maid and buy coal by the ton. We thought that "Treat" might even be a sketch; Susan had said it was. Tom told Maura that we would like to have "In Passing" (1936), "Autobiography of a Drummer" (1935), "In the Beginning" (1937), and "Homage to Shakespeare" (1937). Since Susan had expressed the opinion that "Beginning" and "Drummer" were not only immature and inferior but were also actually sketches and not stories at all, we thought Mrs. Cheever might be willing to let us publish them. If we could have those four stories in addition to "Expelled" and "Frère Jacques," we would give up the four 1940s stories we had been given and drop the appeal. We considered "Homage to Shakespeare" such a strong story that we thought we might be able to call the book *Homage to Shakespeare and Other Stories.* We knew that "In Passing" and "Drummer" were in the public domain, and at the time we believed that "Homage" was, too—although we discovered later that the status of "Homage" was murky. One of the ironies of this stupid situation was that we were not allowed to include the public domain stories, over which Mrs. Cheever had no control, in a volume over which the judge had declared that she had complete control.

Maura called Tom back to say that Mrs. Cheever loved "Homage," "In Passing," "In the Beginning," and "Autobiography of a Drummer" and had no intention of letting us publish them. This comment added to the rich fabric of the dispute. Maura said that Mrs. Cheever wanted us to look at Cheever's first collection, *The Way Some People Live*. This raised our hopes. The book had not been well received when it was published in 1943, Gottlieb had included none of those stories in his omnibus collection, and the consensus among the Cheevers and Gottlieb was that nothing in that book was valuable. We had a xeroxed copy of the collection because Kiley had ordered us to count the words in it, so we read it and concluded that, although as a collection it was disappointing, some of the stories were certainly worth reprinting.

In the middle of March, Maura phoned to tell Tom that we could have only "Expelled," "Frère Jacques," and "Treat"; if we did not accept those, she said, the discussion was at an end. She called again a week later to ask Tom to join her in an "expedited appeal." Whatever that was, it came to nothing.

Meanwhile, I was working feverishly on Hella Haasse's novel, which had remained untitled until I went in to have my teeth cleaned and presented the dentist with a list of tentative titles that everyone in the office was arguing about ("The Forest of Longing"? "The Forest of Expectations"? "In a Darkling Wood"?). I told the dentist, Rob Savin, that we would use the title he chose, without further discussion. He chose *In a Dark Wood Wandering*. So that settled that. In April, Hella Haasse came to Chicago to go over the final manuscript with me. We were fortunate that, through Franklin, Gayle Feldman of *Publishers Weekly* became interested in the book—partly because of its unusual history, having been locked in a closet for twenty-five years—and Chris Goodrich was assigned to do a "Trade News" story on it. Hella and I flew to New York for a luncheon interview. Lunch was delicious, and Hella was impressively charming and erudite. So the novel got a good send-off with an in-depth interview with Hella in the trade magazine.[1] And we needed it because if this book did not sell, we could not possibly stay in business.

Since the ABA convention was held in Washington that year, we were able to arrange a reception for Hella at the Dutch Embassy. We invited booksellers and the press. This was one of the more dreadful evenings of our lives—one that still gives us nightmares. We envisioned an informal event, with a few words from the author, a lot of mingling, and the kind of food and drink you usually get when you go to a reception at 6:30. However, the embassy's cultural attaché had a different vision: he envisioned a lecture, with rows of seats and a podium and nothing to eat; just a glass of wine when the lecture was over. And the attaché's vision was what everyone got after a hard day on the convention floor. Mary Jo implored the attaché to let us bring in food at our expense, but he was adamant in his refusal.

Hella gave a lecture that covered her entire career. Because she had been writing since the end of World War II, it was a lengthy lecture, and because none of her books had been published in this country, we were treated, on empty stomachs, to a painstaking description of a lot of Dutch titles. While she was talking, a torrential thunderstorm broke; thunder crashed, and jagged streaks of lightning lit the room through an enormous window. Hella talked on, undaunted. We sat in the front row, afraid to look behind us and make eye contact, in a kind of frozen, dreamlike state—the sort of dream where you want to open your mouth and scream, but nothing comes out.

The embassy, which looks like a gigantic college gymnasium, was tucked away in an obscure corner of the countryside; it was decidedly off the beaten path, so those who had not made an early escape were stranded there, drinking wine, when the lecture finally ground to a halt. A few cabs trickled into the driveway—an appropriate verb because the downpour continued all evening—but we eventually had to hire a couple of limousines to carry exhausted booksellers back to the city. Hella and her husband got a lift from the cultural attaché, who remarked as they left that he thought everything had gone very well. Everybody else got home around midnight. Nobody attacked us physically, which must mean that most booksellers are extraordinarily civil people.

When we bravely manned our booth the next morning, some booksellers, who had luckily left the embassy proceedings in the first hour, dropped by to tell us how great it had been. Franklin dropped by to tell us that at least one book review editor who had been stranded in the embassy had decided to forget that he had ever heard of Hella Haasse. Bob Stein dropped by to say hello. In retrospect, he said, we probably should have tried to settle with the Cheevers; he had apparently blocked out his memory of the Royce Hotel meeting. He mentioned in passing that the Volunteer Lawyers for the Arts, a New York City group, had scheduled a discussion of the Cheever case for July 12 and had invited Martin Garbus and Russell Smith to explain everything. Invitations had gone out, but not to us.

When we got back to Chicago, we contacted the Volunteer Lawyers and asked if one of our attorneys could join the panel. They said all right, without noticeable enthusiasm. But it turned out to be too late for either Paul or Tom to change their schedules, and we were working frantically on *Dark Wood* and could not spare the time—or the money—to go to New York. Fortunately Franklin's friend Michael Kesend, a New York publisher, offered to stand in for Academy. He had been following the case. And a friend of Mary Dennis said she would sit in the audience with a tape recorder. Jordan sent the Lawyers a letter giving our side of the conflict. It did not occur to us to send multiple copies of the letter for distribution.

The program, which was held in the eighth-floor auditorium of the Time & Life Building in Manhattan, began at 7:00. The panel included—in addition to Garbus, Russell Smith, and Michael Kesend—Karen Mayer, a Putnam publishing attorney. It was a lively evening. Garbus distributed a "press packet" containing copies of the contract, the two judicial opinions, and Jonathan Yardley's *Washington Post* article, "John Cheever and the Unforgotten Wish"—the only piece of journalism about the case based solely on conversations with Susan Cheever. "The Chicago press," Garbus announced, "was sympathetic to Academy; the New York press was sympathetic to Mrs. Cheever."

Russell Smith was invited by the moderator to give a précis of the issues. He explained that John Cheever was ashamed of his pre-1947 stories, which he wrote to prevent his family from starving, and that Academy had represented itself as a scholarly press and asked for some obscure 1930s stories and then collected every single story, even sketches, and tried to publish them without reading any of them. Following this précis, the moderator read most of Jordan's letter aloud. Then Garbus took up the story, explaining that two judges many miles apart had given almost identical opinions, until Michael Kesend, who is blessed with a deep, rich baritone voice, broke in to ask for some time for the other side. "The real issue," Kesend said, "is M.O.N.E.Y."

Garbus responded that Kesend didn't know anything about the case: he hadn't been there, there were letters, there was a mountain of depositions, and there had been "elaborate negotiations." When Karen Mayer said she was troubled by this whole thing and thought that the courts might have overstepped their bounds, Garbus said that the court had looked outside the contract in this particular case because of the "fundamental unfairness" of the thing. The judges decided to forget about the contract because they weren't going to let Mrs. Cheever or John Cheever get hurt. "If," Garbus said, "you go on the assumption that judges are idiots, and sometimes that's a fair assumption . . . . " When the chuckles died down, he explained that both these judges were sophisticated and Judge Goettel knew exactly what he was doing.

Someone in the audience asked why Mrs. Cheever had signed the contract. Garbus replied that she had thought Academy was a university press. Kesend interrupted to say that no university press is called "Academy" and anyway Mrs. Cheever knew all about Academy. Why, he asked Garbus, had she given Academy "the worst stories"? Russell Smith said it wasn't a question of best or worst. Academy had talked about "best-kept secrets" and accused Cheever of "keeping his true style secret from the public . . . . " Garbus implied that there was byzantine background stuff that the audience, and certainly Kesend, couldn't possibly know about. Karen Mayer expressed puzzlement about the court requiring a publisher to give up editorial control. Garbus said that the judge had said that Mrs. Cheever could just walk away, but he gave this small press ten or twelve stories because he felt sorry for them. "That ain't bad," Garbus added, in his jovial mode: ten or twelve stories for "ninety dollars" and the publisher could earn "a million three" on it. A book of 120 to 130 pages could be a bestseller. It was "rough justice," he said, but it was fair. Karen Mayer kept raising questions. Two judges, Garbus said, "with no particular bias . . . . Two for two. Can't do better than that." A wave of appreciative merriment greeted this witticism, and the meeting ended.

As Mary's friend was gathering up her things, she heard someone near her remark, "I think it's all about money."

40

"Small Press,
Small Book"

As we had hoped it would, *In a Dark Wood Wandering* brought us in from the wilderness. Hella had a successful tour; Bill Rickman of the Chicago book chain Kroch's and Brentano's was so taken with her when he met her at a party given at the home of the Dutch consul, that he got behind the book and it made the Chicago bestseller list. We sold rights to the English publisher Hutchison for a substantial sum. Buoyed by this, I began work on a second Hella Haasse novel, *The Scarlet City*, which we were to announce for Fall 1990.

In June 1990, the appeals court presented its decision. It was a split decision, and the bad news was that they upheld Kiley's fifteen-story order. The good news was that they found that Mrs. Cheever had no right to demand approval of advertising, promotion, and sales of the book, nor could she limit the number of books printed and sold. They pointed to the clause in the contract that gave the publisher the right to publish "in such style and manner . . . as it deems best." The good news was good news only if we decided to publish Mrs. Cheever's manuscript—a decision that we had not yet made. Mary Jo Reilly had sat in on the oral arguments before the appeals court; we had not been optimistic enough to join her. There were three judges, one of whom, she said, dozed through the process. The judge who seemed most interested in Tom's argument was Charles Freeman, who was later to win a seat on the Illinois Supreme Court. Mary Jo told us that at one point Judge Freeman said, "Small press, small book."

Garbus announced that Mrs. Cheever had now "regained ownership of one hundred John Cheever stories that are conservatively valued at one million dollars." She was also, he added, free to seek statutory and punitive damages in federal court. We were interested to see that our sixty-eight inferior stories had grown to one hundred and that they were now worth a conservative estimate of $1 million. It seemed to us that the months and months of Cheever denigration of these stories, denigration that had been picked up and repeated endlessly by newspapers across the country, might well have affected their salability. "It reminds me of Vietnam," Jordan said glumly. "They are destroying these stories in order to save them."

We were both heartily sick of the whole thing and beginning to toy with the idea of publishing *Depression Stories* so that we could get it over with and concentrate on work. But Tom Leavens and his associate Marc Fogelberg, the appeals lawyer, urged us to go forward and appeal to the Illinois Supreme Court. They said there was about a 10 percent chance of the court's accepting our case, but they wanted to try. After talking it over with everyone who would still listen to us, we decided to go for this final appeal.

This meant reading more Garbus briefs—in which he said, for instance, that Academy had already received $225,000 from an unauthorized paperback sale and that Mrs. Cheever had never called all the stories inferior— and typing pages and pages of responses for the lawyers. While we were embroiled in this, we barely noticed that there were signs of impending significant change in the book world—at least in the retail end. The mall chain bookstores—Waldenbooks, B. Dalton, and Crown Books—were feeling the effects of the recession. The president of Waldenbooks said that traffic was down "at least four percent" in the chain's mall stores. We had stopped shipping to Dalton and Walden in the early 1980s because of numerous headaches connected with servicing them, not the least of which were gurneys filled with returns. We did, however, sell to the Chicago chain Kroch's and Brentano's, which was hit very hard by shrinking incomes in the suburbs. Half of Kroch's twenty stores were in malls: Bill Rickman in an interview said that mall sales had fallen off between 5 and 10 percent in recent months. "The marketplace has changed," Bill said, "and the new mall stores are more tenuous."[1]

Kroch's continued to operate all their stores in their traditional manner, despite this ominous cloud on their horizon, which was eventually to produce a deluge that would drown them. But Barnes & Noble and Crown, taking a leaf from the midwestern chain Borders Books, devised the superstore concept: "gentle lighting," comfortable chairs, coffee bars, and— a real departure—"knowledgeable staff." These huge bookstores would stock five to ten times the number of books in an average mall store: about one hundred thousand titles, eighty thousand more than the B. Dalton and Walden shops. And they would stock what Roger Cohen of the *New York Times* called "recondite titles," which the knowledgeable staff would help the browsing reader to find. "Chains have discovered that the bestseller market is fickle and you have to try to appeal to the solid, regular reader," Constance Sayre, a publishing consultant, was quoted as saying. Attracting readers of Sidney Sheldon, she said, is no longer enough.[2] Roger Cohen noted, possibly with some surprise, that the Borders bookshops "showed that contrary to the prevailing opinion, there may be as high a proportion of avid readers in a middle-class Detroit or Toledo suburb as in New York or Chicago."[3]

Since we were not able to forget the remark of the Waldenbooks official who had told us in the late 1970s not to bother to present our list to him because Waldenbooks was only interested in "blockbusters"—and the top ten blockbusters at that—we found this new concept of bookselling encouraging. Along with it, there seemed to be a certain restlessness in the media with the increasing conglomerization of publishing. In 1990, some thoughtful journalists, apparently under the impression that the "excesses of the '80s" were behind us, cast a jaded eye on the enormous advances, hype, and large print runs that conglomerate money produced at the behest of powerful agents.[4] There was a touch of nostalgia for the days when publishing houses stood for books that reflected "an identifiable set of principles," as Edwin McDowell put it. "For better or for worse," he wrote, "the distinctive images of what houses stand for has largely disappeared, a casualty of changing public tastes, of mergers and consolidation, of the passing of the editorial torch to people less concerned with a house's tradition." He noted that in 1983, *Truly Tasteless Jokes* had been published by a division of Random House, the publisher who had dared to bring out *Ulysses* fifty years earlier.[5]

Some of this melancholy reflection was a reaction to Simon & Schuster's belated jettisoning of *American Psycho* by Brett Easton Ellis, a book that they had apparently accepted in a moment of abstraction and that presented appalling scenes of graphic violence against women. Edwin McDowell commented that the fact that this book was then picked up by Vintage, a division of Knopf, was evidence of the blurred image of many big houses. Other people chose to consider the dropping of Ellis's book, a month before its scheduled shipping, an ominous manifestation of the sinister control of corporations over hapless publishing executives; these people believed that Martin Davis, the chairman of Simon & Schuster's corporate parent, Paramount Communications, had instructed Simon & Schuster publisher Richard Snyder to drop the book. Robert K. Massie, president of the Authors Guild, said that the Guild had predicted that a "black day" like this would occur ever "since giant corporations started buying distinguished American publishing houses." (Mr. Massie, in another context, had been quoted as saying, "The hell with publishers."[6]) Martin Davis denied that he had initiated this act. Mr. Snyder, soon to be jettisoned himself, said he had decided to drop the book after he had read it over the weekend.[7]

Booksellers were faced with the dilemma of whether they should stock *American Psycho*. One said she didn't feel right saying yes, and she didn't feel right saying no. Bill Rickman said he was "repulsed," but he felt "obligated by the First Amendment" to stock the thing. Sonny Mehta, the president of Vintage Books, commented that it was "appropriate given the immense coverage and curiosity" that Vintage bring Ellis's book out "to swiftly reach the widest possible readership."[8] In the event, the book did not do particularly well.

Booksellers were also thrown into an ethical dilemma over Salman Rushdie's *Satanic Verses*, which had infuriated the Ayatollah Khomeini.[9] No one wanted to bend to his wishes, but no one wanted to get blown up either. This book had been auctioned off by our old friend Andrew Wylie: Viking Penguin was the lucky winner, for $800,000, a surprisingly large amount of money for a literary novel written by someone with an unimpressive sales track record. It had received mixed reviews on publication, and some publishing types speculated that if the ayatollah had not issued his threats, Viking Penguin could easily have lost $500,000 on the book. Martin Garbus, who represented Penguin (and who turned up on ABC's *Nightline* because of the affair, thus ruining our evening), explained that Penguin had bid high because they believed *Satanic Verses* was a potential "breakout book" for Rushdie. Garbus also praised Andrew Wylie's "extraordinary skill."[10] The English *Observer* reported that providing security for its staff was costing Penguin $3.2 million a year.[11]

Some authors were shaken by the ayatollah's threats and expressed sympathy for booksellers who had stopped carrying Rushdie's book. Not so Ben Cheever. He said he thought the ayatollah was insane, and he certainly didn't think "you should respond to that kind of person with cowardice. What is a bookstore about if the very first time they're asked to stand by their merchandise they retreat?" he asked. Don DeLillo agreed. He sympathized with the bookstore chains who feared for the safety of their employees "in human terms," but books, he believed, were not like any other product. If the book chain was being run as "strictly a commercial enterprise," he said, those booksellers should "be selling soap instead."[12]

Then there was the firing of André Schiffrin, who for years had run Pantheon, a respected division of Random House. In the resulting uproar, Pantheon authors loyal to Schiffrin took to the streets, and several Pantheon editors resigned in protest. Shortly after that, some Random House editors and publishers accused Schiffrin of ineptitude and paying insufficient attention to the bottom line.[13]

Some months later, Simon & Schuster announced that it had bought a first novel for the impressive sum of $920,000, largely on the strength of endorsements from John le Carré and Joseph Wambaugh. A couple of days later, both authors denied they had ever even heard of the book, *Just Killing Time* by Derek Goodwin, who said he had been duped by someone with a personal grudge against him or by an acquaintance who had worked for the CIA. He said he was mystified about the reason for this plot against him. Simon & Schuster said they were taking the matter "under advisement" and emerged about two weeks later to report that they had decided to drop the book, so the money, one of the highest advances ever offered for a first novel, was never paid. *Just Killing Time*, like *American Psycho*, another ill-fated Simon & Schuster project, was the story of a serial killer—a hot topic that year.[14]

Distaste for conglomerate publishing was to reach a kind of climax in June 1991 with the publication of Jacob Weisberg's article in the *New Republic* headlined on the magazine's cover, "Houses of Ill Repute: The Lost Honor of American Publishing." In the midcentury golden years of publishing, Weisberg said, a publisher such as Random House would issue some schlock to finance worthwhile books. But now, he said, except at some independent houses like Farrar Straus, the situation is reversed: "the literature is an afterthought to the schlock, a garnishing of literary prestige to soothe the conscience and placate the ghosts." And editors had abandoned conscientious editing for acquisitions.

Some of the media angst over conglomerate publishing and inflated advances ($12.3 million from Dell for Ken Follett's next two novels, for instance; more than $20 million reportedly from HarperCollins for three books by Jeffrey Archer) seemed to result not only in nostalgia for the vanished world of Alfred A. Knopf, but in some sympathetic attention to small presses and independent booksellers.[15] When we learned that *Newsweek* was doing a piece on this subject, we urged Franklin to contact them and see if they would include us among the small presses they were going to mention. But Franklin had been so spooked by Garbus's drumfire of contempt for us as "small" that he refused to do anything that would encourage people to think of Academy in those terms. Perhaps it was just as well. The *Newsweek* article talked about the "modest gravy train" onto which, in a slightly mixed metaphor, these small presses had "stumbled." (Among them, *Newsweek* mentioned North Point Press, which was to close down a few months later.)[16] In any case, what we had stumbled onto was more like an ox cart than a gravy train, and we had only recently been able to afford an ox.

So we plodded along until October 1990, when to our amazement, the Illinois Supreme Court accepted our case.

41

"It's Still a Very Good Idea, in the Abstract"

Our case, as Edwin McDowell pointed out in the *New York Times*, had been in the courts for more than two and a half years. Now it was going to continue for a while. "I'm very discouraged," Mary Cheever said. "It's just another long wait."[1] The *Kansas City Star* seemed to agree with her: they headlined their story "Cheever Book Flap Drags on in Courts.[2] Jordan told the press that we had won "a significant victory"; I told them it was "a ridiculous case" but that giving up would be an admission that we had done something wrong, and we hadn't. Garbus was more upbeat than his client. "I would prefer to see it end," he told the Gannett Westchester reporter. "We have been before six different judges who have ruled in our favor. I don't see why we can't win now."[3] We had been before Goettel and Kiley and three appeals court judges, if you count the one who was asleep. That was five. Who, we wondered, was the sixth judge? Perhaps Garbus was referring to a higher realm. Could his Sixth Judge be the final Judge of us all?

In the same interview, Garbus said also that Mrs. Cheever would have met her obligation if *all* the stories she selected had been in the public domain. "She delivered a book that they could have called 'The Uncollected Short Stories of John Cheever,'" he remarked, and she had received only $750 for her work, which included writing introductory material and selecting stories to "illustrate her husband's development as a writer." But royalties were "irrelevant": "Mrs. Cheever feels very strongly that this has nothing to do with money. It has to do with ripping off maybe 100 non-public domain stories." He told the *Chicago Daily Law Bulletin* that Academy claimed sixty-eight stories, of which fifty-six were in copyright.[4] The provenance of Garbus's other forty-four stories remained as mysterious as that of his Sixth Judge.

Franklin told Elizabeth Mehrens of the *Los Angeles Times* that he felt battered. But he was still pleased that he had thought of collecting the stories. "It's still a very good idea," he said sadly, "in the abstract."[5]

In August 1991, the *New Yorker,* edited by Robert Gottlieb, ran a two-part series of what James Warren called "the often melancholy" entries of Cheever's journals, edited by Robert Gottlieb.[6] In the spring of 1991, Susan published *Treetops,* another family history, this time with emphasis on her mother, who, Susan revealed, had had an extramarital affair. That fall Knopf brought out the *Journals* in hardcover. A hint of dismay could be discerned in a few notices of these books by reviewers who remembered the *Letters* and even *Home Before Dark*. In *Time* magazine, Stefan Kanfer commented, "Mary and the children are Cheever's literary executors.* Why would they allow him—as well as themselves—to be so unflatteringly exposed?" Was it revenge, he wondered, or royalties? Robert Gottlieb's explanation was that Cheever had wanted his notebooks published; the family was "simply honoring his wishes."[7]

Lisa Anderson began her profile of the Cheevers in the *Chicago Tribune* with a metaphor that was to recur in other accounts of Cheever activities: "When it comes to the airing of dirty linen in public, the Cheever family might seem to be running the literary equivalent of a laundromat." Susan said her intention was to "bear witness . . . to testify"; Gottlieb praised the family for publishing the journals, an act he called "both courageous and correct." Mrs. Cheever suggested another motive: "I probably shouldn't say this, but this is Susan's livelihood. Who am I to put obstacles in her way in trying to make a living for herself and her children?"[8] Susan, in her midforties, had recently produced a son, named after his father, the columnist Warren Hinckle, whom she had married in a somewhat unusual garden celebration at "Afterwhiles."[9]

Of course, both Susan's book and the *Journals* received some good reviews. Carolyn See called Susan "sturdy and fair-minded, much more than loving, determined to understand."[10] Theodore Solotaroff, in the *Nation*, expressed great admiration for Gottlieb's editing of the journals, which Solotareff had seen in their raw state when they were first put up for auction. He was impressed with what Gottlieb had done with "this badly typed, misspelled and often unstrung prose."[11] This called up for us memories of Ben's comments on his father's fanatical devotion to "neat typing and double spacing" and Ben's belief that if John Cheever were alive, we would have had to move to South America, change our names, and have plastic surgery to escape his wrath over our sloppy Xeroxes.

---

*Mary, as we have seen, was named the sole executor.

Apart from John Cheever's tendencies to single-space journal entries and ignore typos, there was the question, so often broached by Mary Cheever in connection with Franklin, of editorial responsibility. So eminent a literary presence as John Updike, thrilled though he declared himself with the *Journals'* prose and "scandalous frankness," complained that the presentation of the journal selections as a sort of "prose poem," without "a single clarifying note" or any "editorial guidance, frazzled the brain and depressed the spirit."[12]

Mary Gordon loved the *Journals*. She wrote in the *New York Times Book Review* that they were—God help us—a "treasure-trove" of literary riches.[13]

James Wolcott brought up, in *Vanity Fair*, what to us was the interesting question of the effect of their publication on Cheever's reputation. After discussing some of the writer's less attractive literary mannerisms ("what kind of man talks about 'mounting' his wife?"), Wolcott said he closed the book in the "firm hope that Susan and Benjamin Cheever have nothing left to drag out of their father's closet. It's become a cottage industry, carting out the debris." Cheever's life was, Wolcott said, "a mud slide," but these muddy revelations had boosted the writer's "mystique," giving him the image of a "Tortured Artist of our time" and elevating his fiction to "the big league," invoking undeserved comparisons of Cheever's "patchy novels" with the work of Hawthorne and Kafka.[14]

The Cheevers and Gottlieb appeared to us, despite their talk of a fearless presentation of the truth, to agree with Wolcott that everyone loves a sinner. We thought that Bob Hoover, book editor of the *Pittsburgh Post-Gazette,* was, in his review of *Treetops*, closer to the truth. Despite being embarrassingly candid, Susan's book was, he thought, "a must for students of John Cheever," but "with the publication of Cheever's pathetic, miserable diaries, it adds another blow to the reputation of an important fiction writer."[15]

We had been impressed, too, with Robert Boyd's comments on the *Letters:*

> Some of these letters are vital, full of the artistic fire with which Cheever, at his best, could singe the eyebrows of his readers. Others, especially toward the end of the book, are overt and ingenuous confessions of various failings of the flesh that should have been destroyed—indeed, would have been destroyed by recipients (or by an editor) sensitive to the fact that a harshly explicit account of an artist's sex life adds little to the illumination of his

creativity and robs him of the dignity to which every human, famous or not, is entitled.[16]

And, indeed, the *Journals* as well as the *Letters* (to say nothing of *Treetops*, despite Susan's alleged hiring of her own publicist) sold poorly. Those readers who had been charmed by what Wolcott called "the swan-necked shimmer" of Cheever's early stories and who admired, as Michiko Kakutani did, his preoccupation "with the fundamental decencies of life" were apparently not eager to read what the writer did in the bathroom with the door open.

A literary reputation, as I learned during my research on Arnold Bennett, can depend on many things apart from the actual literary value of the author's work. It is fragile, not immutable, and can be seriously damaged by the vagaries of time and taste; the damage can be compounded by negative posthumous comments by the author's contemporaries. The usual impulse of the families of these writers has been to protect them from anything that could be considered an "unseemly" revelation, and—the sisters of both Jane Austen and Walter Pater come immediately to mind—have often been only too willing to slash and burn documents, to the frustration of literary historians. But it occurs to me that some comfort can be taken in the thought that such lacunae might enable the reader to concentrate on the work itself, without the distraction of intimate details of the author's private life.

42

"It's Like Getting a Cancer off Your Back"

Oral arguments before the Illinois Supreme Court were set for March 21, 1991. We took a train to Springfield on the 20th, accompanied by Franklin and Bruce's wife, Julia Anderson, and checked into a comfortable hotel, where we had a sort of Last Supper with Tom Leavens, who left the table early to go up to his room and rehearse his argument.

It had not occurred to us, when the court accepted our case in October 1990, that there would be new justices when the time came for arguments. Tom and Marc Fogelberg hadn't mentioned this as a cause for worry, so we didn't think about it. Illinois Supreme Court justices are elected for ten-year terms; three new justices had been elected in November 1990. These were Michael Bilandic, 67, and Charles Freeman, 56, both Democrats, and James Heiple, 57, a Republican from Pekin, Illinois, and a life member of the National Rifle Association. (Bilandic had been mayor of Chicago until he had been defeated by Jane Byrne because he had been unprepared, to put it mildly, for the mother of all snowstorms.) These three had joined four incumbents: Republicans Thomas J. Moran, 70, and Ben Miller, 54, and Democrats William G. Clark, 66, and Horace L. Calvo, 63. William Clark and Charles Freeman had recused themselves from our case: Freeman because he had heard our case in the appellate court, and Clark because a relative of his worked for Tom's law firm.

There have been attempts in Illinois to replace the system of electing justices with a merit appointment system, but all of these have failed. Some lawyers hoped that the presence of Freeman and Bilandic, who were believed to be more liberal than their predecessors, would improve the court, where there had not been much dissent and not much questioning or comment during oral arguments, and where there was a very high rate of reversal by the U.S. Supreme Court. A few lawyers thought that Heiple would participate in oral arguments more than the others and write more dissenting opinions because he was "an independent thinker."[1]

March 21 was an unseasonably warm, summery day. The court is housed in an impressive two-story building on a leafy street. We ascended a marble staircase to the second floor. There were no bag searches or checks of any kind; the atmosphere was pleasantly relaxed. The hearing room, entered through carved double doors, was beautiful: oak paneling, Corinthian gilt-edged columns, thick red carpeting, and red velvet curtains over venetian blinds on the four tall windows. There were about fifty spectators in the room. Garbus was in the back row, chewing gum. The seven justices filed in. Their first case involved a state trooper who had allegedly committed a tort in responding to a police call. All the justices seemed to take a strong interest in this case, interrupting the lawyers with questions and comments. When that case ended, the two recused justices left the room.

The opposing attorneys were given twenty minutes to present their arguments; after that the plaintiffs' lawyer was given ten minutes in which to respond. If the justices interrupted the lawyers with questions, the time was not extended. Tom went first, using notes, to argue that Kiley's advisory opinion was not valid in Illinois; that he had improperly intruded himself into the editing process; that he had not given Academy the right to judge whether Mrs. Cheever's manuscript was satisfactory in form and content because there had been no manuscript when the trial ended; that he had not considered enough criteria; that Mary Cheever had waived her right to select the stories because of her silence, and that she had not shown good faith and fair dealing in her selection of stories.

The five judges sat quietly. Bilandic was smiling; he seemed to be having a good time. Toward the end of Tom's presentation, Justice Heiple interrupted. "You don't have a valid contract, do you?" he asked. "Isn't it just an agreement to agree?"

"Oh, no," Tom said earnestly. "Oh, no, no, no. It's a valid contract. It's been found valid by two courts." Heiple lapsed back into silence, and Tom finished, obviously shaken.

Garbus came forward, unencumbered by notes and no longer chewing gum. The significance of Heiple's question was not lost on him: he immediately said that the contract was "illusory," a word that must have appealed to Heiple because it turned up later in his opinion. After that Garbus embarked on a kind of stream-of-consciousness defense, beginning with a contemptuous dismissal of Tom, at whom he gestured with his thumb. "He's their fifth lawyer," Garbus said, adding three illusory lawyers to his Sixth Illusory Judge and his forty-four illusory uncollected stories. "He wasn't there. He doesn't know about any of this. He doesn't know anything about publishing." Then he began to talk about Mrs. Cheever's manuscript, describing the plot of "Bayonne" and reading aloud from her headnotes and Susan's introduction.

The judges sat like people in a trance. Bilandic was still smiling. Members of the audience shifted in their seats; some exchanged glances.

Academy Chicago, Garbus said, was "a public domain publisher." It had no full-time editor. Academy wanted to present this book as pure trash, calling Cheever a homosexual writer. There never, he informed the court, had been a nationwide injunction against a book. "They went into federal court and said, 'You can't give us public domain.' The court said, 'Of course you can.'" After this mysterious comment, he noted that Academy had paid $375; earlier he had said that Academy paid $250. "They want to rape Mrs. Cheever's inheritance," he said. "She won't get a nickel. We know that. We acknowledge that." At one point he said that there was "no interest" in these stories; at another point he said that the Cheevers—or possibly Academy? It was impossible to tell—could sell "these stories" for "hundreds of thousands of dollars."

He waved a copy of a book of short stories we had published, *Loose Connections* by Sybil Claiborne. "Here's a typical Academy book," he said. "One hundred fifty pages, eight stories." (*Loose Connections* has 171 pages and *sixteen* stories.) All John Cheever left his wife, he said, were "these stories." "They wouldn't take the money back," he said. "They didn't have a real editor. Franklin Dennis is here, a publicity man. Jordan Miller was in court on Friday, he said he had no idea how many stories there would be . . . . They got into financial difficulties, they decided to grab all the stories. They said it was a gold mine. The best stories are in the Knopf collection. These are early stories, his early period. They talk about public domain," he said to the glassy-eyed judges, "they asked for 'Expelled' and 'Homage to Shakespeare'—they're both in the public domain . . . "*

Despite his obvious distress, not one of the robotic judges would help him out by interrupting him with a question. I felt somewhat the same way I had felt when Mrs. Cheever called us beggars in the court in White Plains. Surely, I thought, even though these men are judges, they can see that some-

---

*"Expelled" is still within copyright. There is a question about the status of "Homage to Shakespeare."

thing is askew here? But after my experience with Judge Goettel—who was appointed, not elected—I had no real confidence that anyone, apart from the uncomfortable citizens in the audience, would wonder about this performance.

In his rebuttal, Tom attempted to refute some of Garbus's points, and then it was over. Garbus left immediately. A friend of Julia's, a resident of Springfield who was with us, spied him descending the marble staircase and said he seemed to be upset, since he was still talking and gesticulating. She also remarked that she thought he was a good lawyer.

We went back to the little preparation room where Tom was packing up. He was greatly distressed. He said that Heiple's question about the contract was a serious one: it meant that Heiple was going to declare our contract invalid. "You didn't mention ICM vetting the contract," I said, to make him feel better. "Oh, I forgot to mention ICM," he said, "I forgot to mention it." He looked at us with a wild surmise. "Maybe you can make some kind of settlement with them before the opinion comes down," he said. "Maybe you can still salvage something."

Horrified, we immediately went into denial. We saw Tom into a taxi and rushed to a pay phone to call the appeals lawyer Marc Fogelberg so that he could tell us that Tom was wrong about Heiple. That worked: Marc said soothingly that Heiple's question didn't necessarily have a dire implication and that even if the court declared our contract invalid, they were required by law to consider a plea for reconsideration.

For some idiotic reason, we felt much better after talking to Marc and went home comforted. Thus we were emotionally unprepared when, on the morning of June 20, a reporter for the *Chicago Daily Law Bulletin* called us at home and told us that the court had reached a unanimous decision and had thrown out our contract. "Oh, my heavens," Jordan said, caught off guard. "That means we lose everything."

This reaction was duly reported in the *Law Bulletin* for that day, along with Garbus's gracious comment that "One of the greatest pleasures in my life is that I will never have to speak to Mr. Miller or his lawyers again." This was wonderful news, he said, adding that "the parties" had spent more than $1 million on legal bills since the summer of 1987. "That means that everybody goes home, everybody goes their own way," Garbus said. "If the contract is unenforceable, that means they don't have a manuscript."[2]

It was Heiple who wrote the decision. Treating the book like an apartment lease or an agreement to buy a tractor, he had found it invalid because "it lacked essential terms": it did not specify the minimum or maximum number of stories or pages necessary for publication; it did not say who would decide which stories would be included; it gave "no date certain" for delivery of the manuscript; it did not define the criteria that would render it "satisfactory to the publisher in form and content"; gave no date certain for publication; no "certainty as to style or manner in which the book will be published"; no indication of the price at which the book would be sold or the length of time the book would stay in print. All these terms, Heiple complained, were "left to the sole discretion of the publisher."

Mrs. Cheever told the press that she was relieved, noting that her legal bills were more than $500,000. To her credit, she seemed to have some inkling that Heiple's decision had the potential to wreak havoc in the publishing business. "I don't think we'll make a lot of money on the stories," she said, "and I don't know that it sets a great precedent. But it was something that we as a family felt we must do."[3]

Despite the fact that he frequently represented publishers, Garbus did not seem concerned about the precedent. "She has total control over the works," he told the Associated Press. "She can decide what she wants to do with them. It's like getting a cancer off your back."[4]

Tom said he was going to ask the court to reconsider its opinion, which he called "devastating" to the publishing industry, since it "virtually wiped out every publishing agreement that is used across the country."[5] It was almost, he said, "as though a book has to be in its final form in order for the contract for publication to be enforceable."[6] Jordan called it "a terrible jolt. We're not ready to concede, but I have no idea what's going to happen next. How," he asked, "can a publisher know how many pages an unwritten book is going to contain until it's written? The implications go way beyond us. It affects every publisher."[7]

To add to the circus atmosphere, Ray Hanania, Cook County reporter for the *Chicago Sun-Times,* wrote a story headlined "Court OKs Publication of Cheever Book," in which he announced that "The Illinois Supreme Court Thursday reversed a lower court order that blocked the publication of a collection of short stories by the author John Cheever. The order allows Academy Chicago Publishers to release *The Uncollected Works of John Cheever* [*sic*]." The result of this item was that we received several congratulatory notes and phone calls, even though Hanania's last paragraph read, "But the Supreme Court ruled that the agreement is not a valid contract because it was vague."[8]

On June 25, Garbus sent Tom a check for $375, in repayment of the advance. The check was drawn on the personal account of Ruth B. Garbus and Martin S. Garbus at the Chemical Bank.

Some weeks after this, a friend of ours met Justice Bilandic at an official function in Chicago and asked him why the court had come down with such a dumb decision in the Cheever case.

"What Cheever case?" Bilandic said.

43

A Hellabaloo

True to his word, in mid-July Tom filed a petition for rehearing with the Illinois Supreme Court, maintaining that Academy Chicago was denied due process when the Court both raised and decided the issue of the enforceability of the contract without any brief from the company. At the very least, Tom and Mark argued, "Academy Chicago must be given the opportunity to present evidence of industry custom and practice to sustain the validity of the contract."

When the story broke, the *Wall Street Journal* asked some attorneys at New York publishing houses for a response. The attorneys' first reaction was that "the ruling may not have broad impact because contracts drafted by major publishers usually are quite explicit."[1] We interpreted that to mean that these lawyers thought, off the tops of their heads, that a small publisher in the boonies might well have drafted a cockeyed contract. But when Tom sent copies of Heiple's decision to publishers and publishers' organizations, the result was what my father-in-law used to call "a hellabaloo."

Grant Barnes, director of the Stanford University Press, sent Tom a letter to be used to bolster our petition, in which he said that Heiple's decision represented "an arbitrary and unfair revision of the basic terms of trade between publishers and their authors" and if allowed to stand would call into question the validity of most agreements that Stanford had with its own authors, since "most if not all of the same alleged defects" that Heiple found in the Academy contract existed in Stanford's standard printed agreement. This could cost Stanford, he wrote, "hundreds of thousands of dollars of investment in staff development costs and other direct costs" because virtually all of its contracts, at least for books yet unpublished, would become unenforceable. He made clear he was not taking a position on the case in any other area.

Grant Barnes sent copies of his letter to officials of the Association of American University Presses (AAUP): Peter C. Grenquist, director; David Bartlett, president; and Elizabeth Hadas, president-elect;—and to Nicholas Veliotes, president of the Association of American Publishers

(AAP). R. Bruce Rich, of Weil, Gotshal & Manges, the law firm represent-ing the Association of American Publishers, wrote a letter to Tom support-ing, as Grant Barnes had, our rehearing petition. It was, he wrote, "of con-siderable concern to AAP and its publisher members" that many of the contract provisions stated by Heiple to be insufficiently specific were not substantially different from the terms contained in many other publishers' contracts for thousands of books published annually in the United States. Customarily the determination of what constituted a "satisfactory" manu-script was left to the "good-faith discretion" of the publisher, as were deci-sions about the price at which a book would be sold and the length of time it would remain in print. Heiple's opinion, the AAP said, did not appear to "take account of the realities of the book publishing process and the con-tractual undertakings that underlie that process," especially since many projects are acquired by publishers "in the conceptual stage" and are devel-oped afterward by the author working with the publisher's editorial staff. Peter Grenquist, executive director of the AAUP, provided a letter agreeing in every way with Bruce Rich.

Garbus did not appear to be much concerned by the Grenquist or Barnes letters: he had always made clear his minimum high regard for university presses. But the AAP's endorsement of our petition lit a fire under him: it was the unkindest cut of all, to mix a metaphor. He sprang into action with a ferocity and persistence that we found somewhat surprising even in him, since, after all, he had now really won his case: there was virtually no chance that the Illinois Supreme Court would reverse itself. It was not known to reverse itself, and any court that could produce a document as eccentric as Heiple's opinion was clearly not going to admit error by paying attention to an argument, however well reasoned. Garbus told *PW* that Academy was "attempting to mislead the industry": standard publishing contracts bore "no resemblance to the alleged agreement which Academy persuaded Mrs. Cheever to sign." Academy's was "an anomalous contract." His complaints floated on the *PW* page in a sea of quotations from Grant Barnes, Bruce Rich, and Peter C. Grenquist.[2]

Still fighting the good fight, he fired off a three-page letter to Parker B. Ladd, director of general publishing for the AAP, addressing him as "Dear Parker" and telling him about "twelve judges in four separate opinions in two states" who found against the contract. Actually, *five* judges on the Illinois Supreme Court had found against the contract, but there were five

judges (including the appellate judge who was asleep) who had *not* found
against the contract. But even so, who were the two illusory judges making
up Garbus's twelve? After some thought we decided they were probably
Supreme Court justices Charles Freeman and William G. Clark, who had
recused themselves from the case. They may have been crushed to discover
that Garbus had not noticed their absence.

Garbus told "Parker" a lot of things that had nothing to do with Heiple:
the Cheevers had never seen the book, which had been prepared "unilater-
ally" over the objections of the author (who had presumably been contacted by Ouija board); "embarrassingly immature" stories had been falsely
advertised; and all those courts had refused to allow Academy to realize
over $1 million in potential profits. But apart from that, Garbus told the
director that he should have written his letter more carefully and not allowed it to be used against "John Cheever's widow." And "Parker's" failure
"to even advise the Cheevers" of what he was doing "was unseemly and
inexplicable."

The Cheevers, Garbus wrote, did all they could to avoid litigation. "They
offered to give Academy a very substantial six (6) figure sum so that Academy could profit on its contract. Academy refused to settle for anything
less than a $1,500,000 payment from the Cheevers and a continuing inter-
est in royalties if the stories were published—a very substantial return on
$375."

After telling this big story, which had nothing to do with the AAP's
objections to Heiple's opinion, Garbus fell back on charm. "We request
that you withdraw your letter," he wrote. "If you want to submit a letter,
please consider sending one which is more appropriate."

Parker Ladd got a letter, too, from Erica Jong ("Dear Parker"), who wrote
in her capacity as president of the Authors Guild on official stationery that
included a list of Guild officers. Not the least of these—surprise, surprise,
as James Warren said—was Susan Cheever. The Guild was "dismayed," it
was "appalled"; the Academy contract was "vague and poorly drafted" and
diverged "fundamentally from industry practice"; "Parker's" letter had done
"grave damage to author/publisher relations." Further, it was incompre-
hensible that "at the very least the AAP could not have used its good offices
to support Mrs. Cheever." The AAP had "undercut the very concept of
authorship," and defending Academy's contract could "only undercut the
AAP's moral authority."

Tom Leavens too wrote to Parker Ladd ("Dear Mr. Ladd") to point out that the contract had been vetted by ICM and found enforceable by four judges in Illinois. Referring to Garbus's "twelve judges in two states," Tom said, "Where Mr. Garbus finds three additional phantom judges . . . is known only to his imagination." This comment added to the exotic overlay of the discussion: where, we wondered, had Tom found *three* phantom judges? We had found a Sixth Illusory Judge in an earlier reference, but with these Twelve Judges, we could find only *two* Garbus phantoms, and these were probably Freeman and Clark. If you wanted to be picky about judges who had actually found the contract invalid, you could come up with *seven* phantoms because only five members of the Supreme Court had actually done that. In one state. We tried to stop thinking about it.

The letter-writing epidemic spread to Nicholas Veliotes, president of the AAP, prompting him to write to Helen Stephenson, executive director of the Authors Guild, to say that he had gotten letters not only from Garbus and Erica Jong but from Mrs. Cheever as well, and he had received Garbus's letter only after it had been distributed to the press. Mr. Veliotes, in what he described as an attempt to "throw some cold water on the conflagration," pointed out that the AAP was reacting only to the unusually broad language of the court and had expressed no opinion about the case itself. This controversy, he said, could and should have been avoided "with the right handling."

Erica Jong, undeterred, wrote to Judge Heiple at his post office box in Pekin, Illinois. In the *Chicago Tribune,* James Warren commented that when Heiple spent $400,000 of his own money to win the seat on the Supreme Court, he had probably never expected to get a letter from Erica ("Fear of Flying") Jong.[3] Anyway, she called the "manuscript acceptability clause" in standard publishing contracts unfairly one-sided and attacked the AAP for questioning Heiple's opinion without "the balance of equivalent input from America's authors."

Scott Meredith weighed in with his own letter, remarking that "if a perfectly valid contract such as this one can be voided on the grounds that the language . . . contains 'omissions, ambiguities, unresolved essential terms and illusory terms,' then virtually every contract in existence at every publishing house can be set aside. And if allowed to stand, this uninformed opinion could destroy the long standing tradition of fair dealing and mutual trust between publishers and authors."[4]

This went on throughout the month of August. On August 20, Jerome S. Robin, chairman of the AAP, wrote to Garbus in response to a letter from Russell Smith—who had added his voice to the swelling chorus—and enclosed a copy of Mr. Veliotes's cold-water letter to Helen Stephenson. Appearing to be fed up, Mr. Robin said that he was aware of letters from Garbus and Smith to various AAP members and to AAP management on this subject and he had decided to answer. He explained once more that the AAP had not misconstrued the Supreme Court's decision and was not insensitive to Mrs. Cheever's circumstances. But, as Bruce Rich's letter had made clear (and Nicholas Veliotes's letter had repeated), the AAP's concerns were limited to the overly broad language of the court and its possible deleterious consequences for the publishing industry. Their concern had, he said, nothing to do with the *result* reached by the court or what Garbus portrayed as Academy's intent to publish and so forth. Their attorneys, Messrs. Weil, Gotshal & Manges, had "repeatedly requested" on the AAP's behalf that Garbus "communicate with them on this legal matter instead of with the laymen to whom you have addressed your correspondence." He trusted Garbus would do so from then on, if there was any further correspondence.

On August 30, Garbus wrote to Heiple ("Honorable Sir"), enclosing a copy of Veliotes's letter to the Authors Guild, which Garbus called "a letter of regret, this time from the President of the AAP," which, Garbus said, "has clarified its position." The implication was that Veliotes "regretted" the AAP position. With this letter to Heiple, Garbus declared victory and in effect left the field.

Earlier in the month, before the letter writing reached fever pitch, Garbus and Russell Smith found time to contribute a five-thousand-or-so-word article to the *New York Law Journal* attempting to prove, as Paul Freehling put it, that we were devils and the Cheever lawyers were angels. The article was ostensibly intended to answer the question, "Will the 'Cheever' Case Affect Other Author/Publisher Relationships?" The answer, unsurprisingly, was "No." Garbus and Smith mentioned Jonathan Yardley's reference to the projected book, which he had never seen, as "a literary scavenger job"; the "$375" advance; Franklin's "obtaining" an introduction to Ben Cheever and suggesting "the possibility of locating and publishing some" of John Cheever's uncollected stories; the Cheevers' perception of Academy as "a small, university-related press"; quotes from Franklin's letters with typos included and italics added; Academy's nefarious attempt to sell rights through Scott Meredith; the illegible Xeroxes; large hunks of Judge Goettel's opinion and pieces of Kiley's decision; and so on. Finally, in the last paragraph or so, the two Cheever lawyers attempted to answer the title question: their response was that the Academy contract was "anomalous," produced by "a maverick publisher" who had tried to publish a book over the objections of the author *and* (my italics) the author's executor and who had "no specific copyright license or other clearly defined contractual right to do so"—well, Garbus and Smith concluded, "that publisher is likely to find itself in court, and is likely to lose."

The Illinois high court, they wrote, agreed with Mrs. Cheever that "'it is time for the parties to go their own ways.'" A footnote informs us that this wording was from an "Appeal Brief of Mary Cheever"; Heiple did not use these words. Some of Heiple's own words are squeezed into the final footnote, accompanied by Garbus and Smith's comment that the Illinois Supreme Court really did not mean to say that publishing contracts must always specify the future price of the proposed book or that contracts must contain a date certain for delivery of a manuscript. All the court was doing, Garbus and Smith said in four-point type, "was simply pointing out" that in "the alleged contract between Academy and Mrs. Cheever there was hardly any agreement on any subject at all."[5]

By September, most of the uproar had died down; a final volley was shot on our behalf by Jennifer Moyer in an editorial in *Small Press* magazine, where she recounted what she called Heiple's "scary precedents" that, if not appealed, could affect "the way thousands of publishers do business."[6] Garbus did appear to consider "small press" a term of opprobrium, saying in the *Law Journal* article that "Academy is referred to in its own trial exhibits as 'a small publishing house,' 'a little house' and 'a small press.'"

In the first week of October, the court rejected our petition for a rehearing, as just about everyone had expected it would. Garbus hailed this "total victory for the Cheevers," who, he said, were "'taking stock' of the situation" and "might consider publishing a book to their liking."[7]

As a coda to this controversy or whatever it was, I have to say that months after Heiple's decision, an author of our acquaintance approached a New York publishing lawyer, saying he wanted to get out of a contract with a major house for a proposed book, a contract in which the terms were necessarily vague, and he wanted to use the Academy/Cheever Illinois Supreme

Court decision to nullify that contract. "Oh, forget it," the lawyer said. "No New York court is going to take that goofy decision seriously. They're too sophisticated."

Another coda was Judge Heiple's subsequent contribution to the history of Illinois jurisprudence. In June 1994, he wrote a decision that made him a household name in Illinois and even nationally. Reversing the findings of two lower courts, this decision dictated the removal of a three-and-a-half-year-old boy from the home of his adoptive parents, where he had lived since he was four days old, and delivered him into the custody of his biological father. Considerable uproar ensued, and Bob Greene, the *Chicago Tribune* columnist, devoted much of his energy to discussions of this and other Heiple decisions and actions. In January 1997, the judge was elected chief justice of the Supreme Court by his colleagues. Shortly after that he was censured by the Illinois Courts Commission because of his behavior toward the police when he was stopped for traffic violations. The upshot was that, under threat of impeachment, Heiple resigned as chief justice. He will remain on the court until his term expires in 2000.[8]

44

"Father Sells Best"

Nineteen ninety-one was drawing to a close; our revels now were ending. Our main concern was keeping out of Judge Goettel's clutches and stopping the depressing flow of legal bills into our bookkeeper Elma Pador's in-basket. We were surprised and pleased to discover that we had some insurance coverage on these bills. Tom Leavens had asked to see our insurance policies and had announced that we were actually covered, although so much time had elapsed before we made this discovery that the response of the insurance company was uncertain.

In October, the *Village Voice* ran a long, well-researched piece on what was now being called the "Cheever cottage industry." It was probably inevitable that the *Letters,* the *Journals, Treetops,* and even *Home Before Dark,* taken together, would give rise to an article like this, which was called "Father Sells Best: In the Dysfunctional Family Olympics, the Cheevers Go for the Gold." The litigation against us fit neatly into the picture. *People* magazine had taken note of it in their 1988 piece on the *Letters,* in which I had helpfully called the Cheevers "venal" and observed that if Mrs. Cheever really wanted to protect her husband's reputation, she would not have allowed the publication of "pornographic homosexual love letters." Garbus was deeply offended by this, and so was Paul, who said later that he had thought that "venal" implied political corruption.

Now in the *Village Voice,* James Ledbetter did not assume, as we did, that these latest revelations would hurt John Cheever's reputation; indeed, he, like James Wolcott—and probably the Cheevers themselves—thought "the public appetite for Cheever's work" would be "whetted by the hoopla surrounding the journals." He mentioned the "cottage industry" and employed the "soiled linen" image: "airing their domestic soiled linen before the public" had "become the family business," he wrote, mentioning not only the nonfiction books but also Ben's first novel, due out in 1992, in which the protagonist "is the son of a famous, alcoholic writer." And to protect the family business, Ledbetter noted, the Cheevers attempted to destroy the competition. They had "almost fanatically tried to cut off outsiders' access to their patriarch's documents and copyrights," spending "three years and $900,000 to keep a book of short stories from being published by a small Chicago publisher, even after Mary signed a contract for the book" and cutting off "an experienced academic biographer who's done loads of research on Cheever, which he eventually had to excise from his book." They had even, Ledbetter wrote, "bullied a Jesuit priest to keep him from giving trial testimony they thought could be damaging." They had made it clear "that Cheever history and the money to be made peddling it, are to be kept all in the family."

The "academic biographer" was, of course, Scott Donaldson, who had a tale to tell Ledbetter. After two years of research, during which Mary cooperated with him, Donaldson was suddenly denied access to "the vast majority" of the journals—a denial based, he said, "on the grounds that they contained material that would be extremely painful for Mary Cheever to read or hear about." When Ben announced that he was going to edit the letters, Donaldson offered him copies of two thousand letters he had found. Ben refused them. And then Donaldson was refused permission to quote from Cheever letters in his own book, even after he offered Ben a percentage of his royalties. Susan admitted that she might have telephoned Donaldson's editor at Random House to tell him that Donaldson did not have permission to use the journals. "I wasn't out to get him," she said, "but we were competing . . . . I wished that he hadn't been writing it."

In the end, after the judicial Salinger decision that forbade extensive quotation—and even paraphrasing—of unpublished material, Donaldson's editor and a Random House lawyer had to go through his entire manuscript and pare down every quote and paraphrase to ten words or less. It took them "two-and-a-half hours to clean up a single page of typescript." The book came out a year late, to essentially good reviews. Susan said that "bad chemistry" took over when Donaldson gradually alienated the family by acting as though he knew more about her father than she did and "bragging" about getting research grants. "The way we've published this material is much, much better than to have them in a biography," she said. The Cheevers, Ledbetter concluded, had a right to make money from their copyrights. But their behavior had opened them to the charge that they were "exploiting their father's reputation, not protecting it."[1]

This was obviously a devastating article and the most complete published to that date on the family's handling of their literary inheritance. It had an impact. When in the spring of 1992 Ben's novel *The Plagiarist* was published, Daniel Max, in the *New York Observer*, commented that the book's "kind reviews" had cheered the "battered and nervous" Cheever family: Ben told Max that he had been afraid that his novel would get bad reviews because of "a lot of stories about the wicked, greedy Cheevers," all that "terrible publicity." And indeed the headline on Max's story was "The Cheever Cottage Industry Takes Patrimoney to the Bank." Max noted that three Cheever projects had been published in the past year alone, "capping an eight-year bull market involving six publishers and"—wait for it—"twelve judges." Max provided some figures about Cheever projects, beginning with *Home Before Dark* ($125,000 advance, 40,000 hardcover copies sold*); then the *Letters* ($75,000 advance, 30,000 copies sold); and the *Journals* ($1.1 million advance, 19,000 copies sold). Then there was the Academy litigation—the $1,500 advance "may have been one of the worst deals in publishing history," by the end of which "the press was regularly portraying the Cheevers as attacking a hapless, small publisher in order to reap greater profits." And then came *Treetops* with "excruciating" revelations about Mary Cheever, whose "creative processes could hardly be deemed of literary interest." The amount spent by the family on the Academy lawsuits varied from Ben and Mary's "roughly $500,000" to Susan's "more fanciful $1 million."†

Max quoted Susan as saying that it would be fitting if they spent all the money they made on the *Journals* defending the case against Academy; Mary Cheever "wonders what her daughter can be thinking of." Then there was the "mystery" of what the family was going to do with the sixty-eight stories that at time of settlement Garbus had estimated to be worth $1 million (a sum he had mentioned before). At that moment—June 1992—Max reported that publishers were estimating the worth of the stories at $500,000, based partly on anticipated profit, partly on goodwill, and partly on the hope of a backlist success. This income would be important to the estate, he wrote, since backlist sales of all John Cheever's books in the U.S. amount

---

*The reader should be aware that figures on "books sold" often do not include "books returned," especially since the process of returning books can last more than a year.

†It seems to me that, taking into consideration the confusion about royalties and agents' fees demonstrated by the Cheevers in their depositions, all these estimates might belong in the realm of fantasy. However, since our legal bills ran around $400,000, I should think that if the Cheevers paid Garbus anything at all, they would have had to have been billed at least $.5 million by him.

to only about 30,000 copies a year—fewer then the sales of Pearl Buck's *The Good Earth*—and total sales generate about $75,000 annually. Despite this, Ben told Max he was still "reluctant" to publish the stories. Susan said she would agree to publish them but only with the warning that "These are not John Cheever stories." Mary Cheever, who Max mistakenly said "calls the shots," said, "It will be a big job to put them all together [but] eventually we probably will publish them."[2]

These Cheever references to the uncollected stories seem to reflect a state of denial or perhaps deep bafflement about the whole project. A few months later, Ben was to tell John Blades of the *Chicago Tribune* that his family had not made up their minds, "but if we do a book, it certainly won't be anything like the one we went to so much trouble and expense to stop."[3] How, one might reasonably ask, could a book of stories by John Cheever be published with the caveat that these John Cheever stories are not by John Cheever? And why would it be "a big job" to put together a book that has already been put together? And how can a book of short stories be completely different from a book of the same short stories?

In the summer, Hillel Italie wrote an Associated Press story, widely reprinted, in which Ben denied that he and his family were "milking the corpse," as he put it; that they were "only in it for the money." He said he was happy to "bust up" the image of John Cheever as "a rich man . . . [who] lived a wonderful life, a life above reproach." He said that if he upset people with the information that his father "drank a lot or that he had male lovers, all right, I'm happy I upset them." And as for the reason the Cheevers "wanted out" from the Academy contract, Ben said, "they were selling the stories as his best, as intensely autobiographica . . . . Originally they had a book they could have published. If they hadn't decided they had a chance to make a couple of million dollars, it would have been all right. We knew the stories were valuable, but we weren't happy with the kind of book they wanted to put out." Hillel Italie found this answer puzzling because it seemed to supply a different reason from the original one, which was that the stories were inferior.

Finally, Italie noted that Cheever's complete journals in three volumes were to be published "by the end of the century" and quoted James Ledbetter on "the dysfunctional family Olympics": "These people get a tremendous amount of mileage from public psychotherapy. It's very sad that this has scarred them so they can't get over it. I think there has to be a limit."[4]

45

Another
Moral Issue

The Ledbetter article, which appeared in the fall of 1991, brightened our days and lifted our spirits as we discussed with Tom the various questions involved in settling the case. He was in touch with Russell Smith, whom we had last seen the previous May when the booksellers convention was held in New York. We had two booths, and Russell and Maura Wogan kept materializing at various spots across the aisle from us, like Peter Quint and the dead governess in *The Turn of the Screw,* grimacing and gesturing in our direction. The motivation behind these actions escaped us, but if they were meant to underscore the nightmare quality of our relationship with Garbus's firm, they succeeded. Tom presented points for a settlement that were acceptable to us—no blame attached to either party, the White Plains action dropped—except for the Cheevers' requirement that we agree never to publish any work by John Cheever. That struck me as unreasonable. "Why," I asked Tom, "should we be the only publishing house in the world that can't publish Cheever's public domain stories?"

Tom agreed that this was unacceptable. His solution was that we should refuse to settle and let the Cheevers take us to court in White Plains. He said he thought the insurance company would pick up the tab for this, including damages, which would be slight, since Goettel himself had said that our "infringement" was not "egregious." I was not convinced: I had visions of Judge Goettel taking our house away, since he was prevented by law from imprisoning us for debt, sentencing us to forty lashes, or ducking us in a pond. Apart from this, as Jordan pointed out, being found guilty of copyright infringement would not look good on our record. So we nixed this plan.

"Listen," I said to Tom, "how about putting a limit on the time we can't publish public domain? How about five years?" Tom took fire at this. "Good idea!" he said. "I'll ask for two years." And, probably because the Cheevers were not eager to hemorrhage more money in another trial and be awarded insignificant damages and more bad publicity, two years was what Tom got. We were convinced that the Cheevers had agreed, too, because they planned to publish our big book within the next two years, thus making our small public domain collection redundant. But still, we wanted the right to publish: it was the principle of the thing. I wouldn't go so far as to say that it was a matter of honor.

So we signed the settlement agreement in January 1992. David Streitfeld announced it in the *Washington Post:* "The most expensive, protracted and vicious court battle to take place in recent years over a book has finally sputtered to an end." Jordan was quoted as saying that he didn't know what his plans would be in two years but "at the moment, the name Cheever makes me feel like George Bush at a Japanese banquet." Martin Garbus said that the Cheevers were elated. "Elated?" Streitfeld asked. "They're elated it's over," Garbus said. But was "elated" really the word he wanted to use? "I think 'relieved' is more accurate," Garbus said.

What we found amazing in this article was that after maintaining in the *New York Law Journal* that the Academy contract was "anomalous" and drawn up by a "maverick publisher," Garbus told Streitfeld: "If it had any more precision—the number of stories, the number of pages, something descriptive like that—the contract would have been fair and binding." Streitfeld summed this up: "What finally turned the case against Academy Chicago was a missing word or two in the contract."[1]

Mrs. Cheever's response to the settlement was that Academy had intended to put out the stories "in chronological order with no idea what they added up to . . . . It would be very bad for the man's reputation to have a lot of inferior stories put out" that way.[2] She was still, as Garbus had once put it, beating a horse. The Authors Guild, too, was still at it, in their Winter 1992 Bulletin. Under the headline "Guild Intervention Effective in Cheever Law Suit," they put forth the claim that the fervent arguments of Erica Jong and Helen Stephenson had caused President Veliotes, Director Parker Ladd, Attorney Bruce Rich, and the AAP Board of Directors "to clarify their position." Martin Garbus thanked Ms. Jong for the Guild's "eloquent, forceful and timely defense of the Cheevers" and warned writers to beware of small presses: "if they're judgment proof (don't have much money), you're finished." One reason Garbus had asked for an injunction against the Academy book, he said, was that he believed the Cheevers would "have trouble collecting damages." And then there were the "very troubling cases in which a small publisher is solvent, but does not follow standard industry practices in editing, publishing or marketing the book. Before signing with a small house, it is well to consult with other authors who recently had books published there."[3]

It is perhaps not necessary to say that Garbus gave no examples of these "troubling cases." Jennifer Moyer took offense at these slurs, pointing out in *Small Press* that financial difficulties were not limited to small presses: witness the collapse of Robert Maxwell's publishing empire and the problems of Grove Press, when it could not be sold. And then there were all those typos and other errors in big press books and big press editors playing musical chairs, going from one publishing house to another. And, she added, many authors preferred dealing with small presses where they received "individual attention and respect for author input . . . carefully-crafted publicity and marketing plans developed for their book alone and its peculiar requirements." She noted that Studs Terkel had left Random House for the New Press and Victor Villaseñor had gone from Putnam to Arte Publico.[4]

Garbus's denigration of small presses did not prevent another bizarre occurrence in this comic saga. We had provided Tom with a ticket to the 1991 booksellers convention in New York, where he spent the first day or two collecting publishers' catalogs and the rest of the time sitting in a chair in our booth clutching the catalogs to his bosom, with a dreamy look in his eye. We urged him to dump the catalogs and get over it, but he was smitten. He later described this ABA experience as a moment of "inspired lunacy" that led him to set up a publishing house called Kairos Press: *Kairos* means "opportune moment" in Greek. His first book was *Hearts and Times,* an oral history of elderly people's memories, converted into free verse by Ross Talarico, a poet friend of his. Tom told John Blades that even though the Cheever case was "definitely a losing proposition," it had only fortified an interest in publishing that he had harbored for years. "Instead of being dejected by all the Millers' setbacks in the Cheever case," Blades wrote, "Leavens said he was encouraged by their 'strength and commitment to publishing.'"[5]

Hearts and Times remains the lone product of Kairos Press, so we have reason to hope, for Tom's sake, that his opportune moment of lunacy has passed.

The Authors Guild, by the way, was not finished with us. In Helen Stephenson's retrospective of her service with the Guild, in the Winter 1993 Bulletin, she mentioned that, among other things, the Guild under her

stewardship, had "intervened on behalf of the Cheever family when a publisher tried to steal the unpublished stories of John Cheever through an
unconscionable contract."[6] This, we thought, was going too far. We contacted yet another lawyer, this time a defamation expert, who said that
under Illinois laws on defamation, the defamer has to mention the defamed by name and this Ms. Stephenson had not done. We accepted this
advice trustingly and did not pursue the matter.

In the spring 1993 Authors Guild Bulletin, Helen Stephenson was still
warning hapless authors to be wary of "small presses" and "small publishers." The distinction between these two is not clear, but she might have
been thinking of nonprofit as opposed to commercial small presses. In any
case, she said that some are "well-intentioned" but "have terrible cash flow
problems," and others are "just plain deadbeats." Authors were advised not
to say—as if anyone would—"Oh, it's not Simon & Schuster, so who
cares?'"

At the end of June 1992, Robert Gottlieb, the literary eminence and
plastic handbag collector, resigned from the *New Yorker,* owned by S. I.
Newhouse, who told staff that he and Gottlieb had reached "an impasse"
over the direction of the magazine. Gottlieb, who was traveling in Japan
when the axe fell, announced no plans for his future, but friends said that
one thing he would not do was return to book publishing.[7] Thus he would
be spending no more time at Knopf, his first love, and also part of the
Newhouse empire. This raised for us the question of whether the Cheevers
would indeed put out what we thought of as Our Book before our two-year
interdiction expired.

It was not a matter of deep concern to us at the time. Jordan had told
John Blades, in December 1992, that it was all over. "We're so demoral-
ized," he said, "that we no longer want to publish anything of Cheever's." It
was a relief to have done with it. But as we wended our way through 1993,
Jordan began to change his mind. Something concrete, he said, really ought
to result from the agony we had endured, besides legal bills and migraines.
Franklin and I were not sure we agreed. What if the Cheevers issued the Big
Book at the same time? we asked. What if they did something horrible to
us? What if the stories we thought were in the public domain were not
really in the public domain?

Jordan submitted our list of public domain stories to Thomson &
Thomson, copyright specialists in Washington, D.C. All proved to be safely

unregistered except for "Homage to Shakespeare," which we had been told by another researcher was in the public domain. There was some question about that, but there was no question about thirteen of the stories, and they were enough for a small book, about the size of the one Judge Kiley had instructed Mrs. Cheever to give to us. Mrs. Cheever had included nine PD stories in her manuscript, but public domain stories she had not given us were "In Passing," "His Young Wife," "The Opportunity," and the really poignant "Autobiography of a Drummer." Substituting these for the protected stories in the volume she had given us ("Brooklyn Rooming House," "Buffalo," "Play a March," "A Picture for the Home," "A Present for Louisa," and "A Trip to the Moon") would, we were convinced, make a better book.

By the fall of 1993, when the time was approaching to announce our books for spring 1994, there was no sign of the big Cheever book, and Jordan had won a nervous agreement from Franklin and me (Bruce and Eric were already in Jordan's corner—or at least Bruce was: Eric was pretty sick of Cheever). So we went ahead and chose an Edward Hopper painting for the front cover and a photograph of Cheever with his dog for the back cover—this had to be a beautiful book—and Jordan called David Streitfeld at the *Washington Post*. Showing somewhat less confidence than he had exhibited with Franklin and me, Jordan told Streitfeld that "the rational side of our brain tells us we shouldn't worry, but the irrational side says we should." In his article reporting that we were going to publish this book, Streitfeld noted that Jordan was exhibiting "some trepidation" because it was rare for a publisher to issue PD material by a living or recently deceased author, partly because there was not that much valuable PD work and partly because it was considered "rather unseemly" in a profession that still clung to its "gentlemanly pretensions." He reminded the reader that a decade earlier, a small New York publisher had issued two collections of PD stories by Louis L'Amour, who had reacted with a lawsuit, which Bantam, his publisher, lost. The defendant publisher was Carroll & Graf, whom "some in the industry" had called "a literary carpetbagger." Streitfeld did not add that the lawyer who had defended this small publisher against L'Amour's charges was Martin Garbus.

The original book of *Uncollected Stories*, Streitfeld wrote, was not "scheduled for publication or even placed under contract." He had contacted Ben who, he said, "didn't seem eager to renew the battle with Academy." "I don't suppose we can stop them from doing a public domain book," Ben said;

"most of the stories in the public domain aren't very good." I was quoted as commenting that we wanted this book for "a sense of an ending. Maybe we labored and brought forth a mouse, but we wanted to show something for all our agony. It's a natural human urge."⁸ You could hardly call that a ringing endorsement of our product, but it was the way I felt.

The next day, Sarah Lyall announced our new book plans in the *New York Times*. Ben, who had had a day to pull himself together, was more voluble than he had been with Streitfeld. He explained that his family "wanted desperately to stop the first book because it was marketed in a way we felt was misleading. We felt they were acting as if these stories were my father's best, and I don't think they are." But he now attempted to put an end to acrimony. A lawsuit, he said, was "like a divorce; everyone loses, really. They took a terrible beating in the courts and we took a terrible beating in the press. If anyone's entitled to the stories that are in the public domain, it's got to be the Millers. As much as we hated each other during the fight, I'd rather it be they than anyone else."⁹ We welcomed this sign that the war, with Ben at least, was over. He maintained this spirit of reconciliation when he talked to John Blades, saying, "As long as they publish them in a reasonable way, without saying they're his best stories, that's fine with me." He expressed relief that the "horrible fight was over" and added, "If anybody's going to publish the public domain stories, it should be Academy Chicago."

We ourselves commented that it had been "an awful, awful experience" and that when it became apparent that the Cheevers weren't going to bring out the stories with another publisher, "considering our agony, it made sense for us to go ahead." We even emphasized the positive. "It was difficult to judge the stories when there were sixty-eight in the book, but now that there are only thirteen, they stand out as individual stories. That may sound like a rationalization," I said (and God knows it was), "but we're rather happy with this little book."¹⁰

This air of sweetness and light did not extend to Martin Garbus, who, although presumably no longer paid to get into the ring, was still throwing punches. He told Sarah Lyall "that although the new book was indisputably legal, Academy's decision to publish the short stories was bad form." "I think there is a moral issue," he said. "Most people would feel that you shouldn't rip off a living author or estate just because his previous representative didn't properly protect his work. Nobody else would do this now or even five years from now."[11] Possibly Garbus had been in the ring once too often. He had apparently forgotten all about his spirited defense of Carroll & Graf's incursion into the Louis L'Amour canon. But, of course, he had more important things on his mind: having spent some time in Czechoslovakia helping (along with forty other lawyers and some scholars) the new government draw up a constitution, he had told the press that he felt like "the Thomas Paine of Prague."[12]

46

"A Fascinating Example of One Writer's Beginning"

In February 1994, we published ten thousand copies of our little book, *Thirteen Uncollected Stories by John Cheever*. Expecting to be assailed by criticism reflecting the Cheevers' complaints about the stories, we buttressed the volume with an introduction by Father Hunt and secured a positive quote from Matthew Bruccoli, which we put on a first page since we did not want to disturb the pristine beauty of the cover. We included an "Editor's Note" from Franklin, paraphrasing some of Cheever's comments from "Why I Write Short Stories" and making a few other points.

The first reviews of a book appear before publication in what are known as "the trade journals": *Publishers Weekly, Library Journal,* the American Library Association publication *Booklist,* and *Kirkus Reviews.* If none of these magazines prints a positive review of a forthcoming book, it is doubtful that libraries, at least, will order it. It was with relief, therefore, that we received excellent prepublication reviews in *Publishers Weekly* ("It is always good to see a great writer advancing in his craft, and it is a shame the collection could not have been more extensive"); *Booklist* ("all fiction collections should consider purchasing this attractively bound and presented little book"); and *Library Journal* ("A fascinating example of one writer's beginning"). Both the *PW* and *Library Journal* reviewers noted—the latter with some surprise—that many of the stories featured "well-observed character sketches" of strong women "at a point of crisis in their lives." We were pleased that the *PW* reviewer singled out "Autobiography of a Drummer" as a story in which "a real voice, capable of remarkable mimicry is emerging. This is a short, painful tale with something of the impact of *Death of a Salesman.*" And "In Passing" *PW* praised as "a touching parable about a crumbling family and a rootless Communist agitator" that has "real force."[1]

The only sour note in this group was sounded by *Kirkus,* and here there was evidence of a kind of ambivalence that was to recur in some other reviews—notably John Updike's in *The New Yorker*—and that may have been a result of the Cheevers' widely reported denigration of our original collection of uncollected stories. The *Kirkus* review mentioned the "years of litigation" and found the thirteen stories "something of a disappointment," being "hardly typical of his best work." The earliest stories were dismissed as "bleak, abstract expressions of social jitters during an anxious era of poverty and decline." But the reviewer could not lightly dismiss "Autobiography of a Drummer" and "In Passing" ("When Cheever begins to find a voice, his fictions become more convincing") or the portraits of "working women at turning points" or even the racetrack stories ("Cruel fate, not dysfunction, reigns in these clever narratives"). Despite this, the reviewer summed up: "At best, middlebrow fiction in the O'Hara-Cozzens mold."[2]

No other reviews of these stories invoked the names of John O'Hara and James Gould Cozzens. Ernest Hemingway and Scott Fitzgerald—Cheever's debt to them was strongly emphasized in Father's Hunt's introduction—were the heavy favorites. A few reviewers found the stories disappointing. Mark Bautz, in the *Washington Times,* found "a near total lack of Cheever" in the stories and suggested they be read "in conjunction" with the *Journals*; Richard Bausch, in the *Washington Post,* could not "help but believe that Cheever himself would not approve of this enterprise" and was "troubled about the publishing of work as uneven as this in a way that purports to represent the author, even in his formative stages."* And finally, Jacques le Sourd, a staff writer for the Westchester County Gannett papers—where Jordan's famous "gold mine" metaphor had first cropped up—noted that "none of these stories is embarrassing, but none is essentia . . . . Rummaging through an artist's early work arouses, at the least, ambivalence . . . . If [Cheever] didn't put these stories in the definitive collection of his best work, why should we read them now?"[3]

This sort of response was not unexpected, but as far as I know, it was limited to these three reviewers. In general, critics expressed gratitude for the publication of these stories, and some expressed a desire to read the rest of the uncollected work. Sven Birkerts, in the *New York Times Book Review,* had some cavils, "but," he wrote, "what fascination there is in reading these thirteen stories in their chronological sequence, and what instruction!"[4]

---

*Bausch's use of the word "purports" echoes Judge Goettel's comment that Academy Chicago specialized in works of "purported literary value." One dictionary definition of this word is that a *purported* claim is "often a false one."

This sentiment was echoed by John Updike at the bottom of the second page of his long review in the *New Yorker:* "Yet it is, as the three introducers promise, fascinating to see a splendid talent grow its wings." This sentence, introducing as it does a serious and mostly positive discussion of the thirteen stories, comes as a complete and rather baffling surprise because it appears on the heels of what seems to be a total dismissal of these stories: "Chronologically arranged, the thirteen begin with some formless, vaguely anticapitalist effusions by a teen-ager and progress to some pat, hokey confections by a young man trying to survive the Depression by selling to the slick magazines." We are told that Cheever had "basically disowned" *The Way Some People Live*, and are asked the rhetorical question, "How much more emphatically, then, would he have disowned 'Thirteen Uncollected Stories'?" The "pretty" Academy book is labeled a "curious consolation prize" awarded to itself by "the obscure Academy Chicago Publishers . . . a mom-and-pop operation." Being in the public domain, the stories "were up for grabs." When the Cheever "heirs" (whose work is characterized as "informative and charming" [the *Letters*] and "acute and affecting" [*Home Before Dark*]), after accepting "a trifling advance, . . . grasped the publisher's plans to print a total of sixty-eight stories—all it could find," they "balked."

But "yet" there is the fascination of watching the growth of those wings, and the rest of Updike's review—the larger part of it—is devoted to a serious appraisal of these thirteen stories. He found merit in them, even in the racetrack stories ("they hold pockets of uniquely Cheeveresque longing and poetry"), even in "Bock Beer and Bermuda Onions" ("the attempt to be vivid works curious wonders in syntax and vocabulary"), and especially in "The Princess," "The Teaser," and "Bayonne" ("all concern women fighting for their lives as age and hard times and mediocrity catch up with them . . . . the relation between a lone female performer and a mass of men is deftly, rather eerily explored from both sides"), and most especially in "Family Dinner" and "The Opportunity" ("They give off Cheever's particular atmospherics—a wry susceptibility, an offhand yet edgy concreteness, a radiance against all odds breaking through a miasma of weary and bitter wisdom").

At the end of this ambivalent essay, Updike suggests that Cheever's "estate might eventually arrange an edition of his uncollected stories more generous and orderly than this baker's dozen born of bitter litigation," an edition that should include not only the "forty uncollected stories from the

New Yorker files" but also all the stories from *The Way Some People Live*, which Updike has already told us Cheever had disowned. Why only the *New Yorker* stories should be included and not those from the *Atlantic Monthly* and other magazines, Updike does not explain, nor does he explain why this edition of thirteen chronologically arranged stories is not "orderly." If, he says, these *New Yorker* stories and those from *The Way Some People Live* were to be brought out in "a handsome, usefully annotated [with Mrs. Cheever's headnotes?] companion to the 1978 'Stories,' posterity would be served and the air of unease that lingers in the wake of the Academy squabble would be dispelled." Thus Updike uneasily approaches the Cheever "estate" (which had closed years earlier) and asks it to be "more generous" than Academy has been.[5]

And, indeed, how sad it was that we could present only these thirteen stories, a fraction of the "treasure trove" that Franklin had uncovered. And how sad that our press, and by extension all small or medium-sized independent publishing houses that do so much to enrich the literary scene, should be denigrated in order to justify the death of a book.

And on that note of sadness, I feel it might be appropriate here to quote from the last paragraphs of "Autobiography of a Drummer," a story remarkable for the feeling it evokes of compassion and of loss:

> . . . The world that I know how to walk and talk and earn a living in, has gone. The sound of the traffic below the window of this furnished room reminds me of that.
>
> We have been forgotten. Everything we know is useless. But when I think about the days on the road and about what I have done and what has been done to me, I hardly ever think about it with any bitterness. We have been forgotten like old telephone books and almanacs and gas lights and those big yellow houses with cornices and cupolas that they used to build. That is all there is to it. Although sometimes I feel as if my life had been a total loss. I feel it in the morning sometimes when I'm shaving. I get sick as if I had eaten something that didn't agree with me and I have to put down the razor and support myself against the wall.

> —*The New Republic*
> October 23, 1935

Sources

Sources

Court Cases

United States District Court for the Southern District of New York
88 CIV 3404 (GLG)
Mary W. Cheever, Susan Cheever, Benjamin Hale Cheever and Federico Cheever,
Plaintiffs v. Academy Chicago, Ltd. d/b/a Academy Chicago Publishers, Defendants

Chapters 13, 23 24, 25, 26

Circuit Court of Cook County, Illinois
County Department—Chancery Division
88 CH 01810
Academy Chicago Publishers, Plaintiff v. Mary Cheever, defendant

Chapters 27, 29, 30, 31, 33, 34, 37

Appeals

Appellate Court of Ilinois, First District, Third Division
1-89-0506

Chapter 40

Supreme Court of Illinois
70587

Chapter 42

Notes

Chapter 4

1. Michael Shnayerson, "How Wily Is Andrew Wiley?" *Vanity Fair*, January 1988, 24–29. All quotes in the following eight paragraphs are from that article.

Chapter 8

1. Martin Garbus, *Ready for the Defense* (New York: Carroll & Graf Publishers, 1987), XII.

Chapter 9

1. O'Malley & Gratteau, INC, "Under the Covers ... " *Chicago Tribune*, March 8, 1988.
2. Billy Goldstein, "Cheever Feud: Random Run," *7 Days*, March 30, 1988.

Chapter 11

1. David Streitfeld, "Cheever Chronicles," *Washington Post Book World*, May 8, 1988.
2. Herbert Mitgang, "Cheever's Widow Suing to Stop Publication of Story Collection," *New York Times*, May 10, 1988.
3. Andrea Chambers, Family feature, *People*, November 21, 1988, 195.
4. "Cheever widow sues publisher," *Chicago Sun-Times*, May 12, 1988.
5. Paul Kirby, "Cheever's widow seeks to block anthology slated for September," *Gannett Westchester Newspapers*, May 12, 1988.

Chapter 15

1. "Cheever Dispute Reaches ABA Floor," *Publishers Weekly Show Daily*, May 28, 1988.
2. Sonja Bolle, Book Trade, *Los Angeles Times Book Review*, June 5, 1988.

Chapter 17

1. Paul Kirby, "Hearing set for August to stop John Cheever anthology, " *Gannett Westchester Newspapers*, June 28, 1988.
2. Edwin McDowell, Book Notes, *New York Times*, June 29, 1988.
3. Direct quotations in the following paragraphs are taken from John Blades,

"Tale of Cheever collection takes an ugly turn," *Chicago Tribune*, July 7, 1988.

Chapter 23

1. Ellie Voldstad, "Family: Early Cheever writings too 'immature' for public perusal," *Mt. Vernon (N.Y.) Daily Argus*, July 10, 1988.

Chapter 28

1. "Judge delays publication of Cheever short stories," *Philadelphia Inquirer*, August 5, 1988.
2. Ellie Voldstad, "Judge delays Cheever decision," *Gannett Westchester Newspapers*, August 4, 1988.

Chapter 29

1. Tracy Young, People/Books column, *Vogue*, August 1988, 214.
2. Jonathan Yardley, "John Cheever and the Unforgotten Wish," *Washington Post*, August 8, 1988.
3. David Streitfeld, "At War Over the Cheever Legacy," *Washington Post*, September 15, 1988.

Chapter 34

1. Bob Schieffer and Gary Paul Gates, *The Acting President* (New York: NAL Dutton, 1990), 369.

Chapter 35

1. Ben Cheever, "The Cheever Chronicle: my father's life in letters," *Esquire*, November 1988, 153–160.
2. John Schmid, "Cheever Collection bound and gagged," *Skyline*, October 20, 1988.
3. Andrea Chambers, Family feature, *People*, November 28, 1988, 193–196.
4. Dick Polman, "John Cheever: The Other Story," *Philadelphia Inquirer*, December 18, 1988.
5. Ruth Pollack Coughlin, "Living in the shadow of Daddy's halo," *Ithaca (N.Y.) Journal*, January 7, 1989.
6. Polman, "John Cheever: The Other Story."
7. Chambers, Family feature.

8. Anne Hulbert, Washington Diarist, *The New Republic*, November 14, 1988.

9. Coughlin, "Living in the shadow."

10. Robert Gottlieb and Frank Maresca, *A Certain Style: The Art of the Plastic Handbag, 1949–59* (New York: Alfred Knopf, 1988). For two interesting discussions of this book, see Carolyn See, "Mr. Gottlieb's Bag," *Washington Post Book World*, December 4, 1988; and John Heilpern, "The Man Who Mistook His Life for a Handbag," *Manhattan, Inc.*, November 1988.

11. Leslie Garis, "Life With the King of Hell," *Mirabella*, March 1991, 84–88.

12. Susan Cheever, *Treetops* (New York: Bantam Books, 1991), 136, 168, 169, 189–193. Apart from the statement that Jordan had had precontract "conversations" with Mrs. Cheever about "five to seven stories," Susan's chapter on the lawsuit is filled with minor, genteel errors. She places the hearing on June 12 instead of July 11 and 12. She calls Franklin "the publisher's representative" instead of the book's editor. She refers to the Chicago circuit court as "the Illinois State Court in Chicago." She says that Judge Kiley ruled "specifically" that the Cheevers' manuscript "satisfied" their obligations, when in fact the judge specifically ruled that the manuscript "did not violate" his order: he specifically rejected Garbus's "satisfied" language. She says also that Judge Kiley "found" for her mother, when in fact her mother had asked that he find the contract invalid and he found it valid.

13. Dan Santow, "The Millers vs The Cheevers," *Chicago*, December 1988, 152.

14. S. Cheever, *Treetops*, 193.

Chapter 37

1. Bill Goldstein, The World of Books, *Newsday*, January 8, 1989.

Chapter 38

1. Herbert Mitgang, "John Cheever's Wife Wins Ruling in Book Dispute," *New York Times*, February 21, 1989, Midwest edition.

2. People, potpourri, *Bend (Ore.) Bulletin*, June 27, 1988.

3. "Academy v. Cheever," Letters, *American Lawyer*, April 1989, 15–16.

Chapter 39

1. Chris Goodrich, "Academy Chicago to Publish Dutch Bestseller 40 Years After Original Publication in Holland," *Publishers Weekly*, April 28, 1989.

Chapter 40

1. Roger Cohen, "Jitters in a 'Recession-Proof' Trade," *New York Times*, December 17, 1990, Midwest edition.
2. Roger Cohen, "B. Dalton Plans to Open Series of Big Bookstores," *New York Times*, September 6, 1990, Midwest edition.
3. Roger Cohen, Ideas & Trends, "If the Written Word Is Really Dying, Who Is Patronizing the 'Superstores'?" *New York Times*, September 30, 1990, Midwest edition.
4. See Trip Gabriel, "Call My Agents," *New York Times Magazine*, February 19, 1989, 45ff. See also Priscilla Painton, "Big Books, Big Bucks," *Time*, June 12, 1989, 44–46. This article includes a boxed essay, headed "The Naughty Schoolboy," about Andrew Wylie, who, the author says, while topping "all mercenary agents in aggressiveness and acerbity," is "the inevitable product of the awkward transition" of publishing "from a cottage industry to multinational business." She quotes Robert K. Massie, a Wylie client and then president of the Authors Guild, as saying, in praise of the agent's methods, "The hell with publishers." Jeanette Walls, in "Wylie Closes the Book on Brodkey," *Newsday*, March 12, 1990, calls Wylie "the Gordon Gekko of agents." In connection with the extension of American conglomerates to the United Kingdom, see "Loss of Bodley Head Fuels UK Disquiet over Conglomerates," *Publishers Weekly*, July 7, 1989. See also Roger Cohen, "Book Business Toes the Bottom Line," *Lenoir (N.C.) News-Topic*, March 28, 1990, and Edwin McDowell, Ideas & Trends, "For Some Authors, Book Publishers Pay Millions Without a Word," *New York Times*, May 20, 1990.
5. Edwin McDowell, Publishing, "Many Houses find Images are Blurred," *Chicago Tribune*, November 18, 1990.
6. Priscilla Painton, "Big Bucks, Big Books," *Time*, June 12, 1989, 46.
7. Edwin McDowell, "Canceling of Ellis Novel Shocks the Book Industry," *New York Times*, November 16, 1990.
8. Mariane Taylor and Kenneth R. Clark, "Book's graphic violence has stores squirming," *Chicago Tribune*, November 17, 1990. See also Carlin Romano, "Publishing house drops controversial novel," *Chicago Tribune*, November 16, 1990; "Writer claims censorship after novel is dropped," *Chicago Tribune*,

November 16, 1990; Edwin McDowell, "Vintage Buys Violent Book Dropped by Simon & Schuster," *New York Times*, November 17, 1990, Midwest edition; and Clarence Page, "There's no need to throw the book at Simon & Schuster," *Chicago Tribune*, November 21, 1990.

9. Herbert Mitgang, "Rushdie Novel Brings Bomb Threats," *New York Times*, January 14, 1989, Midwest edition.

10. Jane Mayer, "Publishers Bemoan Brash Style, Big Bucks of Rushdie's Agent," *Wall Street Journal*, March 28, 1989.

11. Roger Cohen, "Decision Put Off on Rushdie Book," *New York Times*, June 1, 1990, Midwest edition.

12. Joey Asher, "Local authors discouraged by bookstores' timidity," *Gannett Westchester Newspapers*, February 21, 1990.

13. Sherryl Connelly, "1990: One for the Books," *New York Daily News*, December 30, 1990; "We didn't cover the story, we beat it to death," *Variety*, May 30, 1990.

14. Edwin McDowell, "Simon & Schuster Pays $920,000 for a First Novel," *New York Times*, April 11, 1991; idem, "A Spy Novel's Boosters, It Seems, Aren't," *New York Times*, April 13, 1991, Midwest edition; idem, "Simon & Schuster Decides Not to Publish Novel with False le Carré Endorsement," *New York Times*, April 26, 1991, Midwest edition.

15. Paul Nathan, "Dell Pays $12.3 Million for Two Follett Books," *Publishers Weekly*, July 13, 1990, 9; Roger Cohen, "Publishing World Shaken as Advances for Books Soar," *New York Times*, July 16, 1990.

16. Malcolm Jones Jr., with Ray Sawhill, "Grass Roots Gold Rush," *Newsweek*, July 16, 1990; Adam Begley, "Classy, Independent House Looking for Mr. Goodbuyer," *New York Observer*, July 2, 1990; Edwin McDowell, "North Point to Stop Publishing New Books," *New York Times*, November 30, 1990; "North Point Press to End Operations by the Spring," *San Francisco Chronicle*, November 30, 1990.

Chapter 41

1. Peter West, "New chapter in fight over Cheever stories," *Gannett Westchester Newspapers*, October 10, 1990.

2. "Cheever book flap drags on in courts," *Kansas City Star*, October 15, 1990.

3. West, "New chapter in fight."

4. David Heckelman, "Supreme Court to resolve dispute over rights to Cheever short stories," *Chicago Daily Law Bulletin*, October 8, 1990.

5. Elizabeth Mehren, "A Cacaphony of Cheevers," *Los Angeles Times*, December 2, 1990.

6. James Warren, "Gift of the Gab," *Chicago Tribune*, August 9, 1990.

7. Stefan Kanfer, "Jack, Wrench, Hubcap, and Nuts," *Time*, March 19, 1991.

8. Lisa Anderson, "The Never-Ending Stories," *Chicago Tribune*, April 9, 1991, Tempo section.

9. Warren Hinckle, "Why I was 2 hours late for wedding, etc.," *San Francisco Examiner*, June 13, 1989. See also Rob Morse, "Free the Beijing one billion," *San Francisco Examiner-Chronicle*, June 11, 1989.

10. Carolyn See, "More Pruning on Cheever Family Tree," *Los Angeles Times*, March 25, 1991.

11. Ted Solotareff, "The Cheever Chronicle," *The Nation*, November 18, 1991, 616–620.

12. John Updike, "The Waspshot [*sic*] Chronicle," *New Republic*, December 2, 1991, 36–39.

13. Mary Gordon, "The Country Husband," *New York Times Book Review*, October 6, 1991.

14. James Wolcott, "Leave It to Cheever," *Vanity Fair*, October 1991, 94, 98.

15. Bob Hoover, "In Brief: Family Affairs," *Pittsburgh Post-Gazette*, April 27, 1991.

16. Robert Boyd, "Odd Lots of Nabokov's and Cheever's Letters," *St. Louis Post-Dispatch*, September 24, 1989.

Chapter 42

1. Adrienne Drell, "Newcomers seen shaking up high court," *Chicago Sun-Times*, November 8, 1990.

2. David Heckelman, "Court rules against publisher in Cheever case," *Chicago Daily Law Bulletin*, June 20, 1991.

3. Meg Cox and Wade Lambert, "Contract for John Cheever Stories is Nullified by Illinois High Court," *Wall Street Journal*, June 24, 1991.

4. "Author's widow wins suit over story publication," *Arlington Heights (Ill.) Daily Herald*, June 21, 1991.

5. Ibid.

6. Heckelman, "Court rules against."

7. William Grady and John Blades, "Chicago publisher loses bid for Cheever book," *Chicago Tribune*, June 21, 1991.

8. Ray Hanania, "Court OKs publication of Cheever book," *Chicago Sun-Times*, June 21, 1991. James Warren noted the discrepancy between

Hanania's report and the *Tribune*'s correct report in his Media Watch column, *Tribune*, June 23, 1991.

Chapter 43

1. Meg Cox and Wade Lambert, "Contract for John Cheever Stories Is Nullified by Illinois High Court," *Wall Street Journal*, June 24, 1991.
2. Madalynne Reuter, "AAP, AAUP, Support Academy on Contract Issue," *Publishers Weekly*, July 25, 1991.
3. James Warren, Media Watch, *Chicago Tribune*, September 1, 1991.
4. Scott Meredith, Letters, *Near North (Chicago) News*, October 5, 1991.
5. Martin Garbus and Russell Smith, Outside Counsel, *New York Law Journal*, August 6, 1991.
6. Jennifer Moyer, Publisher's Letter, *Small Press*, Fall 1991, 4–5.
7. "Court Rejects Re-Hearing in Cheever Case," *BP Report on the Business of Book Publishing*, October 7, 1991.
8. See Jan Crawford Greenburg, "'Baby Richard' ordered returned to birth parents," *Chicago Tribune*, June 17, 1994. See also Bob Greene columns in the *Tribune* for September 22, 23, and 24, 1996, December 23, 1996, and January 26 and February 16, 1997. Also see Ken Armstrong, "State targets Heiple conduct," *Chicago Tribune*, January 24, 1997, and "Trials, tribulations wrack state's high court," *Chicago Tribune*, January 26, 1997; and Tim Novak, "Top judge accused in ticket flap," *Chicago Sun-Times*, January 24, 1997.

Chapter 44

1. James Ledbetter, "Father Sells Best," *Village Voice*, October 29, 1991.
2. Daniel Maxwell, "The Cheever Cottage Industry Takes Patrimony to the Bank," *New York Observer*, June 22, 1992.
3. John Blades, "Unfinished business," *Chicago Tribune*, December 31, 1992.
4. Hillel Italie, "Cheever Skeletons," *St. Louis Post-Dispatch*, July 5, 1992. This article was widely distributed to newspapers by the Associated Press.

Chapter 45

1. David Streitfeld, "Cheevers, Publishers End Fight," *Washington Post*, January 25, 1992.
2. Michael Meek, "Court battle ends over Cheever's stories," *Mamaroneck (N.Y.) Daily Times*, January 27, 1992.
3. "Guild Intervention Effective in Cheever Law Suit," *Authors Guild Bulletin*, Winter 1992, 3–4.

4. Jennifer Moyer, Publisher's Letter, *Small Press*, Spring 1992.

5. John Blades, "Unfinished business," *Chicago Tribune*, December 31, 1992. See also Andrew Grene, "He sued for the press—now the press suits him," *Chicago Daily Law Bulletin*, December 1, 1992.

6. "Guild Symposium on Tactics for Tough Times," *Authors Guild Bulletin,* Spring 1993, 18.

7. Charles Trueheart, The Talk of the Town, *Washington Post*, July 1, 1992, Style section.

8. David Streitfeld, "Uncollected Cheever Works to Be Published," *Washington Post*, December 13, 1993, Style section.

9. Sarah Lyall, Book Notes, *New York Times*, December 15, 1993.

10. John Blades, "Final chapter," *Chicago Tribune*, December 23, 1991.

11. Lyall, Book Notes.

12. "Czechoslovakia's Paine," *Chicago Tribune*, December 23, 1991.

Chapter 46

1. *Publishers Weekly*, January 17, 1994; *Library Journal*, March 1, 1994; *Booklist*, March 15, 1994.

2. *Kirkus Reviews*, January 1, 1994.

3. Mark Bautz, Books, Short Fiction, *Washington Times*, May 1, 1994; Richard Bausch, "Cheever's Early Earnest Efforts," *Washington Post*, May 19, 1994; Jacques le Sourd, "Cheever tests his wings in early stories," *Tarrytown (N.Y.) Daily News*, April 3, 1994.

4. Sven Birkerts, "A First Glimpse of Cheever Country," *New York Times Book Review*, March 13, 1994.

5. John Updike, Books, *The New Yorker*, May 30, 1994.

Appendix A
The Publishing
Agreement

PUBLISHING AGREEMENT

INITIAL HERE

AGREEMENT made this 15th day of August 1987 , between Academy Chicago Publishers or any affiliated entity or imprint (hereinafter referred to as the Publisher) and ~~the Estate of John Cheever~~ MARY W. CHEEVER and Franklin Dennis of the USA (hereinafter referred to as Author).

WHEREAS the parties are desirous respectively of publishing and having published a certain work or works, tentatively titled The Uncollected Stories of John Cheever

(hereinafter referred to as the Work);

THEREFORE, in consideration of the mutual covenants contained herein, the parties do hereby agree as follows:

1. The Author grants to the Publisher, during the full term of copyright of the Work and all renewals and extensions of copyright, the exclusive right to print, publish, and sell the Work in book form in the English language throughout the world, and the exclusive right to license its publication in all languages throughout the world.

INITIAL HERE

2. The Author will deliver ~~has delivered~~ to the Publisher on ~~or before~~ a mutually agreeable date one copy of the manuscript of the Work as finally ~~revised~~ ARRANGED by the ~~Author~~ EDITOR and satisfactory to the Publisher in form and content. ~~The Author acknowledges that Publisher's acceptance of the Author's manuscript and the Publisher's duty to publish said manuscript is subject to Publisher's right to edit and revise the manuscript to the Publisher's satisfaction. If the Author shall fail to edit or revise the manuscript to the Publisher's satisfaction, the Publisher shall, at its sole discretion, have the right to reject the manuscript and terminate this agreement, or edit, revise, or otherwise modify the manuscript to suit its requirements. In the event the Publisher shall reject the manuscript and thereby terminate this agreement, Publisher and Author shall have no further liability to each other.~~

3. The Author will supply, on delivery of the final revised manuscript and at his or her own expense, all photographs, drawings, maps, tables, charts, or other illustrative material essential to the Work, along with captions to accompany such material, all in a form satisfactory to the Publisher. The Author will supply an index to the Work, if required by the Publisher, within days after his or her receipt of page proofs of the Work. The Author will also obtain, at his or her own expense, written permissions for all items, graphic and textual, from other published and unpublished works incorporated into the Work by the Author, and will deliver such permissions to the Publisher with the final revised manuscript. If any of the foregoing materials are not so delivered by the Author, the Publisher will have the right to charge the Author for the Publisher's reasonable expenses in providing such materials. In the event that the Author fails or refuses to reimburse the Publisher for such expenses, the Publisher shall have the right to deduct such expenses from any sums due from the Publisher to the Author whether under this agreement or otherwise.

4. In addition to those prerogatives reserved to it in paragraph two hereof, the Publisher may edit the manuscript in accordance with the Publisher's standard style of capitalization, punctuation, spelling and usage. The ~~Publisher may, at its sole discretion, alter the title of the Work.~~

5. Within a reasonable time* after delivery of the final revised manuscript, the Publisher will publish the Work at its own expense, in such style and manner and at such price as it deems best, and will keep the Work in print as long as it deems it expedient; but it will not be responsible for delays caused by circumstances beyond its control.   * and a mutually agreeable date

INITIAL HERE

6. The Publisher will apply for copyright in the United States of the Work in conformity with the Copyright Law of the United States and the Universal Copyright convention in the name of ~~the Author~~ and may effect MARY W. CHEEVER any renewals or extensions of copyright provided for by law.

7. If the copyright of the Work is infringed, and the Publisher and the Author agree to join in an action for infringement, the expenses thereof and the net recovery therefrom will be shared equally. If the Author and the Publisher do not agree to proceed jointly, then either party may bring an infringement action and the expenses thereof will be borne solely by such party and any recovery therefrom will belong solely to such party; and if such party is not the registered copyright owner, the other party agrees to be named as co-plaintiff, without assuming any liability for expenses or claim to benefits thereby. The party bringing such a suit agrees to indemnify, defend and hold harmless the other party from any counterclaims, cross-claims or other claims or actions by the adverse parties in any such suit. Each party will notify the other of infringements coming to its attention.

8. The Publisher may use and authorize use of the Author's name, likeness and photograph in connection with advertising, publicizing, licensing and promoting the Work, ~~and the Author hereby waives all of the so-called "moral rights" of authors not only in connection with his name or likeness, but also in connection with any exercise of the rights, licenses and privileges granted or agreed to be granted Publisher under this agreement.~~

INITIAL HERE

9. The Publisher will give the Author AND THE EDITOR on publication, ~~six~~ ten copies ~~of~~ EACH of the regular edition of the Work, or if it is a dual edition, three copies of each, and the Author may purchase for his or her personal use further copies at a discount of 40% off Publisher's list price.

10. The Publisher shall pay to the Author for each copy sold, paid for, and not returned (except as hereinafter set forth):

     a. A royalty on the trade paperback edition of 7% of the cover price.

     b. A royalty on the hardcover editions of ten per cent (10%) of the cover price on the first five thousand (5,000) copies sold;

twelve and one-half per cent (12½%) on the next five thousand (5,000) copies sold;

and fifteen per cent (15%) on all copies sold in excess of ten thousand (10,000).

Copies covered by any other subdivision of this Paragraph, except Subdivision c., shall not be included in such computation.

   c. Where the discount in the United States is more than fifty-two per cent (52%) of the retail price, the Author and Publisher shall equally bear the additional cost in excess of said fifty-two per cent. In no event, however, shall the royalty be less than one-half (½) of the royalty stipulated in Subdivisions a. and b. of this Paragraph.

   d. A royalty of five per cent (5%) of the amount the Publisher charges for all copies of the Work, less returns, sold direct to the consumer through mail-order advertising or circularization, or by radio or television solicitation.

   e. In order that the Publisher may maintain the Work in print for the longest posible time, it is agreed that in any semiannual accounting period in which sales of the Work fall below five hundred copies, a royalty will be payable to the Author of one-half the then current rate of royalty on all copies of the regular edition sold; but this provision will take effect only after one year from the date of original publication of the Work hereunder.

   f. No royalty will be paid for copies furnished gratis to the Author, for advertising or review, for sales promotion use, or charitable or public purposes from which the Publisher receives no proceeds, or for remainders or damaged copies sold at or below cost.

11. The Publisher shall render semiannual statements of account to the last day of June and to the last day of December, and shall mail such statements during the September and March following, together with checks in payment of the amounts due thereon. If less than fifty dollars is due in any accounting period, the Publisher will render no accounting until after the next period in which fifty dollars or more is due. Should there be an overpayment of royalty arising from copies reported sold but subsequently returned, the Publisher may deduct such overpayment from any further sums due hereunder.

   Upon his or her written request, and with not less than thirty (30) days' advance notice to the Publisher, the Author may examine or cause to be examined through Certified Public Accountants the books of accounts of the Publisher insofar as they relate to the sale or licensing of the Work.

   All royalty-statements of account rendered by the Publisher to the Author shall be considered true and accurate unless Author shall deliver to the Publisher a written objection thereto within twenty-four (24) months of the month of mailing, which objection shall state in detail the items on the royalty statement being objected to and the nature of the objection.

   Author's rights to examine Publisher's books and records, with respect to a particular royalty statement of account, shall expire unless such examination is conducted within twenty-four (24) months of the month within such statement is mailed.

   The Publisher may deduct from any funds due the Author any sums that the Author may owe the Publisher, or any advances made by the Publisher for the Author and at the Author's request.

12. The Author warrants that he or she has full power to make this agreement; that the Work has not been previously published; that all rights conveyed to the Publisher hereunder are free of encumbrances; that the Work does not violate any copyright or any other right and contains nothing libelous, obscene, or otherwise unlawful. Nor does the Work, in whole, constitute an invasion of privacy. The Author will indemnify, defend, and hold harmless the Publisher and its licensees against all claims, demands, or suits related to these warranties. The Author will compensate the Publisher for any loss or damage, and for any sums payable in settlement of any claim or judgment, including counsel fees, resulting from a breach of such warranties. The Author and the Publisher will promptly notify each other of any claim, demand, or suit hereunder, and pending the disposition thereof the Publisher may withhold any payments due the Author. If a joint defense is not agreeable, each will be entitled to his or her own counsel. These warranties and indemnities will survive in the event this agreement is terminated.

in book form ∧

13. The Author agrees that during the term of this agreement he or she will not, without the written permission of the Publisher, publish or permit to be published, any material in book or pamphlet form, based on the material in the Work, or which is reasonably likely to injure its sale.

14. ~~If the Author fails to deliver a satisfactory manuscript as agreed, the Publisher will have the right to terminate~~ this agreement and to recover from the Author any expenses incurred in connection with the Work. Until this agreement has been terminated, and until the Author has reimbursed the Publisher for such expenses, ~~the Author may not have the Work published elsewhere.~~

15. The Author further grants to the Publisher, for the same territories and with the same exclusivity described in Paragraph 1, the following additional rights in the Work; and any proceeds derived from the licensing, use, or disposition of these rights, less any expenses incurred in connection therewith and less any fees or commissions paid by the publisher to outside agents, will be divided as indicated below:

INITIAL HERE
FHD
MWC

   a. ~~first serial rights; eighty per cent (80%) to the Author and twenty per cent (20%) to the Publisher;~~

   b. reprint, large-type, and inexpensive-edition rights to other publishers; book club rights, book club digest rights; anthology, lyric, condensation, digest, selection rights; rights for second serial, newspaper syndication and abridged or unabridged versions; fifty per cent (50%) to the Author and fifty per cent (50%) to the Publisher;

   c. rights for editions of the Work published in other languages, and for editions published in the English language outside the United States, fifty per cent (50%) to the Author and fifty per cent (50%) to the Publisher;

   d. rights for filmstrips, transparencies, microfilming, programming, and for any method now or hereafter known or devised for information storage, reproduction, and retrieval; fifty per cent (50%) to the Author and fifty per cent (50%) to the Publisher;

INITIAL HERE
FHD
MWC
OF THE PRINTED PAGE

INITIAL
HERE
F.H.D
M.W.C

e. ~~motion picture and allied rights, radio and television rights, dramatic rights and readings, operatic~~ and musical compositions; ~~fifty per cent (50%)~~ to the Author and fifty per cent (50%) to the ~~Publisher;~~

f. rights for phonograph records, wire and tape recordings, commercial use and adaptations for commercial use; two-thirds to the Author and one-third to the Publisher;

g. no payment will be made to the Author for any use of the Work that the Publisher may authorize without change in any form, including publication by the Publisher or others,
(i) of brief selections to promote sale of the Work;
(ii) for the blind or physically handicapped;
(iii) for education or noncommercial television.

16.   (a) The Work will be considered in print if it is on sale under the Publisher's imprint or under the licensed imprint of another publisher, or if it is under option or contract for publication in another edition.

(b) If at any time after two years from the original date of publication hereunder the Work is out of print as above defined and the Author makes written demand on the Publisher to reissue the Work, the Publisher shall have six months after such written demand to reprint the Work or to contract for its reissue within a reasonable time. Upon the Publisher's failure to cause reissue of the Work, and upon payment to the Publisher of any sums owing from the Author this agreement will terminate and all rights herein granted will revert to the Author, subject, however, to any licenses or options previously granted either party, and to the continuing payment to the Publisher of its share of the proceeds from any such license or options.

17. If after one year from the date of original publication of the Work hereunder the Publisher deems that it is overstocked with copies of the Work, the Publisher may dispose of such overstock at the best price obtainable, and in accordance with the royalty provisions herein.

18. ~~The Author hereby grants to the Publisher the option to publish the Author's next two works of book length on the same terms as in this agreement provided, except that financial arrangements will be subject to mutual agreement of Author and Publisher.~~

19. All notices, statements and payments due the Author under this agreement will be sent to: ~~Franklin H. Dennis (Editor)~~ ~~College Hill Road~~ ~~Montrose, N.Y. 10548~~   MARY W. CHEEVER 96 I CM 40 West 57 th St New York, NY 10019

All notices to the Publisher will be sent to its offices at 425 N. Michigan Avenue, Chicago, Illinois 60611.

20. This agreement will be binding and inure to the benefit of the heirs, executors, administrators, or assigns of the Author and the successor or assigns of the Publisher. The Publisher may assign this agreement, but only in its entirety. The Author may assign any net sums due or to become due to him or her hereunder, but he or she may not assign any other rights or obligations hereunder. This agreement will be construed in accordance with the laws of the State of Illinois, regardless of the place of its physical execution. The Author and Publisher agree that no suit on any cause of action arising out of or related to this agreement will be filed except in Chicago, Illinois.

21. Author and Publisher acknowledge that the commercial success of the Work to be published under this agreement is speculative and nothing herein contained shall be construed as a representation by either of the parties that the Work, after publication, will have commercial success or that any royalties or income will be earned, as a result of such publication.

22. This agreement constitutes the complete understanding of the parties. No modification or waiver of any provision shall be valid unless in writing and signed by both parties.

23. In the event a court of competent jurisdiction should find any one or more of the numbered paragraphs of this agreement void or otherwise unenforceable for any reason, it will not by so finding rule the entire agreement unenforceable but rather will enforce, as written, all those other provisions not objectionable.

24. In consideration and on account of all monies due herein, the Publisher will pay the Author an advance of $1500 (one thousand five hundred dollars), one half on signature, one half on publication.

INITIAL 25. In order to expedite payment of royalties, *AND ADVANCE* the Publisher will divide royalties *AND ADVANCE*
HERE   due equally between ~~The Estate of John ~~ *MARY W. CHEEVER* ~~Cheever~~ and Franklin Dennis, providing
F.H.D   each with accompanying documentation. Each will be paid 50% of all monies due on
M.W.C   dates noted in paragraph 11 of this Agreement.

IN WITNESS WHEREOF, the parties have duly executed this agreement the day and year first written above.

In the presence of

_____
Witness sign here

_____
The Publisher

In the presence of

_____
Witness sign here

_____
The Author MARY W. CHEEVER

In the presence of

_____
Witness sign here

_____
~~The Co-Author~~ Editor

Appendix B
Chronology, Lawyers,
and the Uncollected
Stories List

Chronology

June 15, 1987:   Franklin Dennis contacts Ben Cheever about Academy Chicago collection of John Cheever's uncollected stories

Sept: Mary Cheever, John's widow, signs a publishing agreement with Chicago through International Creative Management

Dec 12:   Franklin Dennis delivers two binders containing Xeroxes of over sixty stories to Mary Cheever to give to Ben

mid-Dec: Ben calls Franklin to tell him he is reading manuscript

Jan 15, 1988:   Ben introduces Franklin to Andrew Wylie in the Algonquin Hotel bar

Feb 22:   Cheever attorney Martin Garbus issues a five-day ultimatum to Academy to give up the contract

Feb 26:   Academy attorney Paul Freehling files a suit for a declaratory judgment in chancery court in Chicago

May 16:   Mary Cheever, Ben Cheever, Susan Cheever, and Federico Cheever file suit in federal court in White Plains, New York, against Academy for copyright and Lanham Act violations

June 10:   Judge Goettel in White Plains accepts Cheever suit

June 15:   Settlement meeting at Royce Hotel in New York

July 29: Auction for paperback rights to Cheever book conducted by Scott Meredith Agency. Dell is top bidder at $225,000

July 1: Judge Goettel sets evidentiary hearing on copyright question

July 2–7: Depositions taken that will serve for both White Plains and Chicago trials

July 11–12: Evidentiary hearing in White Plains

July 29: Hearing before Judge Kiley in Chicago to determine whether he will accept Academy's case

Aug 3: Judge Goettel issues opinion

Aug 10: Judge Kiley agrees to accept Academy's case

Aug 30: Judge Kiley sets trial parameters, trial date of September 15

Sept 15–20: Trial before Judge Kiley in Chicago

Sept 23: Kiley delivers oral opinion

Dec 1: Mrs. Cheever delivers manuscript

Jan 24, 1989: Judge Kiley has left the bench, but returns for hearing on Mrs. Cheever's manuscript

Feb 10: Kiley issues final opinion

Feb 23, 1989: Tom Leavens files appeal

June 1990: Appeals court hands down split decision

Oct: Illinois Supreme Court accepts Academy's case

Mar 1, 1991: Oral arguments before Illinois Supreme Court

June 20: Illinois Supreme Court decision

Jan 1992: Settlement agreement signed by both parties

Lawyers

For Academy Chicago
  In Chicago
  Paul Freehling (Pope, Ballard, Shepard & Fowle)
  Cynthia Johnson

  In New York
  Adam Walinsky (Kronish, Lieb, Weiner & Hellman)
  Tab Rosenfeld

  In Chicago for Appeals
  Tom Leavens (McBride, Baker & Coles)
  Marc Fogelberg

For Franklin Dennis
  Bob Stein (Pryor, Cashman, Sherman & Flynn)
  Tom Ferber

For the Cheevers
  In New York
  Martin Garbus (Frankfurt, Garbus, Klein & Selz)
  Maura Wogan
  Russell Smith

  In Chicago
  M. Leslie Kite, M. Leslie Kite & Associates)
  Jerome Brozak

For International Creative Management
  Sidney H. Stein (Stein, Zauderer, Ellenhorn, Frischer & Sharp)

For the Association of American Publishers
  R. Bruce Rich (Weil, Gotshal & Manges)

From Random House
   Ellis Levine, Senior Counsel

The Uncollected Stories List

Expelled, *New Republic* (Oct 1, 1930).

*Fall River, *The Left: A Quarterly Review of Radical and Experimental Art* (Autumn 1931).

*Late Gathering, *Pagany* (Oct–Dec 1931).

*Bock Beer and Bermuda Onions, *Hound and Horn* (Apr–June 1932).

Brooklyn Rooming House, *New Yorker* (May 25, 1935).

Buffalo, *New Yorker* (June 22, 1935).

*The Autobiography of a Drummer, *New Republic* (Oct 23, 1935).

*In Passing, *Atlantic Monthly* (Mar 1936)

*Bayonne, *Parade* (Spring 1936).

Play a March, *New Yorker* (June 30, 1936).

*The Princess, *New Republic* (Oct 28, 1936).

A Picture for the Home, *New Yorker* (Nov 28, 1936).

Behold a Cloud in the West, *New Letters in America* (1937).

*The Teaser, *New Republic* (Sept 8, 1937).

Homage to Shakespeare, *Story* (Nov 1937).

In the Beginning, *New Yorker* (Nov 6, 1937).

*His Young Wife, *Collier's* (Jan 1, 1938).

Frère Jacques, *Atlantic Monthly* (Mar 1938).

*Saratoga, *Collier's* (Aug 13, 1938).

Treat, *New Yorker* (Jan 21, 1939).

The Happiest Days, *New Yorker* (Nov 4, 1939).

It's Hot in Egypt, *New Yorker* (Jan 6, 1940).

*The Man She Loved, *Collier's* (Aug 24, 1940).

I'm Going to Asia, *Harper's Bazaar* (Sept 1940).

A Present for Louisa, *Mademoiselle* (Dec 1940).

A Bird in the Hand, *Mademoiselle* (Feb 1941).

From This Day Forward, *Mademoiselle* (Oct 1941).

The Pursuit of Happiness, *Mademoiselle* (Feb 1942).

A Place of Great Historical Interest, *New Yorker* (Feb 21, 1942).

*Family Dinner, *Collier's* (July 25, 1942).

Sergeant Limeburner, *New Yorker* (Mar 13, 1943).

They Shall Inherit the Earth, *New Yorker* (April 10, 1943).

A Tale of Old Pennsylvania, *New Yorker* (May 29, 1943).

The Invisible Ship, *New Yorker* (Aug 7, 1943).

My Friends and Neighbors All, Farewell, *New Yorker* (Oct 10, 1943).

Dear Lord, We Thank Thee for Thy Bounty, *New Yorker* (Nov 27, 1943).

Somebody Has to Die, *New Yorker* (June 24, 1944).

A Walk in the Park, *Good Housekeeping* (Oct 1944).

The Single Purpose of Leon Burrows, *New Yorker* (Oct 7, 1944).

The Mouth of the Turtle, *New Yorker* (Oct 7, 1944).

Town House, *New Yorker* (Apr 21, 1945).

Manila, *New Yorker* (July 28, 1945).

Town House—II, *New Yorker* (Aug 11, 1945).

A Trip to the Moon, *Good Housekeeping* (Oct 1945).

Town House—III, *New Yorker* (Nov 10, 1945).

Town House—IV, *New Yorker* (Jan 5, 1946).

Town House—V, *New Yorker* (Mar 16, 1946).

Town House—VI, *New Yorker* (May 4, 1946).

Love in the Islands, *New Yorker* (Dec 7, 1946).

The Beautiful Mountain, *New Yorker* (Feb 8, 1947).

Roseheath, *New Yorker* (Aug 16, 1947).

Keep the Ball Rolling, *New Yorker* (May 29, 1948).

The Temptations of Emma Boynton, *New Yorker* (Nov 26, 1949).

*The Opportunity, *Cosmopolitan* (Dec 11, 1949).

Vega, *Harper's Magazine* (Dec 1949).

The Reasonable Music, *Harper's Magazine* (Nov 1950).

The People You Meet, *New Yorker* (Dec 2, 1950).

The National Pastime, *New Yorker* (Sep 26, 1953).

The True Confessions of Henry Pell, *Harper's Magazine* (June 1954).

The Journal of a Writer with a Hole in One Sock, *Reporter* (Dec 29, 1955).

How Dr. Wareham Kept His Servants, *Reporter* (Apr 5, 1956).

Paola, *New Yorker* (July 29, 1958).

The Habit, *New Yorker* (Mar 7, 1964).

The Leaves, the Lion-Fish and the Bear, *Esquire* (Nov 1974).

The Folding-Chair Set, *New Yorker* (Oct 13, 1975).

The President of the Argentine, *Atlantic Monthly* (Apr 1976).

The Night Mummy Got the Wrong Mink Coat, *New Yorker* (Apr 21, 1980).

The Island, *New Yorker* (Apr 27, 1981).

---

*Stories included in *Thirteen Uncollected Stories by John Cheever.*

Name Index

Incidental mention of principals in the case are not included.

About the Author

Anita Miller earned her Ph.D. in English Literature at Northwestern University, where she taught English for nine years. She is the author of *Arnold Bennett: An Annotated Bibliography, 1887–1932,* and coauthor of *The Fair Women: The Story of the Woman's Building at the World's Columbian Exposition of 1893.*

Dr. Miller has translated three novels by Dutch author Hella Haasse and has edited more than thirty-five books for Academy Chicago, both fiction and nonfiction. She is president and editorial director of Academy Chicago Publishers, which she and her husband founded in 1975.

In 1994, Dr. Miller won the Chicago Women in Publishing "Publishing Woman of the Year" award and in 1996 she received the London Women in Publishing Pandora Award, given to a woman "who had consistently made a significant valuable contribution from which women have benefitted."